SERIAL ENCOUNTERS

CLARE HUTTON is Reader in English and Digital Humanities at Loughborough University, and edited *The Irish Book in English, 1891–2000* (Clarendon Press, 2011). She has published widely on Yeats, Joyce, and the Irish Literary Revival.

T0355468

Serial Encounters

Ulysses and *The Little Review*

CLARE HUTTON

OXFORD
UNIVERSITY PRESS

OXFORD
UNIVERSITY PRESS

Great Clarendon Street, Oxford, OX2 6DP,
United Kingdom

Oxford University Press is a department of the University of Oxford.
It furthers the University's objective of excellence in research, scholarship,
and education by publishing worldwide. Oxford is a registered trade mark of
Oxford University Press in the UK and in certain other countries

© Clare Hutton 2019

The moral rights of the author have been asserted

First published 2019
First published in paperback 2022

All rights reserved. No part of this publication may be reproduced, stored in
a retrieval system, or transmitted, in any form or by any means, without the
prior permission in writing of Oxford University Press, or as expressly permitted
by law, by licence or under terms agreed with the appropriate reprographics
rights organization. Enquiries concerning reproduction outside the scope of the
above should be sent to the Rights Department, Oxford University Press, at the
address above

You must not circulate this work in any other form
and you must impose this same condition on any acquirer

Published in the United States of America by Oxford University Press
198 Madison Avenue, New York, NY 10016, United States of America

British Library Cataloguing in Publication Data
Data available

Library of Congress Cataloging in Publication Data
Data available

ISBN 978–0–19–874407–8 (Hbk.)
ISBN 978–0–19–286462–8 (Pbk.)

Links to third party websites are provided by Oxford in good faith and
for information only. Oxford disclaims any responsibility for the materials
contained in any third party website referenced in this work.

in memory of
Robert Joseph Hutton (1935–2015)

Acknowledgements

I am grateful to the trustees of the Leverhulme Trust for the award of a research fellowship in 2010 which gave me a two-year leave from teaching, and enabled me to undertake the bulk of the archival research on which this book is based. During the fellowship, I became seriously ill with a rare neurological illness—transverse myelitis—which brought things to an abrupt halt, and put much in perspective. I am extremely grateful to the family, friends, and medics who helped me through that difficult time—an illness which lasted more than a year—and who encouraged me to resume writing and research when much seemed in doubt. James Bateman, of the CLEAR unit at Oxford Brookes, gave me first-hand insight into what it is like to know about biomechanics, and was extraordinarily patient and kind. My thanks also to Jane Newman who is a brilliant counsellor and physiotherapist.

My colleagues at Loughborough undertook teaching on my behalf through a long absence, and were very welcoming when I returned. I particularly wish to thank Elaine Hobby, whose support was invaluable in the early stages of this research. Nigel Wood has been a remarkably kind, tolerant, and sage colleague. I want to thank him for his friendship and many conversations in the bistro. Thanks too to Carol Bolton, Chris Christie, Jennifer Cooke, Catie Gill, Nick Freeman, Deirdre O'Byrne, and Wim Van Mierlo.

I now realize that I did not know much about *Ulysses* and textuality when I first outlined this project in the Leverhulme application, and I am very grateful to my Joycean colleagues for the generous ways in which they helped to bring me up to speed. Luca Crispi welcomed me to the genetic fold, and Ronan Crowley pointed me to many relevant sources which I might otherwise have missed, shared his considerable expertise in digital literary studies, and sent many funny and informative emails from Buffalo. Support, encouragement, and advice from Hans Gabler has been both heartening and formative.

When Haines asks Mulligan whether Dedalus has written anything 'for your movement', Mulligan responds with derision, saying that Dedalus is 'going to write something in ten years'. Nowadays I don't think ten years is such a long time, and certainly this book has been brewing for longer than that. Andrew Gibson, a remarkable and inspiring teacher, introduced me to *Ulysses* when I was an undergraduate at Royal Holloway in 1991. Thanks for the continuing conversations which happen at and around London University's Charles Peake *Ulysses* Seminar. Thanks too to the other members of that Seminar, past, present, and occasional, especially Joe Brooker, Finn Fordham, Robert Hampson, Bernard McGinley, Steven Morrison, Len Platt, Helen Saunders, Chrissie Van Mierlo, Katie Wales, and John Wyse Jackson.

Fritz Senn's invitation to join the Genetics Workshop at the Zurich James Joyce Foundation in August 2016 was particularly welcome, and I am very grateful to him and other participants in the workshop, particularly Bill Brockman,

Tim Conley, Daniel Ferrer, Stephanie Nelson, Genevieve Sartor, and Barry Spence. I would also like to thank Frank Callanan, Catriona Clutterback, Anne Fogarty, Nicky Grene, Anne Harpin, Jennifer Hayes, Geert Lernout, Timothy Martin, John McCourt, Katie Mullin, Gareth Petts, Sam Slote, and Dirk Van Hulle for advice, support, and encouragement along the way. The 9.30 congregation at Blackfriars has rallied round on many occasions, and I'd like to thank my friends there: Joshua Dubin, Jenifer Dye, Louise Frith-Powell, John O'Connor, Liz Robertson, Amanda Robson, Tessa Roynon, Maddy Shaw, Halina Simm, Bernadette Urtz, and Aoife Walsh. Thanks also to Claire Gavin, and Selina Guinness in Dublin, and to Anto, Steve, Dan, Gemma, and Elaine, who may be far away but are never far from mind.

A work of this kind could not be undertaken without the support of archivists and librarians. Thanks are due to staff at the following: the Bodleian Library, Oxford; Rare Books and Manuscripts at the British Library, London; the Morris Library at Southern Illinois University, Carbondale; Rare Books and Manuscripts at the New York Public Library; the Archives Department of the University of Wisconsin, Milwaukee; and the Poetry/Rare Books Collection of the University at Buffalo. I am also very grateful for the award of a Visiting Fellowship at the Humanities Institute at Buffalo which enabled me to undertake a crucial tranche of archival work on Joyce's manuscripts. Thanks too to Jacqueline Norton, Commissioning Editor at OUP, for having faith in this project and for being so patient when its delivery was delayed.

The biggest debts are the hardest to express. This work would never have found feet had it not been for the love, support, and encouragement of my husband, Grant Lamond, who has discussed the work on an almost daily basis, often at the Missing Bean. He has also been happy to turn his hand to many things, including finding legal sources and explaining them, locating Joyce materials on AbeBooks and buying them, cooking delicious dinners, doing the washing, and generally keeping the domestic show on the road. Thank you, Joe, Aisling, and Nellie. This book began when you were at nursery, and has been written round the edges of your lives. I won't mind if you never evince an interest in James Joyce. Thanks too to my mother, Bez, for everything. Your checking of the entire typescript was (well and truly) above and beyond the call of maternal duty, but much appreciated.

This book is dedicated to the memory of my father, with love, affection, and many happy memories of Dublin in the rare old times.

Contents

List of Illustrations

List of Tables

List of Abbreviations

The following abbreviations have been adopted for frequently recurring names of publications and places:

CSE
: James Joyce, *Ulysses: A Critical and Synoptic Edition*, 3 vols, ed. by Hans Walter Gabler (London and New York: Garland, 1986). In general, references are only made to the *Little Review* and *U*1922. Where the intervening stages in the post-serial genetic dossier seem particularly pertinent, reference is made to the left-hand pages of the *CSE* by volume number, page number, and line number (thus *CSE*I 140.16 refers to the first volume, page 140, line 16)

EP-JJ
: Forrest Read (ed.), *Pound/Joyce: The Letters of Ezra Pound to James Joyce with Pound's Essays on Joyce* (New York: New Directions, 1965)

EP-JQ
: Timothy Materer (ed.), *The Selected Letters of Ezra Pound to John Quinn* (Durham, NC and London: Duke University Press, 1991)

Gaipa et al., *LRU*
: *The Little Review Ulysses*, ed. by Mark Gaipa, Sean Latham, and Robert Scholes (New Haven, CT: Yale University Press, 2015)

JQ-JJ I
: Myron Schwartzman (ed.), '"Quinnigan's Quake": John Quinn's Letters to James Joyce, 1916–1920', *Bulletin of Research in the Humanities*, 81:2 (Summer 1978), 216–60

JQ-JJ II
: Myron Schwartzman (ed.), "Quinnigan's Quake!": John Quinn's Letters to James Joyce, 1921–1924', *Bulletin of Research in the Humanities*, 83:1 (Spring 1980), 27–66

L I
: *Letters of James Joyce*, vol. I, ed. by Stuart Gilbert (New York Viking, 1957)

L II
: *Letters of James Joyce*, vol. II, ed. by Richard Ellmann (New York: Viking, 1966)

L III
: *Letters of James Joyce*, vol. III, ed. by Richard Ellmann (New York: Viking, 1966)

LR
: *Little Review*. Original copies are scarce. As an alternative, see the facsimile, 12 vols (New York: Kraus Reprint, 1967), the full run of all issues from March 1914 to Spring 1929, or the digital copy of the first nine volumes (1914 to 1922), available at the Modernist Journals Project: http://modjourn.org//render.php?view=mjp_object&id=Littl eReviewCollection. A few issues of the *Little Review* were misnumbered by the original editors. Thus a simple date of issue plus page number has been used for references, including all references to the text of the serial *Ulysses*

P-LR
: Thomas L. Scott and Melvin J Friedman (eds.), *Pound/The Little Review: The Letters of Ezra Pound to Margaret Anderson: The Little Review Correspondence* (New York: A New Directions Book, 1988)

Rosenbach   Clive Driver (ed.), *James Joyce, Ulysses: A Facsimile of the Manuscript*,
                 3 vols (Philadelphia, PA: Rosenbach Foundation, 1975) (with P#, which
                 correlates the manuscript to *U*1922)

SL   *Selected Letters of James Joyce*, ed. by Richard Ellmann (London: Faber,
                 1975)

*U*1922   James Joyce, *Ulysses* (Paris: Shakespeare and Company, 1922).
                 See the digital copy: http://web.uvic.ca/~mvp1922/portfolio/
                 ulysses-shakespeare-co-1922-1st-edn
UWM   *Little Review* records, Golda Meir Library, University of Wisconsin,
                 Milwaukee

Introduction

Many readers of *Ulysses* are familiar with the story of the novel's first publication: it was published in Paris on 2 February 1922, the occasion of Joyce's fortieth birthday, by the American-born Sylvia Beach, who willingly turned Shakespeare and Company, her English-language lending library and book shop, into a publishing house specifically for the purpose of issuing the first edition of *Ulysses*. Joyce did not just write *Ulysses*; he also played a significant role in determining the physical shape of the first edition, an octavo which runs to a lengthy 732 pages. For example, he specified the colour of the cover: the blue of the Greek flag is intended as a subtle reminder of the book's Homeric substructure; and he chose the typeface, Elzevir, after seeing samples of the text set by the printer, Maurice Darantiere, a printer of high-quality limited editions, with a significant reputation for attention to detail. That first edition—which can be downloaded from the website of the Modernist Versions Project—is often cited as one of the icons of high Modernism.[1] Yet that first edition was not the first iteration of *Ulysses* in print. Joyce never visited the US, but *Ulysses* was first published serially in the US periodical, the *Little Review*, between 1918 and 1920. This book discusses the textual and contextual significance of *Ulysses* as it appeared in the *Little Review*.

Ulysses is a work which concludes twice: first with Molly remembering the moment at which she decided to commit to Bloom ('yes I said yes I will yes') and secondly with the epigraph, *Trieste–Zurich–Paris, 1914–1921*. These final words, like the blue cover of the first edition, are an instance of what Gérard Genette would describe as 'paratext', paratextual features being bibliographical elements which adorn 'the fringe of the printed text' and help to determine its 'whole reading'.[2] As Genette argues, epigraphs have a very particular type of effect and function, by offering a commentary on the text 'whose meaning it indirectly specifies or emphasizes'.[3] The epigraph to *Ulysses* asserts that the precise facts of biography, history, and cultural geography might be determinants in the reading and interpretation of the text. It gestures to the significance of Joyce's sustained

---

[1] For the searchable and downloadable digital facsimile of the first edition, see http://web.uvic.ca/~mvp1922/portfolio/ulysses-shakespeare-co-1922-1st-edn. Or see the print facsimile (with the same pagination), James Joyce, *Ulysses* (Alexandria, VA: Orchises Press, 1998) or Jeri Johnson (ed.), *Ulysses* (Oxford: World's Classics, 1993), also a facsimile of the 1922 text, but reduced in size.
[2] Gérard Genette, *Paratexts: Thresholds of Interpretation*, translated by Jane E. Lewin (Cambridge: Cambridge University Press, 1997), 2.
[3] Genette, *Paratexts*, 156, 157.

compositional achievement in the extraordinary circumstances of upheaval and dislocation which the First World War, its aftermath, and related events brought about for the lives of millions, including Joyce and his family. The epigraph might also be read as an aspect of Joyce's self-fashioning. Looking back on what he had written, it was convenient for Joyce to be able to associate the achievement of *Ulysses* with the major events of the period, including not just the 'Great War', but also the Russian Revolution of 1917, the Versailles Treaty of 1919, and, of course, the dramatic events in Ireland: the Easter Rising of 1916, the War of Independence (1919–21), and the ratification of the Anglo-Irish Treaty, which led to the foundation of a twenty-six-county independent Irish state in January 1922, just as Joyce was completing the book.

Most readers agree that Molly's final yes placed alongside *Trieste–Zurich–Paris, 1914–1921* announces the conclusion of *Ulysses* with a flourish. Rather fewer have noted the way in which Joyce's triumphant conclusion glides over the messy material circumstances in which the text was composed. Some of the facts which the epigraph asserts can easily be unpicked. For instance, Joyce appears to have first thought of writing something about *Ulysses* when in Rome in 1906 (*L* II, 190); it is by no means clear that he did much work on the text in 1914; and he completed the early chapters of the work not in Trieste, or in Zurich, but in Locarno (Switzerland) in the closing months of 1917. These small facts suggest the danger of accepting Joyce's version of events, of accepting Joyce as his own interpretive agent. Read against historical fact, the shaped nature of the epigraph also underscores the difficulty of making clear statements about the compositional history of *Ulysses*. Abundant evidence of Joyce's work on the text survives, in the form of notebooks, draft and fair-copy manuscripts, typescripts, and proofs. But most of this enormous and rich archive documents the middle and latter stages in the composition of the work, making it difficult to establish how, when, and why Joyce set about the writing of *Ulysses*.

It is much easier to be precise about the facts of the work's serialization. Joyce first mentioned his work on *Ulysses* to Ezra Pound in June 1915, eighteen months after Pound had written to introduce himself to Joyce and suggest their mutual interest in writing which was 'markedly modern'.[4] The two men did not meet until June 1920, but from 1915 they established a regular correspondence, and Pound became an important supporter for Joyce, backing up his conviction that the manuscript of *A Portrait of the Artist* was 'damn fine stuff' by arranging for the entire text to be serialized in *The Egoist*, one of the London literary journals with which he was informally associated.[5] In the spring of 1917, when Pound became 'European editor' of New York's *Little Review*, Joyce's name was high on his list of essential contributors, along with those of T. S. Eliot and Wyndham Lewis. He wrote encouraging Joyce to send 'Anything you have in your desk',

[4] J to Pound, 30 June 1915 (Yale, unpublished); Pound to J, 15 December 1913, *EP-JJ*, 18.
[5] Pound to J, 17 and 19 January 1914, *EP-JJ*, 24.

'any short stuff you have and that you can afford to sell (magazine rights only) for £2 per thousand words':

> It has always struck me that you could do a unique series of 'portraits', 1000 to 2000 words, Priests in Padua. Students in Dublin, etc. God knows where you have been and what you have gazed upon with your microscopic, remarkable eye. Rough drafts of parts of *Ulysses*, if they wouldn't interfere with later serial publication of the whole.[6]

But Joyce was not the kind of writer to publish 'rough drafts' and, unlike Pound—in terms of his psychology as a writer—did not feel such a need to be part of a movement. He had also recently received the news that he was to be paid an anonymous donation of £200 by 'an admirer' of his writing (*L* II, 389), a gift which undoubtedly buoyed up his confidence, and may have made him less inclined to dissipate his energies by writing for journals.

Over the spring and summer of 1917 Joyce's entire focus was on the composition of *Ulysses*, and the work was still at quite a preliminary stage. Pound began to despair that Joyce would ever contribute anything to the *Little Review*. He wrote to Margaret Anderson, editor of the journal, telling her: 'We may as well take Joyce's name off the announcement list. Heaven knows when he'll get anything done'.[7] But then, just days after what he described to Pound as 'a violent Hexenschuss which incapacitated me from moving for about twenty minutes' (*SL* 227), and days before an iridectomy (an operation to remove part of the iris in his left eye), Joyce wrote to Pound in an uncharacteristically business-like manner and informed him, with regard to *Ulysses*, that he would be prepared to 'consign it serially from 1 January next, instalments of about 6000 words' (*SL* 227). Pound was collaborating with Harriet Shaw Weaver (1876–1961), editor of *The Egoist*, the source of the £200 gift, and the individual who would, in due course, become Joyce's most significant financial supporter.[8] Together Weaver and Pound had hatched a plan for the simultaneous dual serialization of *Ulysses* in *The Egoist* in London and the *Little Review* in New York. The US was not, at the time, a signatory to the Berne Convention, and the rationale for printing in New York was compliance with the 'manufacturing clause' of the 1891 International Copyright Act, which would enable the protection of Joyce's copyright in the US.[9] Joyce, in all likelihood, did not fully understand this aspect of copyright law, and was probably attracted by the prospect of dual serialization because it gave him access to a widely dispersed

---

[6] Pound to J, 9 February 1917, *EP-JJ*, 92.

[7] Pound to Margaret Anderson, 10 August 1917, *P-LR*, 108.

[8] Weaver played a role of fundamental and shaping significance in Joyce's career. Despite a significant archive at the British Library and sources such as John Firth (ed.), 'Harriet Weaver's Letters to James Joyce, 1915–1920', *Studies in Bibliography*, 20 (1967), 151–88 and Jane Lidderdale and Mary Nicholson, *Dear Miss Weaver: Harriet Shaw Weaver, 1876–1961* (New York: The Viking Press, 1970), the relationship remains difficult to interpret, in terms of psychology.

[9] See Robert Spoo, *Without Copyrights: Piracy, Publishing and the Public Domain* (New York: Oxford University Press, 2013), esp. ch. 2, 'Transatlantic Modernism and the American Public Domain', or Wikipedia on the 'International Copyright Act of 1891' for a briefer explanation of the function and rationale of the 'manufacturing clause'.

English-language readership and, as he noted, it would bring 'double fees' (*SL* 227). These arrangements led, eventually, to the first thirteen chapters of *Ulysses* being published in the *Little Review*, as well as the first instalment of chapter 14. The exact chronology can be seen in the following table (see Table I.1), which includes the commonly assigned Homeric titles of the individual chapters, for ease of reference.

That a significantly different version of *Ulysses* was being published and read so long in advance of the work's eventual completion is a fact of evident critical interest. After all, *Ulysses* as serialized in the *Little Review* is a text which Joyce consigned for publication, and not a manuscript which he might have thrown away. Moreover, it runs to a lengthy 122,918 words.[10] But until recent years readers have struggled to access this version of *Ulysses* because original copies of the *Little Review*, printed on cheap and highly acidic paper, tend to be scarce, and only available in research libraries. Copies that survive are often too fragile to consult, being victim to what conservationists dub 'slow fire' (the pages are extremely brittle and crumble to the touch). The Modernist Journals Project (MJP), a major digital humanities project begun at Brown University in 1995, saw the potential for making Modernist periodical literature available in digital form, thus proving (or at least contesting) that

Table I.1. *Ulysses* in the *Little Review*

Chapter no.	Date of *Little Review*
1 ('Telemachus')	March 1918
2 ('Nestor')	April 1918
3 ('Proteus')	May 1918
4 ('Calypso')	June 1918
5 ('Lotus-Eaters')	July 1918
6 ('Hades')	September 1918
7 ('Aeolus')	October 1918
8 ('Lestrygonians')	January 1919
	February–March 1918
9 ('Scylla and Charybdis')	April 1919
	May 1919
10 ('Wandering Rocks')	June 1919
	July 1919
11 ('Sirens')	August 1919
	September 1919
12 ('Cyclops')	November 1919
	December 1919
	January 1920
	March 1920
13 ('Nausicaa')	April 1920
	May–June 1920
	July–August 1920
14 ('Oxen of the Sun') [first instalment only]	September–December 1920

[10] See p. 136–144 below for information on word counts.

'modernism began in the magazines'.[11] In 2010–11 the MJP made available all issues of the *Little Review* from 1914 to 1922.[12] This, together with the 'material turn' in Modernist studies, has led to a renewal of interest in the *Little Review Ulysses* and, in 2015, the publication of an important printed edition of the text from Yale.[13]

Yale's *Little Review Ulysses*, edited by Mark Gaipa, Sean Latham, and Robert Scholes, reproduces all the instalments of Joyce's text as they appeared in the *Little Review*, and includes a general introduction, essays on the composition history, the magazine's context, and a selection of the original letters and comments on *Ulysses* which appeared in the journal. In every respect—including the provision of a full contextualizing history of the *Little Review*, detailed discussion of the composition history of *Ulysses*, discussion of the state of Joyce's text as it appeared in the *Little Review*, and discussion of post-serial revision—*Serial Encounters* aims to complement and extend the scholarship of the Yale edition (and the MJP from which it derived). This involves introducing important new archival finds from a range of sources including the *Little Review* Records at the University of Wisconsin, the currently unpublished Joyce–Pound correspondence at Yale, the John Quinn collection at the New York Public Library, and the Croessmann Collection at Southern Illinois University in Carbondale.[14] It also involves some necessary repetition and clarification of fact, of importance to readers who are not familiar with these resources and the field of Joycean textual scholarship more generally. More specifically, *Serial Encounters* is based on a fresh examination of unpublished, published, archival, and textual sources and, as such, and as a full-length monograph, carries questions about the significance of the serialization to a deeper level than that which was possible in the Yale edition. This is particularly true in relation to the general argument of the book about the contextual and genetic significance of the *Little Review* for the authorship and reception of *Ulysses*.

If the serialization of *Ulysses* is of critical significance for Joyce's authorship, then the appearance of the text in *The Egoist* is, in theory, at least as important as the appearance of the text in the *Little Review*. But the arrangement to publish a serial *Ulysses* in *The Egoist* was less successful than the arrangement to publish in the *Little Review*. During the course of 1919, just three of the chapters were printed in *The Egoist* (2, 3, 6) as well as a portion of chapter 10.[15] In every instance the text had already been printed in the *Little Review*. Thus the *Little Review* serialization is

---

[11] http://modjourn.org/teaching/introduction/intro1_identity.html.

[12] The release schedule is posted at http://www.modjourn.org/about.html.

[13] *The Little Review Ulysses*, ed. by Mark Gaipa, Sean Latham, and Robert Scholes (New Haven, CT: Yale University Press, 2015) (Gaipa et al., *LRU*).

[14] See the Bibliography's 'Archival and Unpublished Sources' for a full listing of works consulted, p. 251.

[15] See all numbers of *The Egoist* for 1919 (Modernist Journals Project, http://modjourn.org). Chapters 2, 3, 6, and an excerpt from 10 appeared in the numbers for Jan.–Feb., March–April, July (chapter 6, part 1), September (chapter 6, part 2), and December respectively. According to Hans Gabler, Chapters 2 and 3 were 'set up from *Little Review*' (*CSE*III 1730) whereas chapters 6 and 10 were set from typescript (*CSE*III 1734, 1740).

more significant, textually and contextually, and is the rationale for the emphasis of this study on the *Little Review*, and not *The Egoist*.

Yet the story of what was going on behind the scenes at *The Egoist* is also fascinating, and thus a few facts are worth reporting here. The reason more of *Ulysses* was not published in *The Egoist* boils down to Weaver having difficulties finding a British printer prepared to print Joyce's text. Under the Newspapers, Printers and Reading Rooms Repeal Act (1869), printers were required to print their name and address on every copy of a book that they printed.[16] It is the printer and publisher—rather than Joyce—who would have been liable in legal proceedings brought, for example, under the Obscene Publications Act of 1857. Printers may not have believed such action to be very likely but they did tend to err on the side of caution because the test of obscenity established in 1868 ('whether the tendency of the matter charged... is to deprave and corrupt') was dangerously vague.[17]

Weaver was level-headed and practical, but it is not clear how effective she was at negotiating within the all-male world of the British printing establishment. What exactly did the printers object to in the opening chapters of *Ulysses*? Did the printers actually read the typescripts Weaver had in hand, or were they prejudiced by hearsay of all the fuss surrounding *Dubliners*? Why were London's literary editors so reluctant to step forward and champion Joyce? Would they have responded differently if the request to print *Ulysses* had come from the male representative of an established literary publisher, rather than a woman of independent means who happened to edit an *avant-garde* periodical? Perhaps, but the evidence of an intensely conservative printing culture is not difficult to discern. For example, Stanley Morison (1889–1967), the typographer noted for designing Times New Roman, turned down the opportunity to print *Ulysses* for the Pelican Press in July 1920, venturing a view of the work as 'mere incomprehensible jabber with only occasional flashes that recall the "Portrait" ' and adding:

> I do feel that much (one-third possibly) of the MS. is too utterly foul to escape possibly prosecution but at any rate considerable disrepute...I do not accuse Mr Joyce of 'immorality' or of making vice appear virtuous—it is his merit to make sexuality supremely disgusting.[18]

Interestingly Morison's response was based on—at most—the typescripts of the first thirteen or fourteen chapters. A detailed reconstruction of the compositional chronology of the text reveals that chapter 14 ('Oxen of the Sun') was being typed in May 1920, by which time Joyce was beginning to concentrate on chapter 15 ('Circe').[19] In July 1920—the moment of Morison's response—Joyce moved to Paris from Trieste. He did not know Morison, who was in London and who could not have had any sense of the four concluding chapters of the book, including

---

[16] Geoffrey Ashall Glaister, *Encyclopedia of the Book*, 2nd edn with a new introduction by Donald Farren (New Castle, DE: Oak Knoll Press; London: The British Library, 1996), 241.

[17] John Feather, *A History of British Publishing* (London: Routledge, 1988), 157.

[18] Stanley Morison to Harriet Shaw Weaver, 20 July 1920 (unpublished, Lilly Library, Indiana University, Bloomington).

[19] J to Pound, 18 May 1920, Yale (unpublished).

chapter 18 ('Penelope'), which Joyce later described, knowingly, as 'more obscene than any preceding episode' ('It turns like the huge earth ball slowly and surely and evenly round and round spinning, its four cardinal points being the female breasts, arse, womb, and cunt', *SL*, 285).

Though the *Little Review* managed to publish twenty-three instalments of *Ulysses* in sequence, the process of publication in New York was fraught with difficulty. Trouble began in January 1919 with the issue containing the first instalment of chapter 8 ('Lestrygonians'). Some copies of this issue appear to have been 'suppressed' (i.e. not posted, and thus withheld from circulation) by officials working for the New York Post Office, who, somewhat unusually, were legally entitled to declare items to be 'non-mailable' if they were deemed to be 'obscene', 'lewd', 'lascivious', 'indecent or immoral'.[20] The *Little Review* had been identified by the Post Office as a 'Publication of Anarchistic Tendency', and was thus being checked with some care by officials looking for a reason to declare a particular issue non-mailable.[21] Some copies of the issues for May 1919 and January 1920 were also withheld by the Post Office—on grounds which remain a little unclear. But it was the issue of July–August 1920 that caused the most significant problems. The daughter of a New York attorney asked her father to complain about the contents of the third instalment of chapter 13 ('Nausicaa'), in which Leopold Bloom masturbates on Sandymount Strand. The complaint was passed to John Sumner, Secretary of the New York Society for the Suppression of Vice, and led, eventually, to the successful prosecution of the *Little Review* editors in February 1921 on grounds of the 'obscenity' of the third instalment of 'Nausicaa'. Both Anderson and her partner Jane Heap were fined $50 and finger-printed, and the serialization of *Ulysses*, which had advanced as far as the first instalment of chapter 14 (of eighteen), came to an abrupt and permanent halt.

This troubled history of production, reception, and suppression underpins the structure of the following study, which divides, in terms of methodology and emphasis, into two halves, Chapters 1 and 2 being contextual and historicist, and Chapters 3 and 4 being textual, genetic, and interpretive. Using a range of unpublished archival sources, as well as the rich secondary literature, Chapter 1 ('The World of the *Little Review*') looks at the foundation, history, and typical content of the *Little Review*, as well as the cultural formation and *mentalité* of those playing a role behind the scenes, including Anderson, Heap, Pound, and Pound's supporter and financial patron, John Quinn. Chapter 2 ('Trial and Error: The Composition and Production of *Ulysses* to April 1921') examines the early compositional history of *Ulysses* and the ways in which the material circumstances of the text's production created a context for the proliferation of error; it also offers a detailed and original account of the trial of the *Little Review* editors, with reference to the surviving legal and archival materials.

The serial text of *Ulysses* is significantly different to that of the first edition of 1922 and Chapter 3 ('The Serial Style and Beyond: From the *Little Review* to

---

[20] *LR*, March 1918, 33.
[21] Paul Vanderham, *James Joyce and Censorship: The Trials of Ulysses* (London: Macmillan, 1998), 18.

Shakespeare and Company') looks at the nature of *Ulysses* as a serial text, and offers an initial view of Joyce's post-serial revisionary practice by close reading the additions made to four pages of the 1922 text. Digital facsimiles have transformed the methodologies of this type of research and an introductory section to Chapter 3 explores this issue in some detail, and focuses, in particular, on text collation in the digital environment, and quantitative approaches to literary analysis. *Ulysses* was written over many years, and in several different locations, and Joyce's text, and his intentions for it, underwent a significant transformation from the moment of his arrival in Paris in July 1920. Chapter 4 ('Paris Departures: Patterns of Post-Serial Ulyssean Revision') puts forward a general argument that there are, in essence, seven types of Ulyssean revision. It then explores this in some detail by looking at the particular post-serial revisions which Joyce made to four chapters: chapter 2 ('Nestor'), chapter 11 ('Sirens'), chapter 5 ('Lotus-Eaters'), and chapter 13 ('Nausicaa').

Given the Yale edition of the *Little Review Ulysses*, intense scholarly interest in Joyce, and *Ulysses* in particular, it is surprising how little attention has been paid to the textual and contextual significance of the serialization. As Kevin Birmingham has recently noted, Richard Ellmann only devotes two pages to the New York trial of 1921, and does not discuss Margaret Anderson in any great detail.[22] Michael Groden's *Ulysses in Progress*, still the most significant study of the genesis of Joyce's text, suggests that the *Little Review* has no 'textual significance'.[23] It is certainly true, from the perspective of traditional scholarly editing, that the *Little Review Ulysses* may be said to be both 'corrupt' (in that it omits text intended by Joyce, and includes many errors) and 'outside the line of transmission' (from author to completed work). Yet to use this kind of reasoning to suggest that the *Little Review Ulysses* has no authority—and thus justify gliding over this phase in the composition of the whole work—is to overlook the significance of the process of serialization for Joyce's subsequent rewriting of the text, and is to ignore the social, cultural, and critical significance of the very first iterations of Joyce's iconic text in print.

As the editors of the *Little Review Ulysses* have noted, the very first readers of *Ulysses* were not those who could afford to purchase the prohibitively expensive limited edition issued by Shakespeare and Company, but were those who read the text serially as it appeared in the *Little Review* and *The Egoist*.[24] Those readers—who were largely American and usually regular subscribers—encountered *Ulysses* not as an iconic and finished masterpiece, but as a gradually evolving serial, which gradually provoked controversy. For those readers *Ulysses* was a work to be continued, to be experienced in a range of serial encounters; a work to be sampled, crucially, alongside writings by other significant authors of the modern era, such as Pound, T. S. Eliot, Yeats, and Dorothy Richardson. They read Joyce not as a lone and isolated pioneer, but as one writer among several who were trying to develop a modern idiom and consciousness for literature during and immediately following the First World War.

[22] Kevin Birmingham, *The Most Dangerous Book: The Battle for James Joyce's Ulysses* (New York: The Penguin Press, 2014), 14; Richard Ellmann, *James Joyce* (1959; Oxford: Oxford University Press, rev edn, 1982), 502–4.

[23] Michael Groden, *Ulysses in Progress* (Princeton, NJ: Princeton University Press, 1977), 7.

[24] Gaipa et al., *LRU*, xi.

Of course those who read *Ulysses* in the *Little Review* included not just enthusiasts, but also those who responded with opprobrium, such as the three judges who tried the editors of the *Little Review* at the Court of Special Sessions in February 1921. That trial, and the events which led up to it, may be interpreted as an aspect of reception; after all, it turned specifically on the question of whether the third instalment of chapter 13 ('Nausicaa') could be judged to be 'obscene' or of 'an indecent character'. The judgment that Anderson and Heap had violated the Penal Law of the State of New York by publishing work considered to be 'smutty' and 'filthy within the meaning of the statute' is a crucial element in the historic reception of the still-to-be-finished work, which had far-reaching implications for both its subsequent publishing and compositional history.[25] For instance, Sylvia Beach's desire to publish the work 'as Joyce wished in every respect' was inspired by an awareness that the work had been 'suppressed four times', a fact pointed out in the prospectus offered to potential purchasers of the first edition.[26]

In the first stages of the serialization, for example during the calendar year of 1918—when Joyce saw to some state of completion the first nine chapters of the work—the process of serialization was clearly both formative and incentivizing. The difficulties of serialization were also highly significant for Joyce's ongoing compositional labour. The legal proceedings against the *Little Review* stretched out between August 1920 and February 1921. Other writers might have given up in the face of such upheaval and controversy but Joyce—who made the decision to equip himself with only a sketchy sense of what was happening and why it might be significant for the publication of the completed work in the US—buried himself in the composition of chapter 15 ('Circe'), arguably the most obscene, and certainly the longest chapter in the book. Using Quinn as intermediary, patron, and agent, he also continued to seek options to publish the work as a whole. Clearly his effort to complete *Ulysses* was driven, at least in part, by his relish for the spirited cultural antagonism it was inspiring.

In addition to being a work of notorious complexity, *Ulysses* is also one of the longest novels in the English language. Errors of various kinds—authorial, transcriptional, and typographical—inevitably began to creep in to the text as soon as Joyce began to prepare his manuscript for publication. As he worked on the final stages of the Paris edition, Joyce became 'extremely irritated' by what he identified as 'printer's errors'.[27] Examples from the 1922 text include, in chapter 1 ('Telemachus'), 'Genera' instead of 'General', 'pantomine' instead of 'pantomime', a missing dash at the beginning of the line to mark conversation, and the slightly French 'aimiably' instead of 'amiably' (*U*1922, 6, 10, 13). Joyce's eyesight was poor; even he could find his handwriting difficult to decipher; and he was working

---

[25] John Quinn to Pound, 21 October 1920, Carbondale. Quinn is describing the reasoning of the magistrate J. E. Corrigan, presented at a preliminary hearing at the Jefferson Market Police Court on 21 October 1920. The judges of the full hearing in Special Sessions (21 February 1921) did not issue a written judgment, and thus their precise legal reasoning is not completely clear, but has to be adduced from newspaper reports and other contemporary accounts.

[26] Sylvia Beach, *Shakespeare and Company* (1959; Lincoln, NE: University of Nebraska Press, 1991), 60. For the prospectus advertising the first edition, see Katherine McSharry (ed.), *A Joycean Scrapbook from the National Library of Ireland* (Dublin: Wordwell, 2004), 102.

[27] J to Weaver, 6 November 1921, *L* I, 176.

with printers who knew little English. Most significantly, as the work was being produced in proof from June 1921 onward, Joyce was continuing to add to the text and his focus was not (or not entirely) on the correction of errors. In a letter of November 1921 which reveals a tellingly disdainful attitude to the business of final proof correction, Joyce told Weaver:

> I am extremely irritated by all those printer's errors. Working as I do amid piles of notes at a table in a hotel I cannot possibly do this mechanical part with my wretched eye and a half. Are these to be perpetuated in future editions? I hope not.[28]

In the meantime, it was decided that the first edition would acknowledge error with an unusual kind of apologia—an italicized prefatory note in the prelims, signed 'S. B.' (Sylvia Beach), and placed prominently on a recto after the title page, and following the notice of limitation. The note reads:

> *The publisher asks the reader's indulgence for typographical errors unavoidable in the exceptional circumstances.* (*U*1922, [vii])

Together with the very obvious typographical errors of the first edition, this note inevitably helped to create the goal of establishing the text of Joyce's final intentions, a goal which led, eventually, to the publication of Hans Walter Gabler's three-volume *Critical and Synoptic Edition of Ulysses* (1984), an important scholarly work which generated significant controversy in the immediate aftermath of its publication, and which is now out of print, and largely ignored or misunderstood. Few of the world's many Joyce scholars have engaged in the work of trying to understand what the left-hand pages of Gabler's edition actually denote; still fewer have grasped Gabler's fundamental aim of raising awareness about:

> the material indeterminacy of texts, the logical impossibility of definitive editions, the involvement of readers as well as editors in the process of texts, the centrality of textuality scholarship to the enterprise of criticism.[29]

Given that Gabler's project is central to all study dealing with the textuality of *Ulysses*, it is necessary to introduce and examine its rationale here, in order to situate this study within its wider intellectual context. It is also important to consider the reasons why the Gabler edition generated such controversy.

'LOST IN THE TRANSMISSION TO PRINT': THE EDITIONS CONTROVERSY

The easiest way to grasp an initial understanding of Gabler's edition is by looking in detail at a textual sample. Here, to begin, is a moment from chapter 3 ('Proteus'), transcribed as written by Joyce in the Rosenbach manuscript, the most significant

---

[28] J to Weaver, 6 November 1921, *L* I, 176.
[29] Hans Walter Gabler, 'What *Ulysses* Requires', *Proceedings of the Bibliographical Society of America*, 87:2 (1993), 187–248 (248).

surviving *Ulysses* manuscript, sometimes referred to as the 'fair copy' because it is a clear copy of the text in Joyce's hand, rather than a working draft.

> Five fathoms out there. Full fathom five they father lies. At one, he said. High water at Dublin bar. Driving before it a loose drift of rubble, fanshoals of fishes, silly shells. A corpse rising saltwhite from the undertow, bobbing landward. There he is. Hook it quick. Pull. We have him. Easy now[30]

This passage of interior monologue sees Dedalus thinking about the moment when a drowned man may be swept ashore somewhere in Dublin Bay, when the tide comes in at about one. In what is presumably Joyce's copying error, the final full stop after 'Easy now' is clearly missing. But the single-word sentence 'Pull.' is clearly present, and is part of a dialogue Dedalus imagines between those recovering the drowned body. From this manuscript, Claud Sykes (Joyce's friend who was strong-armed into the role of being typist) prepared some copies of a typescript which does not survive, except for one page (not, as it happens, the right page).[31] That now lost typescript must have included the word 'Pull.' as the word appears in the *Little Review* version of the text, which was published in May 1918. The *Little Review* omits the comma in the phrase 'At one, he said.' but includes the full stop after 'Easy now.'; it is otherwise exactly as the Rosenbach.

The very prominent reference to Ariel's song in *The Tempest* ('Full fathom five thy father lies') reflects Dedalus's literary sensibility, as do the lexical innovations apparent in the words 'fanshoals' and 'saltwhite', and the wordplay of 'High water at Dublin bar', a phrase from *Thom's* tide tables of 1904.[32] When Joyce came to revise this paragraph he notably added three phrases which intensify the lyricism of what had already been written: 'Found drowned', 'a pace a pace a porpoise', and 'Sunk though he be beneath the watery floor'. The 1922 text, with the new additions marked in **a Semibold font**, reads:

> Five fathoms out there. Full fathom five they father lies. At one he said. **Found drowned**. High water at Dublin bar. Driving before it a loose drift of rubble, fanshoals of fishes, silly shells. A corpse rising saltwhite from the undertow, bobbing landward, **a pace a pace a porpoise**. There he is. Hook it quick. **Sunk though he be beneath the watery floor**. We have him. Easy now.   (*U*1922, 49)

'Found drowned' may reflect a coroner's official verdict for an accidental drowning, as Gifford suggests; that two words with such variant spelling could make such a full rhyme—with stressed vowel and subsequent sounds being identical—is the

---

[30] Clive Driver (ed.), *James Joyce, Ulysses: A Facsimile of the Manuscript*, 3 vols (Philadelphia, PA: Rosenbach Foundation, 1975).

[31] The one surviving page of the original typescript, prepared in January 1918, is at Buffalo. See UB Joyce Catalog at http://library.buffalo.edu/pl/collections/jamesjoyce/catalog/vb2.htm. This page has been reproduced in Michael Groden (ed.), *The James Joyce Archive* (New York: Garland, 1978) (63 vols, hereafter *JJA*), volume 12: *A Facsimile of Notes for the Book and Manuscripts and Typescripts ('Telemachus' to 'Scylla and Charybdis')*, 259.

[32] Don Gifford, with Robert J. Seidman, *Ulysses Annotated: Notes for James Joyce's Ulysses*, rev 2nd edn (London: University of California Press, 1988), 64.

kind of detail to appeal to Dedalus's aspirations as a poet.[33] The same is true of 'a pace a pace a porpoise', a phrase of alliterative onomatopoeia which mimics and imagines the undulations of the drowned corpse (alongside a porpoise, a common sight in Dublin Bay). The added phrase from Milton's *Lycidas*, another very prominent Renaissance text dealing with drowning ('Sunk though he be beneath the watery floor'), works well in context, particularly alongside the existing reference to Shakespeare; this addition might also be identified as an example of Joyce's tendency to make the text of *Ulysses* more encyclopaedic and complete as he revised it for publication in book form.

The evidence of Joyce adding these three phrases can be seen in sets of page proofs now at libraries in Buffalo and Texas (and in the facsimile of these documents in the *James Joyce Archive*).[34] Interestingly these proofs omit the one-word sentence 'Pull.'. This is a tiny adjustment, and its omission does not make a significant difference to the meaning and impact of the whole paragraph. Nonetheless, the question of what Joyce intended is significant. Did he intentionally omit the word 'Pull' or was it omitted by the typesetter in error? If so, why didn't Joyce restore that word as he corrected the proofs? It is possible, of course, that he simply forgot to do so. He may not have conducted a full check of the proof against his typescript—a labour-intensive and tedious process—and he certainly did not verify the proofs against the Rosenbach manuscript, which he was selling, in completed sections, to John Quinn.[35] Another variant in this paragraph is the omitted comma in the phrase 'At one, he said'. This comma plays an important role in tightening the phrase, and is indicative of the precise way in which Dedalus is processing the conversation he had overheard earlier, in which a boatman had discussed the drowned man's expected reappearance ('It'll be swept up that way when the time comes in about one') (*U*1922, 21). It seems unlikely that Joyce would have intentionally omitted the comma, which may have been omitted in the typescript (it is not included in the *Little Review*). Another interesting complication thrown up by study of the proofs for this particular paragraph is the placing of the phrase 'a pace a pace a porpoise'. Should that phrase sit between the words 'bobbing' and 'landward', to make the reading 'bobbing a pace a pace a porpoise landward' (as in the Buffalo proofs)? Or should the phrase be added after 'landward' (as in the later Texas proofs, and the 1922 edition)?

In preparing the *Critical and Synoptic Edition*, Gabler had to make decisions about issues of this kind, and he had to devise a system for doing so. As Gabler himself has explained, the edition took a 'radical editorial stance' towards the 'written and the changing text' by editing *Ulysses* from the manuscripts and documents of

[33] Gifford, *Ulysses Annotated*, 64.
[34] *JJA* volume 22: *Ulysses: A Facsimile of Page Proofs for Episodes 1–6*, 169 (Buffalo) and 215 (Texas).
[35] Quinn made the offer to purchase the manuscript in June 1919, when Joyce was at work on chapter 12 ('Cyclops'). Joyce accepted the offer in October 1919, as he left Zurich to return to Trieste and found himself desperately short of funds. See *JJ-JQ* I, 237, 240. Quinn subsequently sold the manuscript to A. S. W. Rosenbach (1876–1952), a sale which Joyce opposed and resented, as he noted in a letter to Weaver ('a grossly stupid act which is an alienation of valuable property.', 8 February 1924, *L* I, 211).

pre-publication transmission, rather than the first edition of 1922 which he found to be 'non-authoritative' (though he also acknowledged it to be 'the closest approximation to be found in one document of the work at its ultimate stage of compositional development').[36] The three-volume edition—in other words, *the* critical edition—comes with left-hand pages with a 'synoptic display' which Gabler offered 'to the scrutiny of every critical reader and adventurous explorer of the novel'.[37] The 'fathom' paragraph—with its careful echoes of several words from the moment of the boatman's discussion in chapter 1 ('fathom', 'drowned', 'saltwhite', and 'bob', *U*1922, 21)—appears as follows (see Figure I.1):

> Five fathoms out there. Full fathom five thy father lies. At one, he said. ⸀Found drowned.⸀ High water at Dublin bar. Driving before it a loose drift of rubble, fanshoals of fishes, silly shells. A corpse rising saltwhite from the undertow, bobbing ⸀a⸌ pace a pace a porpoise⸀ landward.⸌ There he is. Hook it quick. Pull. ⸀Sunk though he be beneath the watery floor.⸀ We have him. Easy now.

Figure I.1. Excerpt from the *Critical and Synoptic Edition* (Garland Publishing Inc, New York, 1986)

The three sets of raised paired half-brackets with the superscript number 2 indicate that that revision is the addition of new text to the second set of proofs, as already discussed. The superscript 'c' and its reverse 'ɔ' placed around 'pace a pace a porpoise landward' directs readers to consider a footnote marked *TD* which indicates a 'transmissional departure', an 'authorized change or error in a scribal copy, typescript or proof' (*CSE*I xiii). In other words, Gabler has decided that Joyce made a mistake in the Texas proof correction and intended to place his phrase about the porpoise between the words 'bobbing' and 'landward'. On this issue Gabler is probably right: the evidence of the proofs reveals that both Joyce and the printers were confused, and the phrase achieves its strongest mimetic effect between 'bobbing' and 'landward'.

But there are issues of evaluation and editorial choice here, and these came sharply to the fore with the publication and reception of reader's editions of Gabler's text from 1986 onwards. These editions, marketed as *Ulysses* 'The Corrected Text' ('purely publisher's nomenclature' in Gabler's account), reproduced the right-hand pages of the *Critical and Synoptic Edition* without any of the anchoring diacritical symbols, lists of emendations, and historical collations.[38] For readers who were new to Joyce this new edition was *Ulysses*, and given the challenge of the novel on other hermeneutic fronts, the need to work out why the text had had to be corrected did not, perhaps, seem pressing. But established readers found that *Ulysses*

---

[36] Gabler, 'What *Ulysses* Requires', 190; *CSE*III 1894.   [37] *CSE*I vii.
[38] Gabler, 'What *Ulysses* Requires', 187.

'had become a little bit less familiar' and the edition 'forced critics to revise some of their favourite interpretations'.[39]

In Gabler's edition, the 'fathom' paragraph became:

> Five fathoms out there. Full fathom five they father lies. At one, he said. Found drowned. High water at Dublin bar. Driving before it a loose drift of rubble, fanshoals of fishes, silly shells. A corpse rising saltwhite from the undertow, bobbing a pace a pace a porpoise landward. There he is. Hook it quick. Pull. Sunk though he be beneath the watery floor. We have him. Easy now.[40]

The three departures from the 1922 text—the introduction of the comma ('At one, he said'), the placing of the porpoise between 'bobbing' and 'landward', and the introduction of the word 'Pull.'—have been introduced here, owing to their presence, as noted, in the Rosenbach and the proofs. These new readings are also meticulously recorded in the list of historical collations contained in volume 3 of the *Critical and Synoptic Edition*.[41] In theory, then, this example reveals that the new reading text should not have surprised any reader who had come to terms with the contents and procedures of the *Critical and Synoptic Edition*. But in practice the new reading text generated controversy and confusion because readers either did not understand or (less commonly) did not agree with Gabler's editorial procedures.

Ellmann's preface to the Penguin 'Corrected Text' did not help matters: it suggested that the substantive changes to the text were 'obvious improvements', and naively claimed that Gabler aimed 'at an ideal text, such as Joyce would have constructed in ideal conditions'.[42] This preface also coyly suggests that the Corrected *Ulysses* had become 'one of the most concluded books ever written' because it included a forty-three-word restoration in chapter 9 about 'love' being the 'Word known to all men'.[43] It is not quite adequate to account for such an obvious omission—clearly present in the Rosenbach and conspicuously absent in the proofs—through the single word 'eyeskip'. Critics baulked at the editorial and interpretive cruxes which Ellmann appeared to be papering over.[44]

In some respects, the edition controversy turned on the choice of copy-text, the 'chosen original' seen to possess over-riding authority, on which the edition was based.[45] As Gabler had explained, 'an editor chooses as the copy-text for a critical edition a document text of highest overall authority' and his edition had eliminated 'the first edition of 1922 as copy-text' on the grounds of its 'many corruptive departures from the text in manuscript which [Joyce] demonstrably...did not see'.[46] In its place Gabler had constructed (and emended) a copy-text which he termed a

[39] Wim Van Mierlo, 'Reading Joyce In and Out of the Archive', *Joyce Studies Annual*, 13 (Summer 2002), 32–63 (48).

[40] James Joyce, *Ulysses* (The Corrected Text), ed. by Hans Walter Gabler with a New Preface by Richard Ellmann (London: Penguin in association with the Bodley Head, 1986), 41.

[41] *CSE*III 1760.

[42] *Ulysses* (Penguin edition with Ellmann preface), xi, x. For the passage see *CSE*I 427–31.

[43] *Ulysses* (Penguin edition with Ellmann preface), xiv.

[44] Van Mierlo, 'Reading Joyce In and Out of the Archive', 48.

[45] For copy-text see Philip Gaskell, *A New Introduction to Bibliography* (Oxford: Clarendon Press, 1972), 338f, and W. W. Greg, 'The Rationale of Copy-Text', *Studies in Bibliography*, 3 (1950), 19–36.

[46] *CSE*III 1894, 1892; Gabler, 'What *Ulysses* Requires', 193.

'continuous manuscript text' from Joyce's 'autograph notation' as represented in the Rosenbach manuscript and other drafts, the typescripts, and the proofs.[47] This 'continuous manuscript text' was, as Gabler clarified in an important later article, not a real entity but a 'virtual' one which had been 'prepared by abstracting Joyce's manuscript text from the documents of composition and pre-publication submission'.[48] It had been collated from various manuscript sources using TUSTEP, a system of computer programs for text data processing. The *Critical and Synoptic Edition* appeared in 1984, at a time when humanities computing was in its infancy, and the very process of using a computer to facilitate the editing of a text aroused scholarly suspicions. So too did the somewhat arcane and difficult language and sigla of the edition.

Thus the controversy raged, and was fuelled, as Wim Van Mierlo has noted, by 'a certain hysteria', 'widespread unawareness of manuscripts', '*ad hominem* attacks', 'waving of unpublicized lists with alleged corrections', and the inherent difficulty of some of the concepts which are so central to the editing of *Ulysses*.[49] What exactly is a 'collateral revision' or an 'inter-document change'? Why do readers need to know about 'residual authority in the earlier witness', the 'lost final working draft', the difference between a revisional and transmissional change, 'passive authorisation', or what Gabler terms the rule of 'invariant context'? The answer to these questions, and the deeper question of how correct the Gabler edition actually is, need not be of concern here. More than thirty years after the publication of the *Critical and Synoptic Edition*, the edition, particularly in its left-hand pages, continues to be of great significance for any close reading of the text, and continues to demonstrate, in exemplary fashion, the ongoing scholarly problems which Joyce's text poses for all editors. Properly speaking, Gabler's edition is not a 'Corrected Text'—a subtitle assigned by the Joyce Estate and trade publishers—but a non-corrupted one.[50] By placing 'every revisional variant in relation to others', the edition establishes the critical significance of the whole compositional process. It reveals that the completed *Ulysses* has a mosaic-like structure, a structure which was finished (more or less, for the serializations of chapters 1 to 14), and then finished (more or less) again.

This study departs from other work on the textuality and genesis of *Ulysses* by taking the view that the *Little Review Ulysses*—however botched, deformed, and corrupt it may be—is of critical interest. Rooted in a concern for textual historicity, the work argues that the *Little Review* text, which was sanctioned by Joyce and published in his lifetime, has a particular and indubitable authority.[51] With this particular argument in mind—that the historic published editions are authoritative—it is

---

[47] *CSE*III, 1895.
[48] Gabler, 'What *Ulysses* Requires', 197, 201. This article is a response to John Kidd's 'An Inquiry into *Ulysses: The Corrected Text*', *Proceedings of the Bibliographical Society of America*, 82 (1988), 411–584, and is the clearest statement of Gabler's editorial intentions. John Kidd was Gabler's most vociferous critic.
[49] Van Mierlo, 'Reading Joyce In and Out of the Archive', 47, 48.
[50] Van Mierlo, 'Reading Joyce In and Out of the Archive', 50.
[51] Another 'serial' *Ulysses* of historic interest, but beyond the remit of the present study, is that of *Two Worlds Monthly*, a copy pirated by Samuel Roth in 1926–7. The text is available at http://web.uvic.ca/~mvp1922/two-worlds-monthly, and is discussed by Amanda Sigler in 'In Between the Sheets: Sexy Punctuation in American Magazines', in Tim Conley and Elizabeth Bonapfel (eds.), *Doubtful Points: Joyce and Punctuation* (European Joyce Studies 23) (Amsterdam: Rodopi, 2014), 43–66.

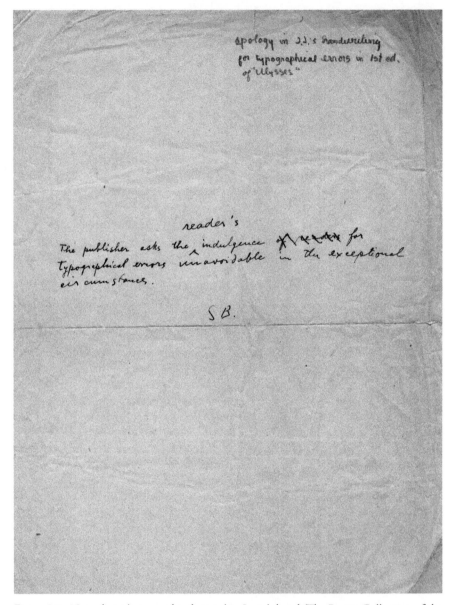

Figure I.2. Note about 'typographical errors' in Joyce's hand (The Poetry Collection of the University Libraries, University at Buffalo, The State University of New York)

worth pointing to a find in the archives, specifically relating to the note ascribed to Beach about errors in the first-volume edition. The Buffalo Joyce Collection—where so many of the drafts, typescripts, and proofs of the first edition are preserved—contains a single-page document, unmistakably in Joyce's hand, which reveals that it was Joyce, rather than Beach, who actually wrote the note about 'typographical errors' (see Figure I.2).

In the months before the publication of the first edition, Joyce, Beach, and Darantiere were clearly engaged in a process of intense collaboration, with Joyce calling to Beach at Shakespeare and Company on an almost daily basis to confer about plans for the edition, borrow books, collect typescripts, discuss ongoing work on the proofs, and sometimes borrow sums of cash.[52] Joyce must have discussed the problem of typographical errors with Beach during that time, and the discussion obviously led to the decision to include this note, which Beach may have asked Joyce to word, given her inexperience as a publisher. The coyness in the phrase 'begs the reader's indulgence' helps to ascribe the authorship of the note to Beach quite effectively; certainly this wording does not sound Joycean. But the material evidence confirms Joyce's hand. Joyce was justifiably proud of the first-volume edition of *Ulysses* and in some respects it is puzzling—given the meticulous care he took with so many aspects of the work—that he allowed this note to advertise the edition's many typographical errors. On the other hand, it is also possible to view this note— the specifics of this piece of 'autograph notation'—as an aspect of intentional authorial strategy, part of Joyce's ploy to position himself as an individual whose work was produced (and could only be produced) in 'exceptional circumstances'.

The note helps to convey an impression—an impression Joyce intended—of the author as a lone genius struggling in exceptional circumstances with inept publishers. By ascribing responsibility for error to Beach, Joyce also neatly occludes his part in creating the material circumstances which contributed so significantly to the errors of the first edition: his determination to write the book exactly as he wished without making any concessions to those of a more conservative mindset; the desire to have that book published on his fortieth birthday; the continued and significant additions to the proofs even as that birthday drew nearer; and, finally, the reluctance to engage with the 'mechanical' part of proof correction, which would have involved checking that the fair copy was accurately represented in the typescript. Error, as Joyce himself recognized, is an inevitable component of all written texts, and this study argues that there is much to be learned from studying the specific error-ridden text of the *Little Review Ulysses*, the context in which it was produced, and the legal controversy which the text generated. In addition, the study argues that the error-ridden and incomplete version of *Little Review Ulysses* can be read instructively against the quite different version of the text which Joyce finalized in Paris in February 1922, in a volume which he would later characterize as the 'usylessly unreadable Blue Book of Eccles'.[53]

---

[52] Sylvia Beach, *Shakespeare and Company* (1959; Lincoln, NE: University of Nebraska Press, 1991), 75.

[53] James Joyce, *Finnegans Wake*, with an introduction by Seamus Deane (London: Penguin Books, 1992), 179.

1

The World of the *Little Review*

INTRODUCTION

Writing prominently on the final page of the *Little Review* for February 1918, Margaret Anderson (1886–1973), principal editor and founder of the *Little Review*, announced that she had 'just received' the first three instalments of Joyce's 'new novel' 'called "Ulysses"'. The text had thus far been read 'by only one critic of international reputation' who considered the work to be 'rather better than Flaubert' and praised its 'compression' and 'intensity'. It carried on the 'story of Stephan Dedalus' (sic) and was, Anderson felt, 'even better than the "Portrait"'; in fact, she was so convinced by the quality of the forthcoming work that she informed readers, with characteristic gush and *brio*, that the 'announcement means that we are about to publish a prose masterpiece'.[1]

Joyce's name—in association with that of Ezra Pound, the 'critic' of Anderson's puff, and 'Foreign Editor' of the *Little Review* for two years from May 1917 to April 1919—had been trailing in the *Little Review* for more than a year before this announcement: Joyce had told Pound about *Ulysses* in progress in June 1915; Pound had told Anderson about the work ('a sort of continuation or at least a second phase of his "Portrait of the Artist"') in March 1917; and the editors had publicly expressed their desire to publish *Ulysses* ('the new novel promised by James Joyce') in October 1917.[2] The American editions of *Portrait of the Artist as a Young Man* and *Dubliners* had been advertised in January 1917, and both Anderson and her partner Jane Heap had separately and very positively reviewed *Portrait* in the *Little Review* of April 1917.[3] Anderson cited extensively and perceptively from the text in support of her view that the *Portrait* 'is the most beautiful piece of writing and the most creative piece of prose anywhere to be seen on the horizon to-day', while Heap heaped praise on the novel as 'a thing of more definite, closer-known, keener-felt consciousness' which maps 'the geography of the body, and how its influences go all the way through'.[4]

The *Little Review* for May 1917 continued to advocate Joyce strongly, with subscribers being offered the chance of a reduced annual subscription to the *Little Review* if they purchased *Portrait* at the same time ('the most important and beautiful piece of novel writing to be found in English today'), an offer which was repeated

---

[1] *LR*, February 1918, [66].

[2] J to Pound, 30 June 1915, Yale; Pound to Anderson, [26 March 1917], *P-LR*, 19; *LR*, October 1917, 42. Arrangements for the dual serialization of *Ulysses* in *The Egoist* and the *Little Review* were formalized by Pound in September 1917 (*P-LR*, [13 September 1917], 122).

[3] *LR*, January 1917, [30].   [4] *LR*, April 1917, 8–10.

several times to the almost exclusively American readership of the *Little Review*.[5] The offer appears to suggest that readers of the *Little Review* and readers of *Portrait* belong in the same cultural constituency. Given the significant cultural distance between avant-garde literary New York in the 1910s and the world depicted in the *Portrait*, the world of Stephen Dedalus' Catholic boyhood and adolescence in Ireland in the 1880s and 1890s, this seems, in hindsight, to be somewhat incongruous. That cultural distance, however, nudges us towards a recognition of what the early US readers admired in Joyce: not (or not necessarily) his realism and vivid cultural specificity, but his use of language, his formal experimentalism, and (for some at least) his candour in writing about sexuality and the body.

In the sixteen years between March 1914 and spring 1929, the *Little Review* appeared seventy-nine times, with publication being most regular and most voluminous between May 1917 and April 1919, when Pound was 'Foreign Editor'. The serialization of *Ulysses* ground to a halt with the number dated 'September–December 1920', and was discontinued completely following the successful trial of the editors in February 1921. Thereafter the *Little Review* appeared less frequently, describing itself as a 'Quarterly' from autumn 1921. In fact, the journal's appearance had been irregular between 1914 and 1920, when it was billed as a monthly, and issues became even more irregular from 1921, with no issue at all in 1927 and 1928. The final issue, a compendium of the views of many contributors, appeared in spring 1929, and noted the particular achievement of serializing *Ulysses*, which Anderson described in a final editorial as 'the master-piece of this time'.[6]

Debate about the facts of this history and the cultural context of the *Little Review* has been lively and engaged, beginning with Jayne E. Marek's groundbreaking study, *Women Editing Modernism: Little Magazines and Literary History* (1995), and leading on to titles such as Mark S. Morrison's *The Public Face of Modernism: Little Magazines, Audiences and Reception, 1905–1920* (2001), Churchill and McKible's *Little Magazines and Modernism: New Approaches* (2007), Scholes and Wulfson's *Modernism and Magazines: An Introduction* (2010), and, most recently, Eric Bulson's *Little Magazine, World Form* (2016).[7] *The Oxford Critical and Cultural History of Modernist Magazines* (2 vols, 2009, 2012) consolidates this scholarly tradition of the 'material turn' (itself a strain of the 'new modernist studies'), and includes an exemplary essay by Alan Golding which argues that the study of modernist periodicals ordinarily works with two models.[8] The first model is that of the 'quotidian', which pays attention to 'mundane daily practices', or

    [5] *LR*, May 1917, [32].   [6] *LR*, spring 1929, 5.
    [7] Jayne E. Marek, *Women Editing Modernism: Little Magazines and Literary History* (Lexington, KY: University Press of Kentucky, 1995); Mark S. Morrisson, *The Public Face of Modernism: Little Magazines, Audiences, and Reception, 1905–1920* (Madison, WI: University of Wisconsin Press, 2001); Suzanne W. Churchill and Adam McKible (eds.), *Little Magazines and Modernism: New Approaches* (Aldershot: Ashgate, 2007); Robert Scholes and Clifford Wulfman, *Modernism in the Magazines: An Introduction* (Princeton, NJ: Yale University Press, 2010); and Eric Bulson, *Little Magazine, World Form* (New York: Columbia University Press, 2016).
    [8] Peter Brooker and Andrew Thacker (eds.), *The Oxford Critical and Cultural History of Modernist Magazines*, 2 vols (Oxford: Oxford University Press, 2009, 2012); for the 'new modernist studies' see Douglas Mao and Rebecca L. Walkowitz, 'The New Modernist Studies', *PMLA*, 123:3 (May 2008), 737–48.

'forgotten writers, ideas, practices, arguments, and so on'. The second model is that of 'avant-garde rupture', which looks at highlights, 'moments of crisis and break', and texts by subsequently well-known individuals whose status 'is measured by the aesthetically revolutionary quality of his or her work'.[9] For the purpose of orienting readers of *Ulysses* who may be new to the field of modernist periodical studies, this chapter seeks to offer a fresh account of the cultural and editorial world of the *Little Review* by re-examining the original archival sources on which a *Little Review* history has to be based, notably including issues of the journal itself, published and unpublished correspondence between those who were involved as either editor or contributor, and autobiographies and memoirs. In terms of chronology, the focus is on two overlapping periods of 'rupture': the period when Pound was actively involved as 'Foreign Editor' (from May 1917 to April 1919); and the period from March 1918 to December 1920, when the serialization of *Ulysses* was underway.

From a methodological perspective, Golding is undoubtedly correct to assert the value of examining the 'quotidian' alongside moments of avant-garde triumph. What was the *Little Review* like before the serialization of *Ulysses*? How was it financed and who was involved? In order to begin to answer these questions, the following account, which is in four parts, begins with 'Editorial Presences', a section which looks at the cultural formation and *mentalité* of those who were initially involved, as well as the journal's origins and general intellectual context. The second part, 'Enter Ezra and "Mon Cher Ami J. Q."', looks at the significance of Pound's appointment as 'Foreign Editor'; the impact of the support given to the journal by John Quinn (1870–1924), New York lawyer and patron of the arts; the evolving political context in which the journal was being produced; and the introduction of the serial *Ulysses*. The third part, 'Association Copy', is an exercise in what might be termed 'adjacent reading'. Building on the work of Gaipa, Latham, and Scholes in the Yale edition, it looks at the nexus of associations between the text of the serial *Ulysses* and some of the other texts and preoccupations of the journal.[10] In the spirit of collaborative criticism and intellectual discourse, the *Little Review* included an occasional column entitled 'The Reader Critic' which printed the queries and views of individual readers. This column—a rich source of information about the first readers of *Ulysses* and their cultural world—is also briefly discussed in 'Association Copy'. Another method of reading the history of the *Little Review*— which complements the generalized reading of associative intellectual structure and mentality—is that of 'sampling', or close reading specific issues of the journal.[11] In the interest of locating the serial *Ulysses* in its original intellectual context in more detail, the fourth part, 'Sample Copy: September 1918 and July–August 1920', examines the issue of September 1918 (when Pound was 'Foreign Editor') and

---

[9] Alan Golding, 'The Little Review' in Peter Brooker and Andrew Thacker (ed.), *The Oxford Critical and Cultural History of Modernist Magazines: Volume II, North America, 1894–1960* (Oxford: Oxford University Press, 2012), 61–84 (62).

[10] See 'The Magazine Context for the *Little Review Ulysses*', Gaipa et al., *LRU*, 381–425.

[11] For comment on methodology see 'How to Read a Magazine' at http://modjourn.org/teaching/introduction/intro3_howto.html.

that of July–August 1920, when Anderson and Heap had freed themselves from Pound's influence.

Looked at from the perspective of genre, the *Little Review* is clearly what is termed a 'little magazine', a type of periodical publication which is considered 'short-lived, committed to experiment, in constant financial difficulties, and indifferent or directly opposed to commercial considerations'.[12] As Brooker and Thacker note, 'little magazines':

> live a kind of private life on the margins of culture as sponsors of innovation and have often raised defiantly the red flag of protest and rebellion against tradition and convention…Such magazines are noncommercial by intent and appeal only to a limited group, generally not more than a thousand persons.[13]

The study of such objects involves engaging with the physical material of the magazine itself and paying attention to what Brooker and Thacker term 'periodical codes', a development of Jerome McGann's concept of 'bibliographical codes'.[14] Periodical 'codes' include: page layout, typeface, price, size, periodicity of publication, use of illustrations, use and placement of advertisements, quality of paper and binding, networks of distribution and sales, modes of financial support, payment practices towards contributors, editorial arrangements, and the type or genre of material published. Yet even if it were possible to recover all of this information in respect of the *Little Review*—and it is not because the archives are incomplete—an understanding of 'periodical codes' would not tell the whole story of the *Little Review*, or the more selective narrative of *Ulysses* in the *Little Review*.[15] The study of periodical codes—a close partner to the traditional concerns of bibliographical or book historical research—needs to be accompanied by the study of what McGann terms 'linguistic codes', i.e. the study of the semiotics and semantics of the texts that actually appeared within the pages of the *Little Review*.[16] The following account proceeds with that need for balance in view.

EDITORIAL PRESENCES

Margaret Anderson's *My Thirty Years' War*, tellingly subtitled *The Autobiography, Beginnings and Battles to 1930 by the Legendary Editor of the Little Review*, is a pertinent place to start. As one of the contributors to the *Little Review* noted, this

[12] Peter Brooker and Andrew Thacker (eds.), 'Introduction', in *The Oxford Critical and Cultural History of Modernist Magazines: Volume I, Britain and Ireland, 1880–1955* (Oxford: Oxford University Press, 2009), 12.

[13] Brooker and Thacker, 'Introduction', 12; Jerome McGann, *The Textual Condition* (Princeton, NJ: Princeton University Press, 1991), 77.

[14] Brooker and Thacker, 'Introduction', 5.

[15] The *Little Review* Records are housed at the Golda Meir Library, University of Wisconsin, Milwaukee. The archive includes some correspondence concerning editorial matters, subscriptions and advertising, letters from Ezra Pound and John Quinn to Anderson and Heap, and a small number of layout materials. Information about who subscribed, what the printing and production costs were, and how finances were managed is particularly limited.

[16] Jerome McGann, *The Textual Condition* (Princeton, NJ: Princeton University Press, 1991), 57.

autobiography is 'written with a breathless rush' and Anderson comes across like 'a character in a book' who is 'not real'.[17] Nonetheless the work is full of interest, and though scant and unreliable in respect of some facts and dates, it provides a solid outline of how the *Little Review* came into existence and is therefore worth reviewing here. To some extent all histories of the *Little Review* draw on this foundational source; Jackson Bryer's PhD thesis ('"A Trial-Track for Racers": Margaret Anderson and the *Little Review*', 1965) is also an important source, as Bryer knew Anderson at first hand, and was working on the *Little Review* when it was still within living memory.[18] Anderson's opening chapter describes her childhood and adolescence, and her conviction that 'life is antagonistic'; that she was born 'to fight the whole system', 'never be a mother', and to be 'quite definitely aloof from natural laws'.[19] Once she had finished college at Columbus, Indiana—where she had studied piano—she formed a plan to 'escape and conquer the world', which led eventually to various jobs on the fringes of Chicago's burgeoning literary culture.[20] These included book reviewing for various publications including the *Chicago Evening Post* and *The Continent*, working at a book store, and working at *The Dial*, a literary review then edited by Francis Fisher Browne (1843–1913), which initiated her 'into the secrets of the printing room—composition (monotype and linotype), proofreading, make-up'.[21] Chicago's literary and artistic culture, epitomized by the Fine Arts Building—Frank Lloyd Wright's iconic art nouveau masterpiece—was flourishing and Anderson was clearly extremely adept at finding strong supporters and artistic friends. She found herself in the midst of the ferment, living a 'marvellous life as literary editor', and regularly attending concerts and plays at Chicago's 'Little Theatre' (which promoted 'new' and experimental dramatists such as Ibsen, Strindberg, and Shaw).[22] But Anderson found that her professional life was not exciting enough; she was 'chafing' under journalistic restrictions, which notably included a directive to condemn Theodore Dreiser's *Sister Carrie* in moral rather than literary terms.[23] Thus she founded the *Little Review*, in order (she said) to 'confer upon life that inspiration without which life is meaningless'.[24]

In *My Thirty Years' War*, which is self-glorifying and disingenuous by turn, Anderson confesses that she was not completely certain as to why the *Little Review* 'was necessary and inevitable'; nor did she know how it would be funded.[25] But she gathered perhaps as much as $450 from advertisers, and the first issue, priced 25 cents, and running to sixty-four pages, appeared in March 1914.[26] By her own

---

[17] Sherwood Anderson, 'Real—Unreal', *The New Republic*, 11 June 1930.

[18] Jackson Robert Bryer, '"A Trial-Track for Racers": Margaret Anderson and the Little Review' (PhD Dissertation, University of Wisconsin, 1965).

[19] Margaret Anderson, *My Thirty Years' War* (1930; New York: Horizon Press, 1969), 3, 4, 5.

[20] Anderson, *My Thirty Years' War*, 11.

[21] Anderson, *My Thirty Years' War*, 28. For the *Dial* see Nicholas Joost, *Years of Transition: The Dial, 1912–1920* (Barre, MA: Barre Publishers, 1967) and *Schofield Thayer and the Dial: An Illustrated History* (Carbondale, IL: Southern Illinois University Press, 1964).

[22] Anderson, *My Thirty Years' War*, 32.   [23] Anderson, *My Thirty Years' War*, 33.

[24] Anderson, *My Thirty Years' War*, 35.

[25] Anderson, *My Thirty Years' War*, 36.   [26] Anderson, *My Thirty Years' War*, 43.

account, that typographically undistinguished first issue—which appeared under
the banner 'Literature Drama Music Art'—'betrayed nothing but my adolescence'.[27]
She had secured an office in the Fine Arts Building—a building designed specifically for working artists—where neighbours and advisors included Harriet Monroe,
the founder, in October 1912, of *Poetry: A Magazine of Verse*, one of the best
known of literary Modernism's 'little magazines'.[28] From the outset, Anderson
wanted to make it clear that the *Little Review* was her own 'personal enterprise' and
was 'neither directly nor indirectly connected in any way with an organization,
society, company, cult or movement'.[29] But by the time of the second issue, the
Little Review had begun to borrow some of *Poetry*'s copy and editorial enthusiasms.
The issue reprints a speech that had just appeared in *Poetry*, an address which
W. B. Yeats made to 'American Poets' during a visit to Chicago. The very act of
reprinting such a specific item implies Anderson's openness to European literary
culture, her tacit support of the advice Yeats is giving American poets ('you are too
far from Paris'; 'I would have all American poets keep in mind the example of
Francois Villon'), and her willingness to cross and explore cultural boundaries.[30]
Poetry had also notably introduced Anderson to Pound, who was resident in
London, and was *Poetry*'s 'Foreign Correspondent'. Though their early letters appear
not to have survived, it is clear that Pound and Anderson began to correspond in
1914, or thereabouts, and that Anderson was supportive of Pound as a poet, and
cultural impresario; *BLAST*, described as 'the street urchin with his tongue in his
cheek', was favourably reviewed in the *Little Review* of September 1914 ('there is
much wisdom in the Manifesto'; 'we cannot be too grateful for Mr Pound').[31]

The financial basis on which the *Little Review* planned to run was, at best, precarious. Anderson had arranged some advertisements, and had obtained the promise of direct funding from her friend, DeWitt C. Wing, who worked as a journalist
for an agricultural journal, and who agreed to pay the printing bill and office rent
from his salary.[32] While Anderson did not 'consider it good principle for the
artist to remain unpaid', *Thirty Years' War* asserts that it was quite taken for granted
that 'the *Little Review* couldn't pay' contributors:

> If they had something we especially wanted they gave it to us before the *Dial* was
> permitted to see it—and pay. The best European writers and painters did the same.[33]

But as Anderson herself acknowledges, this uncomplicated view of the economics
of literary publishing was put to the test by Scott Fitzgerald who met Anderson's
request for a contribution 'with blushes that his stuff was too popular to be solicited

[27] Anderson, *My Thirty Years' War*, 47.
[28] Helen Carr, '*Poetry: A Magazine of Verse* (1912–1936), Biggest of Little Magazines', in Peter
Brooker and Andrew Thacker (eds.), *The Oxford Critical and Cultural History of Modernist Magazines:
Volume II, North America, 1894–1960* (Oxford: Oxford University Press, 2012), 40–60. Early issues
of *Poetry* have been digitized at http://modjourn.org.
[29] *LR*, March 1914, 2.   [30] *LR*, April 1914, 48.
[31] Anderson, *My Thirty Years' War*, 158; *LR*, September 1914, 33, 34.
[32] Anderson, *My Thirty Years' War*, 41; Jackson Robert Bryer, '"A Trial-Track for Racers": Margaret
Anderson and the *Little Review*' (PhD Dissertation, University of Wisconsin, 1965), 21.
[33] Anderson, *My Thirty Years' War*, 44.

by a magazine of the new prose'.[34] Like other authors of his generation, he was being paid for contributions to some of the older and more established journals which published literary texts, such as *Harper's Bazaar* and *Vanity Fair*. Anderson was acutely aware of that market, and the literary culture it promoted; in some respects her aim in establishing the *Little Review* was to set up a non-commercial counter-cultural forum, which, in her own words, would be 'fresh and construct-ive, and intelligent from the artist's point of view'.[35]

Apart from a general interest in literature and criticism, other early and notable editorial 'non-literary' enthusiasms include feminism ('A clear-thinking magazine can have only one attitude; the degree of ours is ardent!'), the support of birth control pioneers such as Margaret Sanger, an interest in the works of Nietzsche, and—most formatively—an interest in anarchism, which came about when Anderson heard Emma Goldman (1869–1940), a leading political activist, lecture in Chicago in the spring of 1914.[36] Anderson knew that Goldman was popularly considered a 'monster, an exponent of free love and bombs' but the two lectures she had heard were inspiring; she turned 'anarchist before the presses closed', rushing to print with an article entitled 'The Challenge of Emma Goldman' in the number for May 1914.[37] Goldman and Anderson became close friends—and may even have been lovers.[38] Whatever the case, their association was to have a lasting and shaping impact on the *Little Review*. Advertisers shied away from being associated with a journal which openly espoused anarchism; Wing, the review's first sponsor, discontinued his financial support on the grounds that it could mean he would 'lose his position'; and other tenants of the Fine Arts Building complained that Emma Goldman was among Anderson's regular visitors.[39] But Anderson was undeterred by such setbacks. A magnetic and commanding personality, she obvi-ously succeeded in talking people into giving funds and sponsorship even if they had no immediate business interest in the *Little Review*. One notes, for example, a whole page ad for 'Goodyear Tires' ('A New Day Dawns in Tires When Men Adopt No-Rim Cuts') in the number for October 1914.[40] George Soule, one of the early contributors, is typical of many supporters in the way he describes being 'bowled over by her vitality, her beauty and her voluble enthusiasm'.[41] Such encounters often led to direct donations.

Nonetheless, the financial situation gradually worsened, and Anderson decided to make a plea for more subscribers. Her campaign took the form of an appeal, printed on a card, and slipped in to the issue of December 1914. It reported a

---

[34] Anderson, *My Thirty Years' War*, 44.   [35] *LR*, March 1914, 2.
[36] For editorial commentary relating to Sanger, see *LR*, April 1915 (2–3), January–February 1916 (21), March 1916 (25), April 1916 (23). Virtually all of the early issues mention or promote Nietzsche in some way.
[37] *LR*, May 1914, 5–9.
[38] See C. Bríd Nicholson, *Emma Goldman: Still Dangerous* (London: Black Rose Books, 2010), especially 'Sex and Sexuality: The Silenced Skein' for the convincing argument that Goldman was bisexual, esp. 170, 176.
[39] Anderson, *My Thirty Years' War*, 56, 75, 74.   [40] *LR*, October 1914, 65.
[41] Cited in Bryer, ' "A Trial-Track for Racers" ', 13.

change of heart by the 'guarantor' who had initially given 'a guarantee of backing for three years', and continued:

> We have reached a crisis; we have come to the point where, if we are to continue, we must have enough money in the bank to pay printers' bills. We are sending out this card to the four thousand people who have expressed an interest in THE LITTLE REVIEW. If half of those people could afford to send us $1.00—if all of them could spare even fifty cents from their Christmas shopping—THE LITTLE REVIEW could get through its second year.[42]

As Golding observes, pleas of this kind 'amount to their own sub-genre' and are 'one of the paratexts by which we can understand the magazine's ethos':

> They are tonally combative and form part of the atmosphere of more-or-less monthly crisis on which the magazine seemed to thrive, its reflections on its own status, problems and triumphs, central to the magazine's identity from the beginning.[43]

Could it really be the case that as many as 4,000 people were 'interested' in the *Little Review* at the end of 1914?[44] If so, how many of those were regular subscribers and where was that readership based? Precise circulation figures are impossible to obtain: the *Little Review* archive, preserved by Jane Heap, and sold by her executors to the University of Wisconsin at Milwaukee, does not contain a list of subscribers, or information about print runs. The number for June–July 1915 contains several pages which are blank but for a note in which Anderson chastises various firms for failing to advertise. One such note—an example of what Golding terms the 'rhetorically self-conscious use of the material page'—mentions '1,000 Chicago subscribers' (see Figure 1.1).[45]

In its context, '1,000 subscribers' may be a deliberate overestimate. Ben Hecht, who contributed significantly to early issues, suggests that 'circulation fluttered around 700' while Max Bodenheim comments that 'circulation never extended beyond 1500'.[46] There were certainly subscribers in other US cities; perhaps 1,000 subscribers in total at this time might be a reasonable estimate. Circulation seems to have been significantly higher by the time of Pound's appointment as 'Foreign Editor'; his correspondence with John Quinn reports a letter from Anderson saying 'it has paid circulation 2500, bookstore sales 600, exchange list 100, office sales 100', i.e. a circulation of approximately 3,300 (of which 100 are complimentary or 'exchange' copies).[47] Quinn's correspondence with the Post Office Solicitor corroborates this approximate estimate, referring to some 'three thousand copies' of the issue for October 1917 being held up by the New York Post Office.[48] There were

[42] *LR*, December 1914, 24.
[43] Golding, 'The Little Review', in Brooker and Thacker (eds.), *The Oxford Critical and Cultural History of Modernist Magazines: Volume II*, 70.
[44] *LR*, December 1914, 24.
[45] Golding, 'The Little Review', in Brooker and Thacker (eds.), *The Oxford Critical and Cultural History of Modernist Magazines: Volume II*, 71.
[46] Cited in Bryer, ' "A Trial-Track for Racers" ', 126.
[47] Pound to Quinn, 8 February 1917, *EP-JQ*, 95.
[48] Quinn to W. H. Lamar, 5 November 1917, UWM.

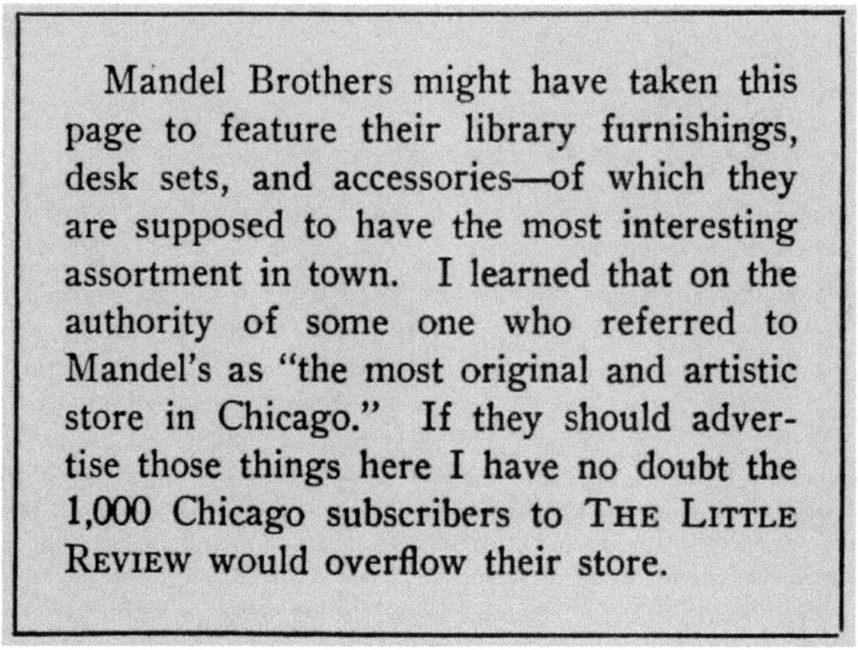

26   *Serial Encounters*

> Mandel Brothers might have taken this page to feature their library furnishings, desk sets, and accessories—of which they are supposed to have the most interesting assortment in town. I learned that on the authority of some one who referred to Mandel's as "the most original and artistic store in Chicago." If they should advertise those things here I have no doubt the 1,000 Chicago subscribers to THE LITTLE REVIEW would overflow their store.

Figure 1.1. Advertisement from the *Little Review*, June–July 1915

(*Little Review*, The Modernist Journals Project (searchable database). Brown and Tulsa Universities, ongoing. http://www.modjourn.org)

only 1,000 copies of the first edition of *Ulysses*; what these circulation figures for the *Little Review* suggest is that the serial text of *Ulysses* had a far wider potential readership than that of the first edition.

In terms of circulation and finance, the *Little Review* appears to have been floundering at the beginning of 1915. But Anderson remained buoyant. As she reviewed the achievements of the *Little Review* in 'Our First Year', she was determined that the journal would 'continue to soar and flash and flame', 'to be young and fearless and reckless and imaginative'. She was extremely good at writing copy which suggested, rather than specified, her aims:

> THE LITTLE REVIEW will strive more and more to be splendidly insane: as editors and lecturers continue to compromise in order to get their public, as book-makers continue to print rot in order to make fortunes, as writers continue to follow the market instead of *doing their Work*, as the public continues to demand vileness and vulgarity and lies, as the intellectuals continue to miss the root of the trouble, THE LITTLE REVIEW will continue to rebel, to tell the truth as we see it, to work for its ideal rather than for a policy.[49]

She supported herself by editing a book page for *The Continent*, and, in the spring of 1915, took the unusual and unconventional decision to reduce her living

[49] *LR*, February 1915, 3.

expenses by following her 'intuition' that she 'no longer needed a house'.[50] Together with her sister, and her sister's children, she pitched a set of tents on the north shore of lake Michigan, and lived there from mid-May until mid-November.[51] Anderson often woke at sunrise, and would 'change from pajamas into bathing suit, plunge into a cold lake, run on the beach'.[52] Later she would dress in the one set of work clothes she owned (a hat, a 'blue tailored suit', and a blouse of 'crepe georgette') and go in to the city where she persevered with the struggle to produce the *Little Review*.[53]

Anderson might have avoided being in such financial straits had she been prepared to accept an offer of perhaps as much as $1,000 from Amy Lowell, the poet, who, in November 1914, wrote to offer capital in return for the privilege of being poetry editor of the *Little Review*.[54] Ezra Pound and Lowell had become bitter enemies in a tussle regarding the nature and definition of Imagism, and while she continued to admire some of his work, she candidly told Anderson she did 'not like his attitude' (hardly a surprising response given that Pound, with typical misogynistic swagger, had dubbed her a 'hippoetess' and her interpretation of Imagism as 'Amygism').[55] Though this offer was accompanied by a meeting in person—Harriet Monroe brought Lowell to Anderson's door—Anderson recalls rejecting Lowell's offer in terms that were barely polite, telling Lowell 'I can't function in "association"':

> No clairvoyance was needed to know that Amy Lowell would dictate, uniquely and majestically, any adventure in which she had a part. I should have preferred being in the clutches of a dozen groups. So I didn't hesitate.[56]

This rejection reveals Anderson's steely determination to make the *Little Review* her 'personal enterprise', come what may. It also shows that Anderson appears to have been willing to become embroiled in Pound's battles long before his formal association with the *Little Review* began. Marek's account of the *Little Review*, inspired by the conviction that 'very few literary histories treat women seriously' and the desire not to merely see 'Anderson as a foil for Ezra Pound', founders on complications of this kind.[57] Anderson clearly *was* influenced by Pound, even before Pound became 'Foreign Editor', and the *Little Review*, run on a very precarious financial basis before Pound's editorial intervention, would almost certainly have run aground had it not been for the subsidy which he brought, a point which Pound made to Joyce ('The only thing is that these women in New York may go bust, and be unable to print the end of the novel . . . The *Little Review* will have to paddle mostly on its own after April. I can't raise any more

[50] Anderson, *My Thirty Years' War*, 59, 88.

[51] Anderson, *My Thirty Years' War*, 88. The dates are queried by Bryer, ' "A Trial-Track for Racers" ', 129n.

[52] Anderson, *My Thirty Years' War*, 89.   [53] Anderson, *My Thirty Years' War*, 90.

[54] Amy Lowell to Margaret Anderson, 18 December 1914, cited in Bryer, ' "A Trial-Track for Racers" ', 172. Lowell writes, 'I should not be able to put more than $1000 into it, my idea really was about $500'.

[55] Amy Lowell to Margaret Anderson, 27 July 1917, *Little Review* records UWM.

[56] Anderson, *My Thirty Years' War*, 61.   [57] Marek, *Women Editing Modernism*, 3, 61.

cash (after the second year's lot runs out) and can't give my time to it without that meagre allowance for self and contributors').[58]

The case for a sensitive feminist repointing of history is much stronger in respect of Jane Heap (1883–1964) whom Anderson met in February 1916. Heap is arguably the most interesting editorial presence within the *Little Review*, particularly vis-à-vis *Ulysses*, and began to contribute to the journal in September 1916.[59] As Holly Baggett has shown, Heap's biography is 'part of the untold story of the *Little Review*', and is shadowy and difficult to recover.[60] Her absence from the record stems, initially at least, from the fact that she rarely signed her name to contributions. Some of her contributions are completely unsigned; others use only her italicized initials in lower case—*jh*—as though to emphasize, in typographical language, the insignificance of her role, and to conceal her gender and identity more generally. In this respect she was at least partly successful. When she wrote to Joyce in January 1920, in order to commiserate with regard to the difficulties the *Little Review* was facing in respect of *Ulysses* and to offer Joyce the very generous sum of '£5 for stories and £1 per page for poems', Joyce had no idea who she was, and could not read her signature.[61] In correspondence with Weaver, Joyce describes this letter as a 'very friendly and complimentary letter' from a 'Mr Heaf or Heap of the *Little Review*' (*SL*, 249). In his initial association with the *Little Review* Pound clearly had no idea who Heap was either, and asked Anderson, on 11 June 1917: 'Who the devil is "jh"? Sherwood Anderson? Or what? I liked his, her, on Joyce in April'.[62] He followed this up a few months later, asking Anderson, 'As policy, what about "jh" signing her name? . . . She writes quite well enough to have a name of her own'.[63] But Heap remained on the side-lines. Although she began to contribute to the *Little Review* in September 1916, she was not specified as an editorial presence until May 1919, and was only then acknowledged as 'advisory board', and not as editor. Her role was far more central than this wording seems to imply, particularly once the journal had become a quarterly from autumn 1921, when she became more or less sole editor until the journal's close in 1929. The failure to acknowledge Heap's significance almost certainly relates to tension in her relationship with Anderson, a tension which is documented in *Thirty Years' War*—which devotes a whole chapter to Heap—and *Dear Tiny Heart*, a collection of letters from Heap to her friend Florence Reynolds (who often made direct donations in order to sustain the *Little Review*).[64]

Late in life Anderson described meeting Heap as the beginning of a 'new and unexpected life that to me was like a second birth'.[65] It is possible that Anderson

---

[58] Pound to J, 12 December 1918, *EP-JJ*, 147.
[59] For Heap's contributions to the *Little Review* of September 1916 see the unsigned column entitled 'And—', 20–1, and her responses to the correspondence of the 'Reader Critic' column, 25–8.
[60] Holly A. Baggett, *Dear Tiny Heart: The Letters of Jane Heap and Florence Reynolds* (New York: New York University Press, 2000), xiii.
[61] Jane Heap to James Joyce, 9 January 1920 (unpublished, Cornell Joyce Collection).
[62] Pound to Anderson, [11 June 1917], *P-LR*, 69.
[63] Pound to Anderson, 10 August 1917, *P-LR*, 111.
[64] Baggett, *Dear Tiny Heart, passim*.
[65] Margaret Anderson, 'Conversation', *Prose*, 2 (1971), 5–21 (6).

associated the relationship with sexual awakening and liberation: in *Thirty Years'*
War she mentions being 'very unrelaxed' about sex in the early days of the *Little*
Review ('all my sex manifestations were expended in ideas').[66] Certainly she identified Heap as 'my obsession—the special human being, the special point of view';
she also describes her mind being 'inflamed by Jane's ideas...This was what I had
been waiting for, searching for, all my life'.[67] For Heap the relationship was also
formative, and an important stage in the gradual formation of her lesbian identity.
Homophobia appears to have contributed to the couple's decision to plan a
sequence of moves in the latter half of 1916. As Anderson recalls, 'Chicago had
had all it wanted from us'; their 'consolidation' had made 'us much loved and even
more loathed'.[68] They moved from Chicago to San Francisco for four or five
months from June 1916, probably in the hope of procuring funding for the *Little*
Review from a woman whom Anderson dubs 'Nineteen Millions'.[69] They then
returned to Chicago for a few months, before moving to New York where they
hoped their 'position would be more commanding' and the *Little Review* could
become an 'international organ'.[70] These moves were not necessarily happy ones
for Heap, who spent her final days in Chicago 'in a coma of regret and indecision'.[71]
Nonetheless, she followed Anderson's lead—for Anderson was clearly the dominant
partner—and the pair had arrived in New York and announced that they were 'getting established' there by March 1917.[72]

Heap's initial involvement in the *Little Review* was administrative. Anderson
appears to have taken little pleasure in 'answering the letters that came in, usually
accompanied by bad manuscripts':

> But Jane adored writing to people. Her first idea in joining the *Little Review* was to be
> its amanuensis. She spent her time answering letters with exaggerated interest (real)
> and in planning new typographies which we never could afford.[73]

Other sources, notably the *Little Review* archive at Milwaukee, and Heap's
correspondence, suggest a division of editorial labour which saw Anderson
become the public face of the *Little Review*—courting writers, seeking funds and
advertisements—and Heap being the worker in the back room, attending to the
more mundane aspects of production, and making occasional editorial contributions.
A letter of July 1917 from Heap to Reynolds vividly evokes the labour involved
in getting the journal to press, the precarious finances, and the intensity of the
relationship with Anderson, here referred to as 'Mart':

> Such a week as we have had—up about 7.30 and at it until one and one thirty. We
> addressed, wrapped, and mailed the magazine here in my room—besides we got out
> 480 letters to prospective subscribers and pleas for renewals...we only had 54 cents

[66] Anderson, *My Thirty Years' War*, 39.   [67] Anderson, *My Thirty Years' War*, 107–8, 122.
[68] Anderson, *My Thirty Years' War*, 136, 107.
[69] Anderson, *My Thirty Years' War*, 113. Based on a letter from Anderson, Bryer identifies 'Nineteen
Millions' as Aline Barnsdell (1882–1946), an American oil heiress best known now for commissioning
Frank Lloyd Wright to build Hollyhock House. See http://barnsdall.org/hollyhock-house/history, and
Bryer, ' "A Trial-Track for Racers" ', 201n.
[70] Anderson, *My Thirty Years' War*, 136.   [71] Anderson, *My Thirty Years' War*, 140.
[72] *LR*, March 1917, 22.   [73] Anderson, *My Thirty Years' War*, 129.

Figure 1.2. 'Light occupations of the editor while there is nothing to edit', *Little Review*, September 1916, drawings by Jane Heap

(*Little Review*, The Modernist Journals Project (searchable database). Brown and Tulsa Universities, ongoing. http://www.modjourn.org)

Figure 1.2. Continued

but there was a letter from Deansie in the mail with $5.00 in it for books…We got out the magazine. We are going to do business with an agency about subs and circulation. We'll make this thing go—Mart had tantrums and almost 'hystics' with heat and weariness—and rage because we have to do the labour. And I had one of my fits of fatal patience—and we walked out hand in hand to our dinners and were good little things—[74]

But the harmony communicated here did not last. Heap appears to have been prone to depression, and Anderson began to have affairs with other women. Heap accused her of egomania ('I'd like to see you once do something that had any consideration in it in any way for another person'), promiscuity ('Whenever she is thrown with those people she has an affair'), and a reluctance to actually engage in the business of editing the magazine:

Mart won't look at the magazine—so I read proof and made the cover etc and went back and forth to the post office with it all.[75]

The relationship appears to have broken down by March 1918, much to Heap's distress ('I have wept much. Suffered much. Written many letters').[76] While the partnership may have been reignited sporadically thereafter, it is clear that the relationship was mainly editorial, and that Heap was undertaking a great deal of the necessary and sometimes tedious work involved in producing the *Little Review* from that time onwards. Holly Baggett has suggested that Heap 'deliberately sought a low profile' and was antagonistic 'toward notoriety' in ways which obviously contrast with Anderson's quest for the limelight.[77] Yet it is also arguable that Anderson—who comes across as remarkably self-centred—wanted to keep Heap in the shadows, and that Heap was happy enough to remain in such a position, given the psychosexual dynamic and history of the couple's relationship.

As Marek has argued, Heap made an important contribution to the spread of avant-garde art in the 1920s.[78] She was trained as an artist and made a significant contribution to the visual identity of the *Little Review*, and particularly to its typography. She drew the cartoons (see Figure 1.2) which accompany Anderson's infamous musings in the issue of September 1916, an issue which opened with blank pages, and described itself as a 'Want Ad'. This gesture followed up Anderson's plangent editorial of the previous month, in which she described the publication of the *Little Review* as a 'ridiculous tragedy' which had failed to come 'near its ideal':

I loathe compromise, and yet I have been compromising in every issue by putting in things that were 'almost good' or 'interesting enough' or 'important'. There will be no more of it. If there is only one really beautiful thing for the September issue it shall go on in and the other pages shall be left blank.[79]

[74] Jane Heap to Florence Reynolds, [July 1917], Baggett (ed.), *Dear Tiny Heart*, 51.
[75] Jane Heap to Florence Reynolds, [postmarked 20 September 1918], and [postmarked 18 August 1918], Baggett (ed.), *Dear Tiny Heart*, 58, 59, 55.
[76] Jane Heap to Florence Reynolds, [postmarked 17 March 1918], Baggett (ed.), *Dear Tiny Heart*, 55.
[77] Baggett (ed.), *Dear Tiny Heart*, 19.
[78] Marek, *Women Editing Modernism*, 93–100. Marek covers the period after the *Ulysses* trial in some detail.
[79] *LR*, August 1916.

Thirty Years' War, somewhat typically, recalls following through on this threat and publishing a magazine 'made up of sixty-four empty pages'; in fact, the issue of September 1916 contained thirteen blank pages, and, as others have noted, reflected an awareness that the *Little Review* had run out of ideas and enthusiasm.[80] Heap's cartoons make virtue of necessity and depict, with some spirit and humour, 'light occupations of the editor while there is nothing to edit'. Activities included collecting firewood, piano practice, 'converting the sheriff to anarchism and *vers libre*', and 'suffering for humanity at Emma Goldman's lectures'.[81]

ENTER EZRA (AND 'MON CHER AMI J. Q'.)

Pound was keeping a sharp eye on the *Little Review* throughout 1916. He was receiving complimentary copies and noted that the content had become 'rather scrappy and unselective'.[82] Some contributors complained of the issue with blank pages ('Don't you think you're asking a little too much of yourself and your contributors?'), but Pound was delighted by the gesture, telling his friend John Quinn, with whom he maintained a regular correspondence, that the journal 'had the nerve to print half a number blank' and had succeeded in eliminating 'the cranks who were associated with the paper at the start'.[83] Pound had contributed 'A Letter from London' in April 1916—more than a year before his formal editorial association with the journal began.[84] In response to Anderson's 'want ad' (or plea for copy), he hastily sent an article protesting against the protective tariff on foreign books imported into the US, 'before you issue another number of your magazine half blank'.[85] This he quickly followed up with a private letter to Anderson in which he asked if 'there is any use my trying to help the *Little Review*'. His intentions for the potential venture were already quite clear, as evidenced by the fact that he specifically wished to know:

> what your circulation (paid and unpaid) is, also how much you lose or can afford to lose, and whether you would make the magazine a 'pays its contributors magazine' if that were possible. And whether you want capital, or on what terms.[86]

At around this time, Anderson's confidence in her editorial direction strengthened: she told readers of the November 1916 issue that the planned move to New York made her 'feel as though we have an entirely new lease on life and were just starting with what we have to say'.[87] Material circumstances continued to be trying, but in a sense that helped to strengthen her determination (as she told readers, 'we may have to come out on tissue paper soon, but we shall *keep on coming out!*').[88] Pound's

---

[80] Golding, 'The Little Review', in Brooker and Thacker (eds.), *The Oxford Critical and Cultural History of Modernist Magazines: Volume II*, 71; see also Ian Hamilton, *The Little Magazines: A Study of Six Editors* (London: Weidenfeld and Nicolson, 1976), 23.
[81] *LR*, September 1916, 14–15.   [82] *LR*, April 1916, 36.
[83] *LR*, November 1916, 27; Pound to Quinn, 8 February 1917, *EP-JQ*, 95.
[84] *LR*, April 1916, 7–8.   [85] *LR*, November 1916, 16–17.
[86] Pound to Anderson, [29 November 1916], *P-LR*, 4.   [87] *LR*, November 1916, 21.
[88] *LR*, November 1916, 21.

sudden enthusiasm to 'help the *Little Review*'—expressed in long-winded letters that were dictatorial in tone—obviously helped to solidify what was already going to be a new departure for the *Little Review*.

As Pound told Joyce, in the letter he wrote to introduce to himself in December 1913, he was interested in finding journals 'that stand for free speech and want (I don't say get) literature'. By that time he was 'informally connected' with *The Egoist*, which did not pay ('we do it for larks and to have a place for markedly modern stuff'), and was the 'Foreign Correspondent' of *Poetry* which paid '2 bob a line' for 'top notch poetry'.[89] He had been introduced to John Quinn by John Butler Yeats, father of the poet, in August 1910.[90] Quinn was a successful New York corporate lawyer who used his considerable earnings to collect art works, and support writers, including Conrad and Yeats, whom he supported through the purchase of manuscripts.[91] By May 1915, Pound was courting Quinn with a view to Quinn's potential sponsorship of a new literary journal ('within limits, an organ at your disposal').[92] Pound had worked out that he wanted an editorial position, recognizing that this would enable him to create a context for his own work, and that of other writers he admired. He had drawn up a prospectus for a monthly journal by August 1915: this, he proposed, perhaps slightly tongue in cheek, could be a 'male review' on the grounds that 'active America is getting fed up on gynocracy'; it could be published under a banner which was bound to cause 'outcry, boycott, etc': 'No woman shall be allowed to write for this magazine' and 'could completely support Joyce, Eliot, Myself and asst-edtr'.[93]

These plans did not materialize, but nor did Pound give up on the idea of trying to acquire an editorial position with a literary journal. He gradually worked out that it would be easier—and cheaper—to have a 'corner' in a journal run by others than to found one on his own. Ironically, of course, this meant collaborating with women, not just Heap and Anderson of the *Little Review*, but also Harriet Shaw Weaver and Dora Marsden of *The Egoist* (which regularly advertised in the *Little Review*, occasionally describing itself, in a slogan which has a Poundian look, as 'a journal of interest to virile readers only').[94] Marsden, who had allowed the *New Freewoman* to be rebranded as *The Egoist* at the beginning of 1914, clearly had some sense of Pound's attitudes. Acting on behalf of *The Egoist* and against Weaver's wishes, she turned down an offer of cash from Pound in exchange for control of her magazine on the grounds that it would reduce 'our editorial powers to zero'.[95]

---

[89] Pound to Joyce, 15 December 1913, *EP-JJ*, 18.   [90] *EP-JQ*, 1.

[91] For a biography, see B. L. Reid, *The Man from New York: John Quinn and His Friends* (New York: Oxford University Press, 1968); for his collections see *John Quinn, 1870–1925: Collection of Paintings, Drawings, Watercolours and Sculpture* (New York: Pidgeon Hill Press, 1926), and *Complete Catalogue of the Library of John Quinn* (New York: Anderson Galleries, 1923), both available via archive.org. A quick impression of Quinn's significance as a collector can be formed from Wikipedia (en.wikipedia.org/wiki/John_Quinn_(collector)), which includes selected images from the art collections.

[92] Pound to Quinn, 21 May 1915, *EP-JQ*, 28.

[93] Pound to Quinn, 26 August 1915, 13 October 1915, 8 September 1915, *EP-JQ*, 41, 53, 48.

[94] See, for example, *LR*, March 1918.

[95] Dora Marsden to Harriet Shaw Weaver, 13 March 1916, Harriet Shaw Weaver Papers, British Library Ms add 57354.

Anderson was less experienced and had to be more expedient: she was more receptive to Pound than Marsden because she did not have a significant alternative source of income. The finances of the *Little Review* were genuinely perilous, and she knew the journal would benefit from Pound's international connections, which had done much for *Poetry*. Contradicting her earlier dismissal of Lowell, Anderson's agreement to collaborate with Pound was a sign that she could 'function in association' if the association happened to suit.[96] The decision to collaborate is also arguably a sign of her confidence that she could work around whatever editorial pressures Pound exerted.

The arrangements for Pound's tenure as 'Foreign Editor' of the *Little Review* were in place by February 1917, and were supported by an agreement that committed Quinn to the payment of $750 per annum to Pound, for two years; of this, $300 went to Pound for his editorial duties, and $450 was to be spent on the payment of contributors.[97] Quinn also made direct donations to the *Little Review*, apparently without Pound's knowledge or approval; he was also instrumental in securing funding from others, including Otto Kahn (1867–1934, a banker and philanthropist).[98] Crucially, neither Quinn nor Pound had met Anderson and Heap before they made their commitment to the *Little Review*. Pound was in London and told Quinn, in a series of typical and slightly chauvinistic asides, that the journal was 'a free field to begin in, unclouded by past sins and associations':

> At present it (the L. R.) has very little matter in it, I doubt the editorial discrimination, *but* it has enthusiasm, which does no harm if there is discrimination somewhere in the concern.[99]

Even at this moment Pound was concerned that the relationships between Quinn and the editors might not run smoothly: he feared that Quinn would wish to influence editorial decisions, and thus decided not to reveal the identity of his 'capitalist' to Anderson and Heap.[100] But this delicate balance of anonymity was not in the interests of either party in New York: Quinn did want to influence the way in which the *Little Review* was being run, and the editors were keen to meet Quinn because they immediately and correctly recognized his potential as a source of direct funding.

---

[96] Anderson, *My Thirty Years' War*, 61.

[97] Pound to Quinn, 8 February 1917, *EP-JQ*, 95; figures from *P-LR*, 13n. It is difficult to be precise about exactly how much money was changing hands as the two men discuss dollars and sterling interchangeably. It is also difficult to work out exactly how much (or indeed if) contributors were regularly paid, but Pound had evidently had some funds for this purpose and thought payment important.

[98] See Pound's article on 'Small Magazines', *English Journal*, 19:9 (November 1930), 689–704 (696), which reveals his dissatisfaction that Quinn gave funds direct to the *Little Review*. There is detailed information about other funders in a letter from Quinn to Anderson, 2 February 1918, written just before Quinn underwent potentially life-threatening major surgery (*Little Review* records, UWM). The letter encloses $400 'as my contribution', and promises $400 from Kahn, and further sums from Max Pam and Mrs James F. Byrne, all of whom were personal friends of Quinn.

[99] Pound to Quinn, 8 February 1917, *EP-JQ*, 95.

[100] Pound to Anderson, 8 February 1917, *P-LR*, 15.

Quinn had met with Anderson and Heap by 2 June 1917, and reported back to Pound. Anderson, he felt, was 'a woman of taste and refinement and good looking', but he took an instant dislike to Heap, whom he described as 'typical Washington Squareite', Washington Square being a kind of haven, as he told Pound, for 'pseudo-Bohemianism'.[101] Things looked more positive later that year, on 31 October, when Quinn wrote to Pound, with regard to Anderson, whom he continued to find attractive: 'She is a damned attractive young woman, one of the handsomest I have ever seen, very high-spirited, very courageous and very fine'. He was clearly very impressed by the ability of the women to keep on pulling issues of the *Little Review* together:

> it is all to their credit that they are making this uphill fight decently and almost alone. I don't know that I have seen any two women who were less maudlin, less sentimental and slushy about it, and more courageous.[102]

Still, he regretted that they were not 'business women' and he frequently took the opportunity to offer them unsolicited editorial advice.[103] For example, on 7 August 1917, the first surviving letter in the *Little Review* archive, Quinn mentions the possibility of censorship, stating: 'I shall, of course, be glad to give you the benefit of my expert advice re any question of censorship you want to submit'. He continues, somewhat imperiously:

> I don't speak of propaganda stuff, pacifism, or non-resistance, or anti-militarism, or any other old ism, which, *me judice*, should not appear in such a fine thing as the *Little Review*... The *Little Review* is for literature and art and music and poetry and not for propaganda, or rather ought not to be for propaganda.[104]

How did Anderson respond to such firm editorial direction and why—given her commitments to feminism and editorial autonomy—was she prepared to tolerate being bossed around by the likes of Pound and Quinn? Initial answers are obvious. Anderson's response was expedient: she needed the money. If one measures the journal in terms of numbers of issues and pages published per annum—a sort of 'distant reading' exercise of the kind proposed by Franco Moretti—it is clear that the *Little Review* was struggling in 1916.[105] That year the *Little Review* was issued seven times, and the total number of pages was 308; some individual issues comprised as few as thirty pages, and those were padded out with lengthy advertisements. 1915 had been much more buoyant: eleven issues and a total of 636 pages. 1917, when Pound started, saw a significant recovery from 1916: eleven issues and a total of 428 pages; and 1918 was the best year of all: eleven issues and 772 pages. Pound's offer to 'help the *Little Review*', dated 29 November 1916, was received after the decision that the journal move to New York—an exodus which 'had been

---

[101] Quinn to Pound, 2 June 1917, 12 January 1917, cited in B. L. Reid, *The Man from New York: John Quinn and His Friends* (New York: Oxford University Press, 1968), 287, 285.

[102] Quinn to Pound, 31 October 1917, cited in Reid, *The Man from New York*, 287–8.

[103] Quinn to Pound, 31 October 1917, cited in Reid, *The Man from New York*, 289.

[104] Quinn to Anderson, 7 August 1917, *Little Review* records, UWM.

[105] Franco Moretti, *Graphs, Maps, Trees: Abstract Models for a Literary History* (London: Verso, 2005), 1.

planned', as Anderson conceded, 'minutely except in its financial aspects'.[106] The Pound-Quinn intervention thus came at an auspicious moment.[107]

Golding is undoubtedly correct in his argument that Pound's association with the *Little Review* 'came to effect a striking revival of...substance and energy'.[108] But it would be wrong to see Pound's arrival as a *de facto* takeover. Pound and Anderson did not meet in person before their editorial association formally began in May 1917. But they corresponded regularly and thus discovered a loose cultural and intellectual association between the world in which Pound defined himself, and his cultural nationalism, and the world of the *Little Review*. Pound clearly admired the spirited editorial tone of the *Little Review*, which is epitomized, for example, by the 'Don'ts for Critics' published in March 1916 (see Figure 1.3), which can be read as a direct response (and compliment) to the hectoring prescriptions of Pound's 'A Few Don'ts by an Imagiste', published in *Poetry* in March 1913.

Don'ts for Critics[*]

(*Apropos of recent criticisms of Imagism, vers libre, and modern poetry generally.*)

ALICE CORBIN HENDERSON

Don't confuse vers libre and Imagism. The two are not identical. One pertains to verse, the other to vision.

Don't attempt to "place" Imagism until you know what it is.

Don't substitute irritability for judgement.

Don't attempt to establish absolutes—positive or negative—by precedents of a half or a quarter of a century, or a mere decade ago.

Don't be a demagogue.

Don't try to speak the last word—you can't.

Don't be dishonest with yourself. Analyze your own inhibitions.

Don't believe that beauty is conventionality, or that the classic poets chose only "nice" subjects.

Don't forget that the age that produced the cathedrals produced also the grotesques.

Don't be afraid to expand.

Figure 1.3. 'Don'ts for Critics', *Little Review*, March 1916

(*Little Review*, The Modernist Journals Project (searchable database). Brown and Tulsa Universities, ongoing. http://www.modjourn.org)

---

[106] Pound to Anderson, [29 November 1916], *P-LR*, 4; Anderson, *My Thirty Years' War*, 142.

[107] Pound to Anderson, [29 November 1916], *P-LR*, 4; Anderson, *My Thirty Years' War*, 142.

[108] Golding, 'The Little Review', in Brooker and Thacker (eds.), *The Oxford Critical and Cultural History of Modernist Magazines: Volume II*, 73.

Anderson, like Pound, was interested in the question of form as it related to modern poetry: the *Little Review* regularly published articles about Imagism, and announced a 'Vers Libre Prize Contest' in April 1916.[109] Most significantly, Anderson shared some of Pound's concerns about the position of literary culture and art within the broader culture of the US: in her case this can be seen, for example, in her gloating allusion to Mitchell Kennerley's victory against the New York Society for the Suppression of Vice, who had unsuccessfully claimed that the novel, Daniel Goodman's *Hagar Revelly*, published by Kennerley, was obscene.[110] In Pound's case, this can be seen, for example, in his 'Letter from London', another contribution dealing with America's 'import duty on books' ('It means insularity, stupidity, backing the printer against literature, commerce and obstruction against intelligence').[111] In short, Pound and Anderson were temperamentally and intellectually close; the cultural preoccupations which they shared could, on occasion, be expressed in writing styles which are strikingly similar, a kind of propagandistic and journalistic bluster.

While Anderson saw Pound as a cultural ally who was worth the investment of an argument, and as an individual whose views and judgements she often broadly accepted and shared, others did not share her conviction of Pound's worth. In apparent response to a request for a contribution, Amy Lowell wrote to Anderson as follows:

> I do not want to put anything in your magazine while you are running those men so hard. Much as I admire some of Ezra Pound's work, I do not like his attitude, and I feel the same about the other contributors, only, in most cases, without the admiration.[112]

Lowell's was no means the only voice to criticize the adoption of Pound; regular subscribers often complained at what must have seemed like an abandonment of intellectual independence. For example, Frank Stuhlman, a librarian from Vernon, New York, felt that 'one of the finest publications in America' had become 'a thing of freaks and fakes, of posturists and squeaking egoists' and recommended that Anderson 'fire Ezra Pound, Joyce and Co., and write in some of yourself... You did splendid work in the early numbers before the hegira to San Francisco'.[113] Anderson was capable of revelling in such criticism while simultaneously resisting it. She thrived on the antagonism the *Little Review* was capable of generating.

The historical, cultural, and political context in which the *Little Review* was being published began to change decisively early in 1917, at around the time that

---

[109] *LR*, April 1916, 40. Two hundred and two poems had been received by November, of which thirty-two were returned (on the grounds that 'they were either Shakespearean sonnets of rhymed quatrains or couplets'); results were promised in 'our December issue', an issue which did not, in fact, appear. The winning entries, by H. D. and Maxwell Bodenheim, were finally announced and printed in April 1917. Anderson was clearly short of copy that month and included several other entries to the competition (see *LR*, April 1917, 11–23).

[110] *LR*, April 1915, 3; for the Kennerley case, see 'Acquit Kennerley in Sex Novel Case', *New York Times*, 10 February 1914, and Dawn B. Sova, *Literature Suppressed on Sexual Grounds* (New York: Facts on File, 2006), 70–2.

[111] *LR*, April 1918, 32.

[112] Lowell to Anderson, 27 July 1917, *Little Review* records, UWM.

[113] *LR*, July 1918, 64.

Pound and (by default) Quinn became editorial presences. Woodrow Wilson had resolved to keep the US out of the war, and was narrowly re-elected President in 1916 on that basis. But diplomatic relations between the US and Germany broke down in February 1917, and Congress voted to declare war against Germany on 6 April 1917. This decision, which brought in its wake conscription—and a vigorous anti-conscription movement spear-headed by Emma Goldman—quickly led to the introduction of the Espionage Act. There were many first-generation German migrants in the US, and the Espionage Act was designed to ensure that they would be patriotic to their new country. It specifically prohibited: the support of America's enemies during wartime; any attempt to interfere with military operations; any action which promoted insubordination; and any action which interfered with military recruitment.[114] Under the terms of that Act, Goldman and her partner Alexander Berkman were arrested on 15 June 1917, and charged with inducing 'persons not to register'.[115] Heap and Anderson attended the ensuing trial, and Anderson circulated a formal letter—written by Heap, but signed by her—protesting that 'protesting' had become 'a crime overnight'.[116] Objecting to conscription, in Heap's eloquent and reasoned argument, had nothing to do with anarchism, and everything to do with the cherished principle of 'free speech', an argument Goldman herself invoked by way of defence in her trial ('We say that if America has entered the war to make the world safe for democracy, she must first make democracy safe in America').[117] These arguments work around the First Amendment to the US Constitution in crucial ways (the amendment which prohibits the making of any law which abridges the freedom of speech). They also point to the complicated and varied political positions held in the US at this precise moment. Quinn, for example, was in favour of US participation in the war, but opposed to conscription, and, of course, opposed to anarchism. His views were shared by Pound. When the US entered the war, Pound told Anderson, with characteristic and emphatic confidence: 'I am very glad America is in AT LAST, and think we should have been in long ago, BUT I prefer volunteer armies'.[118] Anderson and Heap, meanwhile, continued to develop their interest in anarchism, and Goldman's ideas, and were opposed to the war and conscription to an extent which both men failed to grasp. Their committed public support for Goldman cost them in a very real and personal way; they were asked to leave their office in Manhattan's West Fourteenth Street because—by Heap's account—the owners 'are good Americans and won't have that kind of publicity about their building'.[119]

---

[114] See http://www.firstworldwar.com/source/espionageact.htm for the full text of the Espionage Act.

[115] Marian J. Morton, *Emma Goldman and the American Left: Nowhere at Home* (New York: Twayne Publishers, 1992), 87.

[116] Baggett, *Dear Tiny Heart*, 45. The letter, addressed to 'American Citizens', is dated 23 June 1917.

[117] *Trial and Speeches of Alexander Berkman and Emma Goldman in the United States District Court, in the City of New York, July, 1917* (New York: Mother Earth Publishing Association, 1917).

[118] Pound to Anderson, 3 August 1917, *P-LR*, 96.

[119] Heap to Reynolds, [c. July 1917], Baggett, *Dear Tiny Heart*, 46. The issue of July 1917 mentions being 'forced to give up our offices…because we expressed ourselves in regard to the trial of Emma Goldman and Alexander Berkman' (*LR*, July 1917, [32]).

Quinn was aware of the pair's support of Goldman in the trial and even knew of the eviction, but—somewhat naively—he failed to anticipate the extent to which such views, events, and commitments might influence the editorial shape and fortunes of the *Little Review*.[120]

With respect to the suppression of dissenting voices, the Espionage Act added to already significant legal powers vested in officials working at the Post Office, who were charged with upholding section 211 of the Criminal Code (1909) which specifically proscribed:

> Every obscene, lewd, or lascivious and every filthy book, pamphlet, picture, letter, writing, print, or other publication of an indecent character and every article and thing designed... for any indecent or immoral use.

Such items were:

> declared to be non-mailable matter and shall not be conveyed in the mails or delivered from any post-office or by any letter-carrier. Whoever shall knowingly deposit, or cause to be deposited for mailing or delivery anything declared by this section to be non-mailable... shall be fined... or imprisoned... or both.[121]

In practice this gave Post Officials the power to examine any item that was posted in order to assess whether it was 'indecent or immoral', and it encouraged any such official with a prudish mentality to act with zeal. The New York Society for the Suppression of Vice—established in 1873, with a specific mission to monitor compliance with state laws, and work with the courts to bring offenders to justice—was also quite active, and had several members working behind the scenes at the Post Office.[122] What made this situation particularly significant for the *Little Review* was the fact that the postal system was the principal means of distribution, the principal means of reaching subscribers, as there were very few direct sales.

Anderson and Heap were quite attuned to the difficulties of this situation and the way in which 'suppression' had become part of the cultural *zeitgeist*. In April 1917, for example, the *Little Review* included a blank page headed 'The War' with a note, at the foot of the page, which wryly states: 'We will probably be suppressed for this'.[123] This barb appears not to have excited official response, but a few months later, the *Little Review* of October 1917 was declared to be 'non-mailable' by officials at the New York Post Office, and the editors found themselves having recourse to the *pro bono* legal advice which Quinn had offered. The 'suppression' (as it was termed) was due to 'Cantelman's Spring-Mate', a story by Wyndham Lewis which contains a blatant description of a sexual encounter between a British soldier, home on leave, and a woman who becomes pregnant. As Quinn wrote to Anderson at the time, it describes the 'psychology of war times' being 'a pitiless exposure of a man who has become mere animal' which would be 'brutal and

---

[120] Heap mentions visiting Quinn for advice about being evicted in a letter to Reynolds of July 1917 ('there is nothing to do'), Baggett, *Dear Tiny Heart*, 46.

[121] *LR*, March 1918, 33.

[122] Paul Vanderham, *James Joyce and Censorship: The Trials of Ulysses* (London: Macmillan, 1998), 135.

[123] *LR*, April 1917, 4.

horrible to some'.[124] Like Anderson and Heap, Quinn found the fact that the *Little Review* was being 'banned' on account of this story 'appalling', and he appealed to Judge Lamar, the Solicitor for the Post Office Department, on behalf of the *Little Review*.[125] He did not want to make an enormous fuss, and warned Anderson that he was more likely to obtain a 'favorable verdict…by a quiet presentation of the case than by an angry presentation of it'.[126] Yet his letter to Lamar, with its reference to 'gunshot', is not quite so measured as this warning might lead one to expect:

> I have read the story of Wyndham Lewis 'Cantelman's Spring-Mate', and I have not the slightest hesitation in stating my professional opinion to be that it does not come within gunshot of violating the statute or any Federal statute.

He continued:

> I am sure that upon reading the story you will agree with me that there is nothing either lewd or lascivious or indecent in it or anything that is calculated to corrupt the morals of any of the readers of the *Little Review*.[127]

But Lamar was not to be so easily swayed. He referred the case on to Judge Augustus Hand who judged that the story contained a 'degree of detail that does not appear necessary to teach the desired lesson'; in a word, it was 'salacious' and he was disinclined to interfere 'with the discretion lodged in the Postmaster General'.[128] The case was denied. Thus copies of the *Little Review* for October 1917 never reached subscribers.

There was, of course, more to Hand's decision than met the eye. With the Espionage Act in force, the Post Office kept a list of 'subversive literature' which identified the *Little Review* as a 'Publication of Anarchistic tendency'.[129] As Quinn noted, Heap and Anderson had attracted 'Federal officials' attention' by publishing articles by and supportive of Emma Goldman.[130] The US had entered 'a period of spy-hunting and a corresponding spasm of virtue', as Quinn observed; in the circumstances he urged Anderson to act with particular editorial discretion 'because now that attention has been centred upon the *Little Review*, too much care cannot be exercised in studying what you print'.[131]

---

[124] Quinn to Anderson, 5 December 1917, *Little Review* records, UWM.
[125] Quinn to Anderson, 5 December 1917, *Little Review* records, UWM.
[126] Quinn to Anderson, 3 November 1917, *Little Review* records, UWM.
[127] Quinn to W. H. Lamar, 5 November 1917, *Little Review* records, UWM.
[128] 'Judicial Opinion', *LR*, December 1917, 47, 48.
[129] Vanderham, *James Joyce and Censorship*, 18. Vanderham is quoting from records relating to Espionage Act, National Archives, Washington, DC.
[130] John Quinn to Margaret Anderson, 5 December 1917, *Little Review* records, UWM. For material by and relating to Goldman in the *Little Review* see Margaret Anderson, 'The Challenge of Emma Goldman' (May 1914, 5–9); Louise Bryant, 'Emma Goldman on Trial' (September 1915, 25–6); Emma Goldman, 'Preparedness: The Road to Universal Slaughter' (December 1915, 7–12); Emma Goldman, 'Letters from Prison' (May 1916, 17–18); and Jane Heap 'Push-Face' (June 1917, 5–6).
[131] Quinn to Anderson, 5 December 1917, *Little Review* records, UWM. Federal prosecutors brought charges against *The Masses*, a radical socialist monthly, in April 1918 for conspiring to obstruct conscription. A sense of the atmosphere and fervour of the moment can be gleaned from looking at

With regard to the Lewis case, Quinn's response was very much that of a lawyer, who had a fine grasp of legal detail, and a deep respect for the workings of the legal system. He could differ with Judge Hand on the 'merits' of the judgment; but on the 'technicalities' he thought the judgment was right, and he told Anderson so, in a vivid and detailed letter which acknowledges that 'courts do not know everything, and courts cannot overrule the orders of executive departments', and describes war as 'a solvent that destroys all the moralities'.[132] For the others, things could not be so straightforward. How could an official at the Post Office be the 'supreme authority' on a matter of 'intellectual interest'?[133] Pound decided that readers of the *Little Review* needed to be told about the 'grotesque' and 'unthinkable' 'law of our country' and immediately penned an intemperate article on section 211 of the Criminal Code for the issue of March 1918, telling Anderson that it needed to be reprinted 'EVERY MONTH...It is a labour of patriotism wherefrom we must not shrink'.[134] The response of Anderson and Heap was also one of predictable indignation. The *Little Review* of November 1917 carries an editorial headed 'OBSCENITY' in which the editors complain of the Post Office acting with 'excessive zeal'; the issue for the following month cites the Judge's decision at length, and includes Anderson's argument that the Lewis piece should have proceeded to circulation on the grounds that it is 'a piece of Art'.[135] Observing events from the distance of London, W. B. Yeats could afford to be more sanguine and reflective. In a view which proved to be perspicuous, he told Pound (who in turn told Anderson) that 'the suppression of the October number is great luck and ought to be the making of the magazine'.[136] The suppression had renewed Pound's editorial energy and made him all the more determined to 'make the contents so bloody good that we will *simply "have" to go on*'.[137]

These responses to the suppression of the *Little Review* for October 1917—which reveal views shared, more or less, by Anderson, Heap, Pound, and Yeats—highlight the incongruity of Quinn's position as an editorial presence, and underscore the enigma of his ongoing financial support and *pro bono* legal advice. From the outset Quinn—labelled 'mon cher ami' by Pound, in a typical aside—had made it quite clear that he did not want his association with the *Little Review* to be publicly known ('it is simply no one's *damn* business what your finances are or whether you have a guarantor or not').[138] As a practising lawyer, he was far more risk averse than either Anderson or Heap. He needed to be seen as an upstanding citizen, in

issues of *The Masses*, including that of August 1917 which was judged treasonable. See http://dlib.nyu.edu/themasses (a digital copy of all issues), and https://en.wikipedia.org/wiki/The_Masses for an excellent summary and further references.

[132] Quinn to Anderson, 5 December 1917, *Little Review* records, UWM.

[133] Anderson, 'Judicial Opinion (Our Suppressed October Issue)', *LR*, December 1917, 49.

[134] Pound to Anderson, [17 January 1918], *P-LR*, 172. See also 'The Classics Escape', Pound's article, *LR*, March 1918, 32–4.

[135] *LR*, November 1917, 43–4; *LR*, December 1917, 46–9.

[136] Pound to Anderson, [14 December 1917], *P-LR*, 167.

[137] Pound to Anderson, [30 December 1917], *P-LR*, 170.

[138] Pound to Anderson, [20 February 1918], *P-LR*, 183; Quinn to Anderson, 11 August 1917, *Little Review* records, UWM.

order to protect his business interests. As he began to understand the extent of Anderson's earlier commitment to Emma Goldman and her various causes (elliptically referred to in the correspondence as 'M. C. A'.s lamentable past'), he became more jittery and nervous about the subvention he was giving to the *Little Review*, and the prospects for the future of the journal more generally.[139] Why then did he continue to offer financial and legal support to the *Little Review* even after Pound's editorial tenure had ended?[140] There is no obvious answer to this question. But it is clear that the suppression of the *Little Review* on account of 'Cantelman's Spring-Mate' in October 1917 foreshadows the formative events that followed, including the reception of the very first chapter of *Ulysses* by Pound, the four suppressions of the *Little Review* on account of *Ulysses*, and the subsequent trial of the editors on account of the obscenity of 'Nausicaa', at which Quinn represented Joyce and the *Little Review*, somewhat ineffectively.[141]

ASSOCIATION COPY

If the serialization of *Ulysses* in the *Little Review* represents a moment of 'avant-garde rupture', as the logic of Golding's argument suggests, it is a moment which continues for some time.[142] In fact, *Ulysses* was associated with the *Little Review* for three years, between March 1918 (when the first chapter appeared) and February 1921 (when the trial involving the editors was heard). The exercise of what McGann terms 'radial reading' ('decoding one or more of the contexts that interpenetrate the scripted and physical text') is therefore quite extensive.[143] The editors of the Yale edition—the *Little Review Ulysses*—estimate that the twenty-three instalments of the *Little Review* in which *Ulysses* appeared contain 527,536 words, of which *Ulysses* makes up approximately 23 per cent (at 122,285 words).[144] What kinds of cultural, literary, and political association exist between the serial texts of *Ulysses* and the content of the *Little Review* in those twenty-three issues? To what extent is there a cultural 'fit' or 'misfit' between Joyce's work and the works it was published alongside? How does the meaning of *Ulysses* alter if one reads the serial text in the specific context of the *Little Review*, rather than the book form of subsequent editions? Unless one makes an attempt to analyse the material surrounding *Ulysses* in a rigorous and consistent overview, using some of the historicist techniques of 'distant reading' ('in which the reality of the text undergoes a

---

[139] Pound to Quinn, 29 and 30 December 1917, *EP-JQ*, 133.

[140] See Quinn to Pound, 24 September 1920 (cited in Reid, *The Man from New York*, 442) in which Quinn indicates that he has just made another donation of $200. Pound was 'thoroughly surprised' by this action ('I certainly wd. have tried to stop you') (Pound to Quinn, 31 October 1920, *EP-JQ*, 199).

[141] This conclusion chimes with that reached by Joseph M. Hassett in *The Ulysses Trials: Beauty and Truth Meets the Law* (Dublin: The Lilliput Press, 2015), 50. With regard to Quinn's intervention and appeal to Lamar, Hassett argues that Quinn 'failed to grasp the opportunity' of contesting the law at this crucial moment (42). See also Morrisson, *The Public Face of Modernism*, 159f.

[142] Golding, 'The Little Review', 62.

[143] McGann, *The Textual Condition*, 119.   [144] Gaipa et al., *LRU*, 382.

deliberate reduction and abstraction' through the use of 'graphs from quantitative history, maps from geography and trees from evolutionary theory'), it is very difficult to be even handed.[145] In 'The Magazine Context for the *Little Review Ulysses*', the editors of the *Little Review Ulysses* have attempted just that, and have pieced together a general commentary which relates how 'each installment of the novel relates to its neighbouring texts'.[146] Building on that account, the following analysis concentrates on easily identifiable major associative trends between the serial *Ulysses* and the other content of the *Little Review*. The argument readily acknowledges that reading is a matter of interpretation, which reflects the acculturation and personal preferences of the individual reader, and is also offered with the observation that journals, as texts which might be analysed from the perspective of intention, are genuinely complicated cultural artefacts. Most obviously they represent a moment, the moment of their creation, and the agency—at least to some limited extent—of the individuals who edit specific issues, and who make the decisions to bring particular contents together in a particular issue. Those editors, acting solo or, as noted in the case of the *Little Review*, as a somewhat contentious group, bring geographically dispersed authors, texts, concepts, and ephemera into a kind of momentary cultural synergy. While literary historians may come to identify that synergy as a fact of significance, it is important to bear the moment of origin in mind, and not to over-determine the significance of a journal, given that it is multi-authored, contingent, expedient, and ultimately social, both in origin and intention. In other words, it is important to note that a journal, viewed as a document within literary history, is, to an important degree, a document of happenstance.

Yet happenstance can throw up associations between texts which might not ordinarily coincide. Few Joyceans would associate *Ulysses* with the work of William Carlos Williams. But Williams, who was friendly with Pound and interested in Imagism, began to make regular contributions to the *Little Review* in 1917, and in April 1919 commented on his own sense of the evolving aesthetics of literary Modernism as follows:

> There is nothing sacred about literature, it is damned from one end to the other...
> I'll write whatever I damn please, whenever I damn please and as I damn please and
> it'll be good if the authentic spirit of change is on it.[147]

As the editors of the *Little Review Ulysses* note, these comments articulate a project for Williams, and 'might well describe Joyce's aims in *Ulysses*'.[148] They chime particularly well with the contribution Joyce also made to the *Little Review* of April 1919: the first excerpt of chapter 9 ('Scylla and Charybdis'), a narrative which remains challenging to the first-time reader of *Ulysses*, and must have posed a particular challenge to readers of the serial, who were working 'without the benefit of the schemas or a sense of the book's deeper epic structure', and who found themselves confronting a chapter with an extremely difficult and ornate contrapuntal

---

[145] Moretti, *Graphs, Maps, Trees*, 1, 2.   [146] Gaipa et al., *LRU*, 381.
[147] *LR*, April 1919, 8.   [148] Gaipa et al., *LRU*, 407.

narrative style, and much in the way of teasing allusiveness and playfully overt historicity.[149] Williams's explicitly stated aesthetic is a counter to the implicit aesthetic position of *Ulysses*, and shows that *Ulysses*, 'far from being a timeless classic sprung wholly out of its creator's head, belongs to and emerges from a time and place that Joyce shared with other writers'.[150] In other words, it is critically significant that the serial *Ulysses* emerged alongside writings by authors such as T. S. Eliot, Ford Madox Hueffer, and Wyndham Lewis, who are similarly concerned 'with honesty, difficulty, offensiveness, fragmentation and subjectivity', and who also allowed their works to be recruited by Pound, who wished to use the *Little Review* as 'a bomb' which would 'span the Atlantic', 'end America's intellectual isolation', and 'blow up the old house of literature'.[151]

As editors, Anderson and Heap typically eschewed grandstanding editorial statements, preferring instead to let editorial views come across in occasional asides, given in response to readers. Pound was far more assertive. He announced his position as Foreign Editor of the *Little Review* with a lengthy 'Editorial', which describes the history of his relations with other periodicals (including *Poetry*, *The Egoist*, and *Blast*), and explains the rationale for his new commitment:

> I wished a place where the current prose writings of James Joyce, Wyndham Lewis, T. S. Eliot, and myself might appear regularly, promptly and together, rather than irregularly, sporadically and after useless delays.[152]

His purpose was 'to aid and abet *The Egoist* in its work' and he was committed to the venture because he believed Joyce, Eliot, and Lewis were producing 'the most important contributions to English literature of the last three years'; *A Portrait of the Artist as a Young Man*, *Prufrock and Other Observations*, and *Tarr* were 'practically the only works of the time in which the creative element is present', which 'show invention' and 'progress beyond precedent work'.[153] Pound's aim in making such works available to the American readership of the *Little Review* was to educate 'the mass of our contemporaries, to say nothing of our debilitated elders'.[154] By June 1917, just a month after Pound had become Foreign Editor, the *Little Review* had remodelled its format, masthead, and banner to reflect these aims, switching the rather bland strapline of 'Literature Drama Music Art' for the rather more riven and somewhat obtuse 'Making No Compromise with the Public Taste' (see Figure 1.4).[155]

From October 1917, another slogan jostled for readers' attention, this time placed on the contents page: 'The Magazine That Is Read by Those Who Write the Others' (see Figure 1.5). The effect of this statement—particularly as it competes

[149] Gaipa et al., *LRU*, 399; I discuss several of the interpretive issues which this chapter raises in 'Joyce and the Institutions of Revivalism', *Irish University Review*, 33 (2003), 117–32.
[150] Gaipa et al., *LRU*, 381.   [151] Gaipa et al., *LRU*, 391; *LR*, June 1918, 55.
[152] *LR*, May 1917, 1.   [153] *LR*, May 1917, 5.   [154] *LR*, May 1917, 5.
[155] The wording of the banner may have been suggested by Anderson, as Golding notes (Golding, 'The Little Review', in Brooker and Thacker (eds.), *The Oxford Critical and Cultural History of Modernist Magazines: Volume II*, 61). The banner can also be read as a deliberate rebuke to the masthead used by *Poetry* (Whitman's statement: 'To have great poets there must be great audiences too').

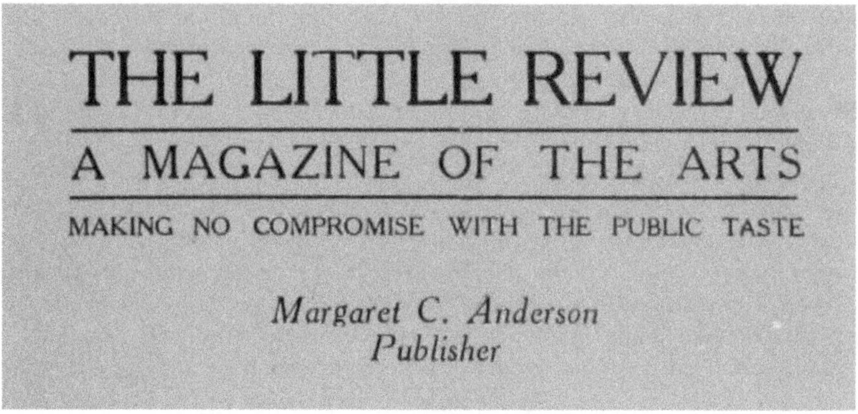

THE LITTLE REVIEW
A MAGAZINE OF THE ARTS
MAKING NO COMPROMISE WITH THE PUBLIC TASTE

Margaret C. Anderson
Publisher

Figure 1.4. Title page masthead and banner, in use from June 1917–March 1921

(*Little Review*, The Modernist Journals Project (searchable database). Brown and Tulsa Universities, ongoing. http://www.modjourn.org)

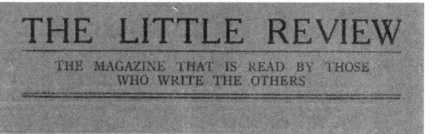

Figure 1.5. Contents page heading and banner, October 1917–April 1919

(*Little Review*, The Modernist Journals Project (searchable database). Brown and Tulsa Universities, ongoing. http://www.modjourn.org)

with the jumble of the contents list, and follows the proclamations of the often vibrantly coloured cover—is rather over-determined and noisy. The wording was recommended by Pound ('I think we can irritate by hoisting [this] flag'), who had both a strong sense of the need to antagonize other editors working within the field of literary journalism and a clear sense of his own position.[156]

Not everyone agreed with Pound, however. Quinn felt that 'Making No Compromise with the Public Taste' was a pointlessly adversarial *défi*, and read it in relation to Joyce's use of language—specifically the words 'scrotumtightening' and 'snotgreen', used in the first instalment of *Ulysses* ('The snotgreen sea. The scrotumtightening sea')—words which were 'hardly', he told Pound, 'a matter of taste'

---

[156] Pound to Anderson, [23 August 1917], *P-LR*, 19.

but 'more a matter of "making no compromise with accepted ideas of decency" '.[157] In the July–August number of 1920, one of the subscribers to the *Little Review* commented that 'Making No Compromise' seemed to 'lack dignity', being 'blatant' and a contradiction of 'the whole spirit of the work', an observation which elicited a response from Jane Heap which revealed that she too felt ambivalent about the banner and the direction in which it seemed to point, describing it 'as one of my compromises for the past three years'.[158]

In ceding some editorial autonomy to Pound, Anderson and Heap compromised with regard to the choice and payment of contributors. In effect they had condoned the creation of a dual economy, comprising the paid (mainly European male, and chosen by Pound) and the mostly unpaid (mainly American, sometimes women and chosen by Heap and Anderson). Pound's group, who appeared in the issues for which he acted as 'Foreign Editor', included Lewis, Eliot, Joyce, Hueffer, and Yeats; they were paid directly by Pound, using the subvention given to him by Quinn. Contributors selected and published by Anderson and Heap in the same period included Richard Aldington, Sherwood Anderson, Djuna Barnes, Maxwell Bodenheim, Hart Crane, Elsa von Freytag-Loringhoven, Ben Hecht, Marianne Moore, Wallace Stevens, and William Carlos Williams. In *Thirty Years' War* Anderson insists that 'no one ever urged me to pay' and in general these non-Poundians appear *not* to have been paid, though some may have been successful in extracting payment on some occasions: a letter from Heap to Reynolds mentions Anderson writing 'checks on an overdrawn bank account', including one for Barnes.[159] Nonetheless it is generally true to say that Pound was paid as both editor and writer, while Anderson and Heap continued to struggle with meagre funds. These funds came from subscriptions and occasional direct donations from Quinn, and others such as J. S. Watson of *The Dial* who appeared at the *Little Review* offices at Christmas 1917 to buy a copy of *Prufrock and Other Observations* (1917)—a volume which Anderson sold—paid with a hundred-dollar bill, and then insisted on taking no change.[160] What income there was had to pay both living and production costs. All the evidence suggests a precarious hand-to-mouth existence, with difficulties paying rent, regular moves from place to place, regular cash-flow crises, and shortages of food. Quinn had urged a policy of 'reserve as to your finances', but Anderson continued to issue urgent appeals for more subscribers, and to make direct editorial comment about the shortage of 'necessary funds'.[161]

The financial situation was not the only editorial compromise. There is no doubt that Anderson and Heap were radical and committed feminists. Nonetheless, some of the issues of the *Little Review* which Pound shaped omitted contributions from women completely, an imbalance which was redressed following his departure in

---

[157] *LR*, March 1918, 5; Quinn to Pound, 14 March 1918, John Quinn Memorial Collection, NYPL.

[158] *LR*, July–August 1920, 32, 33.

[159] Heap to Reynolds, [11 December 1918], Baggett, *Dear Tiny Heart*, 17.

[160] Anderson, *My Thirty Years' War*, 189; the same event is recalled in Heap to Reynolds, [December 1917], Baggett, *Dear Tiny Heart*, 53.

[161] Quinn to Heap, 8 August 1917, *Little Review* records, UWM; *LR*, December 1918, 1.

the spring of 1919. From that moment onwards, the *Little Review* began to promote authors such as Djuna Barnes, Mary Butts, Dorothy Richardson, and the eccentric 'Baroness' (Elsa von Freytag-Loringhoven, a poet and expert in contemporary performance art who appears to have kindled an intense sexual relationship with Heap).[162] As the editors of the *Little Review Ulysses* argue, one of the implications of the shift from Pound's contributors towards this group is that:

> while *Ulysses* was developing in the pages of the magazine, moving away from its initial realistic style and becoming more experimental in later episodes, the magazine in which it appeared was changing as well, featuring more women and more American writers, along with even more aggressively avant-garde art.[163]

From the perspective of a more inclusive history of Modernism, Dorothy Richardson's positioning is of particular significance. *Interim*, the fifth of her novels to describe the London life of Miriam Henderson (a semi-autobiographical self-portrait), began to be serialized in the *Little Review* in June 1919, and ran alongside the serialization of *Ulysses* for an entire year. It is certainly true that the two texts 'exert a strong gravitational pull on one another' and 'draw out the gender differentiation that was increasingly felt in the journal after Pound's departure'.[164]

But is Richardson's work really 'an epic that can stand up to *Ulysses*'?[165] Some readers might say that *Interim* lacks the depth of characterization, allusiveness, lexical creativity, and intense lyricism so evident in Joyce's text. Some of the *Little Review* insiders developed qualms about Richardson as the serialization of *Interim* progressed. John Rodker (1894–1955), the London-based writer and publisher who replaced Pound as 'Foreign Editor' from May 1919, considered Richardson weak in comparison to Joyce ('anyone with a sufficiently sympathetic and cultured brain can follow Joyce and be moved by him; but Miss Richardson's associations are as free as a choppy sea').[166] It is also possible that Anderson did not admire Richardson. Writing in response to a 'reader critic' in March 1920, Anderson suggests a certain *ennui* about Richardson's take on modernist form: 'Richardson is so unlike Joyce that I can't even begin to argue with you—though I am sure there are some five thousand people who will agree with you because Richardson and Joyce have the great soul bond of unconventional punctuation'.[167] That a writer was 'avant-garde' appears to have been more important than their gender. Or, to put it another way, what was published was by no means formulaic, and what the editors might admire could not always be anticipated.

Scholars of Modernism will see a kind of neatness of fit between Richardson and the *Little Review*, given the presence of *Ulysses*. But the facts of Richardson's association with the *Little Review* are complicated. Her work came to the attention of Anderson and Heap because Pound arranged for the publication, in April 1918, of

---

[162] Both Barnes ('an original') and the 'Baroness' (Elsa von Freytag-Loringhoven) were introduced to the *Little Review* in the 'American Number' of June 1918, edited by Jane Heap ('made with no compromise to Margaret Anderson and Ezra Pound'). Mary Butts was introduced in August 1919, and Richardson in June 1919, after Pound's tenure as editor had discontinued.

[163] Gaipa et al., *LRU*, 385.   [164] Gaipa et al., *LRU*, 407.   [165] Gaipa et al., *LRU*, 408.

[166] *LR*, September 1919, 41.   [167] *LR*, March 1920, 62.

May Sinclair's essay on 'The Novels of Dorothy Richardson'.[168] Sinclair—who was also a novelist—was an acquaintance of Pound's and agreed to make a direct donation to the *Little Review* of £10 a year for three years, and to contribute articles 'without payment', an arrangement which Pound described as 'very sporting', while cannily telling Anderson that 'we had better keep this to ourselves, for the present at any rate', an aside which reveals a tacit awareness of the cultural, real, and often gendered economies which were at stake behind the scenes.[169] The very fact that Richardson's work was not included in Pound's issues may be adduced as further evidence of the same types of editorial economy. Pound was happy to have Sinclair's lengthy essay on Richardson for free, as filler in the issue of April 1918— an issue which might otherwise have been thin, given the very short length of the second chapter of *Ulysses*—but he was not prepared to pay Richardson (or for that matter Sinclair) with the funds he had received from Quinn. Anderson and Heap—who do appear to have paid Richardson, in what must have been a rare concession—must have come to resent these subtle and evidently gendered aesthetic preferences, and certainly resented the broader economic position of the *Little Review*, but they remained committed to the enterprise, because editing the *Little Review* kept them in touch with cultural capital and political debate, which is what they valued.[170]

Sinclair's essay on Richardson made literary history by announcing, for the first time, the significance of presenting a 'stream of consciousness' in a literary text, of 'an extreme concentration on the thing felt or seen', of a work which collapses the distinction between 'what is objective and what is subjective' and dispenses with conventional plot: 'there is no drama, no situation, no set scene'.[171] The serialization of *Ulysses*—an event which gave Heap 'a thrill of excitement' and 'an inner circle feeling'—provided ongoing evidence of such literary innovation being a central concern of the *Little Review*.[172] The fact that Anderson and Heap were in a position to continue publishing *Ulysses* even after Pound's term as Foreign Editor had come to an end was, of course, also highly significant for the cultural cachet, ongoing notoriety, and success of their journal. Such success was not easily achieved, however. In *Thirty Years' War* Anderson likens the suppression of *Ulysses* by the New York Post Office to a 'burning at the stake':

> The care we had taken to preserve Joyce's text intact; the worry over the bills that accumulated when we had no advance funds; the technique I used on printer, bookbinders, paper houses—tears, prayers, hysterics or rages—to make them push ahead without a guarantee of money; the addressing, wrapping, stamping, mailing; the excitement of anticipating the world's response to the literary masterpiece of our generation...and then a notice from the Post Office: BURNED.[173]

---

[168] *LR*, April 1918, 3–11.   [169] Pound to Anderson, [22 November 1917], *P-LR*, 161.

[170] Richardson's side of the correspondence survives in the *Little Review* records, UWM. See, for example, that of 7 May 1919, in which Richardson accepts the *LR*'s 'terms for the American serial rights'. My thanks to Adam Guy and Scott McCracken for providing me with scans and transcripts of this correspondence.

[171] *LR*, April 1918, 6, 7, 9, 5.

[172] Heap to Reynolds, [3 October 1918]; Baggett, *Dear Tiny Heart*, 60.

[173] Anderson, *My Thirty Years' War*, 175.

By mid-October 1920, relations between Quinn, Anderson, and Heap had reached an all-time low. Quinn found himself representing the *Little Review* in preliminary hearings alleging the obscenity of the third instalment of chapter 13 ('Nausicaa', which had appeared in the *Little Review* of July–August 1920). He had come to see Anderson and Heap as 'sheer self-exploiters' without any 'disinterested love of literature' who were 'Trying to use Joyce, an artist, as propaganda for their review'.[174] Although not a fair or balanced appraisal, it does point towards Quinn's eventual realization that he could never belong in the same cultural and political world as Anderson and Heap. For Anderson and Heap, whom Quinn terms 'advanced women', the publication of a radical avant-garde literature was part and parcel of a deeper political position, a position which demanded candour about sexual relationships, access to contraception, and equality for women; a position which embraced anarchism, failed to recognize the validity of ordinary laws, and rejected the social, cultural, and economic *status quo*, particularly the participation of the US in the war. The yet-to-be-finished *Ulysses* appeared to chime with some of these views: it was candid about sexuality and the body, and was unafraid of being deemed 'obscene'; it appeared to be anarchic in form; and though it was written in Europe during the First World War, it made absolutely no reference to the war. Viewed from the perspective of deeply rooted cultural politics and mentality, there were multiple associations between the serial *Ulysses* and the individuals who had taken responsibility for publishing it.

Of the political views held by Anderson and Heap, anarchism and opposition to the First World War are the most significant, both as editorial preoccupations and as interpretive frames for Joyce's evolving text. As Anderson and Heap were to learn, it was one thing to be supportive of Emma Goldman before the US entry to the war; but ongoing support after that time—for an individual who had become a notorious household name—meant the *Little Review* attracting official attention, and, as noted, being listed as a 'Publication of Anarchistic tendency'.[175] Anarchism was not a notable editorial preoccupation in the issues for which Pound acted as Foreign Editor, but Anderson and Heap continued to be known as individuals who espoused such views, and thus the *Little Review* (and the serial *Ulysses*) was subject to particularly attentive official scrutiny, as Quinn had warned. Anderson and Heap's position as opponents of war generally, and of the First World War in particular, is notable for a journal which wished—in Heap's words—to 'establish some sort of intellectual connection between America, England and France'.[176] Literary sensibilities had begun to change in Britain, and Europe more generally, almost as soon as the First World War began in August 1914. Anderson was undoubtedly aware of the significance of these changes. She reviewed Rupert Brooke's pre-war *Poems* in March 1914 ('the most important of those young Englishmen who are doing so much for modern poetry', 'essentially a poet's poet').[177] After his death in April 1915, the *New York Times* published a long and

[174] John Quinn to Ezra Pound, 16 October 1920, Carbondale.
[175] Vanderham, *James Joyce and Censorship*, 18.   [176] *LR*, June 1918, 55.
[177] *LR*, March 1914, 31.

detailed article about his poetry and the shaping effect of the war on his writing ('A Genius Whom the War Made and Killed').[178] In contrast, the *Little Review* was carelessly inaccurate about Brooke's death ('Rupert Brooke died of sun-stroke last month in the Dardanelles. There is nothing to be said in the face of such monster horrors') and chose not to review or comment upon *1914 and Other Poems* (1915), which included the war poetry for which Brooke is now remembered.[179]

Between 1914 and 1918, the *Little Review* made virtually no comment on the war, an omission which was noted and praised by a correspondent, 'B. C.' of Kansas, whose letter was printed in the 'Reader Critic' column, a regular feature of the journal from September 1914. This column became an increasingly important forum for the expression of editorial position, and was mainly under Heap's direction from September 1916. Thus it was Heap, not Anderson, who responded to the comment that the *Little Review* 'is the only magazine I have laid eyes on...that hasn't a word in it about this blasted war. How do you do it?'.[180] Pithily, and almost crassly, Heap opined that 'none of us considers this war a legitimate or an interesting subject for Art, not being the focal point of any fundamental emotion for any of the people engaged in it'. She rejected the widely held critical commonplace that the literature of war and suffering is 'deeply touching and of poignant appeal' and offered the view that 'nine tenths of the stuff written is a rotten impertinence to be discouraged'.[181] A surprise find in the *Little Review* archive, consisting of a lengthy letter from Richard Aldington to Anderson, indicates how stringently the editors adhered to their policy of saying little or nothing about the war. Aldington had made several contributions to the *Little Review* before enlisting in 1916, and wrote his letter to Anderson in response to her request for a contribution.

The letter—four pages, handwritten, in pencil—opens with polite conventions, including an apology for leaving it so long before writing ('it must be well over a year since I wrote you'), some scene setting ('I am back in England for a spell, after six months in the trenches'), and a forced comment on imminent military promotion ('They are going to make me an officer, it appears'). Aldington then moves to discussing his 'experiences, state of mind and so on', a topic in which he assumes Anderson 'may be interested'. It casually mentions 'a piece of shell through my steel helmet', 'another piece through my coat collar', 'slight shell-shock twice', and being 'gassed'. It then lists 'quite a number of things' he has learned through the experience of war: '1. To drill. 2. To shoot. 3. To throw bombs and use a bayonet. 4. To swear copiously and obscenely. 5. To sleep anywhere—on floors, the ground, underground, on a mixture of mud & dead "Fritzes". 6. To obey commands. 7. To keep my temper. 8. To box. 9. To command other men. 10. To see dead men without being revolted. 11. To drink French beer. 12. To dig'.

All of these experiences have transformed Aldington's view of himself as a writer:

> I wrote a book of poems & a few articles in the trenches, but they seem rather small beer when contemplated in a detached way in the security of England. Otherwise I've written nothing, save a few translations. The fact is I find it a little difficult not to say

[178] *New York Times*, 12 September 1915.   [179] *LR*, May 1915, 36.
[180] *LR*, August 1917, 25.   [181] *LR*, August 1917, 25.

impossible to compete with people who have gone on living normal lives without assimilating so much crude information & so many experiences. I rather fancy that I must quit writing until this mess is settled or until I can get a more tranquil personality. To this end I have resigned my editorship of *The Egoist* & for a while at least shall not contribute to any periodicals. I may publish my trench poems for a few friends and soldiers. I don't know.

The letter concludes with an apology for being 'extremely egoistic', and comments, in a series of asides, that most war poetry is 'boring and pretentious', and that Aldington 'hates militarism'.[182]

Anderson and Heap were clearly very moved by this letter. In correspondence with Reynolds, Heap mentions 'such a letter from Aldington', quotes what has been said, and confesses how she and Anderson 'had just sat and cried' on receipt of such a vivid and detailed piece of writing.[183] The pair often developed editorial commentary from letters received. That this particular letter did not appear in the 'Reader Critic', where it could have been placed *verbatim*, framed by some comment on 'what has happened to one of our regular contributors' or 'why some writers do not now contribute to periodicals', suggests a very deep commitment to the omission of any significant literary representations of the war, a commitment which Pound obviously did not share (given his decision to publish 'Cantelman's Spring-Mate'). This omission also points to the fact that the First World War had a very different kind of impact in the US, even after the US had joined the effort; as T. S. Eliot pointed out, in a letter to his mother, for Americans the war did not become 'the obsessing nightmare that it is to Europe'.[184] *Ulysses* has been greeted by some Irish readers as a 'central text of national liberation'.[185] Viewed from that critical perspective, and given the events of the Rising of Easter 1916—a key moment for the development of Irish nationalism—the fact that *Ulysses* was first serialized in a journal which largely omitted to acknowledge the significance of the First World War is curiously apt.

Until 9 January 1920, there was no direct contact between Joyce and the editors of the *Little Review*. The serialization of *Ulysses* was being handled and arranged by Pound, recipient of Joyce's typescripts, who relayed them on to New York. Heap felt that there was a 'note of ownership in Ezra Pound's attitude' and opened her very first letter to Joyce by observing this, and confessing that she 'felt much like a

[182] Richard Aldington to Margaret Anderson, 25 August 1917, *Little Review* records, UWM; © The Estate of Richard Aldington. Excerpts reproduced by kind permission of the Estate of Richard Aldington, c/o Rosica Colin Ltd, London. Aldington published some of his war poetry in a volume entitled *Images of War* (1919) in a limited edition of thirty copies (thus 'for a few friends') with watercolour images by Paul Nash. This book has been digitized by the British Library at https://www.bl.uk/collection-items/images-of-war-by-richard-aldington-with-illustrations-by-paul-nash#.

[183] Heap to Reynolds, [July 1917]; Baggett, *Dear Tiny Heart*, 52. This letter has been misdated by Baggett. It records a response to the letter from Aldington and must therefore have been written in late August (at the earliest).

[184] T. S. Eliot to his mother, 28 April 1918, Valerie Eliot (ed.), *The Letters of T. S. Eliot, vol. 1: 1898–1922* (London: Harcourt Brace, 1988), 230.

[185] Declan Kiberd (ed.), James Joyce, *Ulysses* (London: Penguin, 1992), lxv.

robber in starting this letter to you'. She was keen to assure Joyce of the *Little Review*'s good intentions, and wanted to point to the fact that the journal was 'making an audience for your work'.[186] This was being achieved by the steadily advancing serialization of the text, advertisement, review, and discussion of Joyce's other recent works (*Portrait* and *Exiles*), and the 'Reader Critic', which began to publish comments on *Ulysses* in May 1918, two months after the serialization began.[187] As the editors of the *Little Review Ulysses* acknowledge, these comments, which are worth briefly reviewing here, register an awareness of *Ulysses* as 'something unique, even extraordinary'.[188] Responses in May 1918 included one by Israel Solon, a minor writer and contributor, who thought the 'portrait of young Cyril Sargent is marvellous beyond words. He is the most sensitive writer alive'.[189] A similarly positive response came from Daphne Carr in Pittsburgh who wanted to praise the *Little Review* 'for sticking out in these beastly times': 'How grateful I am for "Ulysses"! I call you blessed, even as the rest of the country will some fifty years hence'.[190] Not all of the comments on *Ulysses* were so positive, however. In the very next month, 'R. McM' from Los Angeles asked the editors to justify 'some of Joyce's obscene commonplaces taken from life neither for power nor beauty nor for any reason but to arrest attention'.[191] And in July 1918, the month in which chapter 5 ('Lotus-Eaters') was published, Joyce's work was dismissed as 'punk': 'The much bepraised Joyce's "Ulysses" is punk, Lewis' "Imaginary Letters" are punkier and Ezra Pound is punkiest'.[192] This strain of disapproval continued throughout the duration of the serialization. In January 1919, for example, the month in which the first half of chapter 8 ('Lestrygonians') was published, a Mr Orrick Johns from St Louis wrote that *Ulysses* 'absolutely beggars appreciation', despite only having 'one negligible chapter' (which Johns did not specify).[193]

More than a year later, in March 1920, the serialization had advanced as far as the fourth and final instalment of chapter 12 ('Cyclops')—the moment in the text when Garryowen pursues Bloom ('with his lugs back for all he was bloody well worth. Hundred to five! Jesus, he took the value of it out of him, I promise you').[194] An unnamed subscriber wrote in to describe how the '*Little Review* bewilders me'.[195] The whole journal 'should be preserved as samples of the madness of the present age…To read and see and feel such art leaves one with the same sick nausea and distaste as when one has become a party to some shameful orgy'.[196] In the following month, April 1920, when the first instalment of chapter 13 ('Nausicaa') was published, one subscriber wrote to comment explicitly on the issue of 'obscenity',

[186] Jane Heap to J, 9 January 1920, Cornell.
[187] For an advertisement of Joyce's works published by Huebsch, his American publisher, see *LR*, March 1918 [2]. The *LR* published a discussion of *Exiles* in January 1919 with comments from Heap herself, John Rodker, Israel Solon, and Samuel A. Tannenbaum (20–7).
[188] Gaipa et al., *LRU*, 426. The edition includes a useful sample of the responses to *Ulysses* (426–51).
[189] *LR*, May 1918, 63.   [190] *LR*, May 1918, 64.   [191] *LR*, June 1918, 56.
[192] *LR*, July 1918, 64.   [193] *LR*, January 1919, 64.   [194] *LR*, March 1920, 60.
[195] *LR*, March 1920, 60.   [196] *LR*, March 1920, 61.

the suppression of the number for January 1920 by the post office, and the types of reader attracted to *Ulysses*:

> But why cavil about Joyce at this late day?—it would seems to me that after all these months he could be accepted, obscenity and all, for surely the post office authorities should recognise that a only a few read him, and those few not just the kind to have their moral natures overthrown by frankness about natural functions.[197]

Such comments—which register the shock, bewilderment, and apparent 'obscenity' of *Ulysses*—anticipate both the prosecution and the defence in the trial of February 1921. They are also typically vague about the specificities of Joyce's text. In fact, a careful review of contributions to the 'Reader Critic' column reveals that the number of comments on *Ulysses* appearing in the column varied dramatically from month to month, with some moments in the serialization appearing to elicit no response whatsoever (the case, for example, in issues for October 1918, November 1918, December 1918, February–March 1919, and October 1919), and other moments eliciting multiple responses (the case, for example, in June 1918, July 1918, and January 1919).[198] Within the columns—which represent the very first publicly accessible reader responses to *Ulysses*—several recurring features can be identified.

Readers did not generally comment on specific instalments, engage with the cultural elements of the text, or understand or consider the significance of the introduction of Bloom, and made no attempt to decode the overall evolving plan of the work. No one hazarded a guess as to why the work was called *Ulysses* or commented on the implied Homeric parallel. Nor did readers consider the significance of stylistic disruption, though one did coin the adjective 'Joyceish' (to mean 'wild, involved').[199] Several of those who responded to the challenge of *Ulysses* were writers (Pound's banner 'The Magazine That Is Read by Those Who Write the Others' proved to be on the mark). Apart from Israel Solon, already mentioned, respondents to *Ulysses* included Hart Crane, Marsden Hartley, and, anonymously, and presumably without her permission, Virginia Woolf, whose *TLS* essay on 'Modern Novels' included comments on the serial *Ulysses*, and described Joyce as one among a number of writers whose work:

> attempts to come closer to life, and to preserve more sincerely and exactly what interests and moves them by discarding most of the conventions which are commonly observed by the novelists.[200]

Joyce's break with 'convention' was prized especially by Anderson and Heap, and one of the particularly noteworthy features of the 'Reader Critic' column in respect of *Ulysses* is the detailed responses to the text occasionally made by the editors.

[197] *LR*, April 1920, 61.
[198] 'Reader Critic' began to give way to a column entitled 'Discussion' in mid-1919, but was then restarted in November 1919. Both columns printed the views of readers, though 'Discussion' tended to be more formal, and was usually placed in the middle of the journal, while 'Reader Critic' went at the end.
[199] *LR*, March 1920, 60.
[200] For Marsden Hartley on *Ulysses*, see *LR*, September 1918, 59–62; *LR*, November 1918, 46–50; *LR*, July 1919, 51–5. For Hart Crane on *Ulysses*, see *LR*, July 1918, 65. Woolf's comments appeared under the heading 'The World Moves: From the London Times', *LR*, September–December 1920, 93.

In June 1918, for example, comments from 'S. S. B., Chicago' were printed under the insistently capitalized heading 'What Joyce Is Up Against'. S. S. B.'s description of herself as 'fairly intelligent', coupled with a complaint about the lack of coherence in *Ulysses* ('Each month he is worse than last'), are roundly dismissed by Heap:

> You consider yourself an intelligent, 'well-read' person. Did it ever occur to you to read anything on the nature of writers?...All compulsion exists within the artist...The only concern of the artist is to try in one short lifetime to meet these inner compulsions. He has no concern with audiences and their demands.

Heap's response to another reader in the same issue insists that Joyce cannot be intelligently discussed other than with someone 'who has an intense grip on modern thought'.[201] Similarly, Anderson advised a reader who was inclined to disparage Joyce to simply avoid reading his work ('He isn't so plentiful that you must talk with him on every corner or read him in very magazine you pick up').[202] Responses of this kind—engaged, intelligent, astute, and knowing—created a sense of fuss round *Ulysses*, a sense of coterie, of an evolving interpretive community, with just a few insiders who really understood Joyce and respected his compulsions as an artist.

SAMPLE COPY: SEPTEMBER 1918 AND JULY–AUGUST 1920

If the foregoing section on 'Association Copy' is an attempt to understand the nexus of social, cultural, and political associations between *Ulysses*, its editors, and the *Little Review*, this section on 'sample copy' is an attempt to carry that kind of reading further by looking, more precisely and contextually, at the situation of *Ulysses* within two specific issues of the *Little Review*: that of September 1918 and that of July–August 1920. The editors and contributors to the *Journal of Modern Periodical Studies* (established 2010) have been pioneers in the methodologies of reading periodicals, particularly with regard to 'sampling' (i.e. close reading specific issues of a specific periodical in order to discover broad cultural trends). Reading through this journal, it is clear that the methodologies of this field have changed very quickly as scholars have begun to find new ways of exploiting digital archives, such as those made available through standalone (and academically sponsored) websites such as the Modernist Journals Project, or the much larger (and commercially sponsored) collection of primary historical sources made available by companies such as Gale. Methodology is important here, and for this reason it is worth pausing, for a moment, to point to some important recent insights: Sean Latham's essay 'Unpacking My Digital Library: Programs, Modernisms, Magazines' and Jeffrey Drouin's 'Close- and Distant-Reading Modernism: Network Analysis, Text Mining, and Teaching the *Little Review*'.[203]

---

[201] *LR*, June 1918, 57.   [202] *LR*, March 1920, 62.

[203] Sean Latham, 'Unpacking My Digital Library: Programs, Modernisms, Magazines', in Dean Irvine, Vanessa Lent, and Bart Vautour (eds.), *Making Canada New: Editing Modernism and New Media* (Toronto: University of Toronto Press, 2017), 31–60; and Jeffrey Drouin, 'Close- and

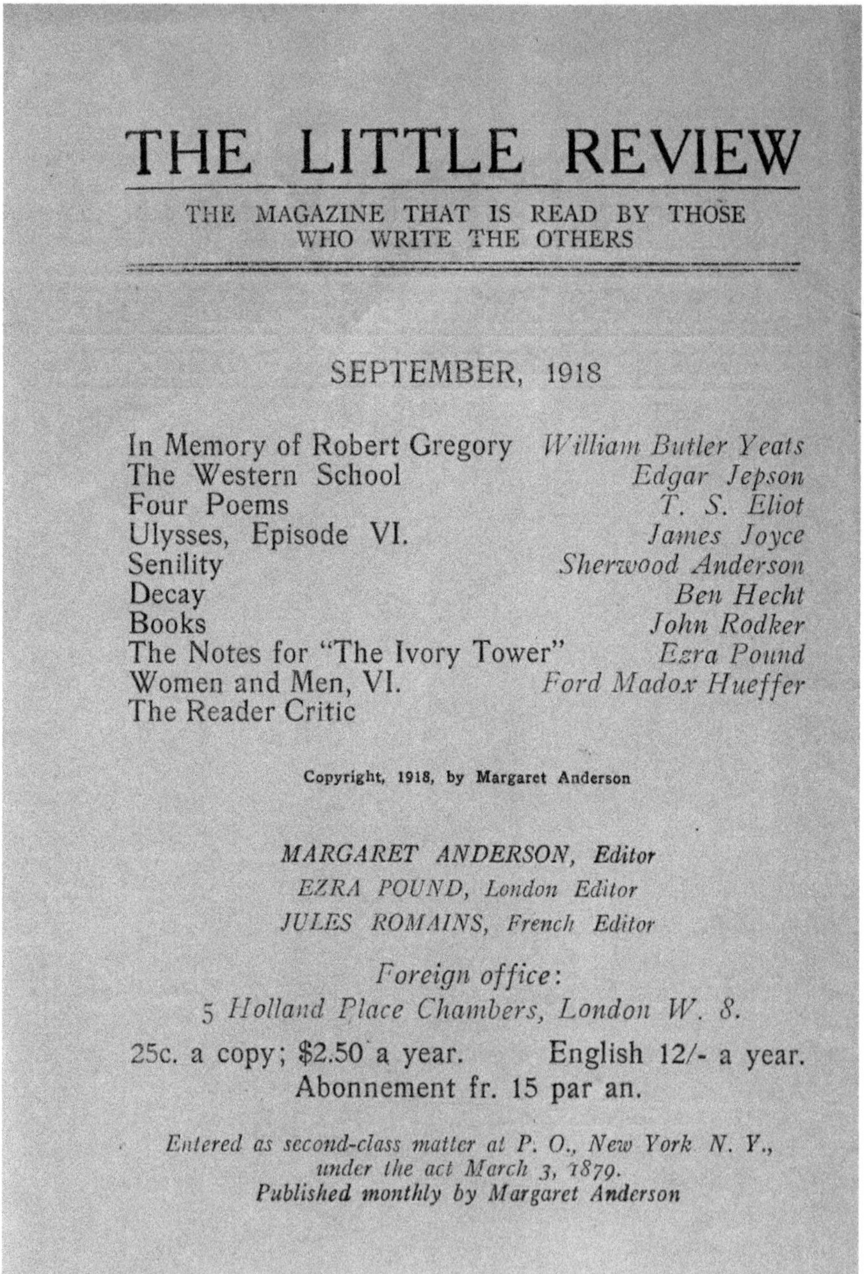

THE LITTLE REVIEW

THE MAGAZINE THAT IS READ BY THOSE
WHO WRITE THE OTHERS

SEPTEMBER, 1918

In Memory of Robert Gregory   *William Butler Yeats*
The Western School   *Edgar Jepson*
Four Poems   *T. S. Eliot*
Ulysses, Episode VI.   *James Joyce*
Senility   *Sherwood Anderson*
Decay   *Ben Hecht*
Books   *John Rodker*
The Notes for "The Ivory Tower"   *Ezra Pound*
Women and Men, VI.   *Ford Madox Hueffer*
The Reader Critic

Copyright, 1918, by Margaret Anderson

MARGARET ANDERSON, Editor

EZRA POUND, London Editor

JULES ROMAINS, French Editor

Foreign office:
5 Holland Place Chambers, London W. 8.

25c. a copy; $2.50 a year.   English 12/- a year.
Abonnement fr. 15 par an.

Entered as second-class matter at P. O., New York N. Y.,
under the act March 3, 1879.
Published monthly by Margaret Anderson

Figure 1.6. Contents page, September 1918

(*Little Review*, The Modernist Journals Project (searchable database). Brown and Tulsa Universities, ongoing. http://www.modjourn.org)

Let's begin with Latham. In 'Unpacking My Digital Library' he suggests that one particular value of reading historical periodicals is that it enables the study of 'emergence', 'a particular kind of complexity that arises not from the individual elements of a system, but only from their interaction'.[204] For scholars of magazines, he suggests 'emergence provides a powerful way of thinking' and 'moments of emergence are exciting, but also provisional, unstable, and sometimes even difficult to capture using our current theoretical and historical frames'.[205] Drouin's essay, 'Close- and Distant-Reading Modernism', pursues the issue of emergence by 'using various techniques in network analysis to read the September 1918 *Little Review*', in order to understand the journal's general emphasis on 'life and vitality' and the specific features of the September 1918 issue, particularly its 'rare mention of the First World War and thematic coherence around death'.[206] These ideas will be returned to in due course.

For the moment, it is important to examine the contents page and date of the September 1918 issue of the *Little Review* (see Figure 1.6). Looked at in hindsight, it is impossible not to be struck by the historicity of that date: September 1918. It was published as considerable Allied advances were being made on the Western Front. The contents page of the issue is dominated by the circle of writers who would come to be known as the 'men of 1914' (Joyce, Pound, and Eliot; only Lewis is missing from Pound's original quartet, and Hueffer, i.e. Ford Madox Ford, might also be admitted to the group).

Looked at more closely this contents page records some attempt to circulate the *Little Review* in France by the listing, for the first time, of an 'abonnement' (subscription) of 15 francs per annum, and of a 'French Editor', Jules Romain (1885–1972), an associate of Pound who hoped that Romains 'would bring in all the best french stuff'.[207] This attempt to expand the reach of the *Little Review* to France is part of Pound's scheme to retain Quinn's subsidy (as he wrote to Anderson, 'we've got to do so damn much in the next 12 months that we CANT BE LET STOP in 1919').[208] This attempt to create an allied international readership needs to be read against the ongoing upheavals of the war, and suggests that American cultural momentum towards Paris had sprung roots even before the war ended, and was born, at least in part, from a desire to create cultural connections even in the face of ongoing atrocities. On the whole, however, the sense of an American readership and writerly circle in Paris dates from the post-war period; Sylvia Beach opened the doors of her English-language reading library and bookshop on 19 November 1919, and recalls receiving many 'pilgrims from America' ('Every day someone whose work I had seen in the *Little Review* or *The Dial* would appear').[209]

Distant-Reading Modernism: Network Analysis, Text Mining, and Teaching *The Little Review*', *The Journal of Modern Periodical Studies*, 5:1 (2014), 110–35.

[204] Latham, 'Unpacking My Digital Library', 43.
[205] Latham, 'Unpacking My Digital Library', 43.
[206] Drouin, 'Close- and Distant-Reading Modernism', 111.
[207] Pound to Anderson, [23 May 1918], *P-LR*, 221.
[208] Pound to Anderson, [23 May 1918], *P-LR*, 221.
[209] Sylvia Beach, *Shakespeare and Company* (1959; Lincoln, NE: University of Nebraska Press, 1991), 23.

Joyce thought of *Ulysses* as a book in three chapters ('Telemachia', 'Odyssey', and 'Nostos'), divided into eighteen individual episodes (three in 'Telemachia', twelve in 'Odyssey', and three in 'Nostos').[210] The excerpt which appeared in the *Little Review* of September 1918, labelled 'Episode VI', appears without any introductory casing and, though complete in itself, is a considerably shorter version of what came to be chapter 6 ('Hades'), as published in 1922. The chapter is a group portrait, and reveals Bloom's social interactions among his male peers. It divides neatly into two halves, with the first meticulously describing the journey across the city by horse-drawn carriage to Prospect Cemetery in Glasnevin, and the second describing the arrival of the cortège, a service of committal in the chapel, and the burial of Paddy Dignam. It concludes with Bloom's thoughts and experiences as he meanders among the gravestones. Apart from the occasional moments of humour, often supplied in Bloom's musings, and through dialogue involving Simon Dedalus ('Most amusing expressions that man finds'), the atmosphere of the text is sombre and elegiac, thus linking, in thematic terms, with the leading text of the September 1918 issue, one of Yeats's elegies for Robert Gregory (1881–1918), Lady Gregory's son, a Major in the Royal Air Force, who was killed in action in January 1918.[211] Though Yeats and Joyce are often viewed as belonging to quite different cultural and literary constituencies, what is striking in viewing the adjacent publication of these two texts is the way in which both build on multiple Irish cultural and historic specificities, which must have been difficult for American readers to grasp.

An implicit recognition of these difficulties, in respect of Yeats's poem, is suggested by the republication of Yeats's obituary for Gregory in the *Little Review* of November 1918, in response to 'so many letters asking for particulars about Robert Gregory'.[212] One such particular is the fact that Gregory died fighting in the war, a fact that is omitted in the poem; the word 'Major', included in the title of the poem in volume editions from 1919 onwards, is not present in the *Little Review*.[213] The poem does not make 'any kind of conventional claim for Robert's death as an heroic contribution to a valiant or necessary war', as James Pethica has argued.[214] Instead it attempts to make 'appropriate commentary' (in its own rather hollow phrase) by promoting a view of Gregory as an all-round Renaissance man ('Our Sidney and our perfect man'), who loved hunting ('with the Galway foxhounds'), painting ('that stern colour and that delicate line'), and craftsmanship.[215] These subtleties suggest the continued significance of close reading, even as Moretti calls for new digital approaches which survey '*all*' of literary history'; for Drouin, Yeats's

---

[210] J to Pound, [n.d., early December 1917], Yale. It is difficult to decide whether to follow his lead on this, as the Homeric titles are omitted in the editions he authorized. For ease of reference, and to avoid confusion, I have referred to the eighteen individual parts of *Ulysses* as chapters, and, following critical consensus, used the Homeric names assigned in the schema.

[211] *LR*, September 1918, 28.   [212] *LR*, November 1918, 41.

[213] W. B. Yeats, *The Wild Swans at Coole* (London: Macmillan, 1919).

[214] James Pethica, 'Yeats's Perfect Man', *The Dublin Review*, 35 (Spring 2009), (https://thedublin-review.com/article/yeatss-perfect-man), 19.

[215] *LR*, September 1918, 4, 2, 3.

poem is one of the *Little Review*'s 'few direct references to the First World War'.[216] For the reading which I am advancing here, this is not a 'direct' reference to the war at all because Yeats had yet to append the word 'Major' to the title. In a sense, this returns, rather neatly, to the importance of Latham's concept of 'emergence', to the importance of seeing the text in its specific and original moment of historicity. The 'First World War', so dubbed, did not become the 'First' world war until (at least) the Second, and the significance of Yeats's use of Gregory as a figure for war elegy did not become apparent until the circulation of his more famous 'An Irish Airman Foresees His Death' (first published in the Macmillan edition of *The Wild Swans at Coole* in 1919). Another small interpretive complication worth mentioning here is the fact that 'In Memory of Robert Gregory' was published in London in *The English Review* in August 1918.[217] In that context, Yeats appears willing to acknowledge the significance of the war. His note, which insists on listing Gregory's distinguished military credentials and honours—'Major Robert Gregory, R.F.C., M.C., Legion of Honour, was killed in action on the Italian Front, January 23, 1918'— appears immediately after the title.[218] Perhaps that note was intended for publication in the *Little Review*. Perhaps it was lost in transmission. Or perhaps, and this seems plausible given Heap's insistence that the war is not 'an interesting subject for Art', the editors decided not to include it.[219]

'In Memory of Robert Gregory' is technically accomplished. As Pethica writes, it has a 'stately rhetoric and architecture', and is written in the Cowley eight-line stanza, in lines which rhyme aabbcddc.[220] But the poem is replete with political and emotional evasion. Lady Gregory had asked Yeats to 'write something down that we may keep', a task which Yeats found particularly awkward given what he knew of Robert Gregory's aimlessness, unionist leanings, and intense cruelty to his wife.[221] Pound was an enthusiastic supporter of Yeats's work, and this poem is one among a number of contributions which he arranged for Yeats to make to the *Little Review*, but Yeats's name is conspicuously absent from Pound's list of essential contributors.[222] This is because Yeats's commitment to traditional stanzaic forms ('I must choose a traditional stanza, even what I alter must seem traditional') meant that he did not fit with Pound's notion of what it meant to be 'markedly modern'.[223]

But T. S. Eliot, writing in French, clearly did. The issue of September 1918 includes four of Eliot's poems: 'Sweeney Among the Nightingales', 'Whispers of Immortality', 'Mr. Eliot's Sunday Morning Service', and (in French) 'Dans le

[216] Franco Moretti, 'The Slaughterhouse of Literature', *Modern Language Quarterly*, 61:1 (2000), 207–28 (208); Drouin, 'Close- and Distant-Reading Modernism', 114.

[217] W. B. Yeats, 'In Memory of Robert Gregory', *English Review*, August 1918, 81–3.

[218] *English Review*, August 1918, 81.   [219] *LR*, August 1917, 25.

[220] Pethica, 'Yeats's Perfect Man', 15, 16.

[221] Pethica, 'Yeats's Perfect Man', 1. It seems that Gregory's enlistment was partly motivated by a desire to escape a conflicted home situation; he was engaged in an extra-marital affair. Even his mother had come to describe him as a 'cad'.

[222] For Yeats elsewhere in the *LR* see the numbers for June 1917, August 1917, October 1918, and January 1919.

[223] For Yeats on traditional stanzaic form see 'A General Introduction for My Work', in W. B. Yeats, *Essays and Introductions* (London: Macmillan, 1961), 522; Pound to J, 15 December 1913 in *EP-JJ*, 18.

restaurant'. These texts represent Eliot's writing after the completion of *Prufrock and Other Poems* (1917) and before *The Wasteland* (1922), and are particularly difficult to interpret without any kind of supplementary authorial or editorial comment, or the inter-referential bibliographical structure supplied within *Poems* (1919), the Hogarth Press volume in which the three English-language texts first appeared. In the *Little Review* context 'Dans le restaurant' looks like the least polished of the four, but it points significantly to Pound's formative role as Eliot's highly attentive close reader and eventual editor of *The Wasteland*. A translated version of the closing eight lines ('Phlébas, le Phenician, pendant quinze jours noyé/Oubliait les cris des mouettes') became the 'Death by Water' section of *The Wasteland* ('Phlebas the Phoenician, a fortnight dead/Forgot the cry of gulls', etc.). Eliot is highly praised in another part of the September 1918 issue: an article by the British author, Edgar Jepson, on what he awkwardly names 'The Western School' of US poetry; Eliot is 'a real poet, who possesses in the highest degree the qualities the new school demands. Western-born of Eastern stock, Mr T. S. Eliot is United States of the United States; and his poetry is securely rooted in its native soil'.[224] This article, a condensed version of 'Recent United States Poetry' which had been published in the *English Review*, had originally been solicited by Harriet Monroe, editor of *Poetry*, but then rejected by her for 'its lack of flattery, its lack of kow-tow to certain local celebrities' (according to Pound, a by no means unbiased participant in this small squabble).[225] Jepson criticizes the work of three poets much praised by *Poetry*—that of Robert Frost, Edgar Lee Masters, and Vachel Lindsay—but as Jane Heap later pointed out, Jepson's article, which Monroe deemed 'egregiously caddish', could hardly be viewed as a serious piece of criticism.[226] Heap explained her reason for being tolerant of Pound, and such petty literary squabbles in a later issue of the journal: he was capable of sending work 'bearing the stamp of originality and permanence'.[227]

Yet the editors could not resist occasional side swipes at Pound's editorial hubris. Pound had contributed 'A Note on the volume completed' to the issue of July 1918, in which he had observed that the *Little Review* 'has got to pay my board and rent etc, and leave me sufficient leisure for my own compositions, or I have got to spend my half time on something more lucrative'.[228] In a subsequent issue, Heap confessed to being 'slightly jarred' by Pound's 'manner of asking for alms'.[229] The 'Reader Critic' of September 1918 plays on that sense of estrangement in an unsigned letter headed 'From California': 'We cannot make any helpful suggestions to Ezra about the rent, but he can solve his board by eating the goose he has cooked for himself'.[230] Both Anderson and Heap had an eye for the sustaining appeal of being transgressive, and this unsigned letter, in common with a few

[224] *LR*, September 1918, 9.
[225] Edgar Jepson, 'Recent United States Poetry', *English Review*, 26 May 1918; *LR*, September 1918, 5.
[226] *LR*, November 1918, 34.   [227] *LR*, November 1918, 37.   [228] *LR*, July 1918, 55.
[229] *LR*, November 1918, 37.   [230] *LR*, September 1918, 62.

others that appeared in the 'Reader Critic', may have been made up.[231] There can be no proof that this was the case (as even a very complete archive is unlikely to 'prove' a hunch of this kind, and the *Little Review* archive is full of gaps). The evidence of fabrication can only be inferential: the barbed tone and witty dialogic style is very much of a piece with what can be seen in the writings of both editors. After all, the 'Reader Critic' was a means by which Anderson and Heap could establish a sense of the *Little Review*'s reading constituency, and it provided a forum in which they could sneer at those who derided the *Little Review*, thus reifying their position as part of the avant-garde. The 'Reader Critic' was also a means by which they could easily fill any spare pages; the economics and logistics of printing meant that they had a fixed number of pages to fill—sixty-four in the case of the September 1918 issue—for which they had to find copy, editorial comment, or advertisements.

Within the sixty-four pages of the September 1918 issue, creative contributions dominate above editorial and critical comment, and run to forty-six pages of the total. The excerpt from *Ulysses* is by far the longest piece of writing, at a little over twenty-two pages, almost a third of the entire issue. The first readers of this text found it particularly challenging. Virginia Woolf, for example, singled out 'the Cemetery scene' for 'flashes of deep significance succeeded by incoherent inanities'.[232] Some assistance in interpretation was offered by the lengthy letter from Marsden Hartley who compares Joyce to 'dot for dot' painters such as Dürer and Seurat, who achieve 'intelligent pointillism'; he thinks of Joyce in terms of 'stylistic radiance', 'humoristic tracery', 'cross-hatching', 'almost too much of vividness'. These comments make it clear that readers need to pay detailed attention to the detail in Joyce. Ultimately, however, Hartley's questions about Joyce also suggest misgivings:

> I wonder if we do not hear the strumming of the mosquitoe's wing a little excessively in Joyce? Is the space around things large enough? Does he care for entirety as much as the whimsie *en passant*?[233]

Pound's comments, which tend to be rather less incisive, dominate the editorial and critical part of the September 1918 issue. For example, the issue includes his 'Notes for "The Ivory Tower"', a continuation from the August number, which summarizes the notes Henry James made for his final and unfinished novel *The Ivory Tower*. A reader unfamiliar with James's practice of theorizing the writing of his fiction would perhaps struggle to make sense of these pages; the challenge is heightened by the fact that this piece is a 'continuation', and appears without any

---

[231] For other examples of possibly made-up letters, see that of 'A. Faun, Paris' ('You have become so sane, so logical, so militant in attacking the obvious') and 'A Proletarian' ('Glad to see your magazine getting more and more revolutionary and courageously attacking the rotten capitalistic order. But why not dot the i's? Why shrink from discussing economic problems?') (*LR*, November 1914, 69, 70). And 'Dear Little Reviewers' in *LR*, May–June 1920, 72, which pitches an ignorant reader of *Ulysses* ('Have you any clue as to when the story will end?') against a rather knowing *jh*.

[232] 'Modern Novels', *TLS*, 10 April 1919.   [233] *LR*, September 1918, 60.

introductory or framing comment. Pound also contributes a lengthy review of 'the American number', that of June 1918, which was edited by Heap alone, 'with no compromise to Margaret Anderson and Ezra Pound'.[234] Pound's comments are digressive, rambling, and self-important; the editors have simply opted to include this letter without editing it, in order to fill the final page. The material form of transmission is relevant here, as Pound's letters to Anderson were very lengthy and were typed like his intended submissions. This made it difficult, sometimes, to establish what was private correspondence, and what was intended for publication, a confusion which the editors used to their advantage if pages needed filling, as here. In total, Pound's editorial commentary runs to about six pages, and thus about 10 per cent of the September 1918 issue, but his voice is more dominant than these facts suggest, because his views are echoed strongly by Edgar Jepson and John Rodker, who contributes a column on 'Books'. One notes, for example, Rodker's endorsement of many French books, including *Mon Chant de Guerre* by Fritz R. Venderpyl ('worth reading because it feels "sound"').[235] The only contributions in this number which appear to have been selected by Anderson and Heap are two short stories: 'Senility' by Sherwood Anderson and 'Decay' by Ben Hecht. 'Senility' vividly evokes the life experiences and reflections of an old man 'in a small Kentucky town'; the piece is full of detail, but it is not clear that it is really finished. 'Decay', a much lengthier story, is rather more satisfying: it describes an evening in the life of Mrs Muznik, a struggling and impoverished mother of eight children, who lives in a grimy urban environment. In some respects the work is an example of naturalism, and could be compared with the early chapters of *Ulysses*, and works such as Lawrence's 'Odour of Chrysanthemums' (which was first published in July 1911).

In July 1920 Joyce moved to Paris, and was continuing work on chapter 15 ('Circe'). Pound continued to support him in many significant and practical ways, but had discontinued being 'Foreign Editor' of the *Little Review* in April 1919, when Quinn's subsidy had officially discontinued. Nonetheless—and without apparent recognition of the significance of these changes—Joyce continued to use Pound as his main means of dealing with the *Little Review*: he sent completed chapter typescripts to Pound, for onward transmission to New York. He also continued to rely on Pound for news of the *Little Review*, regular copies of the journal, and small sums of cash. Meanwhile, Anderson and Heap also continued to struggle. The immediate aftermath of the war had brought a surge in production costs, and saw them appealing, in the double number of May–June 1920, to subscribers for $5,000 ('Are there 1000 people in America who will give $5 a piece to our fund?').[236] Quinn was one of those who received this appeal, and though he was openly hostile towards the *Little Review*, and very hesitant about the ongoing

---

[234] *LR*, June 1918, 62. Editorial notes indicate that one did not need to be American to be included, but merely 'living and working in America'; somehow Joyce—who never visited the US—was included.

[235] *LR*, September 1918, 48.   [236] *LR*, May–June 1920, 76.

serialization of *Ulysses* in that context, he found it difficult to resist a direct plea from Anderson, as he told Pound:

> Miss Anderson blew in to see me early in August without writing or telephoning; dressed in a becoming gray suit...She inquired whether I could help her with Max Pam who had given $400 at my suggestion a year or so ago when I made up that $1600. I finally gave her a check for $200.[237]

Within weeks he would come to regret such generosity, because the District Attorney of New York County received a complaint about the excerpt from *Ulysses* contained in the number for July–August 1920 the third and final instalment of episode 13 ('Nausicaa'). Dated 30 August 1920, the letter of complaint directed attention to 'the passages marked on pages 43, 45, 50 and 51' and continued:

> If such indecencies don't come within the provisions of the Postal Laws then isn't there some way in which the circulation of such things can be confined among the people who buy or subscribe to a publication of this kind? Surely there must be some way of keeping such 'literature' out of the homes of people who don't want it.[238]

Page 43 describes the way in which Gerty McDowell, seated on the Sandymount Strand, leans back both to look at fireworks and to reveal her legs and underwear to Bloom, who is sitting nearby masturbating and reaching orgasm just as the 'Roman candle' explodes ('it was like a sigh of O! and everyone cried O! O! and it gushed out of it a stream of rain gold hair threads...O so lovely! O so soft, sweet, soft!').[239] Page 45 is a passage of Bloom's interior monologue and records his thoughts about what has just happened ('Hot little devil all the same. Near her monthlies, I expect, makes them feel ticklish'), and about menstruation, mutoscope pictures, and women's lingerie more generally. Bloom's ejaculation has made him wet and page 50 begins with him acknowledging this ('This wet is very unpleasant') and moves on to Bloom's thoughts about magnetism, Molly and Boylan, and the waft of Gerty McDowell's perfume which 'Took its time coming like herself, slow but sure'.[240] Bloom's thoughts on smell and sexuality continue to be recorded on page 51 ('Some women for instance warn you off when they have their period. Come near. Then get a hogo you could hang your hat on').[241] The complaint about these particular pages led eventually to the trial of Anderson and Heap with respect to the obscenity of *Ulysses* in February 1921, an event which will be discussed in Chapter 2. For the moment, it is worth concentrating on the other content of the July–August 1920 issue, in order to understand how the *Little Review* had developed in the wake of Pound's departure, and to gain a sense of the bibliographical and cultural environment in which Joyce's apparently controversial text was being published.

Including the cover—on this occasion a very deep blue with gold lettering—the issue of July–August 1920 contains sixty-four pages (see Figure 1.7). Owing to a

---

[237] Quinn to Pound, 24 September 1920, cited in Reid, *The Man from New York*, 442.
[238] The letter to Swann is quoted by John S. Sumner in 'The Truth About "Literary Lynching"', *The Dial*, July 1921, 67.
[239] *LR*, July–August 1920, 43.   [240] *LR*, July–August 1920, 50.
[241] *LR*, July–August 1920, 51.

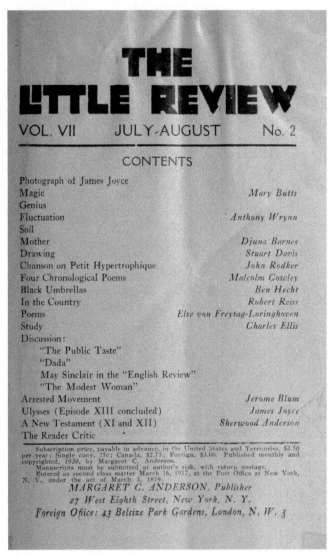

Figure 1.7. Contents page, July–August 1920

(*Little Review*, The Modernist Journals Project (searchable database). Brown and Tulsa Universities, ongoing. http://www.modjourn.org)

change of printer, the contents page has been remodelled slightly, and in comparison to the issue of September 1918, it notably includes more contributors (thirteen writers are listed as opposed to the nine of September 1918), a greater concentration of American writers (including Djuna Barnes, Ben Hecht, and Sherwood Anderson), and contributions by women (Mary Butts, Djuna Barnes, and Elsa von Freytag-Loringhoven).[242]

---

[242] The printing is discussed in Chapter 3, p. 150.

Measured by number of pages, Joyce's presence predominates. Though the final excerpt from 'Nausicaa' could have been given more priority by being placed earlier—it is buried deep in the issue at page 42—Joyce's contribution is, nonetheless, the longest in the issue, accounting for a quarter of the whole at sixteen pages. Joyce's significance is also suggested by his photograph, which appears as a frontispiece, placed, somewhat incongruously, opposite the opening story, 'Magic' by Mary Butts. This photograph, showing a bearded Joyce in his Zurich overcoat, is rather severe and uncharacteristic. The photo had been requested by Heap, who had established a friendly correspondence with Joyce by the spring of 1920.[243] Joyce sent at least two photographs on this occasion and Heap thanked him for them, commenting, in an aside which reveals her ongoing relish for cultural antagonism, that they would enable her to administer another 'shock of vibration'; she planned to send them to 'people who are too disturbed by you' such as the 'the post-office department and several newspaper editors'.[244]

'Magic', the leading story in the issue for July–August 1920, probably came to be positioned in the *Little Review* because the author, Mary Butts, a British modernist (1890–1937), was married at the time to John Rodker. Butts, who was bisexual, was interested in the occult, a fact that is evident from the story, which has never been republished. Butts's journals also reveal that she was an avid reader of other modernist writers, including Yeats, Eliot, and Woolf. Both in style, and through its repeated reference to a 'nailhead' 'sunk in the plaster', 'Magic' appears to invoke Woolf's 1917 story 'The Mark on the Wall'.[245] Butts had declared herself to be 'sick of realism' in December 1919 ('I can do it down to "the curl of an eyelash" ').[246] 'Magic', though more or less conventional in narrative style, is innovative in terms of the kind of reality it attempts to represent: the psychological state of a woman as she is being drawn by a male artist whose pencil is 'inscribing its version of her image'.[247] The woman's sensibility has perhaps been altered by the experience of being at a séance:

> She followed him in briskly, and settled herself for a journey with eyes on the nail. Under the form of a rock she had seen him naked, a pure-shape among the basis of the hills. In bird-shape she had freed herself of his contact... She did not know the rock's significance, but at the end of this observation would come knowledge, and out of knowledge power.[248]

The story may have been inspired by the experience of meeting and being painted by Wyndham Lewis ('whose vitality equals, probably surpasses mine').[249] It also appears to have been influenced by the interior monologue of the third

---

[243] Heap's first letter to Joyce is dated 9 January 1920 (unpublished, Cornell Joyce Collection).

[244] Jane Heap to James Joyce, [late March 1920] (unpublished, Cornell Joyce Collection); for a copy of the other photo sent by Joyce at this time, see Philip R. Yanella, 'James Joyce to the *Little Review*', *Journal of Modern Literature*, 1:3 (1971), 393–8 (396). The pose is rare and uncharacteristic, Joyce in a white jacket, reclining on a chair, staring candidly at the camera.

[245] A point made by Natalie Blondel (ed.), *The Journals of Mary Butts* (New Haven, CT and London: Yale University Press, 2002), 134.

[246] Journal entry for 12 December 1919, Blondel (ed.), *The Journals of Mary Butts*, 124.

[247] *LR*, July–August 1920, 3.   [248] *LR*, July–August 1920, 5.

[249] Journal entry for 9 January 1920, Blondel (ed.), *The Journals of Mary Butts*, 133.

instalment of *Ulysses* (for example, Butts's 'Behind their signatures was the source of signatures, the life which is all life and no death' echoes Joyce's 'Signatures of all things I am here to read, seaspawn and seawrack, the nearing tide, that rusty boot').[250]

Djuna Barnes, who is now mainly remembered for her novel *Nightwood* (1936), had begun her career in New York as a journalist, and made her first contribution to the 'American number' of the *Little Review*, that of June 1918, which Heap had edited. Heap's notes to that number describe Barnes as an 'original', a conviction which led to the *Little Review* publishing what Philip Herring has described as 'arguably the best of the early Barnes' between 1918 and 1921.[251] The contribution to the July–August number of 1920 is a story entitled 'Mother' which, as Herring notes, is an odd title, given that the main character, Lydia Passova, an 'old' and 'perverse' woman, is 'neither a mother, nor motherly'.[252] The story evokes the final days in the life of Passova, the surname being a thinly veiled reference to her Jewishness; she is a lonely pawnbroker, who has a much younger and nervous English lover, but she appears to care more for her 'beautiful angora cat' (who dies), and the jewels and objects she looks after. As Herring remarks, there are some strong passages of careful description:

> She wore coral in her ears, a coral necklace, and many coral finger rings.
>
> There was about her jewelry some of the tragedy of all articles that find themselves in pawn, and she moved among the trays like the guardians of cemetary grounds, who carry about with them some of the lugubrious stillness of the earth on which they have been standing.
>
> She dealt, in most part, in cameos, garnets, and a great many in-laid bracelets and cuff-links. There were a few watches however, and silver vessels and fishing tackle and faded slippers—and when, at night, she lit the lamp, these and the trays of precious and semi-precious stones, and the little ivory crucifixes, one on either side of the window, seemed to be leading a swift furtive life of their own, conscious of the slow pacing woman who was known to the street as Lydia Passova, but to no thing else.[253]

There may be some Joycean echoes here—of the lonely urban lives and emotional sterility depicted in 'A Painful Case' and 'A Mother' in *Dubliners*, of John O'Connell and the cemetery depicted in chapter 6 of *Ulysses*—but the story as a whole fails to resonate because it is not clear why readers should care or be moved by Passova, and the way in which her narrative is communicated.[254] Herring describes this story as 'superior' because no 'metaphysical question rises to the surface', but critics could take the opposite view that this omission is the story's weakness.[255]

---

[250] *LR*, July–August 1920, 5; *LR*, May 1918, 31.

[251] *LR*, June 1918, 2; Philip Herring, *Djuna: The Life and Work of Djuna Barnes* (London: Viking, 1995), 126.

[252] *LR*, July–August 1920, 14, 13; Philip Herring (ed.), *Djuna Barnes: Collected Stories* (Los Angeles, CA: Sun and Moon Press, 1996), 16.

[253] *LR*, July–August 1920, 10.

[254] Barnes's 'Finale' (*LR*, June 1918) describes a laid-out corpse and certainly appears to echo 'The Sisters', the opening story of *Dubliners*.

[255] Herring (ed.), *Djuna Barnes: Collected Stories*, 16.

Barnes appears to have been Heap's lover for a time, and was close to Elsa von Freytag-Loringhoven, another of Heap's avant-garde editorial enthusiasms, whose work had also first appeared in the 'American number' of June 1918.[256] Together with related cultural comment, poetry by 'the Baroness' (as she was titled, by dint of her marriage to a German Baron in 1913) is a significant component within the number for July–August 1920. Irene Gammel—author of the most substantial works on this German performance artist, poet, and sculptor—notes that she has been 'shelved in cultural history under the rubric of eccentricity and madness', and not without reason.[257] *Thirty Years' War* describes the response of the Baroness to the fact that William Carlos Williams refused her sexual advances:

> So she shaved her head. Next she lacquered it a high vermilion. Then she stole the crêpe from the door of a house of mourning and made a dress of it. She came to see us. First she exhibited the head at all angles, amazing against our black walls. Then she jerked off the crêpe with one movement. It's better when I'm nude, she said. It was very good. But we were just as glad that some of our more conservative friends didn't choose that moment to drop in. Shaving one's head is like having a new love experience, proclaimed the Baroness.[258]

Williams's own account of his encounters with the Baroness mentions that she regularly attracted police attention (for assault and indecent exposure), sent him nude self-portraits, and advised that 'what I needed to make me great was to contract syphilis from her and so free my mind for serious art'.[259] Within the pages of the *Little Review* for July–August 1920, the Baroness is hailed editorially as 'the first Dadaiste in New York'; she contributes two poems, 'Holy Skirts' and the 'Marie Ida Sequence', and a lengthier discussion piece entitled 'The Modest Woman' which records, *inter alia*, her response to *Ulysses*. These contributions stand out, typographically, because of their frequent paragraph breaks, use of the 'em' dash (—), and exclamation marks. 'Holy Skirts', praised by Gammel for its 'jagged lines, erotic jolts, and violent intensity', reflects on what the speaker describes as the 'forbidding sexlessness' of nuns.[260] She goes on to reflect on the pointless 'stagnation' and 'Senseless wicked expense' of chastity, and advocates that nuns should:

> make heaven here—
> take steps here—
> to possess bearing hereafter—
> *dignity*.[261]

---

[256] That Heap and Barnes were lovers, and that this created 'some jealousy in the triad' with Anderson, is mentioned in Herring, *Djuna*, 127. No date for the affair is given.

[257] Irene Gammel, *Baroness Elsa von Freytag-Loringhoven: Gender, Dada, and Everyday Modernity: A Cultural Biography* (Cambridge, MA: MIT Press, 2002), 4. See also Irene Gammel and Suzanne Zelazo (eds.), *Body Sweats: The Uncensored Writings of Elsa von Freytag-Loringhoven* (Cambridge, MA: MIT Press, 2011). The spelling of 'Elsa' varies between sources. 'Else' is the norm for the *Little Review*.

[258] Anderson, *My Thirty Years' War*, 211.

[259] William Carlos Williams, *Autobiography* (1948; New York: McGibbon and Key, 1968), 165. According to the chronology in Gammel and Zelazo (eds.), *Body Sweats: The Uncensored Writings of Elsa von Freytag-Loringhoven*, the Baroness (1874–1927) was treated for syphilis in 1896, before the first of her three marriages.

[260] Gammel, *Baroness Elsa von Freytag-Loringhoven*, 8; *LR*, July–August 1920, 28.

[261] *LR*, July–August 1920, 28.

From the perspective of form, this text—which mixes prose with verse—is notably freer and more experimental than the free verse seen, for example, in Eliot's work at this time, and shares its formal qualities with some of the other poetry in the number for July–August 1920, 'Genius' and 'Soil' by Anthony Wrynn, and 'In the Country' by Robert Reiss (both of whom have been lost to literary history, even in the digital age).

In December 1919, Heap had made a particular critical case for the value of work by the Baroness, and her ordinarily 'exalted state', specifying that 'Madness is her chosen state of consciousness. It is this consciousness which she works to produce Art'.[262] In agreement, Maxwell Bodenheim compared the Baroness to the 'intellectual sterilities of a Dorothy Richardson' and praised the way in which 'She does not violate rules: she enters a realm into which they cannot pursue her...Her work, in its deliberate cohesion, shows an absolute and rare normality'.[263] But cohesion is a quality which other readers found wanting. Harriet Monroe, for example, chastised the *Little Review* for not knowing 'when to stop': 'Just now it is headed straight for Dada; but we could forgive even that if it would drop Else von Freytag-Loringhoven on the way'.[264] Anderson was evidently not as persuaded as Heap of the Baroness's genius. *Thirty Years' War* candidly recalls evidence of mental instability:

> The Baroness' mind was of the opposite mold. She would adhere, abstractly, to any subject for three days without exhausting it. When *we* were exhausted—having other things to do, such as publishing a magazine—she would revenge herself against our locked doors by strewing tin cans down the stairs, hurling terrible and guttural curses over her shoulder for three flights.[265]

Yet there is some synergy between the work of the Baroness, the movement of Dadaism, and the evolving *Ulysses*, a synergy which relates both to sexual politics and what has been described as 'the aesthetics of anti-aesthetics'.[266] In her observation that Anderson and Heap 'put the Baroness's genius on a par with that of James Joyce', Gammel may overstate the case: the editors do not seem to have been as organized in their editorial thinking as this comment suggests.[267] But they were drawn to the idea of Dadaism, a movement which has a point of origin in both New York and Zurich. Joyce may not have attended 'the orgies of singing, poetry and dancing' taking place at Zurich's Cabaret Voltaire in the spring of 1916 but it is reasonable to assume that he was aware of the *zeitgeist* which produced the birth of Dadaism.[268] It is also true that some of the stylistic manoeuvres of the later chapters of *Ulysses* can be associated with, or indeed described as, Dadaism. Within the July–August issue, the Baroness's comments on *Ulysses* are an important recognition of that fact, and are addressed, in part, to Helen Bishop Dennis who had objected to Joyce's representation of 'natural functions' (urination, defecation, the

---

[262] *LR*, December 1919, 49.   [263] *LR*, April 1920, 61.
[264] Cited in the *LR*, Spring 1922, 46.   [265] Anderson, *My Thirty Years' War*, 182.
[266] Gammel, *Baroness Elsa von Freytag-Loringhoven*, 10.
[267] Gammel, *Baroness Elsa von Freytag-Loringhoven*, 246.
[268] Gammel, *Baroness Elsa von Freytag-Loringhoven*, 9.

breaking of wind, erections, etc.) not on the grounds of 'morality', or of being a 'prude', but out of a 'desire for privacy'.[269]

Many of the comments made by the Baroness become clear if one understands them as a specific response to Dennis, whose comments on *Ulysses* were also published under the heading 'The Modest Women':

> If I can write—talk—about dinner—pleasure of my palate—as artist or as aristocrat—with my ease of manner—can afford also mention my ecstasies in toilet room!
>
> If you can not—you are invited to silence—by all means! ...
>
> In Europe—when inferiors do not understand superiors—they retire modestly—mayhap baffled—but in good manner. By that fact—that they do not understand—they know their place. They are not invited—of class inferior—the dance is not theirs.
>
> They can not judge—for: they lack real manners—education—class.[270]

These are exactly the kinds of arguments which Quinn would need when it came to the moment of needing to defend *Ulysses*, but Quinn detested the kind of gender activism which the Baroness, Barnes, and Heap had come to represent. It is also significant that the impact of many of the specific points which the Baroness makes about Joyce's value are lost because of the highly experimental mode in which she writes. The editors could have done much to shape, introduce, and explain the Baroness's output (or that of any of the many other authors they published), but they favoured a policy of non-intervention, of accepting manuscripts as submitted, of letting the writers have the last word, all of which excited Quinn's ire ('I said to them, "What are you, stenographers or editors?" But------------ what's the use? It was all wasted').[271]

Readers of modernist periodicals usually work with the assumption that there is a reasonable editorial continuity and stability between one issue of a journal and the next, that the periodical and linguistic codes repeat from one month to another, and that the editorial presences and political commitments evolve slowly and predictably. This would be a reasonable view to take of other modernist journals to which the *Little Review* might be compared, such as *Poetry*, *The Dial*, or *The Egoist*. But the *Little Review* does not conform to the pattern. It changed significantly in the move from Chicago; it changed once Pound became editorially involved; and it changed again once he had departed, and once the serialization of *Ulysses* had ended. In the period from March 1918 to December 1920, *Ulysses* was the *Little Review*'s most significant source of continuity and stability. Indeed it could be argued that *Ulysses* was one of the factors which kept the *Little Review* going, particularly after the departure of Pound. As early as December 1918, Pound had tried to persuade Joyce not to continue with the *Little Review* given the problems the ongoing serialization might confront; Pound was also very quick, once legal action was in train, to denigrate the editorial efforts made by Anderson and Heap ('in general the editrices have merely messed and muddled, NEVER to

---

[269] Helen Bishop Dennis, 'A Modest Woman', *LR*, May–June 1920, 74.
[270] *LR*, July–August 1920, 38, 39.   [271] Quinn to Pound, 16 October 1920, Carbondale.

their own loss').[272] In September 1918 Quinn had prophesied that the *Little Review* 'would be hard put to survive the year', and once legal action had begun in October 1920, he begged Joyce to stop further publication in the *Little Review*, in order to pre-empt further legal repercussions.[273] But Joyce refused to abandon the *Little Review*, as he explained quite deftly in an important letter to Weaver, which remains partly unpublished:

> it seems to me that to do so would be to pass sentence on my own writing and to blame the editors of the review for having published it and to prejudice their position at the next hearing of the court without altering the situation favourably.[274]

Of course Joyce had several valid points here, and had tacitly recognized that the struggle to serialize *Ulysses*—as he had written it—had become part of its meaning. The cultural context in which *Ulysses* was being published was also relevant, as the different editorial phases of the *Little Review* represented conflicting definitions and economies operating within the field of modern literature, all of which could be seen to be relevant to the reception of Joyce's evolving text. One central conflict related to the question of how candid writers could be in exploring ideas about the body, gender, and sexuality. Joyce, like the Baroness, wanted to be 'sexually modern' and told Weaver that any agreement to renege on the *Little Review* would endorse:

> vacillation in the minds of many admirers of the book: and any indication on my part that such vacillation was founded would strengthen it to my detriment.[275]

Another conflict related to whether writers were paid, and here it is interesting to note Yeats candidly telling Rodker that the *Little Review* 'must pay for the pleasure of misprinting our contributions'.[276] For Joyce and for Heap, money did not matter quite so much. The more important struggle was that of continuing to publish, of continuing to be associated with a journal which gave space to 'new systems of art', a struggle which Heap gracefully sustained on a solo basis, long after *Ulysses* had been published as a book, and long after Anderson had lost interest in what she had once prized as her 'personal enterprise'.[277]

---

[272] Pound to J, 12 December 1918; Pound to J (*c.* October 1920), *EP-JJ*, 147, 184.

[273] Quinn to Yeats, 15 September 1918, cited in Reid, *The Man from New York*, 347; Quinn's lengthy letter to Pound (16 October 1920, Carbondale) was intended for onward submission to Joyce, and requested, on page 12, that Joyce cable instructions that publication in the *Little Review* could stop immediately. Quinn commented that such a decision would serve Anderson and Heap 'right, for they have been too fresh, too bumptious and are parading as advanced women by publishing the work of an artist without paying him for it'.

[274] J to Weaver, 10 November 1920. Part of this letter has been published; see *L* I, 149. This particular passage has been omitted and is in the Harriet Shaw Weaver Papers, BL Ms add 57346, folio 15.

[275] The phrase 'sexually modern' is from the Baroness, cited in Gammel, *Baroness Elsa von Freytag-Loringhoven*, i; J to Weaver, 10 November 1920. BL Ms add 57346, folio 15, also omitted from *L* I, 149.

[276] Yeats to John Rodker, 19 June 1919, *Little Review* records, UWM.

[277] *LR*, May 1929, 5; *LR*, March 1914, 2.

2

Trial and Error

The Composition and Production
of *Ulysses* to April 1921

INTRODUCTION

In the opening months of 1914, when Anderson was in Chicago putting together plans for the first issue of the *Little Review*, Joyce was in Trieste, earning a living as a teacher of English. The chain of events which would bring about the formative association between *Ulysses* and the *Little Review* lay in the future. Joyce had yet to make sustained efforts with the composition of *Ulysses*, and was still engaged in the dispute which dogged the first publication of *Dubliners*, a work which he had first considered complete in September 1905.[1] But over the next few years the situation began to improve. Grant Richards, the London publisher, finally published *Dubliners* in June 1914, and Joyce's correspondence with Pound, begun in December 1913, led to *The Egoist*'s serialization of *A Portrait of an Artist as a Young Man*, which began to be published in February 1914, and continued until September 1915. The completed work was published in Britain and the US at the end of 1916, by which time Joyce's financial position as an author had begun to become more stable, partly because he started to receive significant financial support from Harriet Shaw Weaver, and partly because his sudden move from Trieste to Zurich in June 1915—made necessary by the entry of Italy into the First World War—led to him gaining support for his work as a writer from several new sources. As these changes in fortune took hold, Joyce began to work on *Ulysses* more systematically, perhaps around June 1915, when his correspondence first begins to mention completion of particular chapters.[2]

But how and when did Joyce get the idea of writing a novel with the title *Ulysses*? How did he manage to write a work of such volume and stylistic versatility? How did he succeed in writing a work which one of its first readers described as 'cerise abnormal art' with 'no elasticity, no tolerance, no humour'?[3] In order to contextualize the significance of the *Ulysses* serialization in the *Little Review*, and facilitate the interpretation of *Ulysses* more generally, it is necessary to investigate the compositional genesis of the work, its early production history, and the circumstances by which the editors of the serial text became embroiled in an obscenity trial. Thus this

---

[1] J to Stanislaus Joyce, [about 24 September 1905], *L* II, 111.
[2] See, for example, J to Stanislaus Joyce, 16 June 1915 (*SL*, 209), and J to Pound, 30 June 1915, Yale.
[3] *LR*, June 1918, 55.

chapter, which is in two parts, begins by examining 'Phases in the Composition of *Ulysses*', from conception to the moment of April 1921, when Joyce became aware of the judgment against the *Little Review*, realized that the *Little Review* serialization could not continue, and secured Sylvia Beach's agreement to publish *Ulysses*. The second part, '*Ulysses* on Trial: The Moment of February 1921', examines the legal trysts which led to the trial; the event of the trial itself; the tensions and resentments which were simmering in the background; and the repercussions of the judgment for Joyce's authorship in the US.

Joyce's work on *Ulysses* entered a 'most intense' phase of extensive expansion and revision in April 1921, as Gabler argues.[4] Thus, though significant as a terminus for the serialization, April 1921 is also significant as a beginning. The emphasis in this account is on the genesis of *Ulysses* up to April 1921, but events in the compositional chronology are not as neat or as separable as this date suggests. It is also necessary to consider—albeit briefly—what happened to *Ulysses* in the period between the end of serialization and February 1922, when the work was published in volume form; this is accomplished, in the first part of the chapter, through short sub-sections on 'Continued and Post-Serial Drafting' and 'Plans for Publication in Volume Form', and in Chapter 4 which examines patterns of post-serial revision.

PHASES IN THE COMPOSITION OF *ULYSSES*

Michael Groden's *Ulysses in Progress* (1977) examines the novel's stylistic evolution, alongside the manner and circumstances in which Joyce wrote the text. As Groden himself acknowledges, *Ulysses in Progress* is now significantly out of date, owing, in part, to the discovery and acquisition of *Ulysses* manuscripts by the National Library of Ireland in 2002.[5] Nonetheless, the original study remains influential for anyone interested in the composition and publishing history of *Ulysses*, and needs to be briefly summarized here.[6] Even now it remains an ideal book to consult. It is clearly written and full of facts, arguments, and assertions; library copies tend to have been heavily 'gorescarred' (to use a Joycean coinage) by students and scholars searching for quick answers to the challenges which an initial reading of *Ulysses* so obviously poses.

Groden's basic argument is shaped by the view that the composition of *Ulysses* passes through three distinct stages—early, middle, and late—'with the middle stage serving as a bridge between [Joyce's] early interest in character and story and his

---

    [4] *CSE*III 1886.

    [5] Michael Groden, *Ulysses in Focus: Genetic, Textual and Personal Views* (Gainesville, FL: University Press of Florida, 2010), *passim*. But see, in particular, 'Revisiting the "Cyclops" Manuscripts, Part 1', 105–8.

    [6] For the Joyce Papers 2002, see the catalogue at www.nli.ie, collection 68 (ms 36,639); Luca Crispi, 'A First Foray into the National Library of Ireland's Joyce Manuscripts: Bloomsday 2011', *Genetic Joyce Studies*, Issue 11 (Spring 2011) (www.geneticjoycestudies.org); and Michael Groden, 'The Archive in Transition: The National Library of Ireland's New Joyce Manuscripts', in Groden, *Ulysses in Focus*, 14–31.

late concern with schematic correspondences'.[7] In the early stage of the composition of the novel, which Groden equates with chapters 1 to 9 ('Telemachus' to 'Scylla and Charybdis'), Joyce 'developed an interior monologue technique to tell his story'; in the middle stage, comprising chapters 10 to 14 ('Wandering Rocks' to 'Oxen of the Sun'), he 'experimented with the monologue technique and then abandoned it for a series of parody styles that act as "translations" of the story'.[8] Finally, in the last stage—which Groden dates approximately from the moment of Joyce's arrival in Paris in July 1920 and equates with the composition of chapters 15 to 18 ('Circe' to 'Penelope')—Joyce 'created several new styles and revised the earlier episodes'; this last stage of the work 'is marked by his goals of expansion and elaboration' and saw the inclusion of 'many new Homeric and other correspondences to the earlier episodes'.[9]

The problem with this analysis is that it conflates two separable but related topics: the compositional genesis of the text and the story of its stylistic evolution. This leads to some conceptual confusions and difficulties with chronology, which are particularly evident, for example, in Groden's chapter on 'The Early Stage', which looks at the revisions which Joyce made to chapter 7 ('Aeolus'), after it had been published in the *Little Review* in October 1918. By far the most significant of these revisions was the introduction of the sixty-one headings—all in capitals and bold face, as in a newspaper—which Joyce inserted as he revised the text at proof stage between August and October 1921. These headings—which may be, in turn, concise, ironic, disjunctive, parodic, allusive, alliterative, clichéd (or a combination thereof)— offer the most obvious departure from the narrative norm established within the first six chapters of the novel, and encourage readers to think about the very act of reading, and particularly the act of reading newspapers. Though they belong to an early *part* of the novel (chapter 7 of 18), the headings are, of course, a late-stage revision, as Groden himself acknowledges. Thus it is not entirely logical to discuss them in a chapter headed 'The Early Stage'.

The idea of the book moving through early, middle, and late stages makes the compositional process sound simple. In fact, the process of writing *Ulysses* was fraught with complications: Joyce himself described the writing of the book as a 'seven years' sentence', a form of 'ingenious torture' which would be 'enough to upset anyone's mental balance'.[10] A better paradigm for understanding the realization of the work might involve seeing a dynamic interplay between the phases of Joyce's compositional labour—from conception through to the revision of final proofs— and a range of social factors which shaped and influenced Joyce's authorship. This type of critical approach is that proposed by D. F. McKenzie, who remarked, in his

---

[7] Groden, *Ulysses in Progress*, 4. [8] Groden, *Ulysses in Progress*, 4.
[9] Groden, *Ulysses in Progress*, 4, 52. Joyce often referred to the eighteen sections of *Ulysses* as 'episodes' rather than chapters. In the hope of avoiding confusion, I have consistently referred to the sections as chapters, and have followed critical practice in giving Homeric titles as well as chapter numbers.
[10] J to Weaver, 7 October 1921, *L* I, 173; J to Weaver, 24 June 1921, *SL* 284.

pioneering *Bibliography and the Sociology of the Texts*, that a book 'is never simply a remarkable *object*':

> Like every other technology it is invariably the product of human agency in complex and highly volatile contexts which a responsible scholarship must seek to recover if we are to understand better the creation and communication of meaning[.][11]

The following analysis outlines the ways in which the composition of *Ulysses* moved through five principal overlapping phases: (i) conception, (ii) drafting, (iii) serialization, (iv) continued post-serial drafting, and (v) the formation of plans for publication in volume form. At the same time the analysis acknowledges the significance of social factors which influenced the ebb and flow of Joyce's progress, such as the upheavals and opportunities brought about by a series of moves from place to place; the flow of income; health problems; the development and frustration of plans for the dual serialization of the text in *The Egoist* and the *Little Review*; the recurrent suppressions of the *Little Review* and subsequent legal action; the formation and frustration of plans for the publication of the work in volume form in England, and the US; and the formation of the plan to publish the first edition in Paris.

In contextualizing the compositional process, it is important to understand something of the nature of the surviving manuscripts. This material, as Ferrer notes, is of 'overwhelming bulk' and is scattered in several different research libraries (principally the University at Buffalo, New York, the National Library of Ireland, and the British Library).[12] A great deal of what survives has been published, either in facsimile or fully transcribed copies.[13] Yet despite the size of the surviving archive, it is far from complete. Writing to John Quinn from Paris in November 1920, Joyce estimated that he was living at 'the twentieth address' at which he had been at work on *Ulysses*.[14] In the course of moving so frequently one might surmise that he probably threw away or left behind some of the materials which enabled him to write the book. The other important thing to emphasize is that the manuscript material which survives can be divided into broad categories: notes, drafts, 'fair' copies of

---

[11] D. F. McKenzie, *Bibliography and the Sociology of Texts* (1986; Cambridge: Cambridge University Press, 1999), 4.

[12] Daniel Ferrer, 'The Joyce of Manuscripts', in Richard Brown (ed.), *A Companion to James Joyce* (Oxford: Blackwell, 2008), 286–99 (286). Other important sources of information regarding *Ulysses* manuscripts include Michael Groden, 'Before and After: The Manuscripts in Textual and Genetic Criticism of *Ulysses*', in Michael Patrick Gillespie and A. Nicholas Fargnoli, *Ulysses in Critical Perspective* (Gainesville, FL: University Press of Florida, 2006), 152–70; the catalogue of the James Joyce Collection at Buffalo University (library.buffalo.edu/pl/collections/jamesjoyce/catalog), the world's foremost collection of *Ulysses* materials; and Luca Crispi's *Becoming the Blooms: Joyce's Creative Process and the Construction of Characters in Ulysses* (Oxford: Oxford University Press, 2015).

[13] See in particular the sixty-three-volume *James Joyce Archive* published by Garland, 1977–9, and its index (Michael Groden (ed.), *James Joyce's Manuscripts: An Index* (New York: Garland, 1980) (hereafter *JJA*)). Volumes 12 to 27 reproduce most of the *Ulysses* notes, drafts, typescripts, and proofs then known to be extant. See also Philip F. Herring (ed.), *Joyce's Ulysses Notesheets in the British Museum* (Charlottesville, VA: Bibliographical Society, 1972), Danis Rose (ed.), *The Dublin Ulysses Papers*, 6 vols (Dublin: House of Breathings, 2012) and Clive Driver (ed.), *James Joyce, Ulysses: A Facsimile of the Manuscript*, 3 vols (Philadelphia, PA: Rosenbach Foundation, 1975).

[14] J to Quinn, 24 November 1920, *L* III, 30.

completed chapters in Joyce's hand, typescripts, and proofs. Luca Crispi estimates that there are 'over a hundred pages of notes', 'about thirty-nine' drafts in Joyce's hand, 'over eight hundred pages of the Rosenbach faircopy manuscript', 'over one thousand four hundred pages of typescript', and 'over five thousand pages of galley and page proofs for the first edition'.[15] Much of this material is dateable to specific phases in the compositional history of the text and most of it dates from 1917 and later, when work on the book was already underway.[16] Thus in order to establish the compositional history of the text, it is necessary to see the evidence of the manuscript materials against the account of the book's composition which emerges from published and unpublished correspondence which sometimes predates the extant manuscripts. It is also necessary to balance the compositional history against the evidence of Joyce's developing creativity which emerges from studying the published writings that predate *Ulysses* (including *Chamber Music* (1907), *Dubliners* (1914), *A Portrait of the Artist as a Young Man* (1916), *Exiles* (1918), as well as various critical and journalistic writings).[17]

Using the example set by McKenzie's emphasis on the 'sociology of texts', the following account makes an original contribution to genetic scholarship through its emphasis on the significance of the interplay between Joyce's compositional labour, and the social factors which both thwarted and enabled that labour. It builds on the 'invitation to further research' offered by the recent Yale edition of the *Little Review Ulysses*, and presents a clear and accurate overview, in order to contextualize the cultural and textual significance of the original serialization, and prepare the ground for the textually focused arguments of Chapters 3 and 4.[18] The account is a fresh appraisal of the extant sources, which concentrates, in the main, on the facts of the work's compositional genesis that emerge from correspondence and legal documentation. This emphasis arises from the fact that some essential sources—including Joyce's unpublished letters to Pound, Quinn's unpublished letters, legal documents, and the *Little Review* archives in Milwaukee—have not been available to (or consulted by) other scholars.[19] The manuscripts, in contrast, are more well known (and a detailed study of the extant *Ulysses* manuscripts—already begun in Crispi—would produce a different and much lengthier account of the compositional genesis of Joyce's text, which is beyond the remit of the present chapter).[20]

---

[15] Crispi, 'First Foray', 2.

[16] See the appendix to Crispi, 'First Foray', a 'Census of the Extant *Ulysses* Holograph Manuscripts', which includes dates and places of composition (22–3).

[17] See *Occasional, Critical, and Political Writing*, edited by Kevin Barry (Oxford: Oxford University Press, 2000). For an excellent overview of Joyce's textual biography, see Michael Groden, 'A Textual and Publishing History', in Zack Bowen and James F. Carens (eds.), *A Companion to James Joyce* (London: Greenwood Press, 1984), 71–129.

[18] Gaipa et al., *LRU*, 346. Under the heading 'The Composition of *Ulysses*', Gaipa et al., *LRU* includes a set of 'short summaries' (346) which describe the main facts of the work's composition, and post-serial amplification.

[19] These sources are not considered in Gaipa et al., *LRU*.

[20] The chapters of Crispi's *Becoming the Blooms: Joyce's Creative Process and the Construction of Characters in Ulysses* include detailed tables which specify individual manuscript sources used in the

Conception

When did Joyce develop the characters of Leopold and Molly Bloom? At what point did he decide to set the novel on one day, 16 June 1904? At what point in the conception of the work did Joyce decide to write the book in different styles? One means by which it is possible to see the evolving craftsmanship and conceptual work which would lead to *Ulysses* is through generalized manuscript sources such as the forty short texts known as the 'epiphanies' (dating approximately from 1900 to 1903); the 'Trieste Notebook' (also known as the 'Alphabetical Notebook', and dated by Scholes, 1907 to 1909); and the more recently discovered *Ulysses* 'Subject Notebook' which Joyce began to compile in October 1917.[21] The Epiphanies— which were never published by Joyce—consist of two types: small snippets of what appear to have been actual conversations, recorded in dialogue form; and short narrations, mainly in the third person, which dramatize memories, impressions, and experiences. The texts reveal Joyce's formative habit as a note-taker, and his intense interest in crafting literary material out of the details of his everyday life. A few of these texts would subsequently be used for *Ulysses*, though most were put to use earlier, in either *Portrait* or *Stephen Hero*. For example, number 21 describes two women at a funeral, possibly that of Joyce's mother, May, who died in August 1903:

> Two mourners push on through the crowd. The girl, one hand catching the woman's skirt, runs in advance. The girl's face is the face of a fish, discoloured and oblique-eyed; the woman's face is small and square, the face of a bargainer. The girl, her mouth distorted, looks up at the woman to see if it is time to cry: the woman, settling a flat bonnet, hurries on towards the mortuary chapel.[22]

The strange 'face of a fish' (possibly suggesting the pallor of grief), the awry bonnet, and the looked-for gesture of whether 'it is time to cry' recur in chapter 6 ('Hades'), in the description of a woman and girl seen by Bloom as they leave the cemetery at Glasnevin, just as the Dignam cortège arrives. The Epiphany text has notably become more compressed, and more deliberately estranging in its transition to *Ulysses*:

> Mourners came out through the gates: woman and a girl. Leanjawed harpy, hard woman at a bargain, her bonnet awry. Girl's face stained with dirt and tears, holding the woman's arm looking up at her for a sign to cry. Fish's face, bloodless and livid.
>
> (*U*1922, 97)

critical readings. Crispi's readings 'isolate the text of *Ulysses* at particular points in time during the work's at least seven-year genesis' (26).

[21] The Epiphanies are available in James Joyce, *Poems and Shorter Writings*, edited by Richard Ellmann, A. Walton Litz, and John Whittier-Ferguson (London: Faber, 1991), and Robert Scholes and Richard M. Kain (eds.), *The Workshop of Daedalus: James Joyce and the Raw Materials for A Portrait of the Artist as a Young Man* (Evanston, IL: Northwestern University Press, 1965), which also includes a full transcription of 'The Trieste Notebook' whose original is at Cornell University Library (see http://rmc.library.cornell.edu); the 'Subject Notebook' (NLI. MS 36,639/3) has been discussed and described by Wim Van Mierlo, 'The Subject Notebook: A Nexus in the Composition History of *Ulysses*—A Preliminary Analysis', Issue 7 (Spring 2007) (www.geneticjoycestudies.org).

[22] Joyce, *Poems and Shorter Writings*, 181. See Stanislaus Joyce, *My Brother's Keeper* (New York: The Viking Press, 1958), 235 for the suggestion that this Epiphany records a moment at their mother's funeral.

The 'Trieste Notebook' is a series of alphabetically arranged notes, and includes entries on Oliver St. John Gogarty (the model for Buck Mulligan), Ireland, 'Mother', and 'Pappie'. The entry on 'Mother' is particularly moving, and is used almost verbatim in *Ulysses*: 'She came to me silently in a dream after her death: and her washed body within its loose brown habit gave out a faint odour of wax and rosewood and her breath a faint odour of wetted ashes'.[23] In itself, this moment appears to be an elaboration of Epiphany 34 (which begins 'She comes at night when the city is still; invisible, inaudible, all unsummoned') and serves to demonstrate an aspect of Joyce's working methods—the pattern of gradual expansion and elaboration—a process which begins with the taking of a brief note (an experience or a perception), which is then crafted into a short literary text, and finally put to use in the longer literary work, which may in itself be subject to successive draftings.[24] Joyce's ability to use the materials of his everyday life in this way brings to mind an obvious point—that as the origins of *Ulysses* lie in his early experiences, particularly before he left Dublin with Nora on 8 October 1904, a full history of its development is, as Litz has observed, 'a history of his artistic career to the age of forty'.[25] The published prose texts which predate *Ulysses*—*Dubliners* (1914) and *Portrait* (1916)—direct readers to perceive continuities with *Ulysses*. The continuity is not just that of setting (the Dublin of Joyce's youth) but also that of characterization, most obviously in Stephen Dedalus, but also in the minor characters from *Dubliners* who re-appear in *Ulysses*, including figures such as Martin Cunningham, Gabriel Conroy, Hynes, Tom Kernan, Mr M'Coy, O'Madden Burke, and Mr Power. In the early stages of his work on *Ulysses*, Joyce identified this aspect of continuity quite clearly, telling Pound, in a letter which remains unpublished, that *Ulysses* 'is a continuation of *A Portrait of the Artist as a Young Man* after three years' interval blended with many of the persons of *Dubliners*'.[26]

The idea for a story called 'Ulysses' appears to have first occurred to Joyce in September 1906 when he was still working on *Dubliners* and living in Rome. As Terence Killeen and others have noted, 'Ulysses' was to feature a man named Alfred H. Hunter, a real-life Dubliner who worked as an advertising canvasser, and was married to a woman named Marion, who came from a musical family.[27] Hunter may have once lived close to Joyce in north Dublin, and, according to Ellmann, in June 1904 he helped Joyce home one night following a fight in St Stephen's Green which landed Joyce with a 'black eye, sprained wrist, sprained ankle, cut chin, cut

---

[23] Scholes (ed.), *The Workshop of Daedalus*, 103. Cf. *U* 1: 102.

[24] Ellmann (ed.), *Poems*, 194.

[25] A. Walton Litz, *The Art of James Joyce* (London: Oxford University Press, 1961), 1.

[26] J to Pound, 30 June 1915, Yale. In *Dubliners and Ulysses: Bonds of Character* (Novi Ligure, Italy: Edizioni Joker, 2013), David G. Wright estimates that the characters of *Dubliners* make a total of 700 textual appearances in *Ulysses* and argues that *Dubliners* contributes 'a degree of comforting familiarity to help offset some of the novel's strangeness' (35). The vivid characterization and detailed plotting which Joyce devotes to M'Coy, Power, Kernan, Cunningham, and Hynes in *Ulysses* represents a considerable reimagining, revitalization, and extension of their earlier appearances in *Dubliners* (i.e. much more than a 'continuation').

[27] Terence Killeen, 'Myths and Monuments: The Case of Alfred H. Hunter', in *Dublin James Joyce Journal*, 1 (2008), 47–53; and Terence Killeen, 'Marion Hunter Revisited: Further Light on a Dublin Enigma', *Dublin James Joyce Journal*, 3 (2010), 144–51.

hand'.[28] This event may have given Joyce the initial seed for stories of both the Blooms, and particularly Stephen's encounter with Leopold Bloom, but the evidence is scant. By 6 February 1907 Joyce had abandoned the idea of the story—telling his brother Stanislaus, to whom he had appealed for information about Hunter, that 'Ulysses never got any forrader than the title'.[29] He had begun instead to concentrate his energies on writing a fifteenth short story to add to the manuscript of *Dubliners*, 'The Dead', which he completed late in September 1907, after his move back to Trieste. Perhaps it had occurred to him that 'Ulysses' was too good a title to waste on a short story, and he may have felt uncertain about the fate of *Dubliners* and the short story form more generally.[30] In 1906 (as in the opening months of 1914) the meticulously crafted manuscript of *Dubliners* was in the hands of Grant Richards, who was dithering over whether to publish and who had told Joyce, in passing, that *Dubliners* has 'the qualities which do not help a book: it is about Ireland, and it is always said that books about Ireland do not sell; and it is a collection of short stories'.[31]

Other writers might have given up in the face of such disheartening responses, but the sense that he was being thwarted by readers like Richards—as well as his own difficult material circumstances—sharpened Joyce's determination to drive forward, even if he could only do so very gradually. During the six months he spent in Rome—in which he was frequently broke, and often perilously close to being homeless—his plans for writing were gradually advancing. He knew that in order to write with the kind of detail he valued he needed to collect materials documenting life in Dublin, and asked his Aunt Josephine to send 'a Xmas present made up of tram tickets, advts, handbills, posters, papers, programmes & c'.[32] He longed for a map of the city to hang on his wall, picture postcards, and a copy of J. T. Gilbert's three-volume *History of the City of Dublin* (1861).[33] Given these small facts, it is significant that Joyce told a number of correspondents that he had begun work on *Ulysses* while in Rome.[34] Though there is no evidence showing us what he actually did, there is, equally, no reason to doubt the veracity of his account. After all, Joyce's stay in Rome—from August 1906 to February 1907—would have stood out in his memory, as it was a journey into a different kind of life, a period of working as a bank clerk, which took him away from teaching, and the community he had established in Trieste. This time may have enabled him to re-assess his position, to think more clearly about what he had already written, and what he wanted to write, if,

[28] J to Curran, 23 June 1904, *L* I, 55. Richard Ellmann, *James Joyce* (1959; Oxford: Oxford University Press, rev edn, 1982), 161.

[29] J to Stanislaus Joyce, [3 December 1906], *L* II, 197; J to Stanislaus Joyce, 6 February 1907, *L* II, 209.

[30] For the difficulties associated with the publication of *Dubliners*, see Clare Hutton, 'Chapters of Moral History: Failing to Publish *Dubliners*', *Papers of the Bibliographical Society of America*, 97:4 (2003), 495–519.

[31] Grant Richards to J, 17 February 1906, in Robert E. Scholes (ed.), 'Grant Richards to James Joyce', *Studies in Bibliography*, 16 (1963), 139–60, 143.

[32] J to Stanislaus Joyce, 6 November 1906, *L* II, 186.

[33] J to Stanislaus Joyce, 13 November 1906, *L* II, 194.

[34] J to Weaver, 8 November 1916, *L* I, 98; J to Curran, 15 March 1917, *L* II, 392.

in his own words, 'circumstances were favourable'.[35] Perhaps he worked out some sort of general sketch for *Ulysses* as a novel around this time, as well as ideas for individual chapters.[36] It certainly seems probable that as he spent time in Rome's Biblioteca Vittorio Emanuele adding details to the short story 'Grace', he realized he could do more work of this kind: tying *Dubliners*-type stories together, reusing characters he had already conceived, and continuing to write realistic depictions of Dublin's cultural and conversational world.

Joyce first publicly associated his writing with the name 'Stephen Daedalus' by using that name as a pseudonym for the publication of the first three stories of *Dubliners* in *The Irish Homestead* in 1904, 'The Sisters', 'Eveline', and 'After the Race'.[37] Pseudonyms were a common feature of Literary Revival authorship, and were used, in part, to suggest a separation of critical and creative identities. George William Russell, the editor of *The Irish Homestead*, was known as 'AE' (from æon, meaning life or being, and designed to be suggestive of Russell's mystic philosophy); William Kirkpatrick Magee, a minor *littérateur*, and the editor of *Dana*, concealed himself behind the rather floral soubriquet of 'John Eglinton', a point which the narrator of chapter 9 ('Scylla and Charybdis') insists we recognize (see especially *U*1922, 199); and throughout his life Douglas Hyde was known popularly as 'An Craoibhinn Aoibhinn' (which means, though this will sound implausible, the sweet little branch). It is typical of Joyce to choose a pseudonym replete with so much meaning—Daedalus, a legendary inventor, craftsman, and artist, who escaped from Minos with wings made of feather and wax, a feat which could not be copied by his son Icarus, who drowned on that same journey because he disobeyed instructions and flew too near the sun. In using this name to sign his short stories Joyce was suggesting all of this, and was signalling—to himself if not to others—his greater commitment to the longer autobiographical work which was then in progress, *Stephen Hero*, in which Daedalus appears.

Joyce had begun work on *Stephen Hero* in 1903, before planning *Dubliners*, and originally projected a work of sixty-three chapters.[38] He abandoned the project in the summer of 1905 in order to give undivided attention to *Dubliners*, but resumed it again in September 1907, following the completion of 'The Dead'. He was then in a position to reconceptualize the work in hand, and planned *A Portrait of the Artist as a Young Man* in five chapters. But the finished work was still many years off: it would not be completed until 1913 or 1914, some ten or so years following its inception. As Gabler notes, part of the difficulty with completing *Portrait* arose from not quite knowing how or where to finish the account of Stephen's separation

---

[35] J to Stanislaus Joyce, 6 February 1907, *L* II, 209.

[36] See Rodney Wilson Owen, *James Joyce and the Beginnings of Ulysses* (Ann Arbor, MI: UMI Research Press, 1983) who suggests that the nuclei for chapters 6 ('Hades'), 10 ('Wandering Rocks'), and 12 ('Cyclops') had 'potentially been formed' by late 1907, 'as well as Bloom's characteristic psychology' (4).

[37] Published in *The Irish Homestead* on 13 August, 10 September, and 17 December 1904 respectively. Though he was paid the rather generous rate of £1 per story, Joyce did not publish any of the other *Dubliners* stories in *The Irish Homestead*.

[38] 1903, and the other dates noted in this paragraph, are supplied from Hans Walter Gabler in 'The Genesis of *A Portrait of the Artist as a Young Man*', in Philip Brady and James F. Carens (eds.), *Critical Essays on James Joyce's A Portrait of the Artist as a Young Man* (New York: G. K. Hall, 1995), 83–112.

from home, fatherland, and religion.[39] Joyce's original plan for the novel appears to have extended the story beyond Stephen's departure from Dublin, and he intended to include a character named 'Dr. Doherty', an early name for Buck Mulligan, the character based on his sometime friend, Oliver St John Gogarty. *The Workshop of Daedalus* includes a transcription of what has been described as 'a fragment from a late *Portrait* manuscript' which features Dedalus with his 'red-eyed and flushed' mother, seated by the kitchen range of the family home. In a passage of interior monologue, Dedalus recalls 'Doherty's jibes', and Doherty's desire to 'retire to the tower, you and I. Our lives are precious. I'll try to touch the aunt. We are the super-artists. Dedalus and Doherty have left Ireland for the Omphalos—'.[40] What this fragmentary text demonstrates, with its multiple connections to *Ulysses*, is that in the act of completing *Portrait* and discarding this scene, Joyce found that he had overflow materials, which would enable the early drafting of his new novel.

Drafting

As noted earlier, Joyce first indicated that he was engaged in writing *Ulysses* as a novel on 16 June 1915, just a few days before he made his rather hurried move from Trieste to Zurich.[41] He told his brother Stanislaus that he had completed 'the first episode of my new novel *Ulysses*' and that he was planning to write twenty-two 'episodes' in three parts:

> The first part, the Telemachiad, consists of four episodes: the second of fifteen, that is, Ulysses' wandering: and the third, Ulysses' return home, of three more episodes.[42]

The original of this letter is in German as Stanislaus had been interned by the Austrian authorities as an 'enemy alien' because of his outspoken 'Irredentist' politics (he believed that Trieste, largely inhabited by an Italian-speaking population and close to what was then the border with Italy, should be governed by Italy and not Austria-Hungary). When Italy entered into the war against Austria-Hungary on 23 May 1915, the context of living in Trieste changed for Joyce; obtaining control of the city, a major port, was a key strategic goal for both sides. As he found himself being 'exposed to aeroplane raids' and hearing 'cannonades nearly every day', he had little choice but to leave.[43] By 30 June, he had arrived in Zurich, a place he chose to live in as 'the first big city after the frontier' and was settled enough to be able to write to Pound, an increasingly important confidante, to tell him that he was working on *Ulysses* 'of which I have written the first two episodes'.[44] Though there are no extant draft materials for either of these chapters dated to this moment, once again there is no reason to disbelieve Joyce's account: he had written chapter 1 ('Telemachus') in some version by 16 June 1915 and added chapter 2 ('Nestor'),

---

[39] Gabler, 'The Genesis of *A Portrait of the Artist as a Young Man*', 93.

[40] Scholes (ed.), *The Workshop of Daedalus*, 107–8. As he revised *Stephen Hero* for *Portrait*, Joyce changed the spelling of 'Daedalus' to Dedalus.

[41] J to Stanislaus Joyce, 16 June 1915, *SL*, 209.

[42] J to Stanislaus Joyce, 16 June 1915, *SL*, 209.   [43] J to Pound, 30 June 1915, Yale.

[44] J to Weaver, 30 June 1915, *L* I, 82; J to Pound, 30 June 1915, Yale.

which in its finished form is the shortest chapter in the book, by 30 June 1915.[45] At this time, Joyce confessed that he believed himself to be a 'slow writer', a point not borne out by the evidence: Joyce could write quite quickly once he had completed his preliminary work, and established where the writing was taking him.[46]

It is likely that he had spent some of 1914 and the earlier part of 1915 preparing for *Ulysses* by noting, and then drafting, moments of 'epiphany', and by recording notes of his reading. Yet the circumstances in which he was beginning to draft *Ulysses* were hardly ideal. He had had to leave Trieste with just 'a few things and some MSS'; his books and some 'prose sketches' were locked up in his desk in Trieste, which he would not see again until 17 October 1919, when he returned to find the 'upper part' of his former house 'ruined by bombs and my flat . . . let again to a new tenant'.[47] His social and financial circumstances were also now much more unsettled: he did not know anyone in Zurich, had nowhere to live, and had no immediate prospect of either income or employment. But one way or another, Joyce's luck began to turn. He found bits and pieces of teaching, received money from Nora's uncle, Michael Healy, and late in August, just two months after his arrival in Zurich, had heard news that he would receive a grant of £75 from the Royal Literary Fund, to be paid in three instalments 'at intervals of three months'.[48] This award came about owing to the energetic interventions made on Joyce's behalf by both Yeats and Pound, and it enabled Joyce to feel justified in shifting his priorities: he was now a writer who taught to supplement his income, rather than a teacher who wrote in his spare time.

But his career path as a writer was still far from smooth. *The Egoist* finally finished the serial publication of *Portrait* on 1 September 1915, but British publishers kept on refusing to publish the text as a novel.[49] Duckworth and Co. wrote to James Pinker, Joyce's newly appointed London agent, enclosing a reader's report which indicates how difficult it could be for an experimental and modernist text to be accepted, even among high-brow literary publishers. The report was written by Edward Garnett (1868–1937) who, despite being instrumental in helping both Conrad and Lawrence, complained of 'tedious' 'longueurs' in *Portrait*, with the end, in particular, being a 'complete' and 'ineffective' 'falling to bits': 'It is too discursive, formless, unrestrained, and ugly things, ugly words, are too prominent . . . we can only see a chance for it if it is pulled into shape and made more definite'.[50] Pound was so incensed by this report that he refused to forward it to Joyce, telling Pinker 'as for altering Joyce to suit Duckworth's readers—I would like trying to fit

[45] J to Stanislaus Joyce, 16 June 1915, *SL*, 209; J to Pound, 30 June 1915, Yale.
[46] J to H. L. Mencken, 7 July 1915, *L* I, 83.
[47] J to Pound, 30 June 1915, Yale; J to Pound, 9 April 1917, *L* I, 101; J to Pound, 24 October 1919, Yale.
[48] J to Yeats, 1 September 1915, *L* II, 363.
[49] For evidence of British publishers turning down *Portrait* see, in particular, John Firth (ed.), 'James Pinker to James Joyce, 1915–1920', *Studies in Bibliography*, 21 (1968), 205–25 which indicates that the novel was declined by Grant Richards (5 July 1915), and then the firms of Martin Secker (18 August 1915), Herbert Jenkins (25 October 1915), and Duckworth (13 December 1915).
[50] Reader's report enclosed in letter from Cape to Pinker, 26 January 1916, *L* II, 371.

the Venus de Milo into a piss-pot.—…a few changes required'.[51] Weaver was aware of these setbacks and believed that *Portrait* would be best served by 'a proper book-publisher in London with regular machinery for advertisement'; she none-theless offered to publish *Portrait* as a book, using the name of *The Egoist* as an imprint, but then struggled to find a printer willing to print the text in its entirety.[52] Joyce found the drip-drip-drip report of setbacks with *Portrait* a distraction from his work on *Ulysses*. On 10 March 1916, in response to a letter from Weaver reporting that no printer was willing to print 'without deletions', Joyce told Pound:

> In any case I want the book to be published this spring as, until it is out of the way, I cannot continue what I am writing. I had just begun again and now this bad news comes to obstruct me.[53]

Things began to go more smoothly in the latter half of 1916. The deadlock regard-ing *Portrait* finally came to an end in June, when B. W. Huebsch (1876–1964), founder of his own literary publishing business in New York, agreed to publish *Portrait* in the US. He had been introduced to Joyce's work by Grant Richards who had given him a copy of *Dubliners* in the summer of 1914, and was in the position to offer to publish and print *Portrait* 'absolutely in accordance with the author's wishes, without deletion'.[54] In the face of Weaver's ongoing difficulties with British printers, he also undertook 'to supply printed sheets' so that the book could be bound and published by *The Egoist* in London.[55] As these arrangements were being put in place, Joyce moved on with *Ulysses*. On 10 October 1916, he told Weaver, with whom relations were still rather formal:

> I thank you also for your kind inquiry about the book I am writing. I am working at it as well as I can. It is called *Ulysses* and the action takes place in Dublin in 1904. I have almost finished the first part and have written out part of the middle and end. I hope to finish it in 1918.[56]

'First part' here refers to the 'Telemachiad', i.e. chapters 1 to 3; 'middle' refers to the 'Wanderings' or Odyssey, i.e. chapters 4 to 15; and 'end' refers to the 'Homecoming' or Nostos, i.e. chapters 16 to 18. This is clear evidence that Joyce did not write the book in sequence, and that he had 'almost finished' writing some version of the first three chapters by October 1916. The letter makes it sound as if Joyce has a clear plan, and that work is advancing solidly, though the timetable for completion—the 'hope' that the book could be finished 'in 1918'—is admirably imprecise, and proved optimistic.

[51] Pound to Pinker, 30 January 1916, *L* II, 373.
[52] Weaver to J, 30 November 1915, John Firth, 'Harriet Weaver's Letters to James Joyce, 1915–1920', *Studies in Bibliography*, 20 (1967), 151–88 (155).
[53] Weaver to J, 3 March 1915, Firth (ed.), 'Harriet Weaver's Letters to James Joyce', 157; J to Pound, 10 March 1916, Yale.
[54] Huebsch to J, 2 June 1915, *L* I, 81; Huebsch to Weaver, 16 June 1916, *L* I, 91.
[55] British printers were reluctant to print 'risky' books because they were required to print their name and address on every copy of a book that they printed, and would have been liable in any legal proceedings brought, for example, under the Obscene Publications Act of 1857. By arranging to import the printed sheets of *Portrait* from the US, Weaver got round the problem with printers, though she could still have been liable to prosecution as publisher.
[56] J to Weaver, 10 October 1916, *L* II, 387.

There are several explanations for Joyce's optimism on this point. First, he could not foresee the difficulties ahead which would slow progress, particularly the problems with his eyesight, the material daily challenges which continued because of the war, and the upheavals of the moves from Zurich to Trieste to Paris. Second, the 'hope' that *Ulysses* might be finished in 1918 gave him more than two years from the time of writing; this must have seemed like a long chunk of time to finish a book which already existed in partial draft. Third, Joyce's idea for *Ulysses* at this time— October 1916—was for a less ambitious and shorter book than the one he finally produced. Though the book was being drafted, it was also still being conceived. In this regard, it is worth bearing in mind a statement which Joyce made to Pound the following year, on 24 July 1917:

> As regards *Ulysses* I write and think and write and think all day and part of the night. It goes on as it has been going these five or six years! But the ingredients will not fuse until they have reached a certain temperature.[57]

Though he had some sort of general plan or idea for the book, he could not see how it was going to evolve until he had developed the details of his ideas in draft; nor could he see how to 'fuse' the disparate elements of the book, until he had drafts in hand and had tried to work them into some kind of unity.

During the course of 1917, the drafting of *Ulysses* progressed considerably. By 5 April 1917, he had advanced from describing the book as being in three Odyssean 'parts' into describing some chapters in relation to a Homeric parallel.[58] Despite the tribulations and setbacks caused by ill health ('I am not allowed to write much because my eye becomes hard if I strain it'), he told Pound that he had 'managed to finish the draft of Hades' house and also the Lotuseaters and am getting together the notes for the Eolian episode', i.e. chapters 6, 5, and 7 respectively.[59] As noted in Chapter 1, arrangements for Pound's tenure as 'Foreign Editor' of the *Little Review* were in place early in February 1917, when Pound wrote to Joyce offering to 'publish any short stuff you have and that you can afford to sell . . . for £2 per thousand words', including 'Rough drafts of *Ulysses* if they would wouldn't interfere with later serial publication of the whole'.[60] Joyce didn't quite know what to do in response to this invitation. The only part of *Ulysses* that he felt he could offer 'would be the Hamlet chapter, or part of it—which, however, would suffer by excision'.[61] He had given twelve lectures on *Hamlet* between November 1912 and February 1913, and was able to use some of the notes he made for those lectures within chapter 9 ('Scylla and Charybdis'), intriguingly referred to here as the 'Hamlet' chapter, as though he had not yet quite decided, at this stage, the extent to which he wished

---

[57] J to Pound, 24 July 1917, Yale. 'Five or six years' before 1917 may suggest 1912 and an inception of *Ulysses* associated with Joyce's delivery of the *Hamlet* lectures in Trieste. What this evidence suggests, along with the Epiphanies and the Hunter story of 1906, is that *Ulysses* has multiple points of biographical and textual beginning. The inconsistency in Joyce's dating of the inception is testimony to the multiple origins of the work, which began, *inter alia*, in the period when he was still living in Dublin (up to October 1904), during his time in Rome (August 1906 to February 1907), with the Hamlet lectures (November 1912 to February 1913), and as he finished *Portrait* (in 1914).
[58] J to Pound, 5 April 1917, Yale.   [59] J to Pound, 5 April 1917, Yale.
[60] Pound to J, 9 February 1917, *EP-JJ*, 92.   [61] J to Pound, 9 April 1917, *L* I, 101.

to emphasize the Homeric elements of the book.[62] The fact that Joyce was even prepared to *consider* sending that chapter for serial publication may suggest that it was a more advanced and polished draft than other parts of the book. It may also suggest a recognition that the other drafts needed more work, which he was now in a better position to plan given the steady income he knew he would receive, owing to Weaver's anonymously given donation of £50 per quarter for a year, beginning 1 May 1917.[63] Joyce's response to Pound's request for material for the *Little Review* ('the Hamlet chapter, or part of it'), taken with other evidence in the correspondence—particularly his unpublished letter to Pound of 5 April 1917—makes it clear that he had at least six chapters of *Ulysses* in initial draft by April 1917 (1, 2, 3, 5, 6, and 9), as well as the notes for what would become chapter 7 ('Aeolus'), and some 'part of the...end' (i.e. the last three chapters).[64]

Joyce continued to work on *Ulysses* over the summer of 1917, and remained committed to the idea that the book could be realized quite quickly. On 8 August he told Grant Richards, who was publishing *Exiles*, that he hoped to have *Ulysses* 'ready for publication next year'.[65] His progress was hindered to some extent by problems he had with his eyes, which included attacks of iritis in February and April and then a severe attack of glaucoma on 18 August.[66] On 24 August 1917 part of the iris of his left eye was removed, in an operation known as an iridectomy, and he was convalescing for several weeks thereafter.[67] Nonetheless, his plans for *Ulysses* remained active. Attracted by the prospect that he could be paid 'double fees' for the simultaneous serialization of *Ulysses* in both *The Egoist* in London and the *Little Review* in New York, Joyce wrote to Pound on 20 August in order to pin down plans for serialization.[68] He was restless in Zurich, and partly attributed his poor health to its climate ('Perhaps it is this climate which brings to the surface and magnifies every weakness of the body'), and was thus also making plans to get away to work in the small city of Locarno, in Italian Switzerland where the weather was milder.[69] He had settled there by 12 October, and had completed the fair copying of chapters 1 and 2 ('Telemachus' and 'Nestor') before returning to Zurich in early January 1918.[70] Joyce found that he needed to write his work out by hand, and did not, at this stage in his career, type (telling Quinn, who was something of a manuscript fetishist, 'I cannot dictate to a stenographer or type. I write all with my

[62] For the Hamlet materials, see William H. Quillian, 'Shakespeare in Trieste: Joyce's 1912 "Hamlet" Lectures', *James Joyce Quarterly*, 12:1/2 (Fall 1974–Winter 1975), 7–63.

[63] Slack, Monro, Saw and Co. to J, 22 February 1917, *L* II, 389.

[64] Evidence collated from J to Pound, 5 April 1917, Yale; J to Pound, 9 April 1917 (*L* I, 101); J to Weaver (10 October 1916, *L* II, 387). Letters of around this time make no mention of chapter 4 ('Calypso'), the first chapter to feature Leopold Bloom. It seems probable that Joyce also had some version of chapter 4 in draft by April 1917 as it would have been hard to write the continuation of Bloom's day without having a sense of its beginning.

[65] J to Richards, 8 August 1917, *L* II, 401.

[66] J to Weaver, 6 March 1917, *SL*, 224; J to Weaver, 22 April 1917, *L* I, 102; J to Pound, 20 August 1917, *SL*, 226, and *L* II, 390n.

[67] *L* II, 390n.   [68] J to Pound, 20 August 1917, *SL*, 227.

[69] J to Pound, 9 July 1917, Yale.

[70] See J to Sykes, [? November 1917], *L* I, 108; J to Sykes 27 November 1917, *L* I, 109; J to Sykes, [? December 1917], *L* I, 109. Pound knew that chapter 1 was being typed by 7 December 1917 (*P-LR*, 166).

hand').[71] Thus these chapters were typed in Zurich by his friend, Claud Sykes, to whom he was relaying minor corrections in December 1917 and January 1918.[72]

There appears to be a dramatic chronological disjunction between this evidence of the production history of the early chapters of the book and the manuscript evidence of the National Library of Ireland's 'Subject Notebook', the earliest surviving manuscript notebook prepared specially for *Ulysses*, which appears to suggest work at a much more preliminary stage. As Wim Van Mierlo notes, the 'Subject Notebook' can be dated with some precision, as it bears the label of a Locarno stationer, and contains an entry which can be traced to an article in the *Frankfurter Zeitung* of 16 October 1917.[73] The somewhat disparate contents of this notebook, organized under twenty 'subject' headings, range from notes on specific characters (Simon, Leopold, and Stephen) to notes on 'books', 'theosophy', 'Homer', 'words', 'Jews', and 'names and places'. Thus Van Mierlo identifies the notebook 'as a discreet preparatory and creative moment that looks ahead at what was to be written'.[74] But this is not necessarily the case. Joyce clearly had some version of the book in hand several months before he reached Locarno. He also clearly had a filing system of a kind. In an unpublished letter to Pound of 14 October 1916, he mentions 'the bewildering mass of papers for *Ulysses* which I carry in a very large envelope that I possess for the last twelve years'.[75] It is possible that the 'Subject Notebook' represents an attempt to bring order to that 'bewildering mass', an attempt to organize an out-of-control filing system, the kind of initiative one makes after a break from work, or a period of upheaval. Both possibilities are relevant in this case, as Joyce had been forced to stop working for a period after the iridectomy, and had then moved to Locarno. Once he had spent some time going through his 'mass of papers', and transcribing some materials into the notebook, Joyce was in a position to continue with his writing on a more systematic basis. He found he did not need to transcribe everything into the notebook, because the process of going through his papers refamiliarized him with the contours of the writing which already existed, and persuaded him that some of his existing notes and drafts were clear enough for his immediate purpose.

Serialization

Yet Joyce evidently did not have a great deal of the book in hand when he made the commitment to serialization. Of the first ten chapters in the book, there is only draft material for chapters 3 and 9, dateable to autumn 1917 and early 1918 respectively.[76] These chance survivals in what must once have been a much larger archive make it clear that it is accurate to describe what Joyce had in hand before he reached

[71] J to Quinn, 13 May 1917, *L* II, 396. For Joyce and handwriting see Derek Attridge, 'Joyce's Pen', in Richard Brown (ed.), *Joyce, Penelope and the Body* (Amsterdam: Rodopi, 2006), 47–62.

[72] J to Sykes, [? December 1917], *L* I, 109; J to Sykes, [? 22 December 1917], *L* II, 415.

[73] Van Mierlo, 'The Subject Notebook', 3.   [74] Van Mierlo, 'The Subject Notebook', 2.

[75] J to Pound, 14 October 1916, Yale.

[76] Drafts for chapter 3 ('Proteus'): NLI 36,639/07/A and Buffalo V. A 3; drafts for chapter 9 ('Scylla and Charybdis'): NLI 36,639/08/A, B, and C.

Locarno as a kind of 'proto-*Ulysses*', a preliminary and rather rough version of certain chapters in the book.[77] Why therefore did Joyce make the commitment to serialize if the drafting of the book was still at such an early stage, and what gave him the confidence to do so?

There are several possibilities. The prospect of being paid regularly for work as he wrote it must have been very appealing. He had little experience of being treated as a 'professional' author, in receipt of more or less regular and reasonable sums of income in return for completed work; the fact that he uses the language of business in his letter to Pound of 20 August 1917 ('I am prepared to consign it serially from 1 January next, instalments of about 6000 words') implies a desire to be treated as such.[78] As noted, Pound was promising £2 per thousand words for publication in the *Little Review*, and, early in September 1917, as soon as she had heard that Joyce was likely to have *Ulysses* ready, Weaver had hurriedly made arrangements to pay £50 for serial rights to publish the text in *The Egoist*.[79] For Joyce the payment of such sums was a necessary recompense for the loss of earning from teaching, a point he made to Pound as he finalized plans to leave Zurich for Locarno: 'It will be necessary for me to replace in some ways the lessons I forfeit by going away from here'.[80]

Of course the agreement to serialize *Ulysses* was loosely made and not legally binding; though Joyce was very grateful to both Pound and Weaver for their support, he had yet to meet either of them, and they must have seemed far away, in London, the other side of a Europe which was being ravaged by war. Had circumstances forced Joyce to abandon the serial *Ulysses*, the repercussions would not have been great. Though Joyce would later wonder whether *Ulysses* would ever be finished, the prospect of abandoning the work in progress at this early stage was, of course, quite unlikely.[81] On the contrary, the payments he was promised were a push factor in the drive to consolidate *Ulysses* into a publishable form. The loyal support of Weaver and Pound was already having a significant psychological effect on Joyce's confidence and determination to drive forward; now that support was underpinned by actual payment, and promised access to a sympathetic readership. Serialization was thus a win-win situation for Joyce, and was a very important link in the chain of events which led to the realization of *Ulysses*. The process of drafting enabled Joyce to deepen his conception of the work; and the process of serialization enabled him to continue drafting.

In the vast circuit of published and unpublished correspondence which surrounds the arrangements for serialization, submission deadlines were never mooted. But the commitment to serialization meant that Joyce needed to bring system to his working methods, and ensure that he was finishing chapters to his satisfaction in sequence, and with reasonable regularity. He did not necessarily always work on *Ulysses* in sequence, but most of the evidence of his drafting from late 1917 onwards

---

[77] The term 'proto-*Ulysses*' is used by Van Mierlo, 'The Subject Notebook' (40) and echoed by Crispi in his description of NLI 36,639/07/A as a 'proto-draft' of chapter 3 (Crispi, 'First Foray', 12).

[78] J to Pound, 20 August 1917, *SL*, 226.

[79] Weaver to J, 6 September 1917 in Firth (ed.), 'Harriet Weaver's Letters to James Joyce', 177.

[80] J to Pound, 20 August 1917, *SL*, 227.   [81] J to Quinn, 11 March 1920, *L* II, 460.

points to him working systematically, finishing each individual chapter in sequence. For chapters 1 to 9, Joyce's progress with completion—i.e. the process of moving from draft to fair copy, to typed copy, to corrected typed copy submitted and received for serial publication—may be summarized as follows. Chapter 1 ('Telemachus') had been completed by November 1917; Joyce sent it to Sykes for typing, telling him that it needed to be done 'as quickly as possible so that the printers can get to work'.[82] By 19 December the typescript had been received and acknowledged by Pound who admired it immensely ('too serious for me to prattle into criticism. I think it is the only youth that has ever been written down').[83] Chapter 2 ('Nestor') was with Sykes in December 1917, from whom Joyce required three typed copies 'as last time', one to keep for future reference, one for Pound, and the third either for Weaver and *The Egoist*, or for onward submission to the *Little Review*.[84] Pound had received it by 17 January; he later told Quinn he thought it 'inferior' to the first chapter.[85] Joyce hoped to be able to complete chapter 3 ('Proteus') by early January 1918 but progress was delayed slightly by the upheaval of his move back to Zurich, and, as he told Pound, the need to find 'some tolerable quarters'.[86] It was being typed by late January and was sent to Pound on 11 February (who duly pronounced it 'magnificent in spots, and mostly incomprehensible').[87] It is not clear who typed chapter 4 ('Calypso') but Pound had received it 'some days' before 3 April 1918.[88] Joyce had the typescript of chapter 5 ('Lotus-Eaters') in hand by 9 April and intended to send it to Pound the next day; the text was published in the July 1918 number of the *Little Review*, thus it can be assumed that it was relayed from Joyce to Pound within a few days of 9 April, and then sent on to the *Little Review* in what had become a normal pattern.[89] Chapter 6 ('Hades') was being typed—again it is not clear by whom—on 18 May.[90] Joyce planned to check the typescript for corrections, and told Weaver that he anticipated sending it 'in a day or two'.[91] In the event he was unable to do so until late July 1918 owing to another significant period of illness with his eyes, which lasted approximately nine weeks.[92] It is not exactly clear what the problem was, but it may have been iritis in the other eye.[93] He anticipated sending chapter 7 ('Aeolus') soon after his recovery in late July, and

[82] J to Sykes, [? November 1917], *L* II, 108.

[83] Pound to J, 19 December 1917, *EP-JJ*, 128.

[84] J to Sykes, [? December 1917], *L* I, 109; J to Sykes, [? 16 December 1917], *L* II, 413.

[85] Pound to Margaret Anderson, 17 January 1918, *P-LR*, 174; Pound to Quinn of 22 February 1918 in *EP-JQ*, 144.

[86] J to Pound, 6 January 1918, Yale.

[87] J to Sykes, [late January? 1918], *L* II, 416; Pound to Margaret Anderson, 21 February 1918, *P-LR*, 189; J to Pound, 11 February 1918, reproduced in Philip R. Yanella, 'James Joyce to the *Little Review*', *Journal of Modern Literature*, 1:3 (1971), 393–8 (395).

[88] Pound to Quinn, 3 April 1918, in *EP-JQ*, 146.   [89] J to Pound, 9 April 1918, Yale.

[90] J to Weaver, 18 May 1918, *L* I, 113.   [91] J to Weaver, 18 May 1918, *L* I, 113.

[92] See J to Weaver, 29 July 1918 (*L* I, 115), in which J mentions sending 'Hades' to Pound 'with a copy for you a few days ago'.

[93] See Pound to Quinn, 5 July 1918: Joyce's 'wife writes that the iritis has got to his other eye. I suppose he is still laid up as the sixth instalment of Ulysses does not arrive', *EP-JQ*, 154. Joyce would later describe this period as one in which he 'lay dangerously ill and in danger of blindness' (*L* II, 425). In this instance he was not exaggerating: iritis was (and remains) a common cause of avoidable blindness.

had done so 'some days' before 25 August, describing it, somewhat confusingly, as the 'eighth episode'.[94] By 28 August he was at work on what would become chapter 8 ('Lestrygonians'), and told Weaver he had sent it to Pound on 25 October.[95] He had heard little from Pound for several weeks, and wrote to him on 1 November saying, with a little note of menace, that he hoped his work had appeared 'intact' in the *Little Review* (i.e. without alteration by Pound or anyone else); he also promised to send chapter 9 ('Scylla and Charybdis') 'shortly', a commitment he reiterated on 5 December ('Very soon I shall send you the *Scylla and Charybdis* episode (Hamlet) and immediately afterwards the *Wandering Rocks*').[96] In the event he did not finish writing chapter 9 until New Year's Eve 1918, a date he marked on the Rosenbach manuscript with the words 'End of First Part of "Ulysses" '. The typescript was sent to London, and read by Weaver before 25 February 1919.[97]

Looking back over 1918, Joyce must have realized that it was an important year for the composition of *Ulysses*: in a little more than a year he had completed 64,000 words, in nine of what he now knew would be eighteen chapters.[98] This was an impressive rate of production, particularly given the nine-week illness of May/June, and it suggests that Joyce found it relatively easy to finalize the earlier and more novelistic aspects of the book. He anticipated working on the second half of the book with similar *brio*, telling Pound, on 5 December 1918, that the serialization 'should run till the Autumn of next year' 'if regularly sent and printed'. To this rather significant 'if', he added the caveat:

> I cannot possibly deliver any faster than I am doing: I suppose you understand this already. If sometimes a month goes by without my contribution I cannot help it. I cannot send any episode till it is quite finished.[99]

This indicates Joyce's finely balanced attitude to serialization quite clearly. The commitment was motivating him to complete and deliver the work in sequence, chapter by chapter, as fast as he possibly could, but did not persuade him to compromise on quality, or to shape the design of the book specifically for its serial incarnation. If he needed more time, he would simply have to have it, and he expected Pound and others to understand that. Pound, meanwhile, was beginning to have misgivings about his editorial commitment to the *Little Review*. His funding, from Quinn, was due to run out in April 1919, and as he normally had about three months' material in hand, he was unsure what would happen to whatever further chapters of *Ulysses* Joyce had in mind. At the same time he told Joyce that

[94] J to Weaver, 29 July 1918, *L* I, 115; J to Weaver, 25 August 1918, *L* I, 118.
[95] J to Weaver, 26 October 1918, *L* I, 120; J to Pound, 28 August 1918, Yale. Pound had received it by 4 November; see Pound to John Quinn, 4 November 1918 in *EP-JQ*, 164.
[96] J to Pound, 1 November 1918, Yale; J to Pound, 5 December 1918, Yale.
[97] J to Weaver, 25 February 1919, *L* II, 436.
[98] Joyce specified the structure of eighteen chapters in a letter to Pound of 5 December 1918, Yale. He was responding to Pound's query as to whether *Ulysses* would have '24 Odyssean books' (Pound to J, 22 November 1918, *EP-JJ*, 146). He first projected *Ulysses* as a book of twenty-two chapters (J to Stanislaus Joyce, 16 June 1915, *SL* 209), then seventeen chapters (J to Weaver, 31 May 1918, *L* I, 114). For the calculation of word counts by chapter, see p. 139 and 144.
[99] J to Pound, 5 December 1918, Yale.

he hoped *Ulysses* would continue 'forever' and reassured him: 'If there are going to be chapters after April, I will try to bone a few quid more out of someone'.[100] For Joyce, this was reassurance enough. He obviously liked what he had seen of the *Little Review* and did not feel unduly perturbed by Pound's speculation that the *Little Review* 'may go bust'.[101]

Thus Joyce continued to draft the book, and his progress with the completion of chapters 10 to 14 may be summarized as follows. Chapter 10 ('Wandering Rocks') had been sent to Pound 'some days' before 25 February 1919.[102] Pound did not acknowledge receipt, and Joyce wrote trying to prompt some kind of response, observing that he had not seen copies of the *Little Review* 'for some months past'.[103] Chapter 11 ('Sirens') was finished and sent to Pound sometime between 30 May and 10 June 1919.[104] Pound was uncertain about this chapter, telling Joyce that it was 'too long', that he had had enough of Bloom and Joyce's obsessions with the 'arseore-ial' ('one can fahrt with less pomp and circumstance'); he also wondered whether the quality of the chapter was weak because Joyce felt 'bound to send in copy on time? Let the regularity of appearance be damned. If you want more time take it'.[105] With the exception of perhaps the last bit of this advice—to take more time—Joyce paid little heed to Pound's criticisms. He was at work on chapter 12 ('Cyclops') by 19 June and sent it to Pound 'a few days before' he and his family moved back from Zurich to Trieste on 16 October 1919.[106]

Joyce found it difficult to settle back in Trieste, and get started on *Ulysses* again. On 7 November he told his friend Frank Budgen, 'As for *Ulysses*—it is like me—on the rocks'.[107] As McCourt notes:

> Joyce left behind a cosmopolitan Austrian city; when he returned in 1919 he soon came to realize that the rich and varied elements which had provided him with an invaluable workshop for his writing no longer existed.[108]

During this second stay in Trieste, which was to last from October 1919 until his departure for Paris in early July 1920, Joyce and his family lived, somewhat uncomfortably, with his brother Stanislaus, and his sister Eileen, her husband, Frantisek Schaurek, and their two children.[109] He appears to have been still floundering with chapter 13 ('Nausicaa') during December 1919, when he told Budgen that he had yet to write 'a word of *Nausikaa* beyond notation of flappers' atrocities and general plan of the specially new fizzing style (Patent No. 7728. S.P. E.P. E.P. L.P)'.[110] He had started writing this chapter in earnest by 3 January 1920 and completed it 'at 4 am' on 27 January; the typed copy was sent to Pound a few days before

---

[100] Pound to J, 22 November 1918, *EP-JJ*, 146.

[101] Pound to J, 12 December 1918, *EP-JJ*, 147.

[102] J to Weaver, 25 February 1919, *L* II, 436.

[103] J to Pound, [February 1919], Yanella, 'James Joyce to the *Little Review*', 395.

[104] Pound to J, 30 May 1919 and 10 June 1919, *EP-JJ*, 156–9.

[105] Pound to J, 10 June 1919, *EP-JJ*, 158, 159.

[106] J to Weaver, 28 October 1919, *L* II, 455.   [107] J to Budgen, 7 November 1919, *L* I, 130.

[108] John McCourt, *The Years of Bloom: James Joyce in Trieste, 1904–1920* (Dublin: The Lilliput Press, 2000), 247–8.

[109] McCourt, *The Years of Bloom*, 249.   [110] J to Budgen, 3 January 1920, *SL*, 245.

13 February.[111] By then he was already at work on chapter 14 ('Oxen of the Sun'), which was finished and being typed by 12 May 1920.[112] The typed copy was read by Pound during his stay in Sirmione (Italy), where he and Joyce met for the first time on 8 June.[113] According to Joyce, Pound sent the typescript to the *Little Review* 'some weeks' before 22 June, and a few weeks before Joyce's arrival in Paris on 9 July 1920.[114] At this juncture neither Pound nor Joyce could foresee that chapter 14 ('Oxen') was the last chapter typescript which would be sent to the *Little Review*. Nor could they have anticipated the very significant ways in which *Ulysses* would begin to change shape once Joyce had arrived in Paris. Nor could they appreciate the neatness and significance of the fact that the serial *Ulysses* was completed in Zurich (in the case of chapters 1 to 12) and then in Trieste (in the case of chapters 13 and 14), and that the rest of the work would be completed in Paris (in the case of chapters 15 to 18, and then the overall revision of the whole).

Pound had originally asked Joyce to send the *Little Review* 'rough drafts' of '1000 to 2000 words'.[115] In response Joyce made plans to serialize the entire text, in consignments 'of about 6000 words'.[116] Within the surviving correspondence, there appears to be no discussion of the fact that Joyce was now writing chapters of significantly greater length than chapters 1 to 9. He was finding that these latter chapters took much longer to write. Some specific details help to underline this point. The serial versions of chapters 10 to 14 run to approximately 75,000 words in total; over the eighteen months in which they were being completed—January 1919 to June 1920—this equates to a writing speed of about 4,100 words a month.[117] The serial versions of chapters 1 to 9 run to approximately 64,000 words in total; over the fourteen months in which they were being completed—November 1917 to December 1918—this equates to a writing speed of about 4,500 words a month, obviously not that much faster than 4,100 words a month. What had slowed was not particularly the pace of writing, but the rate at which the longer individual chapters were being completed. If chapters 10 to 18 had mirrored the length of chapters 1 to 9, then Joyce could well have finished the novel early in 1920, or thereabouts. The delay in completion points to the fact that the scope of Joyce's ambitions for the book had changed, probably at some point during the first half of 1919. His sense of the timetable makes this clear. In February 1919 he was still clinging to the hope that *Ulysses* might be finished 'this year or early next year'.[118] But by August—when he was at work on chapter 12 ('Cyclops')—he had significantly readjusted his plans, telling Quinn that as each chapter takes 'about four or five months to write', '*Ulysses* will not be finished till the end of next year—if even then'.[119]

[111] J to Budgen, 3 January 1920, *SL*, 245; J to Pound, 27 January 1920, Yale; J to Pound, 13 February 1920, Yale.

[112] J to Weaver, 12 May 1920, *L* II, 464.   [113] Telegram J to Pound, 8 June 1920, Yale.

[114] J to Margaret Anderson, 22 June 1920, in Yanella, 'James Joyce to the *Little Review*', 397; *L* III, 8. See appendix 1 ('The Genesis of *Ulysses* in Typescript') for a summary of the information presented here.

[115] Pound to J, 9 February 1917, *EP-JJ*, 92.   [116] J to Pound, 20 August 1917, *SL*, 227.

[117] See p. 139 for word counts of the serial versions of chapters 1 to 14.

[118] J to Weaver, 25 February 1919, *L* II, 437.

[119] J to John Quinn, 3 August 1919, *L* II, 447.

There is a clear correlation between Joyce's decision to write a *Ulysses* of much greater scope, and the significant shift in his financial position which came about between February and August 1919. On 14 May 1919, Joyce had learnt that he was to receive an anonymous investment of £5,000, which would generate a regular income in his name, regardless of his productivity.[120] This gift, which appeared to bring financial security, lessened the need for Joyce's commitment to serialization because it reduced financial and time pressures, two factors which have a profound shaping and psychological effect on the process of writing. He no longer needed to keep on scrambling to find small sums of cash because he had an income, and the gift of that income had the effect of assuring him that he could write the book exactly as he wished. Indeed Weaver, who did not reveal her identity as the donor of the £5,000 until 6 July 1919—and only then in the face of considerable embarrassment and awkwardness—told Joyce that she most admired his 'searching piercing spirit' and his 'intense instants of imagination' and believed he should be given 'as free scope as is possible in the circumstances'.[121]

John Quinn also decided to offer Joyce financial support around this time. Like Weaver—whose other donations included the four quarterly instalments of £50 from 1 May 1917, £50 for the serial rights to *Portrait*, and £50 for the serial rights to *Ulysses*—Quinn had already given Joyce financial support.[122] Now—on 26 June 1919, when Joyce had written just ten of the eighteen chapters—Quinn wrote and offered to buy the manuscript of *Ulysses* even if unfinished, in which case he would buy it in parts, and pay Joyce drafts 'on account'.[123] In the same letter Quinn mentions that he has written a brief to the solicitor of the New York Post Office Department, which had refused to allow the mailing of the May 1919 number of the *Little Review* on account of 'certain things' in the second instalment of chapter 9 ('Scylla and Charybdis').[124] Of course Weaver, like Quinn, was also actively involved in the struggle to have *Ulysses* accepted. She regularly updated Joyce on the difficulties she was having with English printers; by May 1919—the moment at which Joyce had completed and sent off the first ten chapters of the novel, and at which point she decided to give him £5,000—she had only succeeded in publishing chapters 2 and 3 in *The Egoist*.[125] Quinn and Weaver belonged in vastly different cultural worlds: he was a slightly brash self-made corporate lawyer from a

---

[120] Firth (ed.), 'Harriet Weaver's Letters to James Joyce', 182, n7. Joyce was away in Locarno when the letter from Weaver's solicitors arrived, and received the news by telegram from Nora.

[121] Weaver to J, 6 July 1919 in Firth (ed.), 'Harriet Weaver's Letters to James Joyce', 182.

[122] Slack, Monro, Saw and Co. to J, 22 February 1917, *L* II, 389; Weaver to J, 14 and 28 January 1916; and 6 September 1917 in Firth (ed.), 'Harriet Weaver's Letters to James Joyce', 156 and 177. Monies given by Quinn to Joyce included a 'stake' of £10 in August 1916 sent 'because I am interested in your work'; £20 for the *Egoist* sheets from which Huebsch had set *Portrait*, corrected in Joyce's hand; and £25 for the manuscript of *Exiles* in August 1917. Information from *JQ-JJ* I, 218, 222, 231.

[123] Quinn to J, 26 June 1919, *JQ-JJ* I, 237.   [124] Quinn to J, 26 June 1919, *JQ-JJ* I, 236.

[125] Chapters 2 and 3 appeared in *The Egoist* of Jan.–Feb. (1919) and March–April (1919) respectively. Weaver had arranged the publication of chapter 1 in *The Egoist* of March 1918; she told Joyce that the chapter was 'in type but at the last moment before going to press for the March number they refused to print it—even with deletions. I am trying to find another firm but it will be difficult I know'. Weaver to J, 8 March 1918, Firth (ed.), 'Harriet Weaver's Letters to James Joyce', 179. For issues of *The Egoist* see http://dl.lib.brown.edu/mjp.

modest Irish-American background whereas she was British, and demure, a self-effacing editor and political activist, of considerable independent means. Yet there is a connection in their actions: both were keen supporters of the cause that publishing *Ulysses* had come to represent, and both were prepared to offer Joyce significant financial support. That Joyce was receiving such significant sums of money from individuals who were actively involved in the struggle to publish *Ulysses* must have been a considerable source of consolation and comfort. That Quinn was a lawyer who was prepared to defend the text (for no fee) must also have been particularly encouraging. The money, combined with such editorial and legal support, renewed Joyce's energy and determination to write, indeed to write at length, paying little heed to readers (such as Pound) who found the styles of the latter chapters a bit trying, and the persistent candour about the body and sexuality a bit excessive.

Continued and Post-Serial Drafting

When legal action against the *Little Review* began to unfold in New York in September 1920, Anderson and Heap had in hand the typescript of chapter 14 ('Oxen of the Sun'), which ran to over 19,000 words. Much against Quinn's will, the editors decided to publish the opening section of this chapter—approximately 4,900 words—in the next number of the *Little Review* which they could get to press, that which is dated 'September–December 1920', and which appeared late in November 1920.[126] There was no hurry on Joyce producing chapter 15 ('Circe') because the typescript in hand could have furnished material for another two or three numbers, had Anderson and Heap been able to raise the necessary printing costs (a position which was in doubt). On 10 November Joyce told Weaver that we was 'writing out the final (the sixth or seventh) draft' of chapter 15 which he noted was 'twice as long as the longest episode hitherto, *The Cyclops*'.[127] A month later he was at work on what he described as the '8th draft', and he declared the chapter 'finished' 'at last', and ready for typing, just before Christmas 1920.[128] In its final form, after it had been expanded in proof, and published by Beach as part of the completed novel, chapter 15 runs to just over 38,000 words, or approximately 16.5 per cent of the whole novel (which is more than 266,000 words in total). The fact that the chapter had spiralled to such a significant length is an obvious factor in the time it took for its completion. The unfolding legal action in New York may also have influenced Joyce's progress. He first heard of the proceedings against the *Little Review* on 4 November 1920, when he received a letter from Scofield Thayer, editor

---

[126] 'I hear that after a lapse of several months the *Little Review* came out on 25 November with all the *Oxen of the Sun* episode and an account of the preliminary trial' (J to Weaver, 9 December 1920, *L* I, 150). J's informant was probably Rodker. The legal proceedings were discussed in Heap's 'Art and the Law', and Anderson's 'An Obvious Statement' (*LR*, September–December 1920, 5–16).

[127] J to Weaver, 10 November 1920, *L* I, 149.

[128] J to Rodker, [9 December 1920], *L* III, 32; J to Pound, [? 22 December 1920], [Christmas card], Lilly Library, Indiana University.

of *The Dial*.[129] Within the next few days—before 10 November 1920—he received copies of Quinn's letters to Pound, of 16 and 21 October 1920.[130] By then, as noted, the work on the chapter was already well advanced. It is nonetheless possible to argue, as Weir has demonstrated, that Joyce incorporated a creative response to news of the legal action within the text of chapter 15, particularly after he received further documentation and letters about the trial from Quinn in late June/early July 1921.[131] The 'Messianic Scene' (*U*1922, 453–70)—which was written by Joyce in the summer of 1921, well after the original completion of the chapter—includes references to a 'Reformed Priests' Protection Society' (a possible echo of the Society for the Suppression of Vice) and a 'wealthy American' who 'makes a street collection for Bloom' (a possible representation of Quinn).[132]

The preparation of the typescript of chapter 15 ('Circe') would prove to be a lengthy and difficult process. With the deterioration of his sight, Joyce's hand had become increasingly difficult to read; by his account, four typists looked at the manuscript and 'refused to bother with it'.[133] A fifth was found but her time was limited; she could only find 'an hour or two free in the day to work at it'; thus in early February 1921 Joyce did not envisage the work being completed 'for some weeks more'.[134] By mid-February this typist had produced eighty pages, of a projected 160, when she stopped work because her father had had a heart attack.[135] Joyce spent 'a week or so looking for another typist' and turned to 'the proprietress of a small bookshop' who 'says she will finish it'.[136] At this juncture, towards the end of February 1921, Joyce was not aware of the outcome of the trial against the *Little Review*, and Beach, the willing typist and bookshop proprietress of Joyce's description, had not yet foreseen the possibility of Shakespeare and Company publishing *Ulysses*. No doubt the process of becoming acquainted with the evolving text—at the level of manuscript—was exciting for Beach, who had become a supporter of Joyce from the moment of their meeting in the summer of 1920.

Given the difficulty of reading the manuscript, Beach and 'two or three amanuenses took turns in first preparing a longhand transcription from the autograph'.[137] The text was then typed by a Mrs Harrison, wife of an employee at the British Embassy. On 8 April, or thereabouts, Mr Harrison read some of the manuscript, a portion in Beach's hand, and was so incensed by the content that, according to

---

[129] J to Pound, 5 November 1920, *L* III, 27.

[130] J to Weaver, 10 November 1920, *L* I, 149.

[131] David Weir in 'What Did He Know, and When Did He Know It: *The Little Review*, Joyce, and *Ulysses*', *James Joyce Quarterly*, 37 (Spring/Summer 2000), 389–412. In addition to the letters from Quinn to Pound of 16 and 21 October 1920, Quinn sent Joyce a nine-page typed letter with an account of the trial on 13 April 1921 (*JQ-JJ II*, 32–6); this letter enclosed the letter Quinn had written to Anderson (5 February 1921); a copy of the motion papers for the transfer of the case; a copy of the opinion of the judge denying the motion to transfer the case; and several newspaper reports of the trial. As Weir notes, in all Quinn sent Joyce something like a hundred pages of letters and documents about the trial.

[132] For a fuller version of this argument, see Weir, 'What Did He Know, and When Did He Know It', 401f. Hassett pursues a similar argument in *The Ulysses Trials* (especially 111).

[133] J to Svevo, 5 January 1921, *L* I, 154.   [134] J to Weaver, 4 February 1921, *L* I, 156.

[135] Date from J to Hummel, 14 February 1921, *L* III, 38; length of typescript from *CSE*III 1884; information about typist's father from J to Sykes, [early 1921], *L* I, 158.

[136] J to Sykes, [n.d., early 1921], *L* I, 158.   [137] *CSE*III 1884.

Joyce, he 'tore it up and burnt it'.[138] Joyce had sent a manuscript copy of the chapter to Quinn; he was now faced with the slightly ludicrous situation of having to ask Quinn to 'lend' copies of the missing pages so that an additional copy could be made.[139] Quinn, however, was wary of sending a portion of the manuscript back and arranged for enlarged photographic copies of ten pages to be sent on 18 May.[140] The typing in and around Shakespeare and Company continued, and the typescript became a 'medley of papers and types' with even Joyce thinking it 'very difficult to follow'.[141] A preliminary version was in hand by 17 April 1921 though it was missing the portion 'burned by Harrison', as Joyce explained to Weaver.[142] A more final typescript—incorporating revisions, additions, and the significant additional portion known as the Messianic scene—was in hand by September 1921.[143]

Joyce anticipated that completing the close of the book would be considerably easier than the completion of chapter 15. Shortly after his arrival in Paris, he reiterated his claim that parts of the final three chapters already existed in draft, telling Weaver that 'A great part of the Nostos or close was written several years ago'.[144] On 5 January 1921, just two weeks after chapter 15 was first considered complete, Joyce told Italo Svevo, his friend in Trieste, that chapter 16 ('Eumeus') was 'almost complete' and he envisaged it being ready 'around the end of the month'.[145] The chapter was certainly complete and with a typist by 18 February.[146] As he was working on this text, Joyce was also thinking ahead and planning the remaining work. He needed notes to be sent from Trieste, and asked Svevo to go and retrieve 'an oilcloth brief-case fastened with a rubber band' from his former flat in Trieste.[147] He had received these materials around the middle of March, by which time he was working on chapters 17 and 18 ('Ithaca' and 'Penelope') simultaneously.[148] In November 1920, Joyce told Quinn that he envisaged them being 'short in comparison with the *Circe* episode'; in the event these two chapters became much longer than originally planned, 113 pages, or almost one sixth of the printed book, as Gabler notes.[149] He worked on both texts more or less concurrently until early August 1921, though the evidence of the letters suggests that the composition of chapter 17 ('Ithaca') was the more difficult and time-consuming task. Chapter 18 ('Penelope') was complete by late September 1921.[150] He announced the completion of chapter 17 ('Ithaca'), and thus the completion of the novel, on 29 October 1921.[151]

[138] J to Quinn, 19 April 1921, *L* III, 41; J to Weaver, 9 April 1921, *L* III, 40.
[139] Quinn to J, 5 June 1921, *JQ-JJ II*, 39; J to John Quinn, 19 April 1921, *L* III, 41.
[140] Quinn to J, 5 June 1921, *JQ-JJ II*, 39.   [141] J to Weaver, 17 April 1921, *L* I, 163.
[142] J to Weaver, 17 April 1921, *L* I, 163.
[143] *CSE*III 1885. For a much more detailed account of the compositional genesis of 'Circe', see Ronan Crowley, 'Fusing the Elements of "Circe": From Compositional to Textual Repetition', *James Joyce Quarterly*, 47:3 (Spring 2010), 341–61. As Crowley notes, in terms of manuscript materials, 'Circe' is the most extensively documented of *Ulysses*' eighteen chapters.
[144] J to Weaver, 12 July 1920, *L* I, 143.   [145] J to Italo Svevo, 5 January 1921, *L* I, 154.
[146] J to Linati, 18 February 1921, *L* III, 38, 39.
[147] J to Italo Svevo, 5 January 1921, *L* I, 154.   [148] J to Weaver, 3 April 1921, *L* I, 161.
[149] *CSE*III 1886.   [150] *CSE*III 1887.
[151] Unpublished letter from JJ to Ezra Pound, 29 October 1921, Lilly Library, Indiana University.

But by the time Joyce arrived at this moment—clearly a moment of relief, and of great symbolic significance—he was working on the text in other ways, in what might be described as a composite manner. Darantiere, the printer of the Shakespeare and Company edition, had started to produce proofs for Joyce's approval and correction on 11 June.[152] While continuing to draft the two final chapters, Joyce also now began to correct, revise, and make significant additions to the proofs. Therefore, and in a number of respects, the drafting continued into the proof stage, and was spurred on by the plans for publication in Paris, plans which were unusually generous in allowing Joyce to continue working on finalizing the text well beyond the point at which, conventionally, it might have been considered finished.

Plans for Publication in Volume Form

Established in Paris in November 1919, Shakespeare and Company, Sylvia Beach's English language bookshop and lending library, had become a beacon for American writers and literati fleeing from the atmosphere of intense cultural conservatism in the US of that time. Beach (1887–1962) was the daughter of a Presbyterian minister from Baltimore, and a literary enthusiast and reader of the prominent 'little magazines' of the era, such as *The Egoist* and the *Little Review*. She knew who Joyce was when she found her 'tough little paw' in his 'limp boneless hand' at a party in the summer of 1920.[153] Within days Joyce had become a regular visitor to Shakespeare and Company. In the period between the summer of 1920 and early April 1921, Beach thus found herself gradually learning about the difficulties facing the ongoing serialization of *Ulysses* in the *Little Review*, and the difficulties Joyce was facing in the ongoing composition of the text. It is not clear whether it was Joyce who suggested that Beach publish *Ulysses* or she who offered; as Edward Bishop has established, the surviving drafts of her memoir reveal her 'sculpting the event for posterity'.[154] But it is clear from Beach's correspondence that she had an eye to reputation when the opportunity to publish *Ulysses* came about. Her letters of the time describe the yet-to-be-finished *Ulysses* as a 'masterpiece', which will 'make my place famous. Already the publicity is beginning and swarms of people visit the shop on hearing the news'.[155]

It is also significant that Beach was inspired to publish *Ulysses* because of the difficulties Joyce had faced in the attempt to produce the text elsewhere. As noted earlier, the prospectus offered to potential purchasers of the first edition pointed out that *Ulysses* was 'suppressed four times during serial publication' and promised

---

[152] Dates of proofing (from date-stamps on the originals) are listed in *CSE* III 1913.

[153] Beach, *Shakespeare and Company*, 35. Ellmann dates the meeting to 11 July 1920 (*L* III, 12n). For more information on Beach and Shakespeare and Company, see 'Mapping Expatriate Paris', http://mep.princeton.edu.

[154] Edward L. Bishop, 'The "Garbled History" of the First-Edition *Ulysses*', *Joyce Studies Annual*, 9 (1998), 3–36 (12).

[155] SB to Holly Beach, 23 April 1921 and SB to Marion Peter, 23 May 1921 in Keri Walsh (ed.), *The Letters of Sylvia Beach* (New York: Columbia University Press, 2010), 85, 87.

the text 'complete as written'.[156] In instructing Darantiere, Beach later recalled that she told him:

> to supply Joyce with all the proofs he wanted, and he was insatiable. Every proof was covered with additional text…M. Darantiere warned me that I was going to have a lot of extra expense with these proofs. He suggested that I call Joyce's attention to the danger of going beyond my depth; perhaps his appetite for proofs might be curbed. But no, I wouldn't hear of such a thing. *Ulysses* was to be as Joyce wished, in every respect.[157]

This generosity came at a significant material cost. The day-to-day running of Shakespeare and Company was still dependent on contributions from Beach's sister, Holly, and other members of the family. As *Ulysses* lurched towards publication, Beach found herself especially stretched, and faced with significant printing bills, such as that mentioned in a letter to Holly of 22 September 1921:

> I…have to put every single centime aside to pay the printer of *Ulysses* five thousand francs on the 1st of December. He requires it and naturally the cheques from subscribers will not arrive in time for that first payment.[158]

Beach also found herself having to deal with difficult people, such as Pound, who would later disparage her as one of Joyce's 'flunkies' ('bone ignorant and lacking in tact'), Quinn, who could also be astonishingly misogynistic ('I was made to feel that I was very much to blame for being "another woman" as he called me'), and Joyce himself, who made frequent requests for money, and, in her words, 'had an all-invading way with him'.[159]

In the flurry of excitement which followed Beach's decision to publish *Ulysses* ('it's going to make us famous rah rah!'), Beach had little sense of the nexus of relationships, hostilities, and confused motivations which existed between the individuals who had already played highly significant roles in helping Joyce to realize *Ulysses*.[160] On 10 April 1921 Joyce had told Weaver, somewhat decisively, that Beach's projected Paris edition would 'replace the American one'; in respect of Weaver's projected 'English edition' he suggested, more coyly, that 'it would be to your advantage if that were amalgamated with the Paris one' (*L* I 162). Weaver recognized that plans for publication in the US had been displaced by the outcome of the trial of the *Little Review* editors, but she remained committed to her ordinary English edition, and appears to have advertised to it, as an unpublished letter from Beach to Jane Heap explains:

> Miss Harriet Weaver very foolishly sent out circulars a few months ago announcing an English edition of *Ulysses* at 10/6 'in preparation' which of course affected the Paris edition and held up the subscriptions for a time until she sent out other circulars

[156] For the prospectus advertising the first edition, see Katherine McSharry (ed.), *A Joycean Scrapbook from the National Library of Ireland* (Dublin: Wordwell, 2004), 102.
[157] Beach, *Shakespeare and Company*, 60.
[158] SB to Holly Beach, 22 September 1921, in Walsh (ed.), *The Letters of Sylvia Beach*, 88.
[159] Ezra Pound to John Quinn, 4/5 July 1922 and 21 February 1922 in *EP-JQ*, 212, 205; Beach, *Shakespeare and Company*, 62; Bishop, 'The "Garbled History"', 6. Though she was immensely loyal and dedicated to Joyce, relations became sour, at least intermittently. See esp. her 'unsent' letter to J of 12 April 1927 in Walsh (ed.), *The Letters of Sylvia Beach*, 319–20.
[160] SB to her mother, Eleanor Orbison Beach, 1 April 1921, cited in Lawrence Rainey, 'Consuming Investments: Joyce's *Ulysses*', *James Joyce Quarterly*, 33:4 (Summer 1996), 531–67 (538).

stating that the English edition would not be published until the Paris was completely subscribed. But the whole thing gave a completely false impression as in the first place it will be quite impossible to bring out *Ulysses* in England for many years to come, if ever, which Miss Weaver knows quite well as does Joyce. And in the second place Miss Weaver pledged herself to do everything in her power to obtain the thousand subscriptions to the Paris edition and certainly the announcement of a (fictitious) *Ulysses* edition at 10/6 was not calculated to assist subscriptions.

Pardon me for telling you all this but I hope you will correct the error created by Miss Weaver's circular by informing people who are interested in *Ulysses* that no English edition exists nor is likely to exist.[161]

For the moment, Beach's assertions here were true: Weaver's plans for an 'English' edition did not materialize until October 1922, six months after the publication of Beach's iconic first edition, when 2,000 copies were published under the imprint 'Published for the Egoist Press, London, by John Rodker, Paris'. Given that the sheets for this edition were supplied by Darantiere, and that the paper was French, it might be reasonable to question how 'English' the edition actually was. But the unusually worded imprint is of both symbolic and legal significance. It communicates the endorsement of the London *Egoist*, a point of evident importance for Weaver, who had first begun to make plans for the publication of *Ulysses* in March 1918; it also cleverly evades the risk of prosecution, by specifying Paris as the place of publication, and Rodker—sometime contributor to *The Egoist* and the *Little Review*—as the publisher.[162]

It is very tempting to take the view that *Ulysses*, and chapter 15 in particular, expanded so significantly because Joyce was so uncertain—especially in the autumn of 1920—about the prospects of the work being published in volume form. But planning the publication of the work was clearly psychologically necessary to Joyce. He had begun to plan volume publication in March 1918—when he ceded British rights to Weaver, telling her, in an aside, that 'it is in more senses than one a Greek gift' (*L* I, 112). He continued to make plans even as the dual serialization ran into significant legal and logistic complications. His plans for volume publication in the US began to take shape in July 1919, when he was at work on chapter 12 ('Cyclops'). He had received a letter from Huebsch, who planned to visit London, and wanted to call on Weaver 'with regard to an eventual publication of the book' (*L* I, 127); Joyce was clearly impressed by Huebsch, telling Weaver that Huebsch had 'given me proof of a very friendly and energetic disposition' (*L* I, 126). As noted earlier, it is not clear that Joyce understood that his work needed to be printed and published in the US in order to secure copyright under the terms of the International

[161] SB to Jane Heap, 20 September 1921, *Little Review* records, UWM. The letter, handwritten by Beach, is incomplete. To date I have not located any copies of Weaver's 'circular' in the archives, including the extensive Weaver archive in the British Library.

[162] For Weaver's early attempts to find a British printer for *Ulysses*, see p. 6. Rodker's precise involvement in this *Egoist* edition is hard to pin down. There is some information in Jane Lidderdale and Mary Nicholson, *Dear Miss Weaver: Harriet Shaw Weaver, 1876–1961* (New York: The Viking Press, 1970), 173, 204, and a little more in Birmingham, *The Most Dangerous Book* (245–7). For Rodker's cultural and publishing commitments more generally see Gerald W. Cloud, *John Rodker's Ovid Press: A Bibliographical History* (New Castle, DE: Oak Knoll Press, 2010).

Copyright Act of 1891 (the so-called 'Chace' Act). He was shocked when he met Huebsch in Paris, sometime during October 1920, and Huebsch hinted that 'if a European edition of the book were printed in Paris he could pirate it in New York'.[163] Joyce had developed misgivings about Huebsch and Huebsch's commitment to the publication of *Ulysses* during August 1920.[164] In a letter of gloating self-importance to Stanislaus, he mentions that: 'Huebsch is crying off Ulysses. Miss Weaver writes nobody will print it. So it will be printed, it seems, in Paris and bear Mr John Rodker's imprint as English printer'.[165] This suggests that Joyce was very keen to find a solution to the problem of publishing *Ulysses*, and had spotted the potential for a Paris edition. Rodker knew of *Ulysses* and Joyce through his association with the *Little Review* and was based in Paris for a while.

Meanwhile, Quinn, who was more aware of the legal necessity of publishing in the US, was trying to persuade Huebsch that the way forward was to publish a private edition of the text, priced at $8 or $10 a copy, and 'on better paper and in a better format than he could use with the trade edition'. Huebsch was based in New York, and Quinn told Joyce he had spontaneously called to see him in person, 'on my way from the dentist', and explained 'the practical certainty that if *Ulysses* were published without any alteration of the text, it would be suppressed, involving his arrest and trial'. A private edition was a neat way of side-stepping those complications while a trade edition, Quinn continued, 'is likely to be':

(a) Seized by the New York authorities and the plates and copies confiscated and the publisher indicted and prosecuted.

(b) It is more likely to be prosecuted under the U.S. law, which is even more drastic than the State law, for an indictment in the Federal Courts means almost certain conviction, and conviction there does not mean a suspended sentence, but a heavy fine and jail sentence.

(c) It would be excluded from the mails and express companies, for the statute expressly forbids the sending of prohibited books through the mails.[166]

Quinn paid his unplanned visit to Huebsch 'a couple of months' before the date of this letter, 15 August 1920, and thus before a visit that Huebsch made to London,

---

[163] J to Weaver, 10 November 1920. British Library, add. ms. 57346. The excerpts quoted are not included in *L* I, 149. Huebsch was pointing to the fact that in order to secure copyright in the US, a French publisher would have had to claim *ad interim* copyright protection by applying to the US Copyright Office within eight weeks of the publication in France; and would then have to arrange for the work to be reprinted in the US within four months. Otherwise the work passed into the American public domain. See Spoo, *Without Copyrights: Piracy, Publishing and the Public Domain*, esp. 161–2. J had certainly been given a chance to understand the significance of the manufacturing clause. A letter from Pound to Nora of 10 September 1917 indicates the rationale for dual serialization quite clearly ('The *Little Review* is ready to hold down the American copyright for him, and print to synchronize with the *Egoist*'), *EP-JJ*, 126.

[164] J to Weaver, 16 August 1920, *L* III, 15.

[165] J to Stanislaus Joyce, [29 August 1920], *L* III, 17. At this stage the plan was that Rodker would print and publish the text under the imprint of his own Ovid Press. Pound mentioned the plan to Quinn: 'It will mean a huge job for Rodker if he has to hand print the whole novel, and make it very costly, but at any rate one doesn't face a complete smotheration'. Pound to Quinn, 6 July 1919, *EP-JQ*, 177.

[166] Quinn to J, 15 August 1920, *JQ-JJ I I*, 247, 248.

later that summer, when he called on Weaver and 'seemed very reluctant to have anything to do with *Ulysses*'.[167]

Quinn's *impromptu* visit with Huebsch in June 1920 appears to have been less than helpful. At that moment, the legal case against the *Little Review* had yet to develop. The instalment of chapter 13 ('Nausicaa') which was to cause so much difficulty had yet to be published. Chapter 15 ('Circe') was only just being written, and the completion of chapter 18 ('Penelope')—arguably the most obscene episode of all—was more than a year off. By anticipating and talking about potential complications which Huebsch might face, Quinn was scare-mongering. Clearly this was not helpful to Joyce.

The signs were hardly auspicious, but until the early days of April 1921 both Joyce and Quinn persisted in believing that Huebsch could ultimately be persuaded to publish a private edition of *Ulysses* in the US. That plan, however tentative and impractical, was a crucial factor in the ongoing compositional genesis of the text until 5 April 1921, when Huebsch pointed to the fact that 'A New York court' had 'held that the publication of a part of this in the *Little Review* was a violation of the law'; Huebsch thus told Quinn that he was 'unwilling to publish the book unless some changes are made'.[168] On learning this, Joyce took himself to Shakespeare and Company, where Beach and others were already faithfully copying and typing 'Circe'. That commitment and the flurry of activity it generated had helped to secure Beach's interest in the evolving work and its reception in the US. In that context, he found it easy, to use his own phrase, to arrange 'for a Paris publication to replace the American one' (*L* I, 162).

ULYSSES ON TRIAL: THE MOMENT OF FEBRUARY 1921

Who and what was on trial when the unlikely and unhappy trio of Anderson, Heap, and Quinn arrived at Jefferson Market Courthouse in New York's Greenwich Village on 14 February 1921, for a case to be heard in a Court of Special Sessions before three judges? Was it the specific content of the third instalment of 'Nausicaa', as published in the July–August 1920 issue of the *Little Review*? Or was it the editors of the *Little Review*? Was it Gerty McDowell in her 'nainsook knickers'? Or Leopold Bloom (whose 'careful hand recomposed his shirt')?[169] What are the precise circumstances that led to this trial, and what implications did the judgment have for the *Little Review*, for its editors, and for the future authorship, copyright, and publication of *Ulysses*? Given the extensive range of archival, legal, and textual details which might be brought to bear in answering these questions, as well as several existing

---

[167] J to Pound, 28 September 1920, Yale.
[168] Huebsch to Quinn, cited in Herbert Gorman, *James Joyce* (London: John Lane, 1941), 280.
[169] *LR*, July–August 1920, 43, 46.

analyses which argue for very particular conclusions, it is important, in the first instance, to establish the precise facts, including the facts which led to the trial.[170]

The *Little Review* was being published in an atmosphere of intense cultural conservatism and scrutiny, as argued in Chapter 1.[171] The suppression which occurred in advance of the serialization of *Ulysses*—that of October 1917, of the number containing Wyndham Lewis's 'Cantelman's Spring-Mate'—suggests that it was relatively easy for Post Office officials to declare publications to be non-mailable. Lewis's story is hardly explicit, but even in response to Quinn's appeal the Solicitor for the Post Office had deemed the text to be 'salacious', a decision which reveals that there were probably members of the New York Society for the Suppression of Vice zealously working behind the scenes. The decision also points to the significant cultural power of the social purity movement, and sets the scene for the suppressions of the *Little Review*, in which instalments of *Ulysses* were withheld from postal circulation.[172]

'Suppressed Four Times During Serial Publication'

In all, and for reasons which remain unclear, the New York Post Office appears to have refused to mail:

(1) some copies of the number for January 1919, containing the first instalment of chapter 8 ('Lestrygonians');

(2) the number for May 1919, containing the second instalment of chapter 9 ('Scylla and Charybdis');

(3) the number for January 1920, containing the third of four instalments of chapter 12 ('Cyclops');

(4) some copies of the number for July–August 1920, containing the third and final instalment of episode 13 ('Nausicaa').[173]

---

[170] For accounts of the trial see Anderson, *Thirty Years' War*, 218–26; Birmingham, *The Most Dangerous Book*, 191–8; Jackson R. Bryer, ' "A Trial Track for Racers": Margaret Anderson and the *Little Review*' (University of Wisconsin: PhD, 1965), 384–402; Richard Ellmann, *James Joyce* (1959; Oxford: Oxford University Press, rev edn, 1982), 502–4; Stephen Gillers, 'A Tendency to Deprave and Corrupt: The Transformation of American Obscenity Law from *Hicklin* to *Ulysses II*', *Washington University Law Review*, 85:2 (2007), 215–96; Joseph M. Hassett, *The Ulysses Trials: Beauty and Truth Meet the Law* (Dublin: The Lilliput Press, 2016); B. L. Reid, *The Man from New York: John Quinn and His Friends* (New York: Oxford University Press, 1968), 443–57; Bonnie Kime Scott, ' "The Young Girl," Jane Heap, and Trials of Gender in *Ulysses*', in *Joycean Cultures/Culturing Joyces*, edited by Vincent Cheng, Kimberly J. Devlin, and Margot Norris (Newark, DE: University of Delaware Press, 1998), 78–95; Weir, 'What Did He Know, and When Did He Know It', *passim*. See also *Without Copyrights: Piracy, Publishing and the Public Domain* (New York: Oxford University Press, 2013) where Robert Spoo discusses the copyright status of *Ulysses* as it appeared in the *Little Review*, as well as the trial, 156–60.

[171] See p. 38–42.

[172] For the social purity movement and its significance for Joyce fictions more generally see Katherine Mullin, *James Joyce, Sexuality and Social Purity* (Cambridge: Cambridge University Press, 2003). For more general argument about Modernism, obscenity, and censorship see Celia Marshik, *British Modernism and Censorship* (Cambridge: Cambridge University Press, 2006) and Allison Pease, *Modernism, Mass Culture, and the Aesthetics of Obscenity* (Cambridge: Cambridge University Press, 2000).

[173] Bryer, ' "A Trial Track for Racers" ', 384.

These suppressions—part of the well-worn history of *Ulysses* first touted by Beach in her advertising prospectus ('suppressed four times during serial publication')—need to be considered here in detail. This is necessary for the sake of offering a fresh and original perspective, and important because existing accounts often simply repeat assertions without checking archival facts or considering their implications in detail (a particular problem with the most recent work on this topic, Birmingham's *The Most Dangerous Book: The Battle for James Joyce's Ulysses*).[174] In particular, it is worth focusing on why the work was 'suppressed' on each of these occasions, and whether the evidence of the suppression is reliable and trustworthy. The suppressions must also be understood and located as a prehistory to the trial itself, which evolved over several months, and in a number of different hearings (all of which need explication and interpretation). In short, the *Little Review Ulysses* trial of February 1921 cannot be interpreted without a careful and chronologically organized account of the relevant legal facts and archival sources. Some of these will, of course, already be known to Joyce scholars. Nonetheless, there are multiple missing connections in existing versions of the story. These are filled in here. Using resources from the *Little Review* records at the University of Wisconsin (Milwaukee), papers at the Southern Illinois University in Carbondale, and the Quinn Collection at the New York Public Library, the account also pays particular attention to the pivotal role John Quinn played behind the scenes, a role which has not, hitherto, been fully contextualized.

Suppression 1: January 1919

In a scenario which contrasts vividly with the response to the 'Cantelman' case, the surviving correspondence between Pound, Quinn, and the editors of the *Little Review* makes no reference to the suppression of the number for January 1919, and nor do any of the subsequent issues of the *Little Review*. The one exception to this—indeed the only evidence that the issue was 'suppressed' as such—is a footnote by Anderson in the next issue to be declared 'non-mailable', that of May 1919, which quietly informs readers:

> The Post Office authorities objected to certain passages in the January installment of 'Ulysses' which prevents us mailing any more copies of that issue. To avoid a similar interference this month I have ruined Mr. Joyce's story by cutting certain passages in which he mentions natural facts known to everyone.[175]

This suggests that the Post Office allowed the bulk mailing of the January 1919 issue to proceed, and that some local employee succeeded in stopping the later mailing of additional individual copies, such as those requested by new subscribers. During the course of the 'Cantelman' case, Anderson and Heap had had several furious encounters with local Post Office employees, whom Quinn supposed to be

---

[174] See, for example, Birmingham, *The Most Dangerous Book* on (1) Pound's editorial interventions in respect of 'Calypso' and (2) the *Little Review* suppressions of January 1919 and May 1919, all dealt with, too briskly, at pages 122–5.
[175] *LR*, May 1919, 21n.

'underlings' and 'busybodies'.[176] It seems likely that this particular instance of 'suppression' was brought about by some such individual, acting locally, but with the law more or less on side. It is interesting that Anderson and Heap did not make more of a fuss. The fact that they did not do so may suggest that the individual concerned may have been able to point decisively to some textual detail which could be deemed indecent or immoral, and that the editors took the view that it was not worth a fight for only a few issues.[177] Anderson and Heap would also probably have found it difficult, if not impossible, to enlist the support of Quinn for another battle with the Post Office at this juncture. Quinn had given them a loan of $200 in December 1918, but told Pound that he was so angry at the way they were behaving that he had resolved not to help them further.[178]

Readers of the January 1919 issue of the *Little Review* must have found the opening paragraphs of chapter 8 confusing and difficult to understand:

> Pineapple rock, lemon platt, butter-scotch. A sugarsticky girl shoveling scoopfuls of creams for a christian brother. Some school treat. Bad for their tummies. Lozenge and comfit manufacturer to His Majesty the King. God. Save. Our. Sitting on his throne, sucking jujubes.[179]

Who is narrating this paragraph? What is being specified and why? How does this relate to what readers have already encountered? It does become clear, gradually, in the next few paragraphs, that the chapter is following Bloom, recording his thoughts as he walks through the city. But what is the rhetorical play of this opening part of the text concealing? What is it, a few lines later, that Bloom thinks is 'coming!!', 'coming!!', 'coming!!'? Why does Denis Breen receive a postcard which says 'U. P.'? What is the significance of 'H. E. L. Y. S.'? For a suspicious reader, with a conservative mentality, it would have been easy to form the view that Joyce's unconventional narrative method was a means of concealing details which might, under the terms of the Criminal Code, be deemed 'obscene, lewd, and lascivious'. The war and its immediate aftermath are also relevant here. In a note to Joyce of July 1920 Pound reports the hearsay of an 'ex-govt official' who was 'troubled' by *Ulysses* 'during the war' ('Thought it was all code') and Weir notes that chapter 8 was 'somehow read by the authorities in the context of the Espionage Act'.[180] Files in the National Archives in Washington include a letter, dated 14 March 1919, from an employee of the Translation Bureau (a division of the Post Office) which remarks that 'the creature who writes this *Ulysses* stuff should be put under a glass jar for examination. He'd make a lovely exhibit'.[181]

---

[176] Quinn to Anderson, 3 November 1917, *Little Review* records, UWM.

[177] Though see Birmingham, *The Most Dangerous Book* for a different view (124, and 367n).

[178] Reid, *The Man from New York*, 343. Relations were at a particularly low ebb at this time. Pound told Quinn that Anderson and Heap 'can't be trusted to construct even a single issue' and Quinn had refused to give financial support (Pound to Quinn, 28 December 1918, in *EP-JQ*, 170; Quinn to Anderson, 3 December 1918, *Little Review* records, UWM).

[179] *LR*, January 1919, 27.

[180] Pound to J, [? July] 1920, *EP-JJ*, 182; Weir, 'What Did He Know, and When Did He Know It', 391.

[181] World War 1 Espionage Files, cited by Weir, 'What Did He Know, and When Did He Know It', 391.

In addition to the parts of the text which might have been regarded as coded, Bloom's freewheeling thoughts openly record aspects of life more normally left undocumented, especially with regard to the body and sexuality. For example, he thinks about advertisements and how 'All kinds of places are good for ads' and remembers: 'That quack doctor for the clap used to be stuck up in all the greenhouses'.[182] He reminisces about the way in which Molly undressed after Goodwin's concert at the mansion house: 'Swish and soft flop her stays made on the bed. Always warm from her. Always liked to let herself out'.[183] The language of the epistolary affair he is conducting with Martha Flower also drifts into his consciousness: 'I called you naughty darling because I do not like that other world. Please tell me what is the meaning. Please tell me what perfume your wife'.[184] After his meeting with Mrs Breen, he thinks about Mrs Purefoy giving birth: 'Three days imagine groaning on a bed with a vinegarded handkerchief round her forehead, her belly swollen out. Phew! Dreadful simply! Child's head too big: forceps'.[185] He thinks about the illicit affairs that 'plainclothes men' from Dublin castle have with 'slaveys': 'Squarepushing up against a backdoor. Maul her a bit'.[186] He is troubled by the details of his own intimate life and longs for intimacy, particularly as he reaches the door of the Burton restaurant in Duke Street: 'A warm human plumpness settled down on his brain. His brain yielded. Perfume of embraces all him assailed. With hungered flesh obscurely he mutely craved to adore'.[187] He thinks about the relationship between food and sexuality, and wonders about oysters and their 'Effect on the sexual'.[188] His mood is generally more settled after he has eaten at Davy Byrne's ('I wanted that badly. Felt so off colour') and, as he relaxes, his mind turns to erotic moments he shared with Molly 'under wild ferns on Howth':

> O wonder! Coolsoft with ointments her hand touched me, caressed: her eyes upon me did not turn away. Ravished over her I lay full lips full open kissed her mouth. Yum. Softly she gave me in my mouth the seedcake warm and chewed. Mawkish pulp her mouth had mumbled sweet and sour with spittle. Joy: I ate it: joy.[189]

This passage, taken with all of the others mentioned, as well as the experience of readerly alienation which comes from reading and not being able to follow what is being expressed, may have led to the objections of the anonymous reader at the New York Post Office and the 'suppression' of this issue (though, of course, there is no way to prove this, given the absence of archival evidence).

Suppression 2: May 1919

In the hope of stopping the Post Office from interfering with the May 1919 issue of the *Little Review*, Anderson (or, less possibly, Heap) read the second instalment

---

[182] *LR*, January 1919, 30. [183] *LR*, January 1919, 32. [184] *LR*, January 1919, 35.
[185] *LR*, January 1919, 36. [186] *LR*, January 1919, 37.
[187] *LR*, January 1919, 42. [188] *LR*, January 1919, 46. [189] *LR*, January 1919, 47.

of chapter 9 ('Scylla and Charybdis') with a keen attention to detail, and chose to make deletions.[190] These included:

(1) the word 'pissed' from Mulligan's sentence 'The tramper Synge is looking for you, he said, to murder you. He heard you pissed on his halldoor in Glasthule'.[191]

(2) the phrase 'when he wants to do for him, and for all other and singular uneared wombs, the office an ostler does for the stallion', spoken by Stephen in a passage of comment on Shakespeare's sexual identity.[192]

(3) the sentence 'Sons with mothers, sires with daughters, nephews with grand-mothers, queens with prize bulls' spoken by Stephen in the discussion about incest and the 'mystical estate' of fatherhood.[193]

(4) the subtitle of the play which 'Ballocky Mulligan' purports to read, 'A Honeymoon in the Hand', a reference to masturbation.[194]

In making these deletions, Anderson had paid some heed to Pound's advice—given in January 1918 before the serialization of *Ulysses* had even begun—that she should pre-empt potential difficulties with Joyce's text by leaving 'gaps at the questionable points'.[195] But clearly Anderson did not (and arguably could not) change enough: as Quinn told Joyce, the bulk mailing of the number for May 1919 was 'held up' by the Post Office.[196] Heap later gave Joyce a fuller account, perhaps with a little embellishment of detail:

> Our entire May issue was burned by the Postal Department and we were told brutally that we would be put out of business altogether if we didn't stop 'pulling that stuff'.[197]

Anderson appealed to Quinn, and on this occasion Quinn was prepared to help. He sent a memorandum to Judge Lamar, who was still Solicitor of the Post Office, and received a response on 18 June 1919 which informed him that the decision to withhold the May issue was 'not based solely' on the basis of the instalment of *Ulysses* but 'upon the magazine as a whole, and upon the cuts contained therein as well as the printed matter'.[198] 'Cuts' is here used as an abbreviation of woodcuts, and refers to a set of four sketches of nudes by James Light, and not the 'cutting' of 'certain passages' from Joyce's chapter as acknowledged in Anderson's editorial note of May 1919.[199]

---

[190] It was Anderson rather than Heap who appealed to Quinn in the ensuing debacle, and it thus seems more likely that it was Anderson who made these cuts.
[191] *LR*, January 1919, 19.   [192] *LR*, January 1919, 21.   [193] *LR*, January 1919, 26.
[194] *LR*, May 1919, 34.
[195] Pound to Anderson, [17 January 1918], *P-LR*, 174.
[196] Information from Quinn to J, 26 June 1919, *JQ-JJ I*, 236.
[197] Jane Heap to J, 9 January 1920, Cornell.
[198] Copy of W. H. Lamar to John Quinn, 18 June 1919, *Little Review* records, UWM; see also Quinn to J, 26 June 1919, *JQ-JJ I*, 236.
[199] *LR*, May 1919, 21n.

Voicing a feeling which was shared by Anderson, Heap, and Quinn, Pound was incensed and baffled by Lamar's decision; he told Quinn that he felt that the Post Office had hit on Joyce's 'most intellectual chapter' and that it showed that the officials were 'merely incalculable or rather cranky in just the proportion that the work shows intellectual energy'.[200] He was inclined to agree with his wife Dorothy who had assured him that 'indecency has nothing to do with it'; the 'energy in Joyce...is what upsets people'.[201] With respect to this particular issue of the *Little Review* of May 1919, that seems to be the right judgement. Lamar had not objected to the particular substance of the instalment. His objection was more generalized: there was a sense—which Anderson's note about 'natural facts' had done something to pinpoint—that Joyce's complex contrapuntal narrative style was a stealthy means by which all sorts of 'indecent' 'natural facts' were being acknowledged and discussed.

Within the epistolary circuit which documents these events, some items are missing, including Quinn's memorandum to Lamar, which Pound read and described as 'the best apologia for J. that has been written'.[202] Subsequent correspondence reveals that Quinn had evidently wanted Lamar to recognize Joyce's status as an artist and to that end had enclosed the leaflet of 'Extracts from press notices of *A Portrait of the Artist as a Young Man*'; Quinn had also argued that it was 'regrettable' that the postal laws were being 'construed from the standpoint of "The Convent, Young Girls's Seminary, Young Boys' Sunday Schools" etc'.[203] Anderson's views had been included in this appeal by Quinn: she pointed out that the readership of the *Little Review* was 'composed chiefly of artists, thinkers and men with a passionate belief in the need for an intellectual culture in America', a view Quinn endorsed in describing the *Little Review* as an 'intellectual purgative' not intended for 'young boys and girls'.[204] Anderson and Pound wanted Quinn's memorandum to be printed in *The Egoist* but, somewhat tellingly, Quinn refused this request. As Materer notes, he was not eager to appear in print as a defender of obscenity in literature.[205]

Joyce's response to these events contains another illustrative detail. Quinn had told Joyce that Lamar had 'based his decision in excluding the May number from the mails not merely on your article but on the whole number and "on the cuts contained therein"'.[206] Joyce responded to Quinn with typical disdain:

It is extraordinary that American law allows an employee to penalize a citizen for *not* having committed an offence. I allude to the penalizing of Miss Anderson on account of suppressed passages.[207]

[200] EP to Quinn, 6 July 1919, *EP-JQ*, 176.   [201] EP to Quinn, 6 July 1919, *EP-JQ*, 176.
[202] EP to Quinn, 6 July 1919, *EP-JQ*, 176.
[203] Information in Lamar to Quinn, 19 June 1919, *Little Review* records, UWM; Quinn to Lamar, 18 June 1919, *Little Review* records, UWM.
[204] Quinn to Lamar, 19 June 1919, *Little Review* records, UWM, a letter which cites Anderson.
[205] *EP-JQ*, 178n.   [206] Quinn to J, 26 June 1919, *JQ-JJ* I, 236.
[207] J to Quinn, 3 August 1919, *L* II, 448.

'Cuts' had made Joyce think of Anderson's note about 'cutting certain passages' and not of James Light's woodcuts.[208] Tellingly, Joyce could not read between the lines. He could only see the argument from his perspective: that of the 'great' writer engaged in a battle for freedom of expression, pitched against a conservative and small-minded culture with a censorious mentality. This was Joyce's mythology of self. It was a very powerful and effective self-image, and it was being shared and promoted by the supporters he had gathered in his wake: his patrons, editors, agents, and publishers, a group of individuals which included Pound, Quinn, Anderson, Heap, Weaver, and Edith Rockefeller McCormick.[209] With the exception of Quinn—who did not always write directly to Joyce, acted too late, and was too intemperate and too far away to be effective—that group did not contest Joyce's publication strategies and suggest that it was pointless and unreasonable to allow *Ulysses* to become embroiled in a cat-and-mouse chase with officials of the US Post Office. Nor did anyone challenge Joyce's gradually evolving view of 'American law', or of what it might mean to be published in the US. Nor did anyone suggest that Joyce might venture to the US himself, and find ways of brokering his own publication arrangements, without the sometimes unhelpful interference of endless intermediaries. Had Joyce done so, the fate of *Ulysses* might have been very different. A private edition of the work might even have been published, as Joyce intended, and without textual corruption or editorial intervention.

As it was, *Ulysses* was on a collision course. Though issues of the *Little Review* containing chapters 10 and 11 ('Wandering Rocks' and 'Sirens') were sent to subscribers without difficulty, Anderson sensed that there might be problems with chapter 12 ('Cyclops'). Thus in the November 1919 issue, the first of four issues in which chapter 12 would be serialized, she cut the lines which describe and respond to the way in which a man who has been hanged has an erection ('when they cut him down from the drop it was standing up in their faces like a poker').[210] The omission from the text, marked with an asterisk, directs readers to a note which states: 'A passage of some twenty lines has been omitted to avoid the censor's possible suppression'.[211] There is some interesting linguistic usage in this brief note; for the Post Office was not, or not exactly, acting officially in the role of 'censor'. 'Suppression', the word used so freely by those involved at the time, is not exactly accurate either. Under the terms of the Postal Act of 1879, which divided mail into different categories, the *Little Review* was entered as a periodical which meant that it could be posted, as the title page of every issue affirms, as 'second class matter', a designation which meant that it could attract a much cheaper rate than regular

---

[208] *LR*, May 1919, 21n.
[209] Edith Rockefeller McCormick started to give Joyce money in February 1918, but stopped in October 1919, telling Joyce 'now that the difficult years of the war are past, you will find publishers and will come forward yourself, I know'. See Ellmann, *James Joyce*, 422 and *L* II, 454.
[210] *U*1922, 292; cp. Rosenbach P292. A typescript of this passage does not survive, thus one has to infer what has been deleted by reading the Rosenbach manuscript. For the partial typescripts of chapter 12 ('Cyclops'), see *JJA* volume 13, *A Facsimile of Manuscripts and Typescripts for Episodes 10–13 (Wandering Rocks to Nausicaa)* (New York: Garland, 1977).
[211] *LR*, November 1919, 49.

mail.[212] It was the privileged postal rate which entitled officials at the Post Office to inspect individual copies. The denial of that privileged rate, and of passing through the mails altogether, did not mean suppression per se because other means, such as news stands, book shops, and private courier, could have been used for the circulation of the *Little Review*. In practical terms this may not have been feasible, but it was certainly possible. The battle, after all, was only with the Post Office. If the *Little Review* had not needed to use the postal system, or Joyce had not been published serially, the 'censoring' of *Ulysses* may never have occurred because different standards would have applied. John Quinn recognized this and told Pound (but not Joyce): 'I would stand for anything in a book. But in a monthly magazine I do not think there is quite the same freedom as in a book. I think there is something in that distinction'.[213] But those around Quinn were not temperamentally conditioned to see and accept this kind of reasoning.

Suppression 3: January 1920

In the event the issue of November 1919 passed through the mail without being stopped. This was not necessarily a sign, in itself, that the issue was not 'stoppable', but merely that the Post Office officials, who were dealing with an enormous volume of material every day, had not acted on this particular occasion.[214] But they did act with regard to the issue for January 1920. A detailed account of the legal reasoning for this suppression does not survive, but for one source: a letter from Heap to Joyce, which a lawyer might dismiss as flimsy and biased. Nonetheless, what Heap has to say is the only evidence that can be taken into account, and at any rate her comments are interesting in what they reveal of her as a reader, notably her spirited and engaged perspicuity:

> The January issue was suppressed on your disrespect for Victoria and Edward. We laughed so much reading proof on that episode that we forgot to think of 'obscenity'. The flowery passages are too good—I shall be sorry when Bloom finishes this day.[215]

Within the text Joe Hynes describes the British Royal family—the House of Saxe-Coburg-Gotha, as it was known in 1904—as 'those sausageeating bastards' and Victoria as 'the flatulent old bitch that's dead'.[216] He refers specifically to Edward VII's state visit to Ireland in July 1903, and the particulars of his visit to Maynooth, an occasion when 'the priests and bishops of Ireland' stuck up 'pictures of all the horses his jockeys rode'.[217] Edward was a notorious philanderer and the text acknowledges this in Alf Bergan's wry response: the bishops 'ought to have stuck

---

[212] Stephen Vaughn, *Encyclopedia of American Journalism* (New York: Routledge, 2008), 410.

[213] Quinn to EP, after 3 April 1918, *EP-JQ*, 138.

[214] This was Quinn's reasoning. He had warned Pound that the issue of March 1918 ('scrotum-tightening', 'Ballad of Joking Jesus', etc.) had gone through the mails 'not due to the fact that it was not stoppable' but 'merely due to the general wartime rush of things' (Quinn to Pound, 2 March 1918, qtd in Reid, *The Man from New York*, 345).

[215] Jane Heap to J, [late March 1920], Cornell.   [216] *LR*, January 1920, 55.

[217] *LR*, January 1920, 55.

up all the women he rode'.[218] Vanderham argues that these comments would have been regarded as 'politically subversive', but were Americans really so attuned to sensitivities about the British Royal family?[219] Given the cultural conservatism of the political moment—the fact that there was considerable hostility to immigrants and to radical and communist politics—the citizen's suggestion that the Irish could liberate themselves by putting 'force against force' and calling in the Irish in the US and further afield ('our greater Ireland beyond the sea') might have been deemed more problematic.[220] Interestingly, Joyce's 'disrespect' for Edward—as voiced by Joe Hynes and Alf Bergan in this instalment of the text—develops ideas which had already been written, and deemed problematic, in the *Dubliners* story 'Ivy Day in the Committee Room'.[221] George Roberts, the would-be Dublin publisher of *Dubliners*, had asked Joyce to 'alter the references to the late King'.[222] *Ulysses* was being written in response to the conditions in which the publication of *Dubliners* had encountered difficulties, and, ironically, was encountering similar difficulties, despite the fact that serial publication was taking place in quite a different cultural context.

Relations between Anderson and Quinn had been quite hostile in the period surrounding the suppression of June 1919. Quinn's letters to Anderson—tonally influenced by the fact that they were dictated to a 'stenographer' who captured the draft using a stenotype keyboard, and then typed them for Quinn—could be remarkably self-important, digressive, opinionated, and annoying. In his letter to Anderson of 14 June 1919, for example, he remarks that the dictation of the memorandum for Lamar had made him 'forty minutes late for a dinner engagement' and mentions, in passing, that he thought his brief on 'Cantelman's Spring-Mate' 'was about as good a piece of legal reasoning as I had ever submitted to a Court' (this was the brief which suggested, inappropriately, that Lewis's story did not come 'within gunshot of violating the statute').[223] Subsequent letters describe Light's woodcuts as 'artistic misdemeanours' 'not worthy of publication in any review', and offer views on subjects ranging from British military strategy in the Battle of Jutland ('Mrs Pankhurst...would not have Jellicoed the battle'); women's suffrage ('an absurdity in itself'); sexual relations between men and women; and the 'realistic lingerie advertisements that greet us in every newspaper and magazine'.[224] Given such belligerence, it is easy to see why Anderson ignored Quinn's advice, particularly his warning, as recounted to Pound, that the editors:

> were in danger of having the magazine permanently excluded from the mails...for where a magazine has repeatedly been excluded because of violations of the Act, there comes

[218] *LR*, January 1920, 56.
[219] Vanderham, *James Joyce and Censorship*, 35.   [220] *LR*, January 1920, 55.
[221] In 'Ivy Day', Hynes describes Edward VII as 'a German monarch' and asks, 'What do we want kowtowing to a foreign king?', James Joyce, *Dubliners*, ed. by Hans Walter Gabler and Walter Hettche (New York: Vintage, 1993 and London: Garland, 1993), 109.
[222] George Roberts to Charles Weekes, 31 January 1911, NLI Ms 13272 (3). I discuss this controversy in 'Chapters of Moral History: Failing to Publish *Dubliners*', *Papers of the Bibliographical Society of America*, 97 (2003), 495–519.
[223] Quinn to Anderson, 14 June 1919, *Little Review* records, UWM; cf. page 55.
[224] Quinn to Anderson, 19 June 1919, and 23 June 1919, *Little Review* records, UWM.

a time when under the decisions they are justified in its permanent exclusion... I also warned them that they were likely to be indicted as old and callous offenders.[225]

Anderson and Heap knew that the *Little Review*, which had little to lose in terms of capital, had become engaged in a game of cat-and-mouse with the Post Office. In some respects they understood the particularities of the struggle, including its local and personal dimension, more clearly than Quinn. In fact, they were sufficiently sharp-eyed to be able to see that further legal action would potentially help to consolidate the journal's cultural reputation.

Suppression 4, July–August 1920: Sumner Takes Action

In his argument with Lamar of June 1919, Quinn had attempted to argue that the *Little Review* was 'designed for a particular class and only reaches that class', his hope in reasoning thus being that the Post Office would be 'more liberal' with it.[226] Events ultimately proved this defence untrue, as the person who made the most effective complaint against the *Little Review* was the recipient of an unsolicited copy of the July–August issue for 1920, and the daughter of 'a reputable and leading member of the bar'.[227] Apparently 'shocked' by the content—though one might question the circumstances and coincidences of this story—she had asked her father to complain, which led to the letter of complaint about the third instalment of 'Nausicaa', referring to specific 'passages marked'.[228] The letter, addressed to District Attorney Edward Swann—an elected official responsible for the prosecution of violation of the laws of New York County—was not the beginning of legal action as such; it was merely a letter of complaint, and has to be seen as a suggestion, coming from a well-found source, that legal action should be initiated against the *Little Review*.

One of the more curious anomalies in this mish-mash of events is the fact that neither the name of the lawyer nor that of his daughter survive in the archival record, or any of the existing accounts of events leading to the trial. Did the cash-strapped Anderson really send a lawyer's daughter an unsolicited copy of the *Little Review* in order to bring in subscriptions? This seems unlikely, somehow. How, then, did the third instalment of 'Nausicaa' become ensnared? It is only possible to speculate. Clearly both Heap and Anderson had ways of making themselves conspicuous, particularly to those of a conservative mindset: Heap through cross-dressing, and Anderson through her relentless flamboyance. One senses a local element to Anderson's struggle, a specific vendetta being waged by one of the so-called 'underlings' in the local Post Office. It is possible that Anderson was lured into sending the copy by someone acting under cover for the New York Society for the Suppression of Vice.

---

[225] Quinn to Pound, 16 October 1920, Carbondale.
[226] Quinn to Lamar, 19 June 1919, *Little Review* records, UWM.
[227] Quinn to Pound, 16 October 1920, Carbondale.
[228] The letter is quoted in John S. Sumner in 'The Truth about "Literary Lynching"', *The Dial*, July 1921, 67.

However powerful that Society and the social purity movement may have been, it is also true, as Gillers has argued, that the courts of the era were not entirely comfortable 'with the reach of the concept of obscenity', and 'were divided on how broadly to utilize their power to suppress works of art through conviction of authors and publishers'.[229] Thus Swann—possibly with his eye on re-election—decided not to pursue the matter, but to refer it to John S. Sumner (1876–1971), secretary of the New York Society for the Suppression of Vice, who was a qualified lawyer. In that role, Sumner agreed to act as 'complaining witness', the alleged victim of the crime charged; he did so with some clout because his organization was 'invested by the New York legislature in 1873 with authority to enforce the state's obscenity laws', as Hassett notes.[230]

The Case Develops: Preliminary Actions and Hearings

In order to give the case substance, Sumner needed evidence that the *Little Review* was freely available. It is not clear that he involved the New York Post Office at this juncture. The bulk mailing of the number for July–August 1920 had already occurred, and thus a fourth 'suppression' through the mail would not have been efficacious (and one may doubt that this ever occurred).[231] Instead, Sumner arranged for an 'agent' from his society to purchase a copy at the popular Washington Square Bookshop, something of a *salon* and meeting place for Greenwich Village bohemia; Sumner then proceeded to swear out a warrant against the proprietors of the bookshop, Egmont Arens (1888–1966) and his wife Josephine Bell, who were duly summoned to appear at the local magistrates' court on 17 September 1920.[232] The hearing was adjourned to 4 October, and then again to 18 October, by which time Quinn had conferred with all parties—including Anderson, Heap, Mr Arens, Josephine Bell, and Sumner himself, with whom he took considerable time and trouble by inviting him to lunch, and trying to persuade him to drop the case 'in consideration of having no further numbers appear'.[233] As Quinn told Pound, Sumner was prepared to listen to this 'novel suggestion' but ultimately argued that the case had to proceed because he had been asked to initiate proceedings by the District Attorney.[234] But in accordance with Quinn's wishes Sumner was prepared to offer one concession: rather unusually, he would drop the case against the Washington Square Bookshop, and allow Anderson and Heap to be substituted

---

[229] Gillers, 'A Tendency to Deprave and Corrupt', 244, 270.

[230] Hassett, *The Ulysses Trials*, 75.

[231] I have not located any evidence that the number for July–August 1920 was suppressed by the Post Office. Bryer, '"A Trial Track for Racers"', 384, asserts a fourth suppression but does not give a source. It seems possible that all accounts of 'four suppressions' emanate from the same (not exactly trustworthy) source: the Shakespeare and Company prospectus advertising the first edition, reprinted in Katherine McSharry (ed.), *A Joycean Scrapbook from the National Library of Ireland* (Dublin: Wordwell, 2004), 102.

[232] Quinn to Anderson, 5 February 1921, Carbondale. This is a typed seventeen-page letter, which Joyce saw, and outlines the chronology of legal proceedings against the *Little Review* in considerable detail.

[233] Quinn to Pound, 16 October 1920, Carbondale.

[234] Quinn to Pound, 16 October 1920, Carbondale.

as defendants.[235] The substitution was agreed in court on 4 October 1920, and a preliminary hearing before Magistrate J. E. Corrigan at the Jefferson Market Place Court commenced on 21 October 1920.[236] The purpose of the hearing was for the magistrate to review the evidence and decide whether there was a case to answer: should the matter be dismissed on grounds of insufficient evidence or go to trial in Special Sessions, the New York City court vested with inferior criminal jurisdiction?[237]

From the moment he read the third instalment of 'Nausicaa', Quinn was of the view that conviction was 'certain' and he told Anderson and Heap that this was his view 'repeatedly'.[238] Quinn was, nonetheless, prepared to help defend their case because he cared deeply about Joyce and wanted to see *Ulysses* properly published in the US in book form, with Joyce's copyright secure, and no risk of the text entering the public domain, where it could be easily pirated. It needs to be emphasized that Quinn faced legal proceedings against the *Little Review* from early October 1920, and had to act without much sense of what he described as 'the real question on which everything else turns', namely Joyce's judgement as to when *Ulysses* would be finished.[239] He decided to try and delay proceedings as much as possible, so that Huebsch could publish a limited private edition of an unexpurgated *Ulysses* in advance of the trial. As he explained to Joyce—in a lengthy letter of 19 December 1920—it was possible for US publishers to 'get away with' 'frank' books 'in a privately printed edition' 'that had all been or very largely subscribed before publication'.[240] In response to these suggestions—and without much recognition of the significance that the legal process was potentially set to drive the compositional and publication process—Joyce began to dictate terms that Quinn could offer Huebsch, including a royalty of $3 or $3.50 per copy and a trade discount of only 10 per cent rather than the more standard 33 per cent; he also began to make preliminary arrangement for the book to be set up as far as the end of chapter 15 ('Circe'), and promised to return corrected proofs 'a few days after receipt' (*L*, I, 156).

Meanwhile, in the face of the trial before Special Sessions being called for 12 November 1920, quite quickly after the preliminary hearing before Corrigan, Quinn began to piece together a motion seeking to transfer the case from a hearing before three judges at the Court of Special Sessions (as planned) to a hearing by jury before the Court of General Sessions, which would not be tried, as Quinn told Anderson, for 'a year or so, for it is what is known as a bail case and not a jail case, and jail cases have to be tried first'.[241] Quinn's motion for this transfer—nine foolscap

---

[235] Quinn to Anderson, 5 February 1921, Carbondale.

[236] John Quinn, Attorney for Defendants, 'Affidavit and Notice of Motion for the Transfer of Cause from Court of Special Sessions to Court of General Sessions', 12 January 1921, Carbondale. This document specifies stages in the legal process.

[237] Gillers, 'A Tendency to Deprave and Corrupt', 254.

[238] Quinn to Anderson, 8 February 1921, Carbondale.

[239] Quinn to J, 19 December 1920, *JQ-JJ* I, 260.

[240] Quinn to J, 19 December 1920, *JQ-JJ* I, 260.

[241] Quinn to Anderson, 5 February 1921, Carbondale.

typed pages dated 12 January 1921 and full of legal detail—argues, through the citation of several precedents, that:

> a layman brings to such cases a possibly somewhat different point of view from the court, and that a jury is peculiarly fitted to judge the propriety of permitting or not permitting such books.[242]

Much to Quinn's bitter disappointment, the motion was denied on 2 February 1921.[243] He told Anderson, 'I have tried my best. I have failed...now there is nothing for it but a trial...and instant conviction'.[244] The other lawyers involved in the case had successfully argued that Quinn was playing for time, and refused his request for a further adjournment ('it was a simple case and could be disposed of in a half hour').[245]

Interestingly, Quinn's motion to transfer the case appends, as exhibit A, an affidavit by Sumner sworn to Magistrate Corrigan on 21 October 1920, which extends the charge of 'lewdness and of obscenity' within the July–August 1920 number of the *Little Review* well beyond the four pages initially pointed out to District Attorney Edward Swann.[246] The instalment from chapter 13 only runs to seventeen pages; of these Sumner identifies fourteen as being 'descriptive of scenes of lewdness and of obscenity' and continues:

> said magazine is so obscene, lewd, lascivious, filthy, indecent and disgusting, that a minute description of the same would be offensive to the Court and improper to be placed upon the record thereof.[247]

In response to this argument, the motion to transfer also contains Anderson's sworn affidavit that the 'work was published by us in good faith as a serious contribution to serious, sincere literature' and the further assertion that 'there is all the difference in the world between that work, which is serious literature, and pornography or any of the things forbidden by the statute'.[248] Sumner's affidavit specifies that the editors of the *Little Review* were being indicted under section 1141 of the Penal Law of New York State, article 106 ('Indecency'), which states that it was a 'misdemeanour' to sell, lend, give away, or show 'any obscene, lewd, lascivious, filthy, indecent, or disgusting book, magazine, pamphlet' or to print, utter, publish, 'or prepare any such book'. The offence was punishable by 'not less than ten days nor more than one year imprisonment or be fined not less than fifty dollars nor more than one thousand dollars or both fine and imprisonment for each offense'.[249] Thus the matter before Magistrate Corrigan on 21 October 1920 was to determine

---

[242] Quinn, 'Affidavit and Notice of Motion', Carbondale.
[243] Quinn to Anderson, 5 February 1921, Carbondale.
[244] Quinn to Anderson, 5 February 1921, Carbondale.
[245] Quinn to Anderson, 5 February 1921, Carbondale.   [246] Discussed on p. 109.
[247] Quinn, 'Affidavit and Notice of Motion', Carbondale.
[248] Quinn, 'Affidavit and Notice of Motion', Carbondale.
[249] *Consolidated Laws of the State of New York*, 1909, volume 4 (New York: Lyon State Printers, 1909), 2677–8.

whether there was enough evidence to proceed to trial. Could the final instalment of 'Nausicaa' be deemed 'obscene, lewd, lascivious, filthy'?

Such specificity gestures to one of the reasons why it is difficult to work out who or what was on trial in February 1921. Though the later and more well-known US trial of *Ulysses* in 1933 ('United States v. One Book Called Ulysses') was an action against the book itself, it is more usual for a court to try a person or persons (an action 'in personam') than things or property (an action 'in rem').[250] In February 1921 it was Anderson and Heap, as publishers of the *Little Review*, who were on trial, but the evidence on which Corrigan had to make a decision was that of Joyce's text. In a very real sense, therefore, the initial hearing would be decided by close reading: close reading supported by a legal process which would establish (i) what, if any, offence had been committed and (ii) whether the close reading of Joyce's text suggested that there was a case for trial.

At the preliminary hearing Sumner presented his affidavit which alleges, *inter alia*, that at a meeting between Sumner, Anderson, and Heap which took place on 4 October, the two women had acknowledged that they 'had prepared said magazine' and 'gloried in it'.[251] This meeting probably took place in court; Anderson also remembers meeting Sumner casually, 'walking along Eighth Street where he and I engaged in such a passionate exchange of ideas that we had to go into the Washington Square Bookshop to finish'.[252] Quinn wanted the editors to remain 'inconspicuous, meek and silent' and hoped that he might be able to dissuade Sumner from pursuing the case.[253] That hope was in vain. Through these pre-trial meetings, Sumner had obtained a deep sense of the cultural views the editors held. Corrigan, the magistrate, also had a deep sense of what he was dealing with. He had encountered cases brought by Sumner before. According to Quinn—who may be right on this point—Corrigan was 'one of the most liberal men on the bench': even though Sumner was a lawyer, Corrigan was not inclined to be persuaded by Sumner's testimony alone, and thus made the decision to read the instalment himself in order to form his own judgement.[254]

Quinn was working hard on other matters at this time. Though he was defending Anderson and Heap, he was so certain that the preliminary hearing of 21 October 1920 would lead to a trial that he made the ill-advised and slightly arrogant decision not to appear in person, and opted instead to delegate the matter to a Mr Brigham, a more junior lawyer from his office. On finding that Corrigan was going to go to the trouble of actually reading Joyce's text, Brigham realized that there was a chance the case might be dismissed. He phoned Quinn, who hurriedly made his way to the court so that he could present a defence of *Ulysses* in person.[255]

[250] Actions 'in rem' are more common in US law but rarely occur in the UK (usually only within Admiralty law). An instructive sense of the differences between the two jurisdictions and approaches emerges by comparing two famous obscenity rulings: the US, acting as libellant, tried *Ulysses* (in rem) in 1933; but in England it was Penguin (as publisher, in personam) that was tried in respect of *Lady Chatterley's Lover* in 1960.
[251] Quinn, 'Affidavit and Notice of Motion', Carbondale.
[252] Anderson, *My Thirty Years' War*, 218.　　[253] Anderson, *My Thirty Years' War*, 219.
[254] Quinn to Pound, 21 October 1920, Carbondale.
[255] Quinn to Pound, 21 October 1920, Carbondale.

Describing the court as 'dingy', implying that it was not the kind of court in which he was normally accustomed to appear, Quinn went on to tell Pound about the scene of the hearing in some detail:

> It was rather an amusing scene. There was Heap plus Anderson, plus heaps of other Heaps and Andersons. Some goodlooking and some indifferent. The two rows of them looking as though a fashionable whorehouse had been pinched and all its inmates hauled into court, with Heap in the part of brazen madame. The stage was filled with police officers in blue uniforms with glaring stars and buttons, women and men by twos and threes awaiting arraignment or sentence, niggers in the offing, chauffeurs awaiting hearing; pimps, prostitutes, hangers-on and reporters—also whores, on the theory of 'Once a journalist, always whore.'

> The judge was in his legal chambers, I don't know whether the urinal or judicial water closed abutted on this chambers but I supposed it did. At any rate, chambers struck me as the right place for him to read the July–August number.[256]

Quinn had become distracted by the cultural meaning of the scene before him, and had forgotten that the case might be dismissed. His antipathy to Anderson and Heap, and the cultural world in which they moved, as well as his certainty that conviction was inevitable meant that the defence he mounted was not as well prepared or judicious as it might have been. The hearing, in Quinn's words, had become something of a 'show' and Quinn's argument, which he 'hit out from the shoulder' ('I don't think that there has ever been quite the same kind of speech delivered in a New York court in my time'), caused Corrigan to shake 'with laughter'.[257] But such mirth was to no avail. Corrigan listened patiently, but he had already decided that the case would have to proceed to Special Sessions because he was of the view that 'no one could misunderstand' the part of the text 'where the man went off in his pants' which he judged to be 'smutty' and 'filthy within the meaning of the statute'.[258]

One of the difficulties which Quinn faced was that he had to defend *Ulysses* as a serious literary work on the basis of the final—and sexually explicit—instalment of chapter 13 ('Nausicaa'). It was impossible to argue that the chapter had to be judged in the context of the book as a whole, because *Ulysses* was not yet a completed text. Or, to put it another way, in the eyes of the law the excerpt in the July–August issue *was* the whole.[259] Another difficulty was that Quinn was not as well prepared as he might have been, or familiar with the way in which the magistrates' courts worked. When asked by Corrigan for bail bonds in order that Anderson and Heap might be paroled (rather than jailed pending the next hearing), he had to admit to Corrigan that he had neither provided the bonds, nor

---

[256] Quinn to Pound, 21 October 1920, Carbondale.
[257] Quinn to Pound, 21 October 1920, Carbondale.
[258] Quinn to Pound, 21 October 1920, Carbondale.
[259] Gillers, 'A Tendency to Deprave and Corrupt', 252. Citing a judgment from 1922, which argued that books 'must be considered broadly as a whole', and not individual paragraphs 'which taken by themselves are undoubtedly vulgar and indecent', Gillers notes that the idea that a piece of writing must be judged as a whole was 'just beginning to take hold in the law' at the time the *Little Review* case was heard (252).

known that he needed to do so.[260] Thus arrangements had to be hastily made for the payment of a bond, fixed at $25 per defendant; as neither Anderson nor Heap could pay this sum, it was paid on their behalf by a lawyer from Quinn's office.[261]

February 1921: From Special Sessions to General Sessions and Back

The crucial issue to be determined by the three judges at the ensuing trial, which finally opened at Special Sessions on 14 February 1921, was whether the final instalment of 'Nausicaa' could be deemed 'obscene' under the terms of the 'Cockburn' test used in US obscenity cases of the era, a test which was established, under UK law, in *Regina v Hicklin* in 1868. That test—which became binding on New York courts in 1884, following its citation in *People v Muller*—was:

> whether the tendency of the matter charged as obscenity is to deprave and corrupt those whose minds are open to such immoral influences, and into whose hands a publication of this sort may fall.[262]

As Gillers has noted, this ruling had far-reaching repercussions in 'American case law even when *Hicklin* itself went uncited':

> Several American courts, searching for precedent for their own obscenity cases, subscribed to *Hicklin* with little or no evaluation of alternatives.[263]

But lower courts, in particular, were unhappy with the reach of the *Hicklin*-inspired regime, and, as Gillers argues, 'the tide was turning against Sumner and the Society for the Suppression of Vice toward and after the end of the First World War'.[264] One case, in which Quinn defended a publisher, *US v Kennerley* (1913), deserves particular mention.

Mitchell Kennerley had published *Hagar Revelly*, a naturalistic novel about the sexual choices facing two poverty-stricken sisters in New York City. Though the subject matter is daring, the language dealing with sex is 'only suggestive'.[265] The case, also brought by the New York Society for the Suppression of Vice, was tried by jury at the Southern District Court of New York and all members of the jury were given copies of the novel, and directed to read it in its entirety by the Judge, Learned Hand (1872–1961), who would later become a highly distinguished appeal court judge.[266] The jury declared Kennerley not guilty, and Hand rendered

---

[260] Quinn to Pound, 21 October 1920, Carbondale.

[261] Quinn to Pound, 21 October 1920, Carbondale.

[262] For the significance of *Muller* see Gillers, 'A Tendency to Deprave and Corrupt', esp. 219; Cockburn's test is cited in Gillers, 'A Tendency to Deprave and Corrupt', 228.

[263] Gillers, 'A Tendency to Deprave and Corrupt', 219.

[264] Gillers, 'A Tendency to Deprave and Corrupt', 266.

[265] Dawn B. Sova, *Literature Suppressed on Sexual Grounds* (New York: Facts on File, 2006), 71. Quinn mentions his success in having Kennerley acquitted, describing the case as one 'where I could argue the moral lesson'; by his account it was a 'rather celebrated trial' (Quinn to Pound, 16 October 1920, Carbondale).

[266] Information from Sova, *Literature Suppressed on Sexual Grounds*, 71.

what Quinn later described as a 'scholarly opinion upon the functions of court and jury in such cases'.[267] That opinion, cited at length by Quinn in his motion to have the case against the *Little Review* moved from Special to General Sessions, argued that *Hicklin*, 'however consonant it may be with mid-Victorian morals, does not seem to me to answer to the understanding and morality of the present time'.[268] The opinion is highly relevant to the *Little Review* case, arguing, *inter alia*, that 'truth and beauty are too precious to society at large to be mutilated in the interest of those most likely to pervert them to base uses'; that the word 'obscene' should 'be allowed to indicate the present critical point in the compromise between candor and shame'; and that 'thought' should not be 'fettered' 'by the necessities of the lowest and least capable'.[269] With regard to the trial, and the events which led to it, Quinn might be criticized on several points—his arrogance, the fact that he did not familiarize himself with procedure before appearing before Corrigan, his antipathy to Anderson and Heap and general irritability—but his legal expertise was exact and relevant. By unearthing Hand's scholarly opinion, he was pointing to the fact that the law was muddled, and that rulings in obscenity cases tended to be inconsistent, in the hope that this might bring about a reverse in the case against the *Little Review*.[270]

Quinn attended General Sessions on 17 January 1921, and argued for his motion 'at great length'; when he found that the court was inclined to go against him, he wrote a nine-page memo to the Judge—also on 17 January 1921.[271] Then he could only wait for a decision, which finally appeared on 2 February 1921. As he told Anderson, with understandable annoyance and frustration, the judge's decision— that the case could not be transferred and would thus have to be heard—was 'discretionary and non-appealable'.[272] Quinn was exhausted, and he felt that he had exhausted his legal options for winning the case: his very lengthy letter to Anderson of 5 February 1921—seventeen typed pages—makes this clear.[273] He was suffering from an extremely sore throat and wanted the case, which had been due for hearing in Special Sessions on 4 February, to be adjourned, a request which Sumner refused until Quinn presented yet another affidavit in court, this one pathetically affirming the condition of his throat and his doctor's advice 'about talking very little and only for a few minutes at a time'.[274] Once the adjournment of the trial to 14 February was finally agreed, he wanted a conference with both Anderson and Heap, in order to see 'what position you two should take'.[275] His own position was very clear. All he could do was argue 'along the lines that I did with the magistrate', and as he was of the view that the case could not be won, even on appeal, there was no point in offering 'experts' testimony', witnesses, or 'passages

[267] Quinn, 'Affidavit and Notice of Motion', Carbondale.
[268] Hand quoted by Quinn, 'Affidavit and Notice of Motion', Carbondale.
[269] Quinn, 'Affidavit and Notice of Motion', Carbondale.
[270] The relevance of Hand's opinion is discussed in some detail by Hassett, *The Ulysses Trials*, 40.
[271] Quinn to Anderson, 5 February 1921, Carbondale.
[272] Quinn to Anderson, 5 February 1921, Carbondale.
[273] Quinn to Anderson, 5 February 1921, Carbondale.
[274] Quinn to Anderson, 5 February 1921, Carbondale.
[275] Quinn to Anderson, 5 February 1921, Carbondale.

of comparative literature'.[276] Clearly he rethought this strategy a little, for at the trial—which opened on 14 February 1921 and was then adjourned until 21 February 1921 so that the three judges could read the text—he called two witnesses to the stand: the novelist John Cowper Powys, and Philip Moeller, a director and writer.[277] Both of these witnesses appear to have been found by Anderson and Heap, and Quinn did not prepare them beforehand.[278] This is because he did not think that the testimony they offered would influence the outcome of the trial; he told Anderson quite explicitly that the purpose of the witnesses was to offer evidence 'in mitigation of sentence' (in other words, to reduce the likelihood of Anderson and Heap being imprisoned).[279]

Quinn was deeply familiar with the facts of the case and the relevant case-law and was desperately keen to secure a victory for Joyce's sake. It is nonetheless evident that by the time the case came to trial, he did not want to defend the *Little Review*. His letter to Anderson of 5 February concludes by saying that she might, 'after reading this letter', 'want to have some other counsel defend you'.[280] Though Anderson would have been wise to take this hint, she simply did not have the money or time to do so. Quinn had offered all of his legal advice *pro bono*, and the trial was imminent. When it resumed on 21 February, the prosecution case was argued by Judge Joseph Forrester—a Catholic with an Irish background—who proceeded to denounce the third instalment of 'Nausicaa so vehemently that I thought he would have an apoplectic fit', as Quinn would later tell Joyce.[281] Quinn planned to argue that *Ulysses* was obscene, and that no one could possibly understand it, even himself; but he was faced with a reader who felt that he understood the text, and had become angered by it (in Quinn's description he is 'purple and puffing, his face distorted with rage'). Thus Quinn's defence inevitably fell on deaf ears. Anderson and Heap were convicted; their fine was set at the lowest possible tariff ($50 each) and they were not imprisoned, arguably a sign that the court did not regard their 'misdemeanour' as the most serious crime.

CONCLUSIONS

But these events did have serious implications for those who were involved: for Quinn in his position as Joyce's unofficial agent, for Anderson, Heap, and the *Little Review*, and for Joyce and his potential publishers. From the vast net of archival, legal, and textual facts, it is necessary to draw out several conclusions relating to (1) Quinn's role and effectiveness as a lawyer; (2) Quinn's homophobia; and (3) Joyce's attitude to Quinn, the trial, and the *Little Review* more generally.

[276] Quinn to Anderson, 5 February 1921, Carbondale.
[277] Bryer, ' "A Trial Track for Racers" ', 399. The testimony of a third witness, Scofield Thayer, editor of *The Dial*, was waived because it was considered to be repetitive of evidence already given.
[278] Gillers, 'A Tendency to Deprave and Corrupt', 259.
[279] Quinn to Anderson, 8 February 1921, Carbondale.
[280] Quinn to Anderson, 5 February 1921, Carbondale.
[281] Quinn to J, 13 April 1921, *JQ-JJ II*, 36. The information on Forrester's background is contained in this letter.

In his article on the transformation of American obscenity law—a compelling and impressive article in the field of legal history—Gillers argues convincingly that Quinn might have won the case against the *Little Review* had he tried to 'galvanise "respectable" public opinion extra-judicially'.[282] Specifically, Quinn ought to have made an effort to woo the media, a strategy which 'might have made the press more sympathetic and had an influence on appellate courts or even the trial judges'.[283] But Quinn shunned the opportunity to make publicity related to the case, and was generally keen to avoid becoming known as an 'obscenity' lawyer. When asked for a statement by two journalists as he left the preliminary hearing of 21 October, he walked away ('Statement, hell! I'll make no statement').[284] Otto Kahn, another of the *Little Review*'s financial backers, told Anderson he thought Quinn had been 'rather old fashioned I'm afraid. I should have given you Morris Gest as a publicity agent and had the case on all the front pages', Gest being a successful Broadway producer.[285] According to Gillers, 'Quinn's certainty that the convictions would be affirmed is not defensible. Quinn might have lost, but he also might have won'.[286] Given that the prosecution scared off potential publishers, Quinn could also have appealed against the conviction; and Gillers, in a piece of counterfactual reasoning, argues that 'the chances of reversal were at least fair, certainly better than Quinn believed'.[287] But the question of appeal appears never to have arisen, either with Joyce, or with Anderson and Heap.

Another counterfactual scenario worth considering is the question of what might have happened had Quinn opted not to become involved when Sumner first took action against the proprietors of the Washington Square Bookshop, on 17 September 1920. According to Quinn, at that time Sumner 'didn't know of Joyce or what he had written or how to spell his name'.[288] Quinn was a distinguished lawyer, with an extensive and profitable commercial practice. His intense interest in what Sumner would have identified as a fairly low-level action may well have succeeded in persuading Sumner that there was a more complicated case to answer. There is nothing in the archival record to suggest that anyone objected to the 'substitution' of defendants agreed early in October 1920, but if Anderson and Heap had refused that substitution, the apparently liberal Corrigan *might* have tried to find a way of dismissing the case against Mr and Mrs Arens, perhaps on the grounds of not wishing to open the floodgates, given that any number of New York booksellers could have been deemed guilty of selling publications which might be deemed 'obscene, lewd, lascivious, filthy, indecent'.

---

[282] Gillers, 'A Tendency to Deprave and Corrupt', 263.
[283] Gillers, 'A Tendency to Deprave and Corrupt', 264.
[284] Quinn to Pound, 21 October 1920, Carbondale.
[285] Anderson, *My Thirty Years' War*, 228.
[286] Gillers, 'A Tendency to Deprave and Corrupt', 270.
[287] Gillers, 'A Tendency to Deprave and Corrupt', 265. This is an important conclusion, missed by Kevin Birmingham (in *The Most Dangerous Book*, 168, 194) but echoed by Hassett, *The Ulysses Trials*, who writes of the 'failure of attorney-client communication' (105) and Quinn's lack of 'personal conviction to force the courts to confront the right of *Ulysses* to be heard' (108).
[288] Quinn to Pound, 16 October 1920, Carbondale.

Anderson came to feel that Quinn's strategies had served the legal case poorly. In *Thirty Years' War* she recalls her feeling that Quinn 'was wrong in not wanting us to speak'.[289] Years after the event, she still felt 'we could have given a clearer idea of Joyce's motives than he succeeded in doing'.[290] She also recalls the way in which Quinn argued against the very notion that the case was being tried at Special Sessions, noting her opinion that 'such lack of tact helped him considerably to lose the case'.[291] Both editors had begun to comment on the case against the *Little Review* before the trial of February 1921, with Heap's essay 'Art and the Law', the leading article of the number for September–December 1920, being the pithiest and most engaged of these commentaries.[292] Heap argues that the act of 'trying a creative work in court of law' amounts to a 'heavy farce and sad futility' because judges are not 'qualified to judge even the simplest psychic outburst'.[293] She then proceeds to question the purpose of the society 'for which Mr Sumner is agent'.[294] If its purpose is to protect 'young girls' from 'corruption', does it follow that the 'mind of the young girl rules this country' and why does she have 'such representatives' as Sumner?[295] She notes the ironies of the 'present case' and defends the representation of Bloom as 'a record of the simplest, most unpreventable, most unfocused sex thoughts possible in a rightly-constructed, unashamed human being'.[296] As others have noted, there are some deliberate evasions in this defence, which describes Gerty as 'an innocent, simple childish girl who tends children' and omits to note Bloom's masturbation.[297] But Heap's defence of 'Nausicaa' is ultimately also a plea for more openness about sexuality, and particularly better education for 'young girls', beyond what she characterizes as 'a few obstetric mutterings'.[298] The observations are barbed and understated ('I do not understand Obscenity') and the style is witty, reflective, and focused, in quite significant contrast to Anderson's hectoring and much lengthier 'An Obvious Statement (for the Millionth Time)'.[299] The 'statement' envisages Anderson disagreeing with 'practically everything that will be said in court…both by the prosecution and the defense', and argues that only artists and critics are qualified to judge works of art, and that the only valid judgements

[289] Anderson, *My Thirty Years' War*, 219.   [290] Anderson, *My Thirty Years' War*, 219.

[291] Anderson, *My Thirty Years' War*, 219.

[292] Contemporaneous commentaries on the case include the note in *LR*, September–December, [2] which reports 'our arrest' and describes the case as 'Sumner vs. Joyce'; Heap's 'Art and the Law', Anderson's 'An Obvious Statement (for the Millionth Time)' (both *LR*, September–December 1920, 5–16). For reactions following the trial see Anderson, '*Ulysses* in Court', *LR*, January–March 1921, 22–5; 'Sumner versus James Joyce' by Harriet Monroe, *LR*, January–March 1921, 34; 'The Reader Critic', *LR*, January–March 1921, 61; the advertisement for the Paris edition, *LR*, Autumn 1921, 107; and Heap's note ('Before we could revive from our trial for Joyce's *Ulysses* it was announced for publication in book form. We leap from the field'), *LR*, Autumn 1921, 112.

[293] Heap, 'Art and the Law', *LR*, September–December 1920, 5.

[294] Heap, 'Art and the Law', *LR*, September–December 1920, 5.

[295] Heap, 'Art and the Law', *LR*, September–December 1920, 5.

[296] Heap, 'Art and the Law', *LR*, September–December 1920, 6.

[297] See Scott, ' "The Young Girl," Jane Heap, and Trials of Gender in *Ulysses*', esp. 87.

[298] Heap, 'Art and the Law', *LR*, September–December 1920, 7.

[299] Heap, 'Art and the Law', *LR*, September–December 1920, 6.

are aesthetic, 'not moral, personal nor even technical' (a slightly thin argument, which Joyce himself might have queried).[300]

Nothing in the vast dossier of correspondence documenting the trial records the more informal views of Anderson and Heap at the time. Though it is obvious that the editors had come to resent and dislike Quinn, it is impossible to get a sense of whether they understood the depth of Quinn's homophobia and cultural aversion to the *Little Review*. His typed letter to Pound of 16 October 1920, which was duly passed to Joyce, is quite an extraordinary document; as it has largely been edited out of published accounts, its content needs to be acknowledged, as Scott has argued.[301] The letter is extremely long, running to over 6,000 words, and reviews the whole history of the Pound/Quinn involvement with the *Little Review*, Quinn's numerous meetings with Anderson and Heap, and the legal scuffles Quinn fought on the journal's behalf, and speculates—in considerable detail—as to the likely outcome and repercussions of the prospective preliminary hearing and trial. But what makes the letter extraordinary is the attitudes it reveals to Anderson and Heap and the cultural world in which they circulate, a world centred around Washington Square, and one of:

> buggeries and Lesbianism and God knows what. These people seem to sweat urine and probably urinate sweat. At any rate, they look as though they would stink piss if you got close enough to smell them. That's one of fifty illustrations of their soured piss attitude. I don't mind the aberrations of a woman who has some openness and elasticity of mind, who may be mentally as well as physically plastic, in whose excretions there may occasionally be cream; but by God! I don't like the thought of women who seem to exude as well as bathe in piss, if not drink it, or each other's.[302]

The rant goes on. It characterizes Anderson and Heap as 'sheer self-exploiters' without any 'disinterested love of literature' who were 'Trying to use Joyce, an artist, as propaganda for their review'. It describes the *Little Review* as a 'typical Washington Square monthly fecal discharge' and specifies Quinn's revulsion at the idea of defending 'people who intentionally and stupidly and brazenly and Sapphoistically and pederastically and urinally and menstrually violate the law':

> THEY ARE BORES. They are too damn fresh. They stand for no principle. They are cheap self-advertisers…They are pseudo 'editors.' They add brazen impudence to stark boresome ignorance—ignorance of everything that an 'editor' of even an art-art magazine should know *and feel!*[303]

This revelation of Quinn's abnormal, obsessive, and abhorrent psychology also registers Quinn's sudden awareness of the politics of neighbourhood. From his chambers in Nassau Street, part of New York's financial district, Quinn wanted to collaborate with professional literary editors, who did not mix the professional

[300] Anderson, 'An Obvious Statement (for the Millionth Time)', *LR*, September–December 1920, 9, 10.
[301] Scott, ' "The Young Girl," Jane Heap, and Trials of Gender in *Ulysses*', 81.
[302] Quinn to Pound, 16 October 1920, Carbondale.
[303] Quinn to Pound, 16 October 1920, Carbondale.

with the personal. Instead he found himself thrust into the midst of Washington Square bohemia, defending two women who did not recognize a valid separation between their personal lives and experiences, their sexuality, and their professional editorial commitments. Washington Square—or more accurately Greenwich Village—was only a couple of miles from Nassau Street, but a world away in cultural terms. Quinn knew that the area was associated with social, political, and artistic experimentation, but his description of the preliminary hearing, 'There was Heap plus Anderson, plus heaps of other Heaps and Andersons', suggests that he had not fully realized—and could not accept—the extent to which gay culture had become embedded within Anderson and Heap's locality, and the extent to which they emblematized that culture.[304] Though Quinn's brief was to defend the *Little Review* against the charge of publishing an obscene text, his letter to Pound of 16 October 1920 makes the charges *against* the *Little Review* unusually clear, by including a three-page list of the 'things in different pages...that are objected to'.[305] At his lunch with Sumner on 15 October—boastfully described as a 'tactful talk'— Quinn had 'frankly admitted there were parts in' *Ulysses* which 'should not have been published in a magazine'.[306] This 'tactful talk' almost certainly helped Sumner to develop the case for prosecution. His initial complaint to Swann had only specified four pages in the 'Nausicaa' instalment which he considered objectionable (pages 43, 45, 50, and 51) but his affidavit of 21 October 1920 extends the charge of 'lewdness and of obscenity' to fourteen of the seventeen pages in the instalment (42, 43, 44, 45, 46, 47, 48, 50, 51, 53, 55, 57, 59, 60).[307] The textual trail suggests that Quinn must have helped to clarify Sumner's thinking, as Quinn's letter of 16 October 1920 specifies ten objectionable pages (43, 45, 46, 47, 48, 50, 51, 53, 55, 57) and includes lengthy citations from the text. (See Appendix 2 for this list.)

Quinn's final negotiations with Huebsch were also characteristically unhelpful and volatile. More than a month after the conclusion of the trial on 21 February 1921, Joyce did not have a precise sense of what happened, or what the publishing implications would be. He asked a Dr Collins, a friend of Quinn's, to deliver a letter to Quinn by hand which asked Huebsch for a royalty of 22 per cent, 'one third on signing of contact, 1/3 on delivery of final MS and 1/3 on day of publication'.[308] As Joyce explained to Weaver, he 'stated that this proposal was to be submitted to Mr Huebsch and accepted or refused within two days'.[309] This intervention propelled a final round of negotiations with Huebsch, which, as noted, led to Huebsch

---

[304] Quinn to Pound, 21 October 1920, Carbondale. According to George Chauncey, gay culture became associated with Greenwich Village before the First World War. See 'Long-Haired Men and Short-Haired Women: Building a Gay World in the Heart of Bohemia', in Rick Bear and Leslie Cohen Berlowitz (eds.), *Greenwich Village: Culture and Counterculture* (New Brunswick, NJ: Rutgers University Press, 1993), 151–64.

[305] Quinn to Pound, 16 October 1920, Carbondale.

[306] Quinn to Pound, 16 October 1920, Carbondale.

[307] Appended to Quinn, 'Affidavit and Notice of Motion', Carbondale.

[308] J to Weaver, 3 April 1921, British Library, add. ms. 57346. The excerpts quoted are not included in *L* I, 160.

[309] J to Weaver, 3 April 1921, British Library, add. ms. 57346. The excerpts quoted are not included in *L* I, 160.

making a final decision not to publish *Ulysses*. Though Quinn moved on quickly, he was clearly angry with Huebsch, and taunted him for his timidity, writing to him as follows:

> you may consider this letter as your complete and full 'absolution'. Absolvo te! I might almost add: Ite!—Go!—to or otherwise—the typescript goes to rejoice Joyce. So rejoice yourself and be glad that you escape the long arm of the criminal law and that you won't ever have to stand up in the stinking atmosphere of a New York criminal court and defend your fair name as a husband, if not father, and a publisher and a citizen from the heinous crime of publishing a book with the name of the far wandering Ulysses. 'Twill be a unique book, but so was Ulysses. In it Joyce has drawn a long bow, a bow that no other author living could draw. But don't regret the loss of this unique literary treasure from your list of publications. You will doubtless be able to console yourself with the thought that it is better to lose twenty *Ulysses* than spend thirty days in Blackwell's Island for one.[310]

The fact Quinn took the time to dictate such a letter ultimately suggests a fascinating and deep ambivalence in his attitude towards Huebsch. He was angry at the way matters had turned out with regard to the *Little Review*, angry with Huebsch for not being more daring and for taking so much time in negotiations which ultimately led nowhere, and—arguably—angry with himself for having failed to effectively defend *Ulysses* in court, and find a means by which Joyce's 'long bow' could be published.

Yet Quinn was still keen to see if he could find a publisher for *Ulysses*. Early in April 1921, he had approached Horace Liveright, of the firm Boni and Liveright, and passed him the typescript which Huebsch had finally returned. He was at pains to explain the circumstances in which the book was being written, as he told Joyce:

> I told Liveright that you had worked on 'Ulysses' six or seven years, that you would not finish it until late this spring or early in the summer or midsummer, and that you would not agree to anything like a royalty of $1.50 per volume.[311]

Established in 1917, Boni and Liveright had quickly established a position as an avant-garde publisher of literary Modernism, willing to challenge obscenity and censorship laws. According to Quinn, the New York firm agreed to publish *Ulysses* on 21 April 1921 and started to negotiate terms, by asking for an option on Joyce's 'next three novels, not for limited editions, but for general publication where it would be possible'.[312] But then—on that very same day, 21 April 1921—Quinn received the manuscript of episodes 15 and 16 ('Circe' and 'Eumeus') and asked 'Mr Watson' of his office to read them, with a view to potential publication. Quinn's letter to Joyce of 5 June relays Watson's verdict:

> [He] read enough of the Circe and Eumeus parts in your ms to realise that it never could be published without the certainty of prosecution and conviction. I called up Liveright and told him that his letter of April 21 was impossible, but that I would waste no more time on it for the concluding parts were such that I would not advise

[310] Quinn to Huebsch, 13 April 1921, cited in Reid, *The Man from New York*, 486.
[311] Quinn to J, 13 April 1921, *JQ-JJ II*, 33.   [312] Quinn to J, 5 June 1921, *JQ-JJ II*, 38.

him that it could be published here without the certainty of prosecution and conviction. He said he did not want to be convicted and so he dropped the matter. And that ends Liveright.[313]

The case was closed. Quinn was no longer prepared to help Joyce secure publication in the US, and was notably angry at this moment, telling Pound: 'I've had a hell of a time with Joyce and the *Little Review*. I'm up to date with Joyce and through with Joyce'.[314] The mood did not last. Less than a month later he was in Paris, where he found Joyce in the midst of his work on the proofs for the Paris edition, and suffering a severe attack of iritis. He gave him a 'gift' of 2,000 francs.[315]

One of Quinn's letters to Joyce complains that the case against the *Little Review* 'cost me thousands of dollars personally', made him work harder 'than I have ever worked in my life', and put him into a state where 'feelings' 'were boiling up in me'.[316] Anderson also found that the trial had a significant impact on her mental health. Though the tone and facts of *Thirty Years' War* are not always to be trusted, it is significant that Anderson confesses that after the trial 'I didn't know what to do about my life—so I did a nervous breakdown that lasted several months'.[317] She wanted to end the *Little Review*, feeling that:

> it had begun logically with the inarticulateness of a divine afflatus and should end logically with the epoch's supreme articulation—'Ulysses'.[318]

But this plan was met with 'staggering resistance' from Heap, and thus the *Little Review* continued, and announced in autumn 1921 that it had been 'reorganized' as a quarterly in 'protest' against the suppression of instalments of *Ulysses*.[319] Relations between Anderson and Heap continued to be intermittently hostile. One of Heap's letters to Florence Reynolds mentions a violent row in which Anderson 'took an axe and broke open my trunk' which Heap had locked in order to 'protect my things'.[320] Heap felt that Anderson had 'eliminated herself from my life with this conduct' but the pair must have become reconciled, somehow, as they set sail together to visit Paris, in spring 1923, a trip which gave them the opportunity to meet both Pound and Joyce for the first time.[321] Pound had re-established his connection with Anderson and the *Little Review* in the early months of 1921, in spite of Quinn's dire warnings against doing so.[322] Feeling that the *Little Review* had 'accomplished more in six months than the *Dial* has in a year', he began to contribute to the *Little Review* again and remained editorially committed and named as part of its 'administration' until the number dated Autumn and Winter 1924–5.

---

[313] Quinn to J, 5 June 1921, *JQ-JJ II*, 39.
[314] Quinn to Pound, 15 June 1921, cited in Reid, *The Man from New York*, 488.
[315] *JQ-JJ II*, 43.   [316] *JQ-JJ II*, 34, 35.   [317] Anderson, *Thirty Years' War*, 231.
[318] Anderson, *Thirty Years' War*, 230.
[319] Anderson, *Thirty Years' War*, 230; see *LR*, Autumn 1921, [2].
[320] Jane Heap to Florence Reynolds, [postmarked 24 July 1922], Baggett (ed.), *Dear Tiny Heart*, 79.
[321] Jane Heap to Florence Reynolds, [postmarked 24 July 1922], Baggett (ed.), *Dear Tiny Heart*, 79; information on trip to Paris also in Baggett, 181, n21. Anderson, *Thirty Years' War* describes these meetings, 243–8.
[322] Mentioned in Pound to Anderson, 21 May 1921, *P-LR*, 276.

In response to Quinn's letters of October 1920, Pound had pointed out that in 1919 he had 'severed official connection' with the *Little Review* 'largely at your suggestion, and incidentally because I was fed up'.[323] He felt that Joyce was 'not a particularly reasonable person' and refused to take any 'responsibility whatever' for Joyce's behaviour in the ensuing legal trysts envisaged by Quinn. Joyce was similarly evasive. He did not have a fixed address in Paris in October 1920 when the case against the *Little Review* escalated. Thus Quinn, who was very keen that Joyce agree to stop publishing *Ulysses* in the *Little Review*, directed his letters to Pound, for onward submission to Joyce. Pound certainly co-operated with this request; he forwarded the letters, 'which you need not of necessity read', and recommended that Joyce 'turn the whole matter over to Quinn'.[324] Quinn specifically wanted Joyce to understand that if the third instalment of 'Nausicaa' was 'condemned', the 'whole book would be condemned. Result: no publisher would publish' and the 'careful plans' for Huebsch's 'privately printed edition' would be 'spoiled'.[325] But Joyce was wont to keep his own counsel. He refused to accept the view that a prosecution of the *Little Review* would upset the plans with Huebsch, telling Quinn, in slightly lofty terms:

> I scarcely think that Mr Huebsch as publisher-putative of a private edition will be deterred by any public prosecution of the book as a serial if his edition is safe and lucrative.[326]

With regard to Quinn's request that he withdraw *Ulysses* from the *Little Review*, Joyce did not respond to Quinn directly. Instead he wrote to Weaver, giving detailed reasons for wishing to stick with the *Little Review* (to withdraw *Ulysses* now would be 'to pass sentence on my own writing and to blame the editors for having published it').[327] To some extent his rationale was that of 'I have started so I shall finish'; the unity of publication in the *Little Review* was a cultural and bibliographical fact that mattered to his authorial self-fashioning. Abandoning the journal in its moment of crisis would be tantamount to acknowledging that doubts about the cultural validity of the work were justified: he would be allowing the forces of conservatism to succeed in silencing *Ulysses*, a character whom he described—in what appears to be an acknowledgement of Quinn's obsession with physical secretions— as a 'world-troubling seaman'.[328]

Some of these justifications were not discussed with Quinn, who was furious to find Joyce repeatedly evading and side-stepping such important issues.[329] Writing in direct response to Quinn's lengthy and homophobic ranting, Joyce chose instead

[323] Pound to Quinn, 31 October 1920, in *EP-JQ*, 198, 199.
[324] Pound to J, [*c.* October] 1920, *EP-JJ*, 184. See also J to Weaver, 10 November 1920: 'I have received two very long letters from Mr Quinn of New York concerning *Ulysses* and *The Little Review*', *L* I, 149.
[325] Quinn to Pound, 16 October 1920, Carbondale.
[326] J to Quinn, 17 November 1920, *JQ-JJ I*, 256.
[327] J to Weaver, 10 November 1920. Part of this letter has been published; see *L* I, 149. This particular passage has been omitted and is in the Harriet Shaw Weaver Papers, BL Ms add 57346, folio 15. Discussed above, p. 98.
[328] J to Quinn, 17 November 1920, *JQ-JJ I*, 256.   [329] *JQ-JJ II*, 34.

to emphasize the difficult material conditions of his life ('All October was spent by me in the vain search for a flat'; 'Then I was ill with a kind of influenza'; in Paris 'The food is bad, the cooking worse and the wine is worst of all').[330] Quinn's blatant hostility to Anderson and Heap—evinced, for example, by their repeated depiction as 'pissing rabbits'—is countered by Joyce's explanation that he has had virtually nothing to do with them: 'I never had any letter from Miss Anderson. I had one, I believe, from Miss Heep'.[331] In a move which is deliberate and knowing, he then proceeds to justify the current *impasse* by explaining his attitude to the *Little Review* more generally:

> I do not know much about the L. R. ...I understood that it is or was a review of the better class to judge by its contributors. But if the truth must be told, I never read it (except for my own instalments) so that I have a very hazy idea of its character.[332]

Joyce had been in regular receipt of the *Little Review* from May 1917, the moment when Pound's position as Foreign Editor had begun.[333] His insistence that he only had a 'hazy idea of its character' is hardly to be trusted. Pound briefed Joyce regularly about his plans for the few 'real authors' of his generation; Joyce knew Yeats from his teens, and had met and dined with Eliot and Wyndham Lewis in Paris in the summer of 1920.[334] He appears not to have been particularly interested in the work of many of his modernist peers, and may only have read selectively from Pound's selections in the *Little Review*. But Joyce was, of course, a voracious and sharp-eyed reader, and there is specific evidence (in one of the notebooks) of his reading the *Little Review*.[335] As his lengthy epistle to Quinn developed, he perhaps sensed the implausibility of his claim to having but a 'hazy idea' of the *Little Review*. He decided to change tack, becoming more pragmatic, telling Quinn that he could not 'withdraw *Ulysses*... from further serial publication' because the editors already had in hand the typescript of chapter 14 ('Oxen of the Sun'); any intervention by him would thus be 'useless'.[336] Moreover, John Rodker had recently told him that the *Little Review* was 'suspended or will suspend publication'; if not, he told Quinn, very much tongue-in-cheek, it was possible that the arrival of chapter 15 ('Circe'), '(a tasteful production on which I am now engaged) will decide the matter'.[337]

It seems likely that Joyce found Quinn's letters of October 1920 dictatorial, repetitive, intemperate, and offensive—and one can easily see why he was reluctant to accept advice from a lawyer with such attitudes—but he must also have been pleased to be given such a vivid sense of the kinds of fuss his writing could generate.

[330] J to Quinn, 17 November 1920, *JQ-JJ* I, 254, 255.
[331] Quinn to Pound, 16 October 1920, Carbondale; Joyce to Quinn, 17 November 1920, *JQ-JJ* I, 256.
[332] J to Quinn, 17 November 1920, *JQ-JJ* I, 256. This is hardly candid, and hardly to be trusted. Joyce was receiving copies of the *Little Review* reasonably regularly; while he may not have read every issue from cover to cover, even casual glancing would have enabled him to form judgements and impressions.
[333] His name is included in the 'free list' of subscribers sent from Pound to Anderson, 5 May 1917, *P-LR*, 32. Some of Joyce's original copies of the *Little Review* are in Buffalo.
[334] Pound to Mrs Joyce, 10 September 1919, *EP-JJ*, 126; *L* III, 17.   [335] See below p. 242.
[336] J to Quinn, 17 November 1920, *JQ-JJ* I, 256.
[337] J to Quinn, 17 November 1920, *JQ-JJ* I, 256.

He was, for example, 'much amused' by the description of the magistrate Corrigan in his 'judicial chambers'.[338] The specific evidence of the three-page list of excerpts from chapter 13 ('Nausicaa'), appended to the letter of 16 October, must also have been particularly useful in pinpointing the kinds of detail that generated the greatest opprobrium. In some sense the furnishing of that kind of detail—of reception, of reading, of engaged response to what had already been written and published—enabled the ongoing composition and subsequent revision of the text, a pattern which makes the production of *Ulysses* highly unusual within book history. From that perspective, it is also significant, as noted earlier, that the fraught and difficult circumstances of serial publication served as a catalyst for the publication of Shakespeare and Company's unexpurgated first edition.

Quinn was of the view that *Ulysses* was 'a very unique piece of art, but it is not a work of art to be published in a magazine, for the background as well as the frame and lighting are important in showing a piece of art'.[339] For the other collaborators who made the serial publication of the *Little Review Ulysses* possible, things could not be so clear cut. Pound, for example, commended the *Little Review* for having 'pure heart *à outrance*' and argued that its pages revealed that 'the new thing that is to be durable does not spring up without roots'.[340] He also sensed that serial publication had made Joyce 'better known than a private publication in book form' and believed that the process had 'helped Joyce to get on with writing his book'.[341] Joyce did not understand the significance of the manufacturing clause, and did not foresee the repercussions of Beach's failure to claim copyright protection for his work in the US.[342] Nor did he know that the legal case investigating Bloom's masturbation pitched Cockburn against Learned Hand. But he did understand that the process of serialization was of formative and fundamental significance to the genesis of *Ulysses*. Quinn's regular updates from New York, coupled with the lively discussion in the *Little Review* 'Reader Critic' columns, enabled him to gain a sense of his readers, of the evolving legal, cultural, and literary frameworks in which his work was being published, and—most crucially—facilitated and inspired the ongoing composition of the work, a point which will be explored in the textually focused readings of Chapters 3 and 4.

[338] J to Quinn, 17 November 1920, *JQ-JJ I*, 256.
[339] Quinn to Pound, 16 October 1920, Carbondale.
[340] Ezra Pound, 'Small Magazines', *English Journal*, November 1930, 689–704 (697, 704).
[341] Pound to Quinn, 31 October 1920, *EP-JQ*, 199.
[342] If Joyce had allowed Huebsch to print an expurgated version of the text, he could have had what Spoo terms 'a secure American copyright in the entire work' (162). For more information on this and the subsequent publishing and copyright history of *Ulysses* in the US, see Spoo, *Without Copyrights: Piracy, Publishing and the Public Domain*, esp. chapters 4 and 6.

3

The Serial Style and Beyond
From the *Little Review* to Shakespeare and Company

INTRODUCTION

The *Little Review Ulysses* is of critical interest for several reasons: as an aspect of literary history which reveals the specific significance of periodical production for the development of Modernism; as a distinctive and early version of *Ulysses* intended by Joyce for publication; and as a clear and easily accessible point of comparison with the fuller 'final' version of the novel, as published by Shakespeare and Company. This chapter is concerned with the style and nature of *Ulysses* as a serial, and begins to characterize the multiple ways in which Joyce changed the text for the volume version of 1922. The work examines the genesis of *Ulysses* in print in the period between March 1918, when the first chapter of the novel appeared in the *Little Review*, and 2 February 1922, the date when the first volume edition of *Ulysses* was published in Paris.

The scholarly models for writing about textual variation and revision are quite diverse, and are worth reviewing here. Some are as old as literary teaching itself, and involve the field most would refer to as 'close reading', a phrase with a slightly vexed critical history, and a practice which has been transformed by the digital revolution, as Michael Hancher has observed.[1] Schoolchildren are still sometimes asked to 'close read' by comparing and contrasting two poems on the same theme; the practice of comparing and contrasting two variant versions of the same text (two versions of *King Lear*, for example) is a similar exercise. The task in hand is a case of spotting the differences between the two texts, describing those differences, and attempting to account for their critical significance. So far, so easy. But this becomes much more complicated if the texts are lengthy, and they exist in more than two versions. What is the relationship between the variant texts and how can one unravel the tangled textual history in an intelligible and accurate manner? All too quickly the problem becomes one of trying to describe multiple sources, of too much evidence, of variants pointing in multiple interpretive directions.

---

[1] Michael Hancher, 'Re:Search and Close Reading', in Matthew K. Gold and Lauren F. Klein (eds.), *Debates in the Digital Humanities* (Minneapolis, MN: University of Minnesota Press, 2016), 118–38. Hancher writes that 'large digital libraries . . . afford a greatly improved access to minute particulars—thanks not to data mining but to datum mining'. He continues: 'Keyword search, now ubiquitous, is taken for granted, like flying in an airplane. And yet, like the airplane, it has been a game-changer' (118).

Critique génétique, or genetic criticism, concerns itself with such issues. Within the field of Joyce studies, Daniel Ferrer and Michael Groden are pioneers, while Luca Crispi, Ronan Crowley, Finn Fordham, and Dirk Van Hulle are among a group of younger scholars who have adopted, and continue to refine, this approach.[2] Described as a 'true child' of French structuralism, genetic criticism differs from a more traditional textual or manuscript scholarship through its emphasis on what the study of drafts and manuscripts may reveal about the whole creative process.[3] The manuscript and draft sources are not simply to be regarded as a key which might usefully unlock some hidden meaning in the finished work. Instead the genetic critic pursues the 'broader goal of reconstructing and analysing a chain of writing events', seizing and describing 'a movement, a process of writing that can only be approximately inferred from the existing documents'.[4] As Deppman, Ferrer, and Groden have explained:

> Such an ambitious programme required a new critical vocabulary. It seemed especially important to do away with the philological notion of 'variant,' which implies *one* text with alternative formulations. To make a clean break, Bellemin-Noël used the neologism 'avant-texte' to designate all the documents that come before a work when it is considered as a text and when those documents and the text are considered as part of a system.[5]

For *Ulysses,* the genetic dossier of 'avant-textes' is particularly voluminous, including, as noted in Chapter 2, notes, drafts, 'fair' copies of completed chapter drafts, typescripts, and proofs.[6] In the face of so much evidence, it is difficult to know what to prioritize: should a genetic scholar of *Ulysses* pursue the study of a particular set of documents, a particular chapter, a particular theme or *leitmotif,* or aim to work more generally, across a broader range of materials and issues? Luca Crispi has proposed an emphasis on character and character formation in his recent and pioneering genetic study of *Ulysses.* His *Joyce's Creative Process and the Construction of Characters in Ulysses* explores the conception and evolution of Molly and Leopold Bloom in the work's wide range of surviving notes and manuscripts.[7] Geneticists 'privilege historical development and context in contrast to a conception of a synchronous or timelessly present text', but Crispi, like other scholars in the field, acknowledges that the genetic approach, beyond its historicist and textual foundations, could underpin a wide range of 'critical perspectives and interpretive insights'

---

[2] See *Genetic Joyce Studies,* www.geneticjoycestudies.org, published annually since 2001.

[3] Jed Deppman, Daniel Ferrer, and Michael Groden, 'Introduction: A Genesis of French Genetic Criticism', in Deppman, Ferrer, and Groden (eds.), *Genetic Criticism: Texts and Avant-Textes* (Philadelphia, PA: University of Pennsylvania Press, 2004), 2.

[4] Deppman, Ferrer, and Groden, 'Introduction: A Genesis of French Genetic Criticism', 11.

[5] Deppman, Ferrer, and Groden, 'Introduction: A Genesis of French Genetic Criticism', 8. Note the distinction, implied here, between 'work' (the published piece) and 'text' (the manuscript or typescript precedents). In practice, scholars (especially non-geneticists) often use these terms interchangeably.

[6] See above, p. 74–75.

[7] Luca Crispi, *Becoming the Blooms: Joyce's Creative Process and the Construction of Characters in Ulysses* (Oxford: Oxford University Press, 2015).

(such as narratology, linguistic analysis, psychoanalysis, deconstruction, and so on).[8] The key issue is the study of the avant-texte in a temporal dimension, and the isolation of what can simply be described as 'meaningful variation'.[9]

Deppman, Ferrer, and Groden are keen to emphasize the origins of genetic criticism in France, to note that 'the German-, English- and French-language traditions of textual criticism have been dominated by different models', and to point to the ways in which Anglo-American editorial scholarship has been 'pragmatic and not theoretically self-conscious' insofar as it sees 'textuality and intention as unproblematic'.[10] But D. F. McKenzie (1931–99), a New Zealander, and Professor of Bibliography and Textual Criticism at Oxford until 1996, was certainly attuned to the possibilities of the genetic approach. *Bibliography and the Sociology of Texts* (1986) argued for a scholarly practice in which the concerns of textual and manuscript scholarship attend to the specificities of book history (and *vice versa*). McKenzie's arguments could not 'solve' the problems that textual editors may face in trying to produce non-corrupted editions, but they did usefully point to the 'social' element of *all* texts by suggesting that:

> each reading is peculiar to its occasion, each can be at least partially recovered from the physical forms of the text, and the differences in readings constitute an informative history. What writers thought they were doing in writing texts, or printers and booksellers in designing and publishing them, or readers in making sense of them are issues which no history of the book can evade.[11]

These insights—the ideas of 'meaningful variation' of 'differences in readings' constituting an 'informative history'—are crucial planks within the analysis that follows, analysis which concentrates on the genesis of the *Ulysses* text *in print* between 1918 and 1922, in order to discover the critical significance of 'differences in readings', and to try and gain a general sense of how and why Joyce revised his text.

From the perspectives of authorship and reception—important concepts for bibliographers, textual scholars, book historians, and geneticists—the *Little Review Ulysses* is a particular type of avant-texte, commanding particular critical attention. Within the vast dossier of materials which document the genesis of *Ulysses*, it represents a pre-final version of the text which Joyce intended for publication. Each serial instalment, adding to the previous, represents the evolving text of *Ulysses* in a set of isolatable moments within the composition of the work as a whole. Scholars who wish to parry on this issue—to dismiss the textual and critical significance of the serial text—may argue that the *Little Review Ulysses* does not represent the text as intended by Joyce, and point to the ways in which the serialization is so evidently

---

[8] Deppman, Ferrer, and Groden, 'Introduction: A Genesis of French Genetic Criticism', 5; Crispi, *Becoming the Blooms*, 27.

[9] Deppman, Ferrer, and Groden, 'Introduction: A Genesis of French Genetic Criticism', 11.

[10] Deppman, Ferrer, and Groden, 'Introduction: A Genesis of French Genetic Criticism', 10, 5.

[11] D. F. McKenzie, *Bibliography and the Sociology of Texts* (1986; Cambridge: Cambridge University Press, 1999), 19.

corrupt. But the very idea of textual 'corruption' implies that the text might once have existed in an error-free and pristine form. In respect of *Ulysses* this was never the case: as Gabler notes, 'no manuscript exists as one document that contains a text of the work as fully written and finally revised'.[12] Joyce himself characterized the *Little Review* as a 'review of the better class': the serial text represents the version which the unique and challenging circumstances of his residence in wartime Zurich, and then post-war Trieste, allowed him to achieve.[13]

During the process of serialization, Joyce was meticulous about the completion of each chapter. It is reasonable to assume that the chapter typescripts prepared for serialization represented work in a state that was as complete as could be managed in the circumstances. This does not mean the typescripts could not ultimately be revised (as indeed they were). But it makes sense—a kind of bibliographical and pragmatic sense—to see the serial text as a text of interim intention, and the volume text (of 1922) as a text of final intention (however problematic those terms may be). It certainly is the case that the *Little Review Ulysses* is corrupt; it is also the case, as noted in the introduction, that the 1922 *Ulysses* was riddled with authorial, non-authorial and transcriptional errors, despite the care that Joyce, Sylvia Beach, and Maurice Darantiere took in its preparation.[14] In comparing the serial *Ulysses* with that of 1922, one is therefore comparing two corrupt editions of the work. This comparison involves omitting to consider some documents in the post-serial genetic dossier. But that omission is worthwhile because it enables a clear view of the critical significance of the two original printed texts of *Ulysses*, a view which escapes from such complications as the incomplete but nonetheless voluminous archive, lost notebooks, lost final working drafts, and so on. Instead the emphasis is simply on the differences between the two historic first editions of the text, on what can be understood, critically, by observing the variations between those two editions.[15]

Joyce complained of passages being 'mutilated', 'omitted', and 'hopelessly mixed' in the *Little Review* and insisted that prospective volume publishers, including Beach, begin afresh by setting the text 'consigned in typescript'.[16] During 1918, 1919, and 1920—as the serialization progressed—he continued to make notes and intended to work the material of those notes into the text of *Ulysses* as circumstance allowed.[17] He also kept copies of his original typescripts and made additions to them (by hand) as he prepared for volume publication in Paris. These typescript additions, which are generally rather minimal, can be observed in the collection of typescripts preserved at Buffalo, or the facsimile reproductions of *JJA* volumes 12,

---

[12] Hans Walter Gabler, 'What *Ulysses* Requires', *Proceedings of the Bibliographical Society of America*, 87:2 (1993), 187–248 (197).

[13] Joyce to Quinn, 17 November 1920, qtd in *JQ-JJ I*, 256.   [14] See above, p. 15–17.

[15] In general references are only made to the *Little Review* and *U*1922. Where the intervening stages in the post-serial genetic dossier are thought to be of particular critical relevance, reference is made to the left-hand pages of the *CSE* which record, *inter alia*, the successive stages of revision Joyce made in typescript and proof.

[16] J to Quinn, 11 March 1920, *L* II, 459; J to Weaver, 25 February 1920, *L* I, 137.

[17] For Joyce as a notetaker and the compositional process of *Ulysses* see Luca Crispi, 'The Notescape of *Ulysses*', in Ronan Crowley and Dirk Van Hulle (eds.), *New Quotatoes: Joycean Exogenesis in the Digital Age* (Leiden: Brill, 2016), 75–87.

13, and 14.[18] Looked at more broadly, it is clear that the circumstances in which the work was being written and prepared for publication were significant for the kinds of plans Joyce was making for revision. In this regard, it is worth reviewing the evidence of a particular moment—that of November 1920. At that time, Quinn was in negotiation with B. W. Huebsch about the potential New York edition and Joyce, meanwhile, was finding it difficult to settle in a suitable Parisian apartment and had reluctantly returned to an expensive 'maison meublée'.[19] Joyce wrote to Quinn and complained that he found himself now writing *Ulysses* 'at the twentieth address...and the coldest'. He continued:

> The complete notes fill a small valise, but in the course of continual changings very often it was not possible to sort them for the final time before the publication of certain instalments. The insertions (chiefly verbal or phrases, rarely passages) must be put in for the book publication. Before leaving Trieste I did this sorting for all episodes up to and including *Circe*.[20]

'Complete notes' which fill a 'small valise' is one of those throwaway phrases which remains tantalizing to genetic scholars of *Ulysses*: it suggests a significant post-serial authorial archive (much of which now appears to be lost) and a grand system and plan for the revision of the text (which is difficult to reconstruct). Crucially, this letter also suggests that Joyce regarded the chapters of the work which he had finished by this time (1 to 14) as finished enough, but for the business of adding a few 'insertions' (a comment which makes the revisions sound minor, which is not the case, as I shall argue).

Joyce clearly planned to do some of the 'inserting' work on proof. The same letter to Quinn continues:

> The episodes which have the heaviest burden of addenda are *Lotus-eaters*, *Lestrygonians*, *Nausikaa* and *Cyclops*. Therefore I must stipulate to have three sendings of proofs (preferably a widemargined one to be pulled), namely:
> (1) A galley-page proof of all the book up to and including *Circe*.
> (2) A similar proof of the three chapters of the *Nostos*.
> (3) A complete proof of the book in page form.[21]

In the event, of course, Joyce never got to work on the Huebsch edition envisioned here. But from early June 1921 he did get to work extensively on the proofs of the Paris edition, marking as many as 5,000 pages of proof and working himself into a

---

[18] See http://library.buffalo.edu/pl/collections/jamesjoyce/catalog/v.htm, which describes the 'printers' typescripts' received and typeset by Darantiere from June 1921 onwards. This element of the dossier is incomplete. It is nonetheless fascinating to study chapter typescripts for chapters which are subsequently revised quite heavily (such as chapter 6 ('Hades') and 7 ('Aeolus')) and to see how few of the revisions were undertaken before Joyce consigned his text to Darantiere. Typescript additions can also be studied through the left-hand pages of the *CSE*.
[19] J to John Rodker, 10 November, *L* III, 29.
[20] J to Quinn, 24 November 1920, *L* III, 30–1.
[21] J to Quinn, 24 November 1920, *L* III, 31.

state of 'proof fever', a phrase he added to the proof of chapter 7 ('Aeolus'), in a knowing act of 'self reflexive materiality', under the heading:

ORTHOGRAPHICAL

Want to be sure of his spelling. Proof fever. Martin Cunningham forgot to give us his spellingbee conundrum this morning.   (*U*1922, 117)[22]

A sense of that 'fever' is communicated vividly in a letter to Weaver of October 1921:

A few lines to let you know I am here again with MSS and pencils (red, green and blue) and cases of books and trunks and all the rest of my impedimenta nearly snowed up in proofs and nearly crazed with work. *Ulysses* will be finished in about three weeks, thank God, and (if the French printers don't all leap into the Rhone in despair at the mosaics I send them back) ought to be published early in November.[23]

This suggests the intensity of the final stages of the compositional process, and points to the significance of the 'small valise' in which Joyce had stored notebooks and lightly revised typescripts in preparation for the moment of general revision in advance of publication in volume form. Working from that valise (or trunk or case) with coloured and lead pencils, dipping pen and ink, Joyce revised *Ulysses* significantly. Given the extent of some of the revisions—such as those for chapter 5 ('Lotus-Eaters')—it is surprising to find that Joyce did not, at this stage, generate either a new manuscript or a new typescript of the text he now intended for publication. That he did not do so suggests the economies of labour and the pressures of the moment in which he was working. Manuscripts take hours to copy, and Joyce's eyesight was poor. New typescripts would have involved the trouble of finding and working with typists, and he had already had trouble enough with those who were working on chapter 15 ('Circe'), as noted in Chapter 2.[24] With Darantiere and Beach at hand and willing to help, he clearly felt that the chapter typescripts he had were serviceable enough, and used them as the initial means of textual transmission to Darantiere, and then revised, incrementally, on successive proofs.[25] At the same time he continued to make use of notebooks and notesheets which recorded his thoughts, as well as notes from his reading, and acted as lexical

[22] Ronan Crowley, 'Proof ∧ Finder: Page Proofs', *Genetic Joyce Studies*, 8 (Spring 2008), www.geneticjoycestudies.org; see also Ronan Crowley, 'Proof ∧ Finder: Placards', *Genetic Joyce Studies*, 8 (Spring 2008), www.geneticjoycestudies.org. For Joyce at work on the proofs of *Ulysses*, see also Michael Groden, *Ulysses in Progress*, esp. 101–14; chapter 4 of Hannah Sullivan, *The Work of Revision* ('Joyce and the Illogic of Addition') (Cambridge, MA: Harvard University Press, 2013); and Daniel Ferrer and Jean-Michel Rabaté, 'Paragraphs in Expansion', in Deppman, Ferrer, and Groden (eds.), *Genetic Criticism: Texts and Avant-Textes*, 132–51. The estimate of 'over five thousand pages' is given by Luca Crispi, 'A First Foray into the National Library of Ireland's Joyce Manuscripts: Bloomsday 2011', *Genetic Joyce Studies*, 11 (Spring 2011), www.geneticjoycestudies.org, page 2.
[23] J to Weaver, 7 October 1921, *L* I, 172.   [24] See above, p. 93.
[25] For chapters 1 to 14, the extant manuscript drafts including, for example, the portions of the Rosenbach and the materials now at the NLI predate serialization.

and conceptual aide-memoires.[26] These repositories and the authorial working practices which they communicate would be worth significant bibliographical and genetic scrutiny. The rewriting on proof—attending to the vexed question of whether Joyce planned his revisions or wrote them spontaneously—would also be a particularly rich seam to investigate. But that kind of detailed investigation is beyond the remit of what follows. What is offered here is an account of how the work of *Ulysses* changed *for readers* in its journey from New York to Paris. It involves focusing on very particular aspects of the genetic dossier—the two authorially sanctioned historic first printed editions of the text—and trying to locate 'meaningful variation' in the difference between those editions.

Towards the Digital Genetic: Models for Reading Ulyssean Revision

If geneticists insist on the 'temporal' dimension of the genetic dossier—an argument which is implicit here in the emphasis on what happened to *Ulysses* in the period between March 1918 and February 1922—it is also imperative to acknowledge the significance of a more recent temporality for genetic scholarship, namely that afforded by the digital era. As noted in the Introduction, the digital copy of the *Little Review*, including all published instalments of *Ulysses*, was made available by the Modernist Journals Project in 2010–11.[27] For any scholar interested in what is termed 'material Modernism', this resource is extremely useful.[28] The digital copy of the 1922 *Ulysses* was released by the Modernist Versions Project, chapter by chapter, between June 2012 and June 2013.[29] Most other sources for the genetic study of *Ulysses*—the manuscripts, notebooks, typescripts, and proofs—currently need to be consulted within their respective holding libraries, or a specialist research library which holds the sixty-three volumes of the *James Joyce Archive*.[30] The availability of the *Little Review Ulysses* and the 1922 text in digital form means that the genesis of *Ulysses*—hitherto quite a specialist topic—is accessible to anyone who can access the web.

Digital copies transform the possibilities of traditional research, a point explored at length in a recent introductory book on this topic, Adam Hammond's *Literature in the Digital Age* (2016).[31] Both the serial and volume text of *Ulysses* are in PDF,

[26] For notebooks see NLI 36,639/3, 4, 5A and 5B and Buffalo V. A. 2A and 2B. For the notesheets, see Herring (ed.), *Joyce's Ulysses Notesheets in the British Museum*.

[27] The release schedule is posted at http://www.modjourn.org/about.html.

[28] Original copies of the *Little Review*, printed on cheap and highly acidic paper, tend to be scarce. Those that survive are sometimes preserved through a programme of page-by-page deacidification, a process which laminates the original and makes it look as if it has been dipped in flour.

[29] The release schedule is posted at http://web.uvic.ca/~mvp1922/you-schedule.

[30] Most of the original material is in Buffalo (see http://library.buffalo.edu/pl/collections/james-joyce/catalog) and is available in the facsimiles of Michael Groden (ed.), *James Joyce Archive*, 63 vols (New York: Garland, 1977–9), but not online. The NLI's Joyce Papers (2002) are online (http://catalogue.nli.ie). The Rosenbach Museum in Philadelphia (https://www.rosenbach.org) holds the most important manuscript of *Ulysses* in fair copy. This is not currently available online. The *CSE* collates many of these sources but is out of print.

[31] Adam Hammond, *Literature in the Digital Age* (Cambridge: Cambridge University Press, 2016).

'portable document format', which preserves the colour and dimension of the original texts, and makes it possible for today's on-screen readers to gain some sense of what it was like to experience these texts in their original bibliographical form. These digital facsimiles are also searchable (using the 'find' function within Adobe Reader), making it possible for any reader to find any word known to be in the text, to find it recurring, and to extend from there into a deeper kind of engagement with the text. These developments are highly significant: they create the possibility for a whole host of new and productive interactions between print-based and digital resources.

In the pre-digital era the word 'collation' had a quite tightly defined and special meaning for bibliographers: it involved the systematic recording of textual variation between editions or manuscripts. In the case of 'lengthy texts', even as determined a scholar as Gaskell could find this process to be 'appalingly laborious...and one liable to a good deal of error'.[32] But both the Modernist Journals Project and the Modernist Versions Project have followed the 'build, create and share' mantra of the Digital Humanities movement and made the text elements of their PDFs available as simple files. These files, which might once have been hoarded in the project backroom, are TEI XML, in the case of the *Little Review*, and txt or docx, in the case of the 1922 edition.[33] Their availability makes it possible to collate the points of variation between the two texts digitally, using a software programme such as Juxta, Collatex, the Versioning Machine, or TXSTEP.[34] Even more simply, it is possible to collate the variants between the serial and 1922 *Ulysses* by downloading and then saving the respective and individual source texts in Microsoft Word and then proceeding through Tools, Track Changes, Compare Documents, and Highlight Changes. This technique can display Joyce's 'insertions' and deletions, and original text, all in one document (see Figure 3.1).[35] Digital Humanities—DH to those on the inside—has become a vibrant intellectual field with an innovative and often acronymic language: hackathons, unconferences, webinars, crowdsourcing, and TEI. Asking Word to collate the differences between the serial and 1922 *Ulysses* is, perhaps, a 'quick and dirty' type of 'data visualization'. Collatex or TXSTEP would undoubtedly be able to do more, but Word is a quicker and more accessible way to collate two variant texts if the purposes are critical, rather than editorial.

For the purposes of illustration, let's compare two visualizations of a textual sample. Figure 3.1 has used Microsoft Word to collate the serial version of the

[32] Philip Gaskell, *A New Introduction to Bibliography* (Oxford: Clarendon Press, 1972), 357.

[33] For the *Little Review*, see the MJP 'Lab File Repository', http://cds.library.brown.edu/projects/mjplab; for the 1922 text, see http://web.uvic.ca/~mvp1922/the-algorithmic-ulysses.

[34] www.juxtasoftware.org; http://collatex.net; http://v-machine.org; www.tustep.uni-tuebingen.de/tustep_eng.html. Of these, TXSTEP, a development of TUSTEP which was used by Gabler and his team to produce the *CSE* in the early 1980s, seems to be the most sophisticated. There is, however, quite a learning curve involved in becoming acquainted with this programme. See YouTube: W. & T. Ott: TXSTEP: an integrated XML-based scripting language for scholarly text data processing.

[35] Save the texts chapter by chapter, labelling them consistently (e.g. 'LR1' for *Little Review* chapter 1 and 'Paris1' for chapter 1 of the 1922 text). Under Tools, Track Changes in Word, select Compare Documents. Insert LR1 under 'Original Document' and Paris1 under 'Revised Document'. The highlighted text is what was added post-serially. The way in which the results are displayed can be usefully manipulated from within Options under Highlight Changes.

BYBy lorries along SirsirJohn Rogerson'sRogerson's quay Mr. Bloom walked soberly, past Windmill lane, Leask'sLeask's the linseed crusher'scrusher's, the postal telegraph office. Could have given that address too. And past the sailors'sailors' home. He turned from the morning noises of the quayside and walked through Lime street. By Brady's cottages a boy for the skins lolled, his bucket of offal linked, smoking a chewed fagbutt. A smaller girl with scars of eczema on her forehead eyed him, listlessly holding her battered caskhoop. Tell him if he smokes he won't grow. O let him! His life isn't such a bed of roses! Waiting outside pubs to bring da home. Come home to ma, da. Slack hour : won't: won't be many there. He crossed Townsend street, passed the frowning face of Bethel. El, yes: house of: Aleph, Beth. And past Nichols'Nichols' the undertaker's undertaker's. At eleven it is. Time enough. Daresay Corny Kelleher bagged that job for O'Neill'sO'Neill's. Singing with his eyes shut. Corny. Met her once in the park. In the dark. What a lark. Police tout. Her name and address she then told with my tooraloom tooraloom tay. O, surely he bagged it. Bury him cheap in a whatyoumay call. With my tooraloom, tooraloom, tooraloom, tooraloom.

Figure 3.1. Variant openings of chapter 5 ('Lotus-Eaters'), collated by Word (used with permission from Microsoft)

opening paragraph of chapter 5 ('Lotus-Eaters'), as published in the *Little Review* in July 1918, with the version of this paragraph as it appeared in the volume text of 1922. The text which Joyce added, post-serially, is shown in grey; deleted text is also in grey, with strikethrough: ~~grey~~. This collation—which reveals that Joyce has added the portrait of the children at Brady's cottages and embellished the characterization of Corny Kelleher, the undertaker and 'police tout'—points to one of the problems that comes about in asking a machine to read a text. Word has identified the difference between the curved possessive apostrophe used by the *Little Review* (') and the straight type used by Darantiere ('); as a result, all words with possessive apostrophes have been deleted and rewritten, a distraction which can lead to the view that more has been changed—authorially—than is actually the case. These are the kinds of difficulties which Shillingsburg memorably characterizes as 'noise' in his account of 'The Dank Cellar of Electronic Texts'.[36] Other small points of typographical variation have also been picked out: BY (in *Little Review*) becomes By; Mr. becomes Mr; Sir becomes sir; the undertaker's (without a full stop in the *Little Review*) gets a full stop in 1922.

---

[36] Peter Shillingsburg, *From Gutenberg to Google* (Cambridge: Cambridge University Press, 2006), esp. 20.

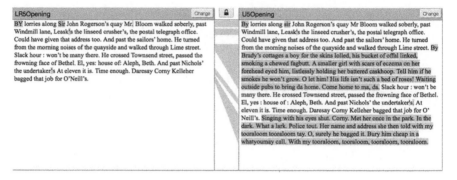

Figure 3.2. Variant openings of chapter 5 ('Lotus-Eaters'), collated by Juxta, side-by-side view
(Image generated by Juxta collation software: http://juxtacommons.org, sponsored by NINES (http://nines.org) at the University of Virginia)

Figure 3.2 has used Juxta to collate the same portion of text and displayed the results in a side-by-side view. The points of difference which exist between the two texts are highlighted in both windows, and the points of similarity are evident in the plain unhighlighted text. Juxta is certainly a very useful tool, and admirably succeeds in its aim of producing visualizations which facilitate the study of textual variation. But it is perhaps better suited to the study of shorter texts, and seems to have been designed with the needs of poetry readers in mind. In particular and in the experience of this user, it can crash when given chapter-length sections of *Ulysses* to collate, a technical glitch which Word seems to avoid. Within Digital Humanities, text and data visualization is a rapidly developing field with a number of different approaches; a recent book on the topic includes chapters on topic modelling, visualizing document similarity, and visualizing document content.[37] In that arena, the visualizations of Word and Juxta are not sophisticated, and are only useful because they encourage readers to grapple with the realities of both macro revision, and minute or micro revisions (which may or may not be authorial; every case is different). Another issue worth mentioning here is that visualizations, no matter how impressive they are to look at, are a form of graphical representation which still usually require interpretation. Certainly this is true in respect of Figures 3.1 and 3.2, which represent points of textual similarity and difference in need of detailed critical reflection and scrutiny.[38]

Joyce found ways to revise the typescript texts he had prepared for serialization very significantly but did not generally find it necessary to delete material which he had committed to the page for serialization. If he does delete, it is usually only a short phrase, then substituted by a modified version, a rephrase of the same idea to make the grammar work. Given such authorial practice, and the availability of the

---

[37] Nan Cao and Weiwei Cui, *Introduction to Text Visualisation* (Paris: Atlantis Press, 2016). See also http://textvis.lnu.se, an interactive text visualization browser.
[38] The issue of close reading with computers is, of course, a very topical subject. For recent reflections, see Martin Paul Eve, 'Close Reading with Computers: Genre Signals, Parts of Speech and David Mitchell's *Cloud Atlas*', *SubStance*, 46:3 (2017), 76–104. See also Martin Paul Eve, *Close Reading with Computers* (Stanford, CA: Stanford University Press, 2019).

relevant texts in digital form, it is possible to use word counting in order to gain a sense of how *Ulysses* expanded in its journey from being a serial to being a finished novel. The first fourteen chapters of *Ulysses* are approximately 137,275 words. Once these chapters had been revised for the 1922 text, they had expanded to approximately 159,362 words, an increase of 22,087 words or approximately 16 per cent. Table 3.1 expresses this in tabular form:

Table 3.1. Word counts: *Little Review Ulysses* compared to 1922 *Ulysses*

	Little Review Ulysses chs 1 to 14	1922 *Ulysses* chs 1 to 14	Extra words	% Increase
Number of words	137275	159362	22087	16%

Quantitative approaches to literary analysis have been controversial, even in recent times ('big data is coming for your books...the algorithmic analysis of novels...is necessarily at the limit of reductivism').[39] But this simple chart reveals the extent of Joyce's revision, and the extent of the 'close reading' task involved in comparing the serial and volume versions of *Ulysses*.

How can one close read the addition of more than 22,000 words? The very question assumes an understanding of what was there before the additions were made—that a reader has a firm critical sense of *Ulysses* as a serial, and of the text's meanings. But Joyce's text was designed to bewilder. As he reputedly said himself: 'I've put so many enigmas and puzzles that it will keep the professors busy for centuries, arguing over what I meant'.[40] Quite apart from such deliberate hermeneutic snares, there are practical challenges involved in trying to write clearly about the significance of multiple and often minute textual changes, which a critic may more easily *see* than describe, explain, or interpret. The argument that follows—which is necessarily tentative, and necessarily incomplete—uses facsimile page images and digital highlighters in order to explore Joyce's additions, and mixes a range of traditional and newer critical approaches, including: genetic criticism, the 'sociology of texts', quantitative analysis, and distant reading. 'Digital genetic'—a phrase which is something of a tease and a deliberate fudge, in that it encourages the recognition that all genetic scholarship is now, at least to some extent, digital—is another way of describing the approach.[41]

Katherine Hayles has described three different kinds of reading that are emerging in the digital age: *close reading* (the cognitive mode traditionally associated with the humanities, focused on a single cultural object for a relatively long time); *hyper reading* (the kind of reading that occurs most often online, which includes skimming, scanning, fragmenting, and juxtaposing texts, and alternating flexibly between different information streams); and *machine reading* (the analysis of text

---

[39] Stephen Marche cited in Hammond, *Literature in the Digital Age*, 87.
[40] Ellmann, *James Joyce*, 521.
[41] 'Digital Genetic Joyce' was the title given to a series of linked panels at the symposium of the International James Joyce Foundation in London in June 2016.

through the application of computer algorithms).[42] The arguments that follow blend all of these kinds of reading. They have been generated by moving back and forth between print and digital: from the real physical bibliographical artefacts to printed facsimile copies; from the left-hand pages of Gabler's pioneering (and yet to be rivalled) *Critical and Synoptic Edition* to the folio pages of the *James Joyce Archive*; from string searches in digital facsimile to skim reading of multiple sources, including text collations generated in Microsoft Word.

While it is undoubtedly true that computers are good at counting words, it is also true that the machine is only as reliable as the information it is given. Table 3.1, above, obfuscates the fact that not all of chapter 14 ('Oxen of the Sun') was published in the *Little Review*. The typescript of approximately 19,320 words—longer than any of the other serialized chapters—was sent to the *Little Review* by Pound, sometime in early June 1920.[43] The first instalment, of approximately 4,963 words, was published in November 1920, in a number dated 'September–December 1920'; given the length of the typescript in hand, it is possible that the editors envisaged two or three further instalments. In order to estimate the length of the *consigned* version of this typescript it is necessary to count the words in (1) the published portion of text (4,963 words), (2) the unpublished portion of text as preserved at the *Little Review* archive in Milwaukee (pages 10 to 28 of the original typescript, 12,873 words), and (3) the two pages of the typescript which are not with the original Milwaukee typescript, but survive in a carbon copy in the Joyce Collection in the Poetry Collection, University at Buffalo (1,384 words).[44] As noted above, this makes the version of chapter 14 consigned to the *Little Review* approximately 19,320 words. The 1922 version of the chapter is 20,296 words, an increase of 976 words or 5 per cent, a figure which is significantly less than the 16 per cent average increase identified in the revision across the first fourteen chapters of the work.

'Reductivism' and the removal of 'refinement' are not unreasonable charges to make against some aspects of quantitative literary research.[45] Word counts of the serial and volume texts of *Ulysses* cannot reveal what has happened in respect of deletion and rewriting; nor can they address the issue of when and why Joyce changed his text; nor can they account for the evolution of the text as traceable in multiple avant-textes. But, at a stroke, the word counting of *Ulysses* can do something which might otherwise take years to discover: it can crudely reveal the extent of Joyce's post-serial revision. Thus the following chart uses word counts to calculate percentage increases between the serial and volume texts of *Ulysses* on a chapter-by-chapter basis (see Table 3.2).

This chart is offered as a kind of lever to open up the question of how Joyce revised *Ulysses*. But *caveat lector* on four fine points. First, as noted above, the chart counts the whole of chapter 14 ('Oxen of the Sun'), rather than just the portion which was serialized (4,963 words). The total number of words of *Ulysses published*

[42] Cited in Hammond, *Literature in the Digital Age*, 19.

[43] J to Margaret Anderson, 22 June 1920, in Yanella, 'James Joyce to the *Little Review*', 397. Discussed above, p. 90.

[44] Buffalo V.B.12.a.i; pp. [8r]–[9r].   [45] Hammond, *Literature in the Digital Age*, 87.

Table 3.2. Percentage increases from serial to 1922 *Ulysses* by chapter

Chapter:	*Little Review*:	*Ulysses* (1922):	Extra words:	Increase:
1: Telemachus	7025	7374	349	4.9
2: Nestor	4332	4530	198	4.5
3: Proteus	5480	5705	225	4.1
4: Calypso	4941	5943	1002	20.2
5: Lotus-Eaters	4541	6406	1865	41
6: Hades	8428	11106	2678	31.7
7: Aeolus	8532	10164	1632	19.1
8: Lestrygonians	9944	12713	2769	27.8
9: Scylla and Charybdis	10898	11914	1016	9.3
10: Wandering Rocks	11441	12670	1229	10.7
11: Sirens	11540	12333	793	6.8
12: Cyclops	16642	21521	4879	29.3
13: Nausicaa	14211	16687	2476	17.4
14: Oxen of the Sun	19320	20296	976	5
Total number of words	137275	159362	22087	16

in the *Little Review* is approximately 122,918. Second, though the word counts (in Microsoft Word) have been checked, they are, of course, automatic: the algorithm of what counts as a word and what counts as a space might be different in another programme. Third, though 137,275 is a reasonable estimate of how many words were *consigned* to the *Little Review*, it is not an absolutely accurate total. This is because the *Little Review* editors and printer corrupted Joyce's text in various ways, an issue which will be explored forthwith. Fourth, one might have a slightly more accurate set of figures—and thus a slightly more refined sense of Joyce's revisionary practice—were it possible to count the number of words consigned to the *Little Review* in typescript; those totals could then be compared to the number of words in the Rosenbach fair copy. This is not possible because a full set of *Ulysses* typescripts does not survive, and the Rosenbach does not exist in digital form.

Even if it were possible to do this, to gather and number crunch all of the relevant data, the results—the chapter-by-chapter percentage increases—would not be significantly different, and the point here is not the small detail but a few broad insights which arise from looking at the expansion of Joyce's text from a quantitative perspective. Before proceeding to analyse the detail of what emerges from Table 3.2, one further immediate observation needs to be made: the chapters consigned to the *Little Review* varied dramatically in length, with chapter 2 ('Nestor') being the shortest (4,332 words) and, as noted, chapter 14 ('Oxen of the Sun') being the longest (19,320 words). Figure 3.3—which represents the serialized chapters by length in a bar chart—reveals a general trend of extension in length as work on the serial text progressed (with the exception of a longer than average opening chapter ('Telemachus'), and slight dips for chapter 4 ('Calypso') and chapter 13 ('Nausicaa')).

This upward trend in length arguably suggests that Joyce was still developing ways to write the book, and becoming more enthralled by its stylistic experiments, as he committed it to print. More elaborately, it is plausible to argue that Joyce wrote longer episodes once he began to abandon the 'initial style', and started to

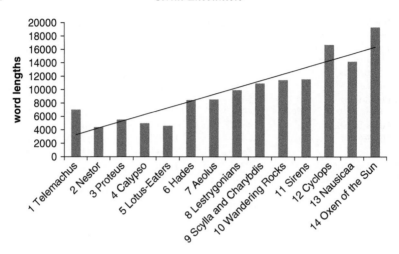

Figure 3.3. *Little Review Ulysses* by word extent

work to establish new narrative norms and voices (a process that happens gradually, beginning, perhaps, in chapter 9, 'Scylla and Charybdis'). This argument—a narratological explanation for the lengthening of the serialized chapters—has been put forward by Eric Bulson, who suggests that the third-person narrators of chapters 10 ('Wandering Rocks'), 12 ('Cyclops'), 13 ('Nausicaa'), and 14 ('Oxen of the Sun') 'describe only to delay the passing hour'.[46]

In revising *Ulysses* after he had completed individual chapter typescripts for serial publication, Joyce clearly reworked some chapters more significantly than others. He did not make significant revisions to the opening three chapters of the work, a point he made himself in correspondence with Weaver: 'Not much change has been made in the *Telemachia* (the first three episodes of the book)'.[47] In November 1920 he thought that the chapters with the 'heaviest burden of addenda' would be chapter 5 ('Lotus-Eaters'), chapter 8 ('Lestrygonians'), chapter 12 ('Cyclops'), and chapter 13 ('Nausicaa').[48] Joyce was accurate in anticipating these heavy revisions, though interestingly the revisions to chapter 13 ('Nausicaa', increased by 17.4 per cent) are less extensive than those made to chapter 5 ('Lotus-Eaters'), which increased by 41 per cent, the most significant extension to a serialized chapter, in terms of percentage. It is also interesting that Joyce did not foresee, in November 1920, the extent to which he would revise chapters 4 ('Calypso'), 6 ('Hades'), and 7 ('Aeolus'). While the precise chronology of Joyce's *commitment* to revision is more or less impossible to piece together, the available evidence suggests that the experience of planning and then carrying out revision to the text occasioned further spontaneous revision, with a ready pen, in *currente calamo*. For a writer whose eyesight was so problematic, the experience of seeing the text in printed proof form was clearly formative and inspirational.

---

[46] Eric Bulson, '*Ulysses* by Numbers', *Representations*, 127 (Summer 2014), 1–32 (19).
[47] J to Weaver, 7 October 1921, *L* I, 172.   [48] J to Quinn, 24 November 1920, *L* III, 31.

Of the fourteen chapters consigned for serial publication, seven were only subject to what might be described as 'minimal revision', with percentage increases of approximately 10 per cent or less. Chapter 3 ('Proteus'), which was being typed in Zurich by late January 1918 and was published in the *Little Review* that May, appears to be the most minimally revised of all chapters (with a percentage increase of just 4.1 per cent).[49] It is extraordinary that Joyce was able to achieve what might be characterized as a relative textual and stylistic stability for this chapter *four years* before the work as a whole was published in volume form, and at a moment when so much of the composition of the work lay in the future. Arranged in ascending order by extent of percentage increase, the other six minimally revised chapters are: chapter 2 ('Nestor', 4.5 per cent); chapter 1 ('Telemachus', 4.9 per cent); chapter 14 ('Oxen of the Sun', 5 per cent); chapter 11 ('Sirens', 6.8 per cent); chapter 9 ('Scylla and Charybdis', 9.3 per cent); and chapter 10 ('Wandering Rocks', 10.7 per cent). The other seven chapters were revised more extensively, in a process of what could be called 'macro revision', with percentage increases of 17 per cent or more.[50] In ascending order of percentage increase, the seven 'macro' revised chapters are: chapter 13 ('Nausicaa', 17.4 per cent); chapter 7 ('Aeolus', 19.1 per cent); chapter 4 ('Calypso', 20.2 per cent); chapter 8 ('Lestrygonians', 27.8 per cent); chapter 12 ('Cyclops', 29.3 per cent); chapter 6 ('Hades', 31.7 per cent); and chapter 5 ('Lotus-Eaters', 41 per cent). Expressed in tabular form, this is as follows (see Table 3.3):

Table 3.3. Minimal to macro revision by chapter, in ascending order by per cent

Chapter:	*Little Review:*	*Ulysses* (1922):	Extra words:	Increase:
3: Proteus	5480	5705	225	4.1
2: Nestor	4332	4530	198	4.5
1: Telemachus	7025	7374	349	4.9
14: Oxen of the Sun	19320	20296	976	5
11: Sirens	11540	12333	793	6.8
9: Scylla and Charybdis	10898	11914	1016	9.3
10: Wandering Rocks	11441	12670	1229	10.7
13: Nausicaa	14211	16687	2476	17.4
7: Aeolus	8532	10164	1632	19.1
4: Calypso	4941	5943	1002	20.2
8: Lestrygonians	9944	12713	2769	27.8
12: Cyclops	16642	21521	4879	29.3
6: Hades	8428	11106	2678	31.7
5: Lotus-Eaters	4541	6406	1865	41

[49] For the evidence of typing, see J to Sykes, [*late January? 1918*], *L* II, 416.

[50] Minimal and macro revision are, of course, approximate terms. But there is a clear numerical gap between chapter 10 ('Wandering Rocks', increased by 10.7 per cent, designated as a chapter exemplifying 'minimal revision') and chapter 13 ('Nausicaa', increased by 17.4 per cent, designated as a chapter exemplifying 'macro revision').

One way of reading *Ulysses* is to consider the early chapters of the finished work—say, up to chapter 10, but excluding chapter 7—as exemplifying a kind of naturalism, a naturalism of a specifically Joycean and Ulyssean kind. The naturalism of these chapters, written in what is sometimes referred to as the 'initial style' (Joyce's own coinage), is gradually disrupted by another prime aesthetic impulse of the work, the impulse of radical style, which can be seen, for example, in the ventriloquizing narrative alternatives of chapters 11 ('Sirens') to 17 ('Ithaca').[51] It is tempting to take the view that Joyce was assured, for the serial version of the work, in the composition of the naturalistic chapters, and that he simply revised the text post-serially by imposing new layers of stylistic complication on what had already been committed to print. But—as the chart above suggests—the very minimal revisions to some of the stylistically challenging chapters, notably chapter 14 ('Oxen of the Sun', increased by 5 per cent) and chapter 11 ('Sirens', increased by 6.8 per cent), indicate that Joyce was committed to stylistic difficulty and disruption, and knew how to achieve it (in some respects and in certain chapters) when he was preparing the serial version of the text.

Writing to Weaver in August 1919, and in response to her view that chapter 11 ('Sirens') seems 'not quite to reach your usual pitch of intensity', Joyce comes close to expressing his stylistic purpose in *Ulysses*:

> I did not know in what other way to describe the seductions of music beyond which Ulysses travels. I understand that you may begin to regard *the various styles of the episodes* with dismay and prefer the initial style much as the wanderer did who longed for the rock of Ithaca. But in the compass of one day to compress all these wanderings and clothe them in the form of this day is for me *only possible by such variation* which, I beg you to believe, is not capricious.[52]

'Various styles' and 'variation' are particularly interesting terms here. As he prepared the text for serialization, Joyce had not quite settled on how far he wished to pursue 'variation'. In preparing for publication in volume form, it is notable that he revised chapter 7 ('Aeolus', increased by 19.1 per cent) and chapter 12 ('Cyclops', increased by 29.3 per cent) quite extensively, in order to amplify stylistic difficulty and disruption.

With regard to the naturalistic chapters, Joyce only made minimal revisions to those involving Stephen: chapters 1 ('Telemachus', increased by 4.9 per cent), 2 ('Nestor', increased by 4.5 per cent), 3 ('Proteus', increased by 4.1 per cent), and 9 ('Scylla and Charybdis', increased by 9.3 per cent). He was building on the world of *A Portrait of the Artist as a Young Man* and clearly had a very certain sense of the mental and cultural world in which Dedalus operates, and a very certain sense of the plots in which Dedalus would be involved. In a sense Stephen had already been fixed in print. As Joyce told Budgen: 'He has a shape that can't be changed'.[53] But

---

[51] J to Weaver, 6 August 1919, *SL*, 242.

[52] Weaver to J, 6 July 1919, in Firth (ed.), 'Harriet Weaver's Letters to James Joyce', 182; J to Weaver, 6 August 1919, *SL*, 242, italics mine.

[53] Frank Budgen, *James Joyce and the Making of Ulysses* (1934; Bloomington, IN: Indiana University Press, 1960), 105. Joyce made this comment in response to Pound's complaint, made after reading episode 11, 'Sirens', that 'Bloom had been disproportionately on...Where in hell is Stephen Tellemachus [*sic*]?' (Pound to Joyce, 10 June 1919, *EP-JJ*, 158).

the development of Bloom's consciousness, by contrast, represented a considerable opportunity for rewriting. The naturalistic chapters involving Bloom (especially chapters 4 ('Calypso'), 5 ('Lotus-Eaters'), 6 ('Hades'), and 8 ('Lestrygonians')) were heavily revised post-serially. Many volume readers of *Ulysses* form their understanding of Bloom on the basis of close reading the naturalism of these early chapters in the work. But as the dramatic increases to these chapters by percentage imply, the serial texts are quite different. The volume versions of these chapters move at a different pace, demanding a slower and more deliberate kind of readerly attention, a deeper and more sustained intellectual and emotional engagement.

Quantitative approaches to literature 'defamiliarize texts' and 'help scholars identify features they might not otherwise have seen'.[54] Certainly it is interesting to note the relatively low position of chapter 7 ('Aeolus') within the ranking by percentage increase of macro revised chapters. Geneticists have long seen chapter 7 as the most 'radically altered' of the serialized chapters: writing in 1977, Groden identified it as the chapter 'to receive the greatest burden of augmentation'.[55] But judged by percentage increase, the extension of 'Aeolus' (by 19.1 per cent) is not as significant as the extensions to some of the naturalistic chapters involving Bloom (4, 5, 6, and 8). By the logic and reckoning of percentage increases, chapter 5 ('Lotus-Eaters') is the most heavily revised chapter of all: its overall length increased by 41 per cent. But the chapter was particularly short in its serial iteration (4,541 words, the second shortest chapter, after chapter 2, 'Nestor'), thus its extension does not have such an impact on the final shape of the work. In contrast, Joyce's additions to chapter 12 ('Cyclops') extend what was already a very lengthy chapter (16,642 words) by a further 4,879 words, an increase which made it the longest of the serialized chapters (in its finished form, longer even than chapter 14, 'Oxen of the Sun').

Numbers, of course, can be made to tell different stories. Eric Bulson's 'Ulysses by Numbers' pursues a quantitative analysis of Joyce's text, but—on the whole— arrives at very different conclusions to those offered here, including the argument that Joyce and Pound had a 'serial agreement' that Joyce was 'writing month after month in order to meet deadlines', was 'measuring as he wrote', and that he initially thought of the text in terms of 'a limit of 6000 words per installment', a figure which Bulson attributes to 'the average episode length in the 1879 Butcher and Lang prose translation of Homer's *Odyssey*'.[56] As noted earlier, the agreement with the *Little Review* was vague and Joyce did not feel pressured to keep deadlines, particularly with Pound telling him to 'Let the regularity of appearance be damned. If you want more time take it', and Heap writing encouragingly to say that they were 'making an audience for your work', and were keen to have the next instalment, but were meanwhile 'cutting it up into smaller sections to avoid gaps'.[57] Social factors of this kind have to be laid against what numbers may appear to reveal.

In this regard, it is necessary to acknowledge that in concentrating on what word counts might reveal about the revision of the serial *Ulysses*, one is overlooking a more

[54] Hammond, *Literature in the Digital Age*, 89.   [55] Groden, *Ulysses in Progress*, 64.
[56] Bulson, '*Ulysses* by Numbers', 10, 5, 6, 8.
[57] Pound to J, 10 June 1919, *EP-JJ*, 159; Jane Heap to J, 9 January 1920, Cornell.

obvious point: the vast post-serial extension of the text through the composition of the last four chapters of the work, chapters 15 ('Circe') to 18 ('Penelope'), which Joyce worked on and completed in Paris, during the latter half of 1920 and most of 1921.[58] These four chapters added a further 107,449 words to the text of *Ulysses*. In fact, these last four chapters represent, in numerical terms, 40.2 per cent of the 1922 text as a whole, which is approximately 266,811 words. Chapter 15 ('Circe'), which Joyce claimed to have written out 'nine times from first to last', is by far the longest of all chapters in the work, at 38,064 words, or 14 per cent of the whole.[59] This numerical expansion can be expressed more clearly in the following chart, which tabulates the lengths of the four final chapters, and calculates those lengths as a percentage of the completed work (see Table 3.4).

As Ronan Crowley has argued, a salient feature of chapter 15 is its 'conspicuous and sustained recurrence to the earlier episodes of *Ulysses*', a point Joyce himself acknowledged in his suggestion that the 'hallucinations' were 'made up out of elements from the past, which the reader will recognize if he has read the book five, ten or twenty times'.[60] 'Phrasal ligatures' and *leitmotif* weld the final part of the work with the portion of text actually serialized: approximately 122,918 words, as noted, or 46 per cent of the whole.[61]

A concentration on the ways in which *Ulysses* differs in print between the *Little Review* serialization and the Shakespeare and Company volume text of 1922 may not seem adequately representative, particularly to scholars who wish to know more about the critical significance of the genetic dossier for the shape of the final work as a whole. But as Crowley and others acknowledge, the final chapters of the work 'advance a set of stylistic concerns beyond the compass of the first fourteen episodes of *Ulysses*' and see Joyce embrace a 'writing method characterized by encyclopedic expansionism'.[62] The analysis that follows, which is in two parts, explores the prehistory to 'expansionism', and the ramifications of 'encyclopedism' for the rewriting of the serialized chapters. The first part, 'Textual Features of *Ulysses* as a Serial', comments on the nature of *Ulysses* as a serial, in terms of style and content,

Table 3.4. A numerical view of the completion of *Ulysses*, post-serially

Chapter:	*Ulysses* (1922):	% of 1922 as a whole:
15: Circe	38064	14.2
16: Eumeus	22808	8.5
17: Ithaca	22509	8.4
18: Penelope	24068	9
chs 15 to 18 total	107449	40.2

[58] For the compositional chronology of chapters 15 to 18, see pp. 92–95.

[59] J to Quinn, 7 January 1921, *L* I, 156.

[60] Ronan Crowley 'Fusing the Elements of "Circe": From Compositional to Textual Repetition', *James Joyce Quarterly*, 47:3 (Spring 2010), 341–61 (341).

[61] 'Phrasal ligatures' is in Crowley, 'Fusing the Elements of "Circe"', 343. To calculate 46 per cent, I have divided 122,918 (the portion published in the *Little Review*) by 266,811 (the total word count of the 1922 text) and multiplied by 100.

[62] Crowley, 'Fusing the Elements of "Circe"', 342.

and looks at the intentional and unintentional corruption of the serial text by the various intermediaries who were involved in the process of its transmission (such as typists, the printer of the *Little Review*, and Pound). The second part, 'Variants Visualized: Pages from "Telemachus", "Hades", "Aeolus", and "Cyclops" ', introduces the nature of Joyce's post-serial revisionary practice by close reading the additions made to sample pages of the 1922 text. This serves as an introduction to the more general account of post-serial Ulyssean revision developed in Chapter 4.

TEXTUAL FEATURES OF *ULYSSES* AS A SERIAL

Readers familiar with the finished *Ulysses* will, on initial inspection, find the serial text to be strikingly similar to the text they know. Virtually all of the quintessential features of the finished text are immediately apparent in the serial version. The chapter settings—in other words, the 'where, when, and who' of each of the fourteen serialized chapters—are those of the final text. The first chapter ('Telemachus') is set at the Martello Tower; the second ('Nestor') in and around the Dalkey school where Stephen Dedalus teaches; Bloom's domestic world is introduced in chapter 4 ('Calypso'); he attends Paddy Dignam's funeral in chapter 6 ('Hades'), and wanders the streets of central Dublin looking for and then finding lunch in chapter 8 ('Lestrygonians'). Chapter 10 ('Wandering Rocks') is a panoramic survey of various characters simultaneously wandering the streets of Dublin, whereas chapter 11 ('Sirens') focuses on Bloom while introducing the musical entertainments of the Ormond Hotel. And so on. The chapters are quite dramatically different in kind, but each of the first nine chapters (at least) preserves an Aristotelian unity of action, and time, taking place over roughly an hour. Unity of 'place'—a concept which relates quite exactly to setting action in one specific location—is not quite so obvious, because there is movement between places in narration (Bloom's trip from Eccles Street to Dlugacz butcher, for example). Yet the idea of adhering to the unities was obviously an important structuring principle for the work, and Joyce clearly made that commitment in the serial iteration of the text. In fact, Joyce's commitment to the unities in the early chapters is more obvious in the serial version, because chapter 7 ('Aeolus'), set at the newspaper office, reads as a stronger part of the narrative continuum in its presentation without the interruption of the headings.

All of the main characters who feature in the finished work appear in the serial version.[63] The vivid characterization—communicated through narration, character interaction, dialogue, and interior monologue—is also strikingly familiar to any

---

[63] Two new named minor characters are added to the early chapters of the work post-serially: Mrs Miriam Dandrade, the 'Divorced Spanish American' who sold Bloom her 'black underclothes' (*U*1922, 153); and Denis J. Maginni, 'professor of dancing' (*U*1922, 146, 211, 226, 243). Unnamed characters who are added post-serially include, in chapter 6 ('Hades'), the street organist on Berkeley Street who plays the 'Dead March from *Saul*' as the Dignam cortège passes (*U*1922, 94), the 'old tramp' who empties 'dirt and stones out of his huge dustbrown yawning boot' (*U*1922, 96), and, in chapter 10 ('Wandering Rocks'), the 'elderly female' who leaves 'the building of the courts of chancery' (*U*1922, 227). In the case of Dandrade and Maginni, Joyce appears to have made these additions in order to deepen the hallucinations of chapter 15 ('Circe'). For Dandrade in 'Circe', see *U*1922 502, 545; for Maginni in 'Circe', see *U*1922, 535–7.

reader familiar with the final text. The dialogue in particular—in terms of trajectory, content, and humour—seems to be exactly the same. As Scarlett Baron has observed in her essay on 'Beginnings', 'Joyce excels at individuating his characters' thoughts' and his third-person narration is often 'shaped by syntactical and idiomatic elements appropriated from the gravitational field of the nearest person'.[64] In the serial text the characters speak and think with 'their own characteristic idiom and syntax', in a manner which will be familiar to readers of the finished work.[65] With the exception of chapter 7 ('Aeolus'), which is radically altered owing to the introduction of the headings, the paragraph structure of the serial text can appear to be that of the finished version: this is because Joyce tended to add text within established paragraphs rather than writing completely new ones (though there are a few exceptions here).[66]

Joyce made few remarks on the unity of *Ulysses* as a whole, but did once tell Pound that he was writing the work 'as Aristotle would say, by different means in different parts', a strategy which makes the work appear to 'begin again in every episode', as Baron has argued.[67] That sense of each chapter being its own stylistic world—of the novel as a set of linked short stories or novellas—was established in the serial text, and is communicated, in part, by the very distinctive opening paragraphs, and equally elegant and conclusive chapter endings. Those opening and ending flourishes appear to be the same in the serial text. For example, Bloom's musing on 'Poor Dignam!' concludes the serialized version of chapter 4 ('Calypso'), and the 'superior' 'very reverend John Conmee' is to be encountered in the very first sentence of the serialized chapter 10 ('Wandering Rocks'). Martin Cunningham and his hat initiate the serial version of chapter 6 ('Hades'), whereas Mulligan the 'sweettoned' 'Usurper' concludes the serial version of chapter 1 ('Telemachus'). Bloom arrives at the gates of the National Museum and feels 'Safe!' ('Ah soap there I yes') at the end of the serial version of chapter 8 ('Lestrygonians'); his very loud fart, which erupts while he reads Robert Emmet's last words, concludes the serial version of chapter 11 ('Sirens') ('Pprrpffrrppffff. *Done*'). Such striking and prominent points of stability can lull the reader into thinking that Joyce has changed very little.

Plot elements established in the serial text include micro-narratives (minor stories, such as the story of 'The man that was drowned'.); macro-narratives (such as the story of Molly's affair with Boylan); actual events (such as Bloom's attendance at Paddy Dignam's funeral, and Stephen's Shakespeare speech at the National Library); and psychological events (such as Stephen's thoughts about his mother, or Bloom's reflections on Rudy). In terms of plot, it is the micro-narratives and psychological events (rather than the macro-narratives and actual events) which are embellished in post-serial revision.

---

[64] Scarlett Baron, 'Beginnings', in Sean Latham (ed.), *The Cambridge Companion to Ulysses* (Cambridge: Cambridge University Press, 2014), 60, 58.

[65] Baron, 'Beginnings', 60.

[66] For examples of completely new paragraphs added to the text post-serially, see *CSE*I 2.273–6; 6.316–20; 7.1–19; 7.1042–9; 8.401–5; 10.56–60; 10.625–31; 10.907–10; *CSE*II 12.925–38; 12.1438–64.

[67] *L* I, 101; Baron, 'Beginnings', 53.

Allusiveness is another quintessential feature of *Ulysses*. Looking at the serial text visually, one can see multiple instances of Joyce including indented italicized quotation from a multiplicity of sources. This can be seen, for example, in the following moment, featuring Bloom feeding the gulls, from the serial text of chapter 8 ('Lestrygonians'):

> He threw down among them a crumpled paper ball. Elijah thirtytwo feet per sec is come. Not a bit. The ball bobbed unheeded on the wake of swells, floated under by the bridgepiers. Not such damn fools. They wheeled, flapping.
>
> *The hungry famished gull*
> *Flaps o'er the waters dull.*
>
> That is how poets write, the similar sounds. But then Shakespeare has no rhymes: blank verse. The flow of the language it is. The thoughts. Solemn.
>
> *Hamlet, I am thy father's spirit*
> *Doomed for a certain time to walk the earth.*
>
> —Two apples a penny! Two for a penny![68]

The quotations—a poem apparently written by Bloom, and a prominent reference to *Hamlet*—are a modulation of narrative voice, and modulation of voice, a key feature of the volume *Ulysses*, is also a key feature of the serial text. Serial readers had to learn to understand Joyce's deliberate habit of withholding information which would make the significance of what is happening clearer. They also had to learn to negotiate difficult and disjunctive shifts from third-person narration, to first-person stream of consciousness, to dialogue, to stylistic oddities and disruptions whose point of view is difficult to discern.

All of these challenges can be seen in the following excerpt from the serial version of chapter 2 ('Nestor'):

> His hand turned the page over. He leaned back and went on again, having just remembered of Him that walked the waves. Here also over these craven hearts his shadow lies and on the scoffer's heart and lips and on mine. It lies upon their eager faces who offered him a coin of the tribute. To Caesar what is Caesar's, to God what is God's. A long look from dark eyes, a riddling sentence to be woven and woven on the church's looms. Ay.
>
> —*Riddle me, riddle me, randy ro.*
> *My father gave me seeds to sow.*
>
> Talbot slid his closed book into his satchel.
> —Have I heard all? Stephen asked.
> —Yes, sir. Hockey at ten, sir.
> —Half day, sir. Thursday.[69]

At Stephen's request Talbot is reciting Milton's *Lycidas*, using a book as an occasional prompt. The third-person narration notes that Sargent has 'turned the page over' and records where he is in the recitation (at the line 'Through the dear might of Him that walk'd the waves', itself a citation from the gospel of Matthew). The narration then shifts from third to first person as Stephen begins to think, perhaps about God. Apart from its evident emotional intensity, it is difficult to pinpoint the exact meaning of the passage which begins 'Here also over these craven hearts his shadow lies, and on the scoffer's heart and on mine'. 'To Caesar what is Caesar's', a phrase which confronts the difficulty of dividing loyalties between church and state, is from the gospels and may indicate that Stephen's train of thought has been inspired by the citation in Milton. Stephen suddenly and disjunctively remembers a snatch of lines from a riddle; this is insistently recorded in italic and prepares readers for the actual riddle which he will pose to the class. But readers are given little time to process any of this because the narration suddenly shifts again: away from recording the psychological events of Stephen's memory and consciousness, and back to the 'actual' events of the classroom scene.

Even now a passage of this kind is difficult to unpick and brings to mind Derek Attridge's observation that 'our activities as readers are usually more complex than the terms in which we represent those activities to ourselves'.[70] For serial readers of the work, the challenges would have been considerably greater because they did not have access to the critical traditions and resources which facilitate first readers of *Ulysses* in our time (such as printed editions which include introductions and annotations; Joyce's schema; websites such as SparkNotes.com and Wikipedia; and printed works such as Blamires' *The New Bloomsday Book*, Gifford's *Ulysses Annotated*, and Killeen's *Ulysses Unbound*).[71] As Sigler has argued, the experience of reading the serial text 'would have been fundamentally different from our own'.[72] In part, this is because the experience of reading any work of fiction in serial form is quite different to the experience of reading the finished volume version.

In the latter half of the nineteenth century part publication of a literary text within a cultural journal dedicated to more general content was commonplace. In that scenario, the serial reader was likely to be more casual, and came to the work with a different 'horizon of expectations' in comparison to a volume reader; they were simply reading a serial—an ephemeral publication—and not making the investment of time, effort, and concentration involved in reading the longer work.[73] The instalment may only have been one among a number of the texts of interest to the reader which was jostling for attention. The instalment or part—held in the hand—was the whole for that moment, even if the reader was aware that the work was being continued, or was to 'to be continued'. The serial reading experience was also different in terms of temporality (because the serial reader had

---

[70] Derek Attridge, 'Reading Joyce', in Derek Attridge, *The Cambridge Companion to James Joyce* (Cambridge: Cambridge University Press, 1990), 5.

[71] Harry Blamires, *The New Bloomsday Book: A Guide Through Ulysses* (London: Routledge, 2nd edn, 1988); Don Gifford and Robert J. Seidman (eds.), *Ulysses Annotated: Notes for James Joyce's Ulysses*, rev edn (London: University of California Press, 1988); Terence Killeen, *Ulysses Unbound* (Dublin: Wordwell, 2004).

[72] Amanda Sigler, 'Archival Errors: *Ulysses* in the *Little Review*', in *Errears and Erroriboose: Joyce and Error*, edited by Matthew Creasy (European Joyce Studies, 20) (Amsterdam: Rodopi, 2011), 73–87 (78).

[73] 'Horizon of expectation' (German Erwartungshorizont) is a term devised by Hans Robert Jauss and designates the shared set of assumptions which can be attributed to any given generation of readers. See J. A. Cuddon, *A Dictionary of Literary Terms and Literary Theory* (Oxford: Blackwell, 2013), www.blackwellreference.com.

to wait for gaps of time to pass between the appearance of instalments); and different in terms of materiality (because the text was mediated in a different kind of material code, usually that of a cheap publication).

An understanding and anticipation of these factors—which are part and parcel of the culture of serialization—has often been crucial in shaping authorial practice. Dickens is a key example. Following *Oliver Twist* (1837–8), which was initially envisaged as a shorter work, and poorly plotted as a result of enthusiastic extension during the process of serialization, Dickens made the commitment to plan his serializations with far greater care. From *Dombey and Son* (1846) onward he wrote instalments to a precise and preset length, and many of the features of his style—memorable character names, descriptive chapter titles, detailed repetition of character traits, and repeated summaries of plot action—are attributable to the fact that his works first appeared in serial form. The serial *Ulysses*—which disdains readerly expectation and need in a classically modernist manner—made no such concession to readers. There was no repetition between the instalments. There was no statement as to what the eventual length of the work would be (because no one—not even Joyce—knew). There was no explanation as to why the book was called *Ulysses*.

Readers of long novels are often in the habit of flicking forward in order to gauge where the book might be going, and get a sense of how much effort is going to be needed. For serial readers of *Ulysses*, it was, of course, impossible to flick forward and it was tricky—unless they kept earlier numbers to hand—to flick back. In sum, the serial reading of *Ulysses* must have been a particularly challenging experience. Anderson and Heap could have done a great deal to help by offering potted summaries of what had happened thus far ('Mr. Joyce appears to have left Stephen Dedalus wandering on a beach, but now introduces a Mr. Leopold Bloom and his cat at breakfast'). But Anderson and Heap were often at loggerheads, and vacillated between gushing but gnomic statements of appreciation ('Joyce has perfected a technique which eliminates description') and editorial carelessness, particularly in respect of the presentation of the text.[74] As Sigler has noted, errors even included mislabelling individual episodes: the opening of chapter 10 ('Wandering Rocks') was labelled 'Episode IX' in June 1919.[75] This must have been particularly confusing: where is the scene set—the National Library or the streets of Dublin? Tricky though this must have been, it is worth remembering that mistakes entered the intended serial text of *Ulysses* at various points in the process of production, and this particular error could have been introduced by someone else.

The serial *Ulysses* was subject to corruption—the introduction of unintended error or intended textual change—at *every stage* in its production, including the very earliest stage when Joyce himself prepared a 'fair' copy from his working draft. At that stage of authorial copying, as is the case with every writer who 'writes out'

[74] *LR*, July 1918, 65.

[75] Amanda Sigler, 'Archival Errors: *Ulysses* in the *Little Review*', in *Errears and Erroriboose: Joyce and Error*, edited by Matthew Creasy (European Joyce Studies, 20) (Amsterdam: Rodopi, 2011), 73–87 (74); *LR*, June 1919, 34.

a new copy of something considered finished, Joyce could and did accidentally make small mistakes, which he may or may not have then attempted to restore in the various stages of revision. After copying, the text went to a typist, an individual who played a crucial role in producing a chapter typescript; these typists were often amateur and sometimes worked as a 'pool', as Ronan Crowley has noted.[76] The typescripts which survive suggest that the typists could and did introduce error, which Joyce may or may not have subsequently corrected. Further and deliberate textual change could be introduced as the serial text went through what can be described as an 'editorial' phase, as it was passed from Pound (in London, or on travels in Europe) to Anderson and Heap (in New York). The 'typographical phase'—the final phase in the process, which saw the serial text being set up for printing—was another point at which error could be introduced. At each stage—manuscript copying, typing, editing, and printing—the potential for textual change, for departure from Joyce's intended original, increased.

Some of the most obvious textual corruptions in the serial *Ulysses* were introduced by the printer of the *Little Review*, a Mr Dushan Popovich, a Serbian (b. 1869 in Serbia), who had arrived in the US in 1892 with his wife Draga, who was from Hungary.[77] Anderson describes Popovich (misspelling his name 'Popovitch') as the 'cheapest printer in New York', and Pound regularly attributed the errors in the *Little Review* to the printer's 'serbo-croatian optic'.[78] Such disparagements understate the significance of Popovich's achievements, including his painstaking patience with the editors of the *Little Review*, and his cultural and political commitments, evidenced by his role as editor and publisher of a range of bilingual newspapers. Titles included the *Serb Sentinel*, begun in 1902, and 'Devoted', as its masthead proclaimed, 'to the mutual understanding between Americans and Yugoslavs, Serbs, Croats and Slovenes'.[79] Content included articles in Serbian, printed in the Cyrillic script, and occasional articles in English.

Popovich was known as 'Popo' to friends, who included Jane Heap. A letter from her to Florence Reynolds recalls working at the December 1918 issue of the *Little Review* in his workshop all day and going out:

> to get a piece of pie for him...no family to bring him any they hate him because he is not 'reech'.[80]

That Popovich was still active as a bilingual printer, publisher, and editor in 1941— when he changed the title of his daily *Yugoslav News* to the *Serbian Daily* in protest against Yugoslavia signing the Axis Accord—is testament to his tenacity, typographical skill, and political acumen.[81] He appears to have been a campaigner for

[76] Ronan Crowley, '"It Is Hard to Believe in Typescript": The Typewriter and Transmissional Departure in Joyce's *Ulysses*', unpb.
[77] Information from the US Census of 1910, accessed via www.mocavo.com.
[78] Anderson, *My Thirty Years' War*, 157; Pound to Anderson, 2 February 1918, *P-LR*, 182.
[79] Information from the Library of Congress Catalogue (http://lccn.loc.gov/sv93017041).
[80] Heap to Florence Reynolds, [December 1918], Baggett (ed.), *Dear Tiny Heart*, 73.
[81] 'Serbian Newspaper Drops Name "Yugoslav" in Protest Here Against the Axis Accord', *New York Times*, 28 March 1941, 9.

the rights of workers, and seems to have stopped printing the *Little Review* in January 1920. The issue of March 1920 states 'we have lost our temperamental printer' and records him writing to Anderson and Heap, saying, 'Do you not know we had war? Workingman is now king'.[82] It is strangely appropriate to find the first printer of *Ulysses* being a left-leaning progressive multi-lingual who was committed to cultural pluralism. In terms of cultural formation, Popovich has something in common with Bloom, who rails against the perpetuation of 'national hatred among nations' (*U*1922, 317), and Bloom's father, Rudolf Virag, who was born in Szombathely, Hungary (*U*1922, 634).

A sense of the challenges which the *Little Review* printing of *Ulysses* posed for Popovich can be obtained by comparing evidence of the work in transmission with the text as it was published in the *Little Review*. This procedure—the straightforward comparison of manuscript, typescript, and serial text—may sound simple. This is not quite the case, because the fourteen chapter typescripts from which Popovich typeset each instalment—unique copies which may have included deletions and additional markings by Joyce, the typist, Pound, Anderson, and Heap—do not survive.[83] But the *Ulysses* typescripts which survive—mainly in Buffalo—are carbon or ribbon copies of what Popovich originally had in hand, and are thus useful enough for the purposes of comparison. The status of the autograph fair copy manuscript poses another bibliographical snag, as it is not clear that Joyce's typists were routinely working from that document, the Rosenbach manuscript, which, according to Gabler, mixes fair copy (chapters 1 to 9, 11 to 16) and draft (chapters 10, 17 to 18).[84] Again, it is necessary to ignore this potential complication—the complication of a 'lost final working draft'—and to value the Rosenbach for what it is: an extant 'autograph of the work', a 'collective manuscript' of the 'individual episodes as written out over a period of four years', and, most significantly, unique evidence of the work in progress.[85]

Of the first three chapters in the novel, only two pages of typescript survive, a carbon copy of a single sheet from chapter 2 ('Nestor'), and a carbon copy of a single sheet from chapter 3 ('Proteus').[86] These sole survivals provide interesting evidence of the early typists' difficulties, including problems with formatting dialogue, and a lack of uniformity in the positioning of tab stops (in the case of 'Nestor'); and a lack of spacing after punctuation marks (in the case of 'Proteus', a fact which markedly reduces the legibility and intelligibility of one of the most

---

[82] 'Some of the Causes for the Omission of the February Number', *LR*, March 1920, [64]. There is a clear shift in the typographical style between the issues of January 1920 and March 1920; January 1920 appears to be the last issue printed by Popovich. His complaint to the editors, printed in the number for March 1920, also registers a dissatisfaction about rates of pay ('If you would pay me three thousand dollars I will not make good word. This is other times. I wrote you about this many times').

[83] Printers usually marked up the copy from which they worked, and the typescripts would have become grubby with ink smudges, etc. Joyce's typescripts almost certainly became part of Manhattan's garbage.

[84] *CSE*III 1868.   [85] *CSE*III 1868.

[86] Buffalo V. B. 1 and Buffalo V. B. 2 respectively (see http://library.buffalo.edu/pl/collections/jamesjoyce/catalog). Reproduced in *JJA* volume 12: *A Facsimile of Notes for the Book and Manuscripts and Typescripts ('Telemachus' to 'Scylla and Charybdis')*, 237, 259.

challenging chapters in the novel).[87] The typescript evidence of chapter 4 ('Calypso') is worthy of more sustained study, as one of the two partial copies which survive runs to eight typed pages. This typescript—Buffalo V. B. 3. A—thus provides more extensive early evidence of the particular difficulties Joyce's typographical and lexical innovations could pose, and of the learning curve Joyce and his typist had to go through to produce this crucial intermediate version of *Ulysses* (which was, of course, the sole means by which Pound, Weaver, Anderson, Heap, and Popovich could access Joyce's text).[88] Joyce's response to this particular typescript is not on record, but a letter to Weaver of March 1918 mentions sending chapter 1 ('Telemachus') to Pound and apologizes:

> for the very bad typescript. I shall try to have the following episodes done better. I hope it is legible in spite of the typist's mistakes.   (*L*, I, 112: 20 March 1918)

He must have felt a similar despair on seeing the first typescript page of chapter 4 ('Calypso'). Undoubtedly the work of an inexperienced typist, the page includes the ugly striking out of several presumably mistyped words; the separation (into two words) of compounds which Joyce wrote as one word (e.g. liver slices rather than liverslices); mistranscription (e.g. bumpy instead of humpy); the insertion of whole line spaces where none are needed (in four places); an inconsistent use of tab stops (to denote paragraph indentation); and the omission of an exclamation mark after 'Mkgnao' and of an apostrophe in 'didnt'.

The other seven pages of this typescript are slightly more assured, though mistakes certainly continued. Joyce was aware that manual typewriters of the era could erase mistakes: Deasy, typing his letter about the foot and mouth disease, is to be seen prodding 'the stiff buttons of the keyboard slowly, sometimes blowing as he screwed up the drum to erase an error'.[89] But such a system could not erase errors on multiple carbon copies, thus the only option was to cross out manually, strike through, or overtype a line of XXX across the mistakes. Other errors, in addition to crossings-out on the typescript, include inconsistent spacing following punctuation marks; the omission of letters in words at the end of the line (as the typist accidentally typed beyond the right-hand margin—manual typewriters of this era did not automatically justify the margins and return, and instead required a manual 'carriage return'); spelling errors; the omission of words Joyce intended (such as oozed, in the phrase 'A kidney oozed bloodguts'); and the substitution of the word the typist thought, instead of what Joyce actually wrote (a common mistake in copying; e.g. 'country' Leitrim instead of 'county' Leitrim and 'draft' instead of 'draught').[90]

---

[87] These typescripts are discussed by Crowley, 'The Typewriter and Transmissional Departure in Joyce's *Ulysses*', who argues that 'Joyce's texts never come unmediated', and discusses the particular features of these two pages.

[88] Buffalo V. B. 3. A; reproduced *JJA*, vol. 12, 261–8.   [89] *LR*, April 1918, 40.

[90] This paragraph builds on an understanding of the bibliographical features of manual typewriters. For an introduction to this topic, see https://en.wikipedia.org/wiki/Typewriter and model demonstration videos on YouTube.

From a typographical perspective, two other features of 'Buffalo V. B. 3. A' are particularly notable. The first is Joyce's preference for the use of the French tiret (—), long or 'em' dash, at the beginning of a slightly indented line of dialogue.[91] As the keyboards of early typewriters did not include longer dashes, Joyce's typist might have followed the standard convention of using two dashes (- -) to signify the tiret Joyce wrote in the fair copy. The typist was consistent in the indentation of dialogue but the tirets—a significant departure from the stylistic norm of inverted commas—had to be marked in by hand, an intervention which created the possibility for omission and inconsistency, and led to the presentation of speech often being riddled with error (either through the omission of indentation or omission of the tiret). The second notable feature in the typescript is the denotation of italic, another important signifier of meaning in Joyce's text. Following established convention, Joyce's manuscript includes underlining of texts to be italicized in print (such as *Love's Sweet Song*, the title of the song Molly will sing, and *O, Milly Bloom, you are my darling*, the poem Bloom imagines as he thinks of his daughter). Typewriters of the era could not produce italic, and thus the typist followed Joyce's implicit instruction by copying the underlining of the manuscript, and appears to have been consistent in the eight pages of the chapter 4 typescript which survive. It is, however, very easy to see how this system of 'underline for italic' could facilitate the proliferation of error (as underlining on a typewriter was achieved by backspacing, and then using the underline key; it was easy to forget and, if you did forget, difficult to rectify).

Joyce's typists worked with the benefit of having Joyce and his manuscript near to hand. Popovich was a world away in Manhattan, and had no such guidance. Apart from one postcard, addressed to Pound and dismissed by him as evidence that Joyce had 'run wode', Joyce appears to have given little instruction on the way in which he wished to see his work presented.[92] The postcard, dated 11 February 1918, was forwarded by Pound to the editors in New York, and reads:

> I hope you are now better and out again. I shall be looking forward to a letter from you. I sent you this morning the third (and last) episode of the Telemachia. The spelling and grammatical construction used by me are to be followed by the printer even when words are misspelled and the grammar is at fault.[93]

A printer reviewing the text referred to here, the serial chapter 3 ('Proteus'), could point to a wide range of potential technical 'faults' in spelling and grammar, such as 'whusky' (not whiskey, or whisky), 'Hray' (not Hurray), 'Oomb'

---

[91] For Joyce and punctuation see Elizabeth Bonapfel and Tim Conley (eds.), *Doubtful Points: Joyce and Punctuation* (Amsterdam: Rodopi, 2014). Apart from the tiret Joyce also appears to have wanted dialogue to be set flush left and not indented, though dialogue in the 1922 text is, in fact, indented. The *CSE* sets dialogue flush left, as though to suggest a more seamless blend with narration. The dialogue tirets in the Rosenbach are in the left margin, outside the 'box' of the writing.

[92] Pound to Anderson, 21 February 1918, *P-LR*, 189.

[93] Joyce to Pound, 11 February 1918, in Philip R. Yanella, 'James Joyce to the *Little Review*', *Journal of Modern Literature*, 1:3 (1971), 393–8 (395). The original of this card is in the *Little Review* records, University of Wisconsin, Milwaukee. Yanella mistranscribes 'grammatical' as 'mechanical', corrected here.

not 'Womb', as well as multiple compounds ('snotgreen', 'strandentwining', 'cleanchested', 'bigdrumming', 'dryingline', 'groatsworth', 'sanguineflowered', 'tobbaccoshreds', 'pushedback', 'shellcocoacoloured', 'shellgrit', 'ghostcandled', 'gumheavy', 'corpsegas').[94] The nonlexical deviations ('Feefawfum'), foreign loan words and phrases (*'Qui vous a mis dans cette fichue position?'*), onomatopoeia ('wayawayawayawayawayaway'), and multiple citations (*'And no more turn aside and brood'*) would have been similarly striking.[95] But Joyce's intention in writing such forms must have been understood by Popovich, who correctly typeset *all* of these examples in chapter 3. This is not to suggest that Popovich's typesetting was by any means perfect: typographical and transcription errors are evident on every page of the *Little Review* iteration of this chapter, and Sigler's general point that the *Little Review Ulysses* was 'couched in the medium of error' remains valid.[96] But Popovich, like Joyce's typists, clearly made a significant effort to make sense of Joyce's challenging text, and to accept and follow its lexical, citational, and typographical innovations. As he relayed Joyce's specific directions to the *Little Review*, Pound was a little disparaging ('Joyce has run wode, as per enclosed p.c') and less than clear ('I suppose we may as well let him have his own way'); but those in New York—Popovich included—were more sympathetic, and more inclined to accept the linguistic novelties and typographical challenges of Joyce's text.[97]

Popovich began to print the *Little Review* in May 1917, two months after publication in New York was announced, a fact which is evident from the shift in typographical style between the issues April and May 1917 respectively. Popovich's typesetting makes more use of interlinear spacing, and has a stronger 'Arts and Crafts' look, which is particularly evident in the display type.[98] Anderson's account of that summer—the summer of 1917, when the *Little Review* was being remodelled editorially, and in terms of its typography and house style—paints a harmonious picture of days spent among Popovich and his family:

> He had two daughters. They all took a personal interest in the magazine. We went to their shop in East Twenty-third Street and helped with the setting-up to gain time—and lost much time helping the daughters to read Wyndham Lewis. On Sundays to push things along we often took our lunch and spent the whole day in the print shop, correcting proof, setting type, even folding pages for the binder. It was a good life.[99]

---

[94] *LR*, May 1918, 'whusky' (34), 'Hray' (35), 'Oomb' (42); the fourteen compounds listed here appear in successive pages of chapter 3 (*LR*, May 1918, 31–44). These forms have been compared with the Rosenbach.

[95] *LR*, May 1918, 'Feefawfum' (39), *'Qui vous a mis dans cette fichue position?'* (35), 'wayawaya-wayawayawayaway' (42), *'And no more turn aside and brood'* (43); cp. with Rosenbach.

[96] Amanda Sigler, 'Archival Errors: *Ulysses* in the *Little Review*', in *Errears and Erroriboose: Joyce and Error*, edited by Matthew Creasy (European Joyce Studies, 20) (Amsterdam: Rodopi, 2011), 73–87 (73).

[97] Pound to Anderson, 21 February 1918, *P-LR*, 189.

[98] Popovich did not sign his work but compare the issue of April 1917 with that of May 1917. The main text font may be the same, though there has been a shift in size and the later issue has more interlinear space; the design of the cover, display font and running head, is also new. While announced as being published in New York, it looks like the issues of March and April 1917 were printed by whoever regularly printed the journal to that date, presumably a Chicago printer.

[99] Anderson, *My Thirty Years' War*, 157.

But things appear to have been rather less harmonious in the spring of 1918, when the *Little Review* began serializing *Ulysses*. Anderson and Heap were exasperated by Quinn, who could be hectoring and dictatorial. Pound found himself having to defend Quinn and felt that his own editorial efforts were underappreciated ('What do I get for this job anyhow').[100] While excited by the arrival of the first chapter of *Ulysses* ('too serious for me to prattle into criticism. I think it is the only youth that has ever been written down'), Pound regretted that manuscripts by the other writers he wanted for the *Little Review* were not coming through ('Hueffer is dead, absolutely dead with army. Eliot is dead with his bank. Lewis wanders about').[101] He felt, in February 1918—the month before the first chapter of *Ulysses* appeared— 'bored to death with being any kind of editor'.[102] As noted earlier, the relationship between Anderson and Heap also began to disintegrate at around this time.[103] While Anderson continued to be the point of contact with Pound, Heap's letters characterize Anderson as antagonistic and disengaged from the business of editing ('She doesn't even edit properly any more').[104] Heap, meanwhile, was engaged in the practical challenges of bringing out the journal, and often worked closely with Popovich. A letter of December 1918, for example, notes 'Mart' taking the day off to have lunch with Gladys (a new lover), and Heap being faced with:

> Nothing to do but address the magazine, go to Popo & order paper, attend to the door and telephone…and scrape together money for all this.[105]

It appears to have been mainly Heap, working with Popovich, who oversaw the presentation of Joyce's text in the *Little Review*.

The serial text of chapter 4 ('Calypso') appeared in the *Little Review* of June 1918. The small differences which exist between that text and the eight extant pages of typescript (Buffalo V. B. 3. A, described above) point to the kinds of choices and dilemmas Heap and Popovich faced as they set to work on the very first appearance of Leopold Bloom in print.[106] For example, Joyce's typist (following the manuscript) wrote 'Mr' Leopold Bloom, whereas Popovich, aiming for a crisp and grammatically correct opening to the chapter, inserted a point after the first 'Mr.', and was consistent in using points following titles thereafter (Mr. O'Rourke, Mrs. Marion Bloom, etc.). Joyce's desire for the omission of points in this position—much like his insistence on tirets—suggests his concern with the look of his work on the page, and his desire for the typography of his work to be spare and uncluttered. As Bloom prepares Molly's breakfast, the cat's mewing gradually

---

[100] Pound to Anderson, 20 February 1918, *P-LR*, 183, 184.

[101] Pound to J, 19 December 1917, in *EP-JJ*, 128; Pound to Anderson, 20 February 1918, *P-LR*, 187. 'Hueffer' is a reference to Ford Hermann Hueffer, who changed his name to the less Germanic Ford Madox Ford in 1919.

[102] Pound to Anderson, 20 February 1918, *P-LR*, 186.   [103] See above, p. 32.

[104] Heap to Florence Reynolds, [Postmarked 17 March 1918], [December 1918], Baggett (ed.), *Dear Tiny Heart*, 55, 73.

[105] Heap to Florence Reynolds, [Postmarked 11 December 1918], Baggett (ed.), *Dear Tiny Heart*, 70.

[106] The typescript Buffalo V. B. 3. A corresponds to *LR*, June 1918, 39–47, stopping in the midst of the Blooms' conversation about metempsychosis at 'Yes. What's that?'. Comments here are based on a comparison of these excerpts from the typescript and serial texts.

becomes more insistent: 'Mkgnao!', 'Mrkgnao!', 'Mrkrgnao!'. The typist transcribed these different forms correctly, but Popovich omitted the second 'r' in the third mew (setting 'Mrkgnao!' instead of 'Mrkrgnao!'), and omitted the tiret, and extra indentation, which should have preceded the first.[107] Another transcriptional error which swims to the eye, and suggests the different ways in which serial readers navigated *Ulysses*, is the sentence 'Yet, yes' instead of 'Yes, yes' in the passage which expresses Bloom's sudden longing for home:

> To smell the gentle smoke of tea, fume of the pan, sizzling butter. Be near her ample
> bedwarmed flesh. Yet, yes.[108]

This could be a typo, though the fact that the phrase makes sense in context—with the change in just one letter indicating the difference between hesitation ('yet') and affirmation ('yes')—may suggest the possibility of it being an 'interpretive' correction of the kind proposed by Sigler.[109]

Hyphens, including the 'soft' type inserted by the typist where a word was split between lines, and the 'hard' variety used to create temporary linkages, also posed particular problems. While Popovich generally accepted Joycean compounds, he could, understandably, become confused. The typist, for example, hyphenated 'liver-slices' in the third line of Joyce's text, but then copied Joyce in joining 'crustcrumbs'; Popovich, presumably aiming for consistency, hyphenated both: 'He liked thick giblet soup, nutty gizzards, a stuffed roast heart, liver-slices fried with crust-crumbs, fried cods' roes'.[110] He had to remember to omit the 'soft' hyphens inserted by the typist (such as in 'plaint-ively', cumbersomely split by the typist) and to insert them where needed in his own setting.[111] Popovich also had to work out what to do with difficult cases. The typist, for example, had separated Joyce's 'twenty eight' in the phrase 'Valuation is only twentyeight'. Popovich opted to hyphenate: 'twenty-eight'.[112] Joyce, momentarily forgetting the logic of his own rules for joining linked words in order to omit hyphens, opted for 'willow patterned' in the phrase 'A kidney oozed bloodguts on the willow patterned dish'.[113] Popovich copied the typist in opting to include a hyphen here.

No matter how skilled, typesetters always make mistakes in individual letters or 'literals'.[114] The *Little Review* printing of 'Calypso' conspicuously includes 'Gibraltr', 'brgiht', 'arry' (instead of Larry), 'eitrim' (not Leitrim), 'bdeeders' (not breeders), and 'crad' (not card).[115] Given the multiple typographical complexities

---

[107] *LR*, June 1918, 39.   [108] *LR*, June 1918, 45.

[109] Sigler, 'Archival Errors: *Ulysses* in the *Little Review*', 74, 76. The clearest example of 'interpretive' correction is the substitution of 'Nother' with 'Mother' in the 'curious' blue telegram Dedalus received in Paris: 'Mother dying come home father' (*LR*, May 1918, 37). Joyce clearly wrote 'Nother' in the manuscript. It is possible, of course, that 'Mother' was introduced in the typescript (which does not survive).

[110] *LR*, June 1918, 39.

[111] *LR*, June 1918, 39, 41. Examples of line-split hyphens on page 41 include 'foot-leaf', 're-fracts', 'fen-nel', 'head-piece', 'can-vassing'.

[112] *LR*, June 1918, 44.   [113] Rosenbach, P57.

[114] Philip Gaskell, *A New Introduction to Bibliography* (Oxford: Clarendon Press, 1972), 111.

[115] *LR*, June 1918, 40, 41, 42, 42, 43, 45.

and stylistic innovations of the text, the uneven quality of the typescripts from which Popovich was working, and the level of accuracy in the printed text, it is clear that considerable energy *was* devoted to proofing, presumably by Heap, Popovich, and family working as a team (with occasional assistance from Anderson). That team picked up many errors, but clearly could not and did not catch everything. Popovich, after all, had been patronized on grounds of being a 'cheap' printer, and probably worked at typesetting with little assistance: relying on him to eradicate all of the 'literals' was a case of Anderson and Heap asking too much. It is also significant that some of the mistakes which may appear to be those of Popovich actually entered the text earlier. Leitrim being a 'country' rather than a county was the typist's error, which Popovich was hardly in a position to correct. 'Mullinger' (rather than Mullingar)—another Irish geographical typo—was also introduced by the typist, and serves as a reminder that the text was finding its very first readers a long way from home. The comma, omitted in the sentence 'The crooked skirt swinging whack by whack by whack', was omitted by the typist and thus omitted by Popovich.[116] Joyce himself vacillated over the spelling of 'tea' in the phrase 'Simon Dedalus takes him off to a tea, with his eyes screwed up'.[117] The correction to 'tee' was introduced in the first edition of 1922 (*U*1922, 56).

Popovich was castigated by Anderson for being 'temperamental'.[118] But the evidence of Heap's letters suggests that Popovich was tolerant of frequent delays in payment, and may even have contributed towards costs (one letter refers to rent being 'in arrears one month—Popo to pay part in advance').[119] Popovich was also an extremely easy target for Pound's ire ('IT IS *NO* good this printing-sloppiness') but Pound, like Anderson, ought to have taken more responsibility for the production of the *Little Review*.[120] But Pound was far away in London, knew that Quinn's financial support was crucial, and—in the wake of the controversy surrounding the publication of Lewis's 'Cantelman's Spring-Mate'—had yet to decide how much risk he was prepared to take with regard to potential further 'suppressions' by the Post Office.

Pound was clearly aware, from the outset of the serialization, that *Ulysses* was likely to lead to further suppressions of the *Little Review*. After all, the Lewis case had had the effect of making the officials at the Post Office more likely to examine individual issues of the journal. Yet Pound regarded the publication of Joyce's first chapter as a matter of cultural necessity. After reading the typescript of that chapter, he told Joyce:

> I suppose we'll be damn well suppressed if we print the text as it stands. BUT it is damn wellworth it. I see no reason why the nations should sit in darkness merely because Anthony Comstock was horrified at the sight of his grandparents in copulation, and there after ran wode in a loin cloth.[121]

[116] *LR*, June 1918, 43.　　　[117] Rosenbach, P56.
[118] Anderson, 'Some of the Causes for the Omission of the February Number', *LR*, March 1920, [64].
[119] Heap to Florence Reynolds, [Postmarked 11 December 1918], Baggett (ed.), *Dear Tiny Heart*, 71.
[120] Pound to Anderson, 10 June 1918, *P-LR*, 232.
[121] Pound to J, 19 December 1917, in *EP-JJ*, 129.

A fortnight later, with the niggle of Comstockery still at the front of his mind, he told Anderson—never an individual to avoid controversy—that Joyce was someone 'Whom we have got to print. Suppression or no suppression'.[122] Another fortnight passed, during which time Pound had begun to reconsider. Quinn had engaged him in a lengthy exchange about what it was appropriate to publish in a magazine, and Pound had begun to have qualms about the serialization of the first chapter of *Ulysses*.[123] Thus he wrote to Anderson, who had the typescript of the first chapter in hand:

> It might be well to leave gaps, at the questionable points, well marked. Saying 'until literature is permitted in America' we can not print Mr. J's next sentence. Mr. J is the author of 'the Portrait' etc. recognized as literature but he lacks the sanction of 'age'.
>
> He refers here to tribal customs of the Hebrews, often mentioned in Leviticus.
>
> He refers here to certain current statements of the New Testament. He refers here to natural facts, doubtless familiar to the reader.
>
> This might help more than anything else to enlighten our public.[124]

'Tribal customs of the Hebrews' 'mentioned in Leviticus' is a reference to the fact that Mulligan describes God as 'the collector of prepuces', i.e. the collector of the foreskins of the circumcised.[125] This is something which Mulligan says 'casually' out of mock deference to Haines, and is prompted by Haines's interest in the collection of folklore. The reference to 'Current statements of the New Testament' is an attempt to prompt Anderson to delete Mulligan's 'ballad of Joking Jesus' ('I'm the queerest young fellow that ever you heard./My mother's a jew, my father's a bird') which Haines himself identifies as 'rather blasphemous', and which Quinn identified as problematic once he had read the chapter in print.[126]

Anderson almost certainly had not read Joyce's text as carefully as Pound, and may not have fully understood these editorial hints; she was not, at any rate, predisposed to be so assertive as an editor. At the end of this letter—which sees Pound deferring final editorial responsibility to Anderson—Pound adds:

> A few unexpurgated copies might also be struck, but not sent through the post. Or they could be printed NOT bound into the review at all.[127]

This impractical suggestion would have involved the editors in the costly business of getting Popovich to print two versions of the text, and it is little surprise that Anderson responded by changing nothing in Joyce's opening chapter. Pound's thinking at this time, January 1918, when the printing of the serial *Ulysses* had yet to begin, was muddled and unclear. He was broadly in favour of making deletions to Joyce's text, but had yet to work out that Anderson was unlikely to make such changes without specific prompts.

---

[122] Pound to Anderson, 30 December 1917, *P-LR*, 171.
[123] For Pound's response to Quinn, see his letter of 29 and 30 December, *EP-JQ*, 132–5.
[124] Pound to Anderson, 17 January 1918, *P-LR*, 232.   [125] *LR*, March 1918, 13.
[126] *LR*, March 1918, 18, 19. Quinn's response is noted in *EP-JQ*, 138. See also above, p. 46.
[127] Pound to Anderson, 17 January 1918, *P-LR*, 232.

As Joyce's chapter typescripts began to arrive regularly, Pound's editorial attitudes began to change. At the end of March 1918, he made significant changes to the typescript of chapter 4 ('Calypso'), as Vanderham and others have noted.[128] He was clearly pleased with the expurgation of 'Calypso', telling Quinn, who continued to goad him, that he had written to Joyce and explained 'my reasons for thinking the said lines excessive'.[129] Pound's specific complaint related to Joyce's 'detailed treatment of the dropping feces'. He had no qualms in telling Joyce 'you overdo the matter':

> I'm not even sure 'urine' is necessary in the opening page. The idea could be conveyed just as definitely. In the thing as it stands you will lose effectiveness. The excrements will prevent people from noticing the quality of things contrasted. At any rate the thing is risk enough without the full details of the morning deposition.[130]

Pound coupled this response with editorial action. He went through the typescript and deleted all of the cues which make it obvious that Bloom has gone into the garden in order to empty his bowels in the outdoor toilet. He made cuts to the text in several places—deleting about 147 words in total—beginning by deleting the phrase 'of his bowels' from the end of the line 'He felt heavy, full: then a gentle loosening'.[131] The *Little Review* omits the description of Bloom undoing the waistband of his trousers, and then undoing his braces; it omits the description of the outhouse with its 'mouldy limewash and stale cobwebs'; it omits the description of how Bloom sits 'asquat on the cuckstool' and begins to quietly read from an old number of *Titbits*; and it omits the description of how 'He allowed his bowels to ease themselves quietly as he read, reading patiently', and then 'tore away half the prize story sharply and wiped himself with it'.[132] What was a carefully written and complicated text, building to a culmination over three pages, becomes, in the context of the *Little Review*, a text that does not make full sense. One can see this clearly in the following example, which shows the last page of the chapter as it appeared in the *Little Review* (see Figure 3.4).

The first two paragraphs here (beginning 'Rubbing smartly' and 'Evening hours') are interior monologue which continue Bloom's ruminations about his domestic life: his memories of a 'bazaar dance', and of the charged moment when Molly first met Blazes Boylan ('Is that Boylan well off?'). Bloom has these thoughts as he continues to sit on the toilet. This is clear in the Rosenbach manuscript, and in the 1922 text (*U*1922, 67).[133] But it is not clear here because Pound has omitted a

---

[128] See Paul Vanderham, *James Joyce and Censorship: The Trials of Ulysses* (London: Macmillan, 1998), 20–7, and Mark Gaipa, Sean Latham, and Robert Scholes (eds.), *The Little Review Ulysses* (New Haven, CT and London: Yale University Press, 2015), 355–6.

[129] Pound to Quinn, 3 April 1918, *EP-JQ*, 147.

[130] Pound to J, [29 March] 1918, *EP-JJ*, 131.   [131] *LR*, June 1918, 50.

[132] A typescript of this passage does not survive, thus one has to infer what has been deleted by reading the Rosenbach manuscript P64–7. It is possible (though perhaps not likely) that some of the details intended by Joyce were corrupted or omitted by the typist. These corruptions are also noted by Vanderham, *James Joyce and Censorship*, 169–70 and in Gaipa et al. (eds.), *The Little Review Ulysses*, 355–6.

[133] Rosenbach, P67.

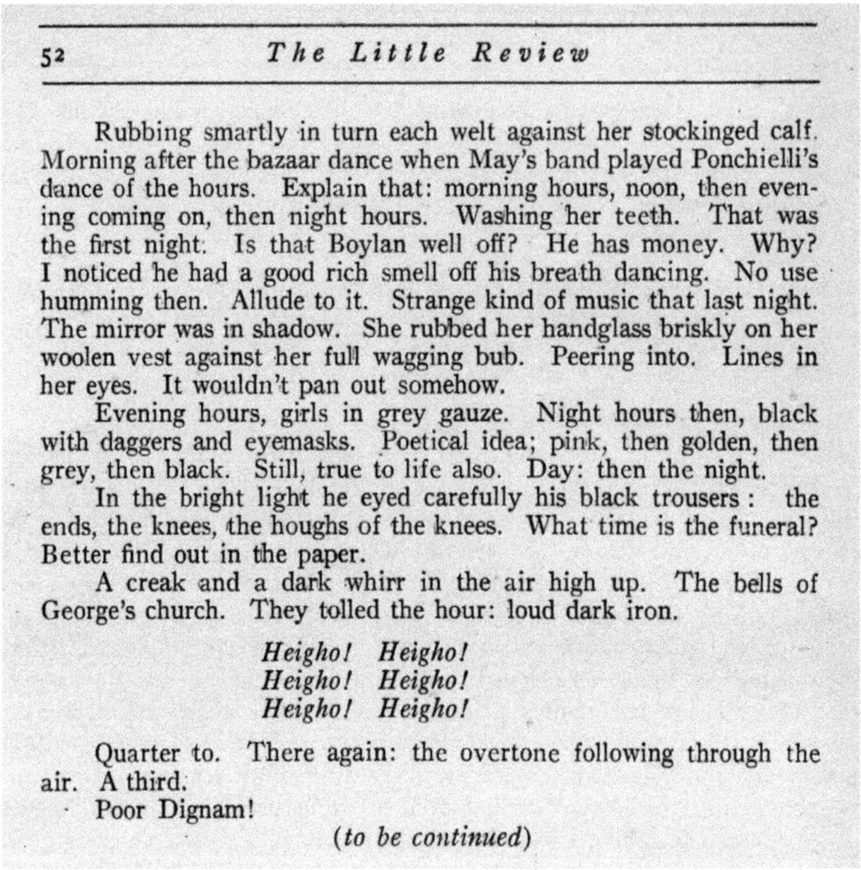

Rubbing smartly in turn each welt against her stockinged calf. Morning after the bazaar dance when May's band played Ponchielli's dance of the hours. Explain that: morning hours, noon, then evening coming on, then night hours. Washing her teeth. That was the first night. Is that Boylan well off? He has money. Why? I noticed he had a good rich smell off his breath dancing. No use humming then. Allude to it. Strange kind of music that last night. The mirror was in shadow. She rubbed her handglass briskly on her woolen vest against her full wagging bub. Peering into. Lines in her eyes. It wouldn't pan out somehow.

Evening hours, girls in grey gauze. Night hours then, black with daggers and eyemasks. Poetical idea; pink, then golden, then grey, then black. Still, true to life also. Day: then the night.

In the bright light he eyed carefully his black trousers : the ends, the knees, the houghs of the knees. What time is the funeral? Better find out in the paper.

A creak and a dark whirr in the air high up. The bells of George's church. They tolled the hour: loud dark iron.

Heigho! Heigho!
Heigho! Heigho!
Heigho! Heigho!

Quarter to. There again: the overtone following through the air. A third.

Poor Dignam!

(to be continued)

Figure 3.4. *Little Review*, chapter 4 ('Calypso'), June 1918, final page

(*Little Review*, The Modernist Journals Project (searchable database). Brown and Tulsa Universities, ongoing. http://www.modjourn.org)

three-sentence paragraph of omniscient narration, which should follow the word 'night', and describes what happens before Bloom emerges into 'the bright light' and starts to examine his black trousers:

He tore away half the prize story sharply and wiped himself with it. Then he girded up his trousers, braced and buttoned himself. He pulled back the shaky door of the jakes and came forth from the gloom into the air.[134]

In June 1918, the month in which this mutilated version of 'Calypso' appeared, Pound wrote to Anderson and complained about Popovich:

What is the use of having stuff that has more care per square inch than the current novelists use per square mile, IF the bloody printer is to reduce it to guff. A misprint

[134] Rosenbach, P67.

that makes sense is the worst. A mis-spelling or a word spelled 'word' don't matter, but to make hash of whole paragraphs is TROPPO!!!![135]

But Pound's own deletions from Joyce's text—a text which has a great deal of care per square inch—are a clear example of making 'hash of whole paragraphs'. The expurgated 'Calypso' is full of non sequiturs. Readers must have wondered why Bloom was in the garden; and the paragraph which describes him reading 'Something new and easy' from *Titbits* must have been impossible to follow owing to the deletion of the description of Bloom sitting down and opening his magazine.[136] Readers of modernist literature are accustomed to thinking of Pound as a good editor because of the formative work he did on Eliot's *Waste Land*, but this example shows Pound's editorial proclivities in quite a different light. It is also interesting that Pound has not been following the advice given to Anderson: to annotate deletions and leave 'gaps at the questionable points'.[137]

While this is by no means the only cut which Pound made to the serial *Ulysses*, it is one of the most interesting, illustrative, and important because it pitches editorial motivation against aesthetic judgement. Beyond being an editor, Pound was a fellow artist and, as such, felt that he could tell Joyce where he had strayed into 'simply bad writing':

> Bad because you waste the violence. You use a stronger word than you need, and this is bad art, just as any needless superlative is bad art. The contrast between Blooms interior poetry and his outward surroundings is excellent, but it will come up without such detailed treatment of the dropping feces.[138]

Crucially, Pound could justify his aesthetic preferences by pointing to potential problems with 'suppression' and his letter to Joyce—which does not fully acknowledge the extent to which he has tampered with the text—catalogues the risks of the *Little Review* being 'suppressed too often', namely 'the damn'd stoppage of all our stipends', and the possibility of being 'suppressed finally'.[139] Pound had yet to meet either Anderson or Joyce, was trying to work out what kind of role he could play as Joyce's editor, and was doing so in a difficult context of publication. He seems to have been particularly affronted by Joyce's interest in the representation of excrement: it is highly likely that it was Pound who deleted the detail of Tatters the dog who 'pissed' from a 'cocked hindleg' in chapter 3 ('Proteus') and he candidly told Joyce that he disliked the 'fahrt' which concludes chapter 11 ('Sirens').[140]

---

[135] Pound to Anderson, 10 June 1918, *P-LR*, 232.   [136] *LR*, June 1918, 51.
[137] Pound to Anderson, 17 January 1918, *P-LR*, 232.
[138] Pound to Joyce, [29 March] 1918, *EP-JJ*, 131.
[139] Pound to Joyce, [29 March] 1918, *EP-JJ*, 131.
[140] The ms read 'Along by the edge of the mole he dawdled, smelt a rock and from under a cocked hindleg pissed against it. He trotted forward and, lifting again his hindleg, pissed quick short at an unsmelt rock' (Rosenbach, P46–7). This description has been mangled in order to omit the word 'pissed' in the *Little Review* (May 1918, 41). For comments on 'fahrt' as 'climax of chapter' and his preference for 'classic detachment' and the 'Racinian off stage', see Pound to J, 10 June 1919, *EP-JJ*, 158–9.

Pound's other deletions from the serial *Ulysses* seem to have included:

(1) the word 'cunt' from chapter 4 ('Calypso'). Joyce's description of the Dead Sea—'the grey sunken cunt of the world' became 'the grey sunken belly of the world'[141]

(2) the phrase 'a stump of black gutta-percha wagging limp between their haunches' from the description of the 'gelded' horses in chapter 5 ('Lotus-Eaters')[142]

(3) the word 'venereal' from the phrase 'an army rotten with venereal disease' in chapter 5 ('Lotus-Eaters')[143]

(4) the phrase 'Has her monthlies probably' in chapter 5 ('Lotus-Eaters')[144]

(5) the phrase 'Where the bugger is it?', spoken by Bantam Lyons, in chapter 5 ('Lotus-Eaters')[145]

(6) the concluding phrase in chapter 5 ('Lotus-Eaters') which describes Bloom contemplating his pubic hair and genitals floating in the bath ('saw the dark tangled curls of his bush floating, floating hair of the stream around a languid floating flower')[146]

(7) the word 'wet' from the sentence 'Mr Bloom with careful hand recomposed his wet shirt' in chapter 13 ('Nausicaa')[147]

(8) the words 'up', 'sawdirty girl', 'love sticky', and 'met' from the sentence 'O sweety all you little white up I sawdirty girl made me do love sticky we two naughty darling she him half past the bed met him pike hoses frillies for Raoul' (in chapter 13, 'Nausicaa').[148]

What is fascinating about this catalogue of unacknowledged textual change, particularly in hindsight, is Pound's prudery. Pound may have been keen to promote the *Little Review* as the magazine that makes no 'compromise with the public taste', but when he actually began to read *Ulysses* he was evidently affronted by Joyce's candour. Another fascinating aspect of what is happening here is the lack of consistency in editorial practice. Why delete the word 'pissed' and retain 'scrotum-tightening'? Why omit 'pubic hair' and allow references to 'incests and bestialities'? Why omit the reference to Bloom's 'wet shirt' and retain 'This wet is very unpleasant' and 'My fireworks. Up like a rocket, down like a stick'?[149]

'Pissed' appears to have been a particularly problematic word for Joyce's first editors. As noted in Chapter 2, it is omitted in Mulligan's allusion to Synge ('the

---

[141] Rosenbach, P44. This deletion is listed by Vanderham in the appendix to *James Joyce and Censorship*, 169–210.

[142] Rosenbach, P42. Not listed as a Poundian intervention by Vanderham, *James Joyce and Censorship*, 170. A typescript of this chapter does not survive, thus one has to infer what has been deleted by reading the Rosenbach manuscript.

[143] Rosenbach, P38.   [144] Rosenbach, P43.

[145] Rosenbach P82; cp. *LR*, July 1918, 48.   [146] Rosenbach P83; cp. *LR*, July 1918, 49.

[147] Rosenbach, P353; cp. *LR*, July–August 1920, 46. Pound explicitly acknowledged this cut in a letter to Quinn, 8 November 1920, *EP-JQ*, 102 ('I did myself dry Bloom's shirt').

[148] Rosenbach P364; cp. *LR*, July–August 1920, 57.   [149] *LR*, July–August 1920, 50, 47.

> Quickly, warningfully Buck Mulligan bent down:
> — The tramper Synge is looking for you, he said, to murder you. He heard you . . . . . . on his halldoor in Glasthule. He's out in pampoe ties to murder you.
> — Me! Stephen exclaimed. That was your contribution to literature.

Figure 3.5. *Little Review*, chapter 9 ('Scylla and Charybdis'), May 1919

(*Little Review*, The Modernist Journals Project (searchable database). Brown and Tulsa Universities, ongoing. http://www.modjourn.org)

tramper Synge') who apparently heard that Dedalus 'pissed on his halldoor in Glasthule'[150] (see Figure 3.5).

Interestingly, this omission from chapter 9 ('Scylla and Charybdis') was made after the Post Office's first actual suppression of the *Little Review* owing to *Ulysses*, the suppression of January 1919. The deletion is one among three omissions marked with an ellipsis, and acknowledged in a footnote signed 'M. C. A.'.[151] As noted earlier, Pound had advised Anderson ('M. C. A.') to 'leave gaps at the questionable points' in the text of *Ulysses*, and to explicitly acknowledge the context in which cuts were being made, advice she did follow, though not until more than a year later, and only after an actual 'suppression'.[152] But Anderson was only intermittently involved in the serialization, and evidently neither she nor Heap wanted to make many changes to Joyce's text.

In the serial versions of both chapters 9 and 12, Joyce uses ellipsis to denote tailing off, interruption, and unsayable things in a number of speeches. When Lyster is summoned to help Bloom in the Library, for example, he says: 'Certainly, certainly, certainly. Is the gentleman......?' ... 'Is he....? O, there!'[153] Similarly, in chapter 12, the citizen reads a list of births and deaths from the *Irish Independent*, concluding 'Cockburn, at the Moat house., Chepstow...', Alf Bergan mentions a postcard with 'u.p.: up on it to take a li...', and Bob Doran, refusing to believe news of Dignam's death, says, 'What about....?'.[154] Anderson's explicit acknowledgements of changes to the text, included in the issues of May 1919 and November 1919 respectively, together with the marking of 'gaps' with ellipses, make it impossible, from the second instalment of chapter 9 onwards, to distinguish between ellipses which are editorial, and those which are deliberately written in and intended by Joyce.[155] Reading the serial version of the text, one cannot help but feel that elements of the text are being withheld, that the serial *Ulysses*, which would officially be deemed 'obscene' by a New York court in February 1921, has elements which happen, as in Greek theatre, 'ob scena', literally off or away from the scene.[156] Anderson's

---

[150] *LR*, May 1919, 19. See above, p. 104.   [151] *LR*, May 1919, 21.

[152] Pound to Anderson, 17 January 1918, *P-LR*, 232.   [153] *LR*, May 1919, 19.

[154] *LR*, November 1919, 43, 44, 45.

[155] For the two notes, see *LR*, May 1919, 21n and *LR*, November 1919, 49n.

[156] The etymology of obscene is in doubt, though a Latin root seems more likely. The Greek root, if a folk etymology, has been cited so frequently that it appears to have become true.

notes have the impact of enhancing that sense, and the ellipses added to Joyce's text increase its hermeneutic challenges.

Against Pound's policy of silent editing Anderson and Heap are to be commended for being explicit in acknowledging most of the changes they made to Joyce's text. Until January 1920, when Heap made her first contact with Joyce, Joyce had little sense of his editors.[157] Nor did he understand who was changing his text. When he noticed the changes made to chapter 4 ('Calypso'), he wrote to Weaver, instructing her to tell Huebsch, his prospective US publisher, that:

> the fourth episode of *Ulysses* as published in the June issue of the *Little Review* is not my full text and that the excised paragraphs must be reinstated and the altered words restored in any proof he may set up.[158]

Weaver wrote to Huebsch as requested, noting the corruptions in 'Calypso' and adding that there were also problems with 'the third episode' where sentences had 'also been excised...these should be restored too'.[159] Joyce had received Pound's typed letter of complaint about 'Calypso', which acknowledges, in a handwritten addendum, the cuts Pound had made to the text ('Hence these tears'); but even with such evidence in front of him, which pointed to the need for an argument with Pound and not the *Little Review*, Joyce insisted on believing that responsibility for the deletions lay with his New York printer, telling Forrest Reid that 'the American printers have mutilated it here and there but I shall see that the few passages excised are restored if it costs me another ten years'.[160] This set of exchanges reveals how vague and muddle-headed Joyce could be; they also communicate Joyce's remarkable, ego, wilfulness, and determination.

Yet those around Joyce continued to want to help. Huebsch wanted to know how the text had been altered and consulted with Anderson; he duly reported to Weaver:

> Miss Anderson says that the excisions in *Ulysses* had been made in pencil in the copy that she received and she is under the impression that they represent Mr Pound's ideas. She says that she made absolutely no changes herself.[161]

This letter, together with Heap's very first letter to Joyce of 9 January 1920—which expresses 'our pleasure and pride in printing you' and apologizes for the 'recent deletions'—is a really crucial piece of editorial evidence, and shows that Anderson and Heap were far more liberal and laissez-faire than Pound in respect of Joyce's text.[162] They did not begin to change the text until the *Little Review* had actually been suppressed on account of *Ulysses*. When they changed the text, they did so reactively, generally making explicit note of the context for intervention. Pound, in contrast, was more proactive, and he attempted to justify his deletions on aesthetic grounds, sometimes seeing them as mere suggestions on which either Anderson or Joyce could decide to act. But after making deletions in chapter 4 and—almost

[157] See above, p. 28.   [158] J to Weaver, 29 July 1918, *L*, I, 116.
[159] Weaver to Huesch, 11 August 1918, *L* II, 419.
[160] Pound to J, [29 March] 1918, *EP-JJ*, 131; J to Forrest Reid, 1 August 1918, *L* II, 117.
[161] Huebsch to Weaver, 31 October 1918, *L* I, 121.
[162] Jane Heap to J, 9 January 1920, Cornell.

certainly—chapters 3 and 5 (one is working from inference, not hard evidence, here), Pound came to see and accept that it was impossible to eliminate the candour from *Ulysses* and he more or less stopped trying. After reading chapter 13 ('Nausicaa'), he explained his attitude to Quinn:

> Joyce has sent on another chapter, excellent start but think he gets a bit too too too at the end of it. Have suggested slight alteration, but see perfectly well that if every possible physical secretion is to be affichéd in course of the work, even this calamity must happen to Mr Bloom. Perhaps *everything* ought to be said ONCE in the English language. At least J seems bent on saying it. Who am I to tamper with a work of genius. For bigod genius it is in parts.[163]

In a sense this reveals Pound's changing attitude as a reader. In fact, all of this evidence—of small corruptions in the serial *Ulysses*—is evidence of reading, and is important in this regard. Pound's first response to *Ulysses* was as a writer, a writer who felt entitled to make suggestions for the way in which the evolving work might be changed or improved. This is evident, for example, in his comments on the serial version of chapter 3 ('Proteus'):

> It is too full of meat to read all at once. Ought to be a division mark of some sort, possibly before the dog comes in. Mere matter of convenience. But even my titanic intellect wants a pause somewhere in the 14 pages.[164]

Anderson and Heap were more inclined to accept Joyce at face value, to accept and publish the text in the spirit in which it was offered. The few letters from Heap to Joyce which survive are friendly and encouraging ('The flowery passages are too good—I shall be sorry when Bloom finishes this day').[165] Popovich, the easiest of this group to malign, made hapless and 'literal' mistakes in setting Joyce's text but, like Anderson and Heap, was also inclined to accept Joyce's lexical innovations and sexual candour. His corruptions are often telling, and critically interesting. How was he to know—moreover, where could he even check—the spelling of a word like 'pampooties'?[166]

While traditional scholarly editing dismisses the *Little Review Ulysses* on the grounds of it being corrupt, and lying 'outside the line of transmission', a genetic scholarship—which attends to the significance of the whole writing process—identifies the preparation and publication of the serial text as being clearly formative for Joyce. Serialization enabled Joyce to fix a number of stylistic stabilities for *Ulysses*, and to see some of the hallmarks of the work being corrupted in the process of transmission. The corruption of the text inspired rewriting, a point one can see quite clearly in the revision to the toilet scene in chapter 4 ('Calypso'). In the text intended for serialization Bloom does not contemplate slowing the action of his bowel movement ('No great hurry. Keep it a bit'); nor does he describe the deliberate action of the movement, and time it as he reads ('Quietly he read, restraining himself, the first column, and, yielding but resisting, began the second'); nor does

---

[163] Pound to Quinn, 21 February 1920, *EP-JQ*, 185.
[164] Pound to J, 7 June 1918, *EP-JJ*, 143.   [165] Jane Heap to J, [late March 1920], Cornell.
[166] 'Pampoe ties' in the *LR*, May 1919, 19.

he think about the size of the stool ('Hope its not too big bring on piles again. No, just right. So. Ah!'); nor does he have a piss ('while feeling his water flow quietly'); or sit 'calmly above his own rising smell' (*U*1922, 66, 67).[167] These post-serial additions—points of departure to set against the points of stability and corruption which can be identified in the serial text—are evidence of the work becoming more explicit in response to the context of it being 'mutilated' (to use Joyce's term) in its first printed version. Candid, socially motivated rewriting of this kind is part of a bigger pattern of revisionary practice, one which needs a more general critical investigation.

VARIANTS VISUALIZED: PAGES FROM 'TELEMACHUS', 'HADES', 'AEOLUS', AND 'CYCLOPS'

One means by which this task can be tackled, initially at least, is to think of the work visually—to think how the first thirteen and a quarter chapters looked in book form when the volume text was first published in Paris on 2 February 1922, and then to consider how much of that text was added post-serially. The new text can be identified by creating a digital collation, as discussed above, or by creating a collation manually. All of the major changes can be highlighted on a paper copy, or by using a mouse-directed digital highlighter (such as the ones available in Adobe). Though this task is labour intensive—it involves comparing and contrasting the first 376 pages of the 1922 text with the corresponding portions of the serial text—it is also relatively simple.[168] Once a preferred method of working is established, the collation is relatively quick to do, and enables readers to identify points of corruption (in both the *Little Review* and the 1922 text), points of stability (features shared by both texts), and points of departure (or moments in the 1922 text which are new). In terms of pattern, the resulting 376 'highlighted' pages can be read visually and grouped into three broad categories:

(1) pages which are unrevised, or which received only very minimal revision post-serialization;

(2) pages with significant post-serial revision, addition, and rewriting; and

(3) pages where the text has been extensively rewritten post-serialization.[169]

The broad categories of minimal, significant, and extensive revision can be identified in a series of four pages from the 1922 text, in which the post-serial additions have been highlighted. Page 14 from chapter 1 ('Telemachus') has very little highlighting, and is a good example of minimal revision (see Figure 3.6).

---

[167] See also *CSE*I 134.30; 136.2; 136.5.

[168] As the *Little Review* serialization stopped after just one instalment of chapter 14, at the word 'whenceness' (*LR*, September–December 1920, 92), the highlighting stops at the corresponding position in the 1922 text (*U*1922, 376).

[169] Another way in which one can come to terms with the genesis of *Ulysses*, and the critical significance of the compositional chronology, is, of course, to study the left-hand pages of the *CSE*. In that case one would not be studying the genesis of *Ulysses* in print, but its genesis from manuscript to volume form.

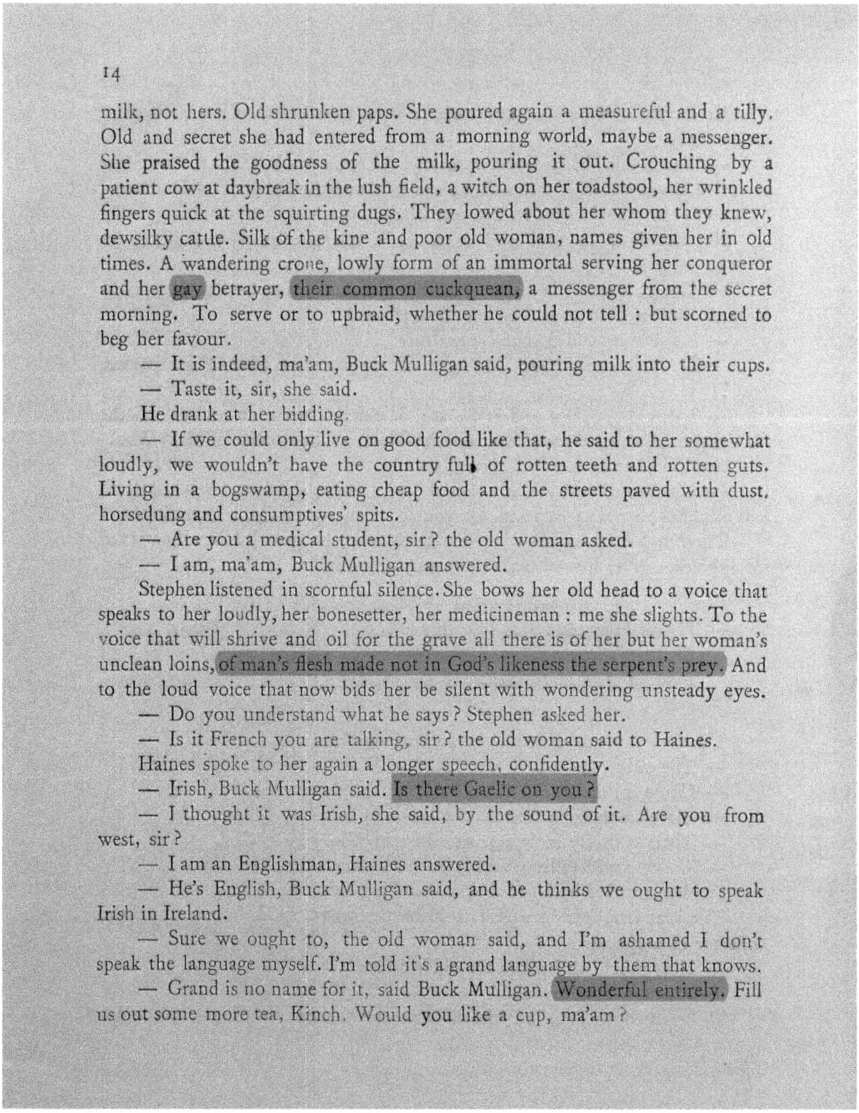

14

milk, not hers. Old shrunken paps. She poured again a measureful and a tilly. Old and secret she had entered from a morning world, maybe a messenger. She praised the goodness of the milk, pouring it out. Crouching by a patient cow at daybreak in the lush field, a witch on her toadstool, her wrinkled fingers quick at the squirting dugs. They lowed about her whom they knew, dewsilky cattle. Silk of the kine and poor old woman, names given her in old times. A wandering crone, lowly form of an immortal serving her conqueror and her gay betrayer, their common cuckquean, a messenger from the secret morning. To serve or to upbraid, whether he could not tell : but scorned to beg her favour.

— It is indeed, ma'am, Buck Mulligan said, pouring milk into their cups.

— Taste it, sir, she said.

He drank at her bidding.

— If we could only live on good food like that, he said to her somewhat loudly, we wouldn't have the country full of rotten teeth and rotten guts. Living in a bogswamp, eating cheap food and the streets paved with dust, horsedung and consumptives' spits.

— Are you a medical student, sir ? the old woman asked.

— I am, ma'am, Buck Mulligan answered.

Stephen listened in scornful silence. She bows her old head to a voice that speaks to her loudly, her bonesetter, her medicineman : me she slights. To the voice that will shrive and oil for the grave all there is of her but her woman's unclean loins, of man's flesh made not in God's likeness the serpent's prey. And to the loud voice that now bids her be silent with wondering unsteady eyes.

— Do you understand what he says ? Stephen asked her.

— Is it French you are talking, sir ? the old woman said to Haines.

Haines spoke to her again a longer speech, confidently.

— Irish, Buck Mulligan said. Is there Gaelic on you ?

— I thought it was Irish, she said, by the sound of it. Are you from west, sir ?

— I am an Englishman, Haines answered.

— He's English, Buck Mulligan said, and he thinks we ought to speak Irish in Ireland.

— Sure we ought to, the old woman said, and I'm ashamed I don't speak the language myself. I'm told it's a grand language by them that knows.

— Grand is no name for it, said Buck Mulligan. Wonderful entirely. Fill us out some more tea, Kinch. Would you like a cup, ma'am ?

Figure 3.6. Page 14 from the 1922 *Ulysses*; post-serial additions highlighted
(Modernist Versions Project, University of Victoria, http://web.uvic.ca/~mvp1922/about)

The additions, including tiny adjustments to Dedalus's interior monologue and Mulligan's speech, typify some of the very minimal revisions which Joyce made to this chapter. The revisions to Mulligan's speech reveal that Joyce does sometimes revise dialogue, and they are particularly interesting. In the serial version Joyce has portrayed the cultural politics of the Irish language, with Haines the 'Britisher' speaking Irish fluently to a native who mistakes what she hears for French, and then reveals her shame that 'I don't speak the language myself. I'm told it's a grand language by them that knows'.[170] In revising these exchanges, Joyce allows Mulligan to ask the milkwoman a question, but not just any question. 'Is there gaelic on you?' is described by Gifford as a 'west-of-Ireland peasant colloquialism'.[171] This oversimplifies the case: the question is culturally charged—and sounds odd to native speakers of English—because of the highly idiomatic use of 'on you'. The Hiberno-English form is a direct translation from Irish and gestures to the fact that there is no exact Irish equivalent for the verb 'to have' (a direct translation of 'an bhfuil gaeilge agat?' would be 'is there Irish on you?', not 'do you speak Irish?' or 'do you have Irish?'). It is hard to believe that someone in the west of Ireland would actually have used the word 'gaelic' (itself an Anglicism) or have said 'is there gaelic on you?', but Joyce (in real life), like Mulligan (in the fiction), attended performances of the Irish National Theatre Society, and was aware that the quirks of Hiberno-English could be intensified and used to good literary effect. 'Wonderful entirely', another phrase added to Mulligan's interaction with the milkwoman, reveals his ability to switch between British and Irish cultural idioms, as this phrase has a kind of Etonian *hauteur*. These tiny revisions—seven words which could be easily overlooked ('Is there gaelic on you?' and 'Wonderful entirely')—show that Joyce had not fully decided how he wished to handle Mulligan's speech in the serial version of the text, and suggest ways in which even very minimal patterns of revision can be of critical interest.

It is also interesting to note the elaborations to Dedalus's thought patterns on this page. 'Cuckquean' suits Dedalus's poetic sensibility and intellectual deviance. A rarely used Renaissance coinage which derives from the stem of 'cuck-old' + quean, to gain the sense of 'female cuckold', the word was obsolete or at least out of normal written circulation by the 1920s, though it continues to have considerable puissance within the culture of sexual fetishism.[172] Wikipedia is a source here: 'In modern English' cuckquean 'generally refers to a woman whose fetish is watching and deriving sexual pleasure from watching a man having sex with one or several women besides his girlfriend, fiancé, wife or other long-term female sex partner'.[173] Joyce certainly had some sense of this meaning, and knowingly adds the word gay in advance of 'betrayer' (thus 'gay betrayer', *U*1922, 14). Through epithets and analogy ('silk of the kine' and 'poor old woman'), this passage is describing how Ireland, personified as a woman, is 'common cuckquean' to Britain, both her 'conqueror' and 'betrayer'. What Joyce has done here is to add sexual frisson and hermeneutic difficulty to a passage which was already challenging. But the addition is effective, and may be seen as an example of the way in which the text becomes more sexually explicit in revision.

---

[170] *LR*, March 1918, 14.
[171] Don Gifford and Robert J Seidman (eds.), *Ulysses Annotated: Notes for James Joyce's Ulysses*, rev edn (London: University of California Press, 1988), 21.
[172] OED online, 2016.   [173] https://en.wikipedia.org/wiki/Cuckquean.

'Of man's flesh made not in God's likeness the serpent's prey', another Dedalus addition on page 14, is a reference to the book of Genesis and was added on the fourth and fifth proofs—the fifth proof being the final proof for this chapter.[174] In September 1921 Joyce himself described the process of revising the proofs of the early chapters as that of writing in 'a great lot of balderdash' and this addition certainly seems a little slapdash.[175] Stephen is thinking about the way in which the milkwoman responds to Mulligan ('She bows her head'; 'me she slights'). The 'To' at the beginning of the sentence ('To the voice that will shrive and oil her for the grave', etc.) makes sense with the idea of the milkwoman bowing 'to a voice'. The new addition obfuscates that clarity, and makes Dedalus's thoughts more difficult to follow. Further rewriting or more punctuation might have tightened this moment in the text, but Joyce was working at speed and on several chapters simultaneously; according to Gabler's table documenting the dates of proofing, Joyce had completed work on chapters 1, 2, and 3 by 17 September 1921, well in advance of his completion of the work as a whole.[176]

There are multiple examples of pages with significant revision in chapters 4 to 8, and 10, 12, and 13. Page 92, from chapter 6, typifies a pattern of significant revision (see Figure 3.7). With the exception of the completely new paragraph ('Dead side of the street this')—a relatively rare feature of Ulyssean addition—page 92 retains the paragraph structure, and the basic content and trajectory of the dialogue established in the serial text. Without an explicit point of comparison, a seasoned reader might struggle to see what is new here, because the additions mainly involve elaborations and not the introduction of completely new ideas. In a sense, this example reveals points of serial stability (the unhighlighted text) amidst multiple points of departure (the highlighted sections). Or, to put it another way, it shows that the serial text can be seen as a stable structure which Joyce chose to elaborate in part.

Mostly the additions in this example involve expanding Bloom's imaginative and emotional world, and show that Joyce became more involved in the representation of Bloom's psychology after he had completed writing the serial text. We see Bloom thinking more candidly than the other characters about the circumstances of Dignam's death ('Too much John Barleycorn'). We also follow Bloom's train of thought after a cortège flashes by bearing a 'tinycoffin'. Within a few lines, it is made clear that this is the funeral of a 'pauper' ('Only a pauper. Nobody owns', *U*1922, 93); this appears to be the funeral party which the men encounter leaving the cemetery as they arrive ('Mourners came out through the gates: woman and a girl', *U*1922, 97). The circumstances of poverty, illegitimacy, and shame are made clearer in the additions (note 'In a hurry to bury', 'Unmarried', and the coffin is made from 'deal', a word to denote a particularly cheap type of pine). As Bloom thinks about this funeral and who pays for it ('Burial friendly society pays'), his thoughts turn, inevitably, to Rudy. The impact of 'Our. Little. Beggar. Baby.' is

---

[174] *CSE*I 421; for the dates of proofs see *CSE*III, table 1, 1914.
[175] To Robert McAlmon, 3 September 1921, *L* III, 48.   [176] *CSE*III 1914.

92

Mr Power's choked laugh burst quietly in the carriage.
Nelson's pillar.
— Eight plums a penny! Eight for a penny!
— We had better look a little serious, Martin Cunningham said.
Mr Dedalus sighed.
— Ah then indeed, he said, poor little Paddy wouldn't grudge us a laugh.
Many a good one he told himself.
— The Lord forgive me! Mr Power said, wiping his wet eyes with his
fingers. Poor Paddy! I little thought a week ago when I saw him last and
he was in his usual health that I'd be driving after him like this. He's gone
from us.
— As decent a little man as ever wore a hat, Mr Dedalus said. He went
very suddenly.
— Breakdown, Martin Cunningham said. Heart.
He tapped his chest sadly.
Blazing face : redhot. Too much John Barleycorn. Cure for a red nose.
Drink like the devil till it turns adelite. A lot of money he spent colouring it.
Mr Power gazed at the passing houses with rueful apprehension.
— He had a sudden death, poor fellow, he said.
— The best death, Mr Bloom said.
Their wide open eyes looked at him.
— No suffering, he said. A moment and all is over. Like dying in sleep.
No-one spoke.
Dead side of the street this. Dull business by day, land agents, temperance
hotel, Falconer's railway guide, civil service college, Gill's, catholic club, the
industrious blind. Why? Some reason. Sun or wind. At night too. Chummies
and slaveys. Under the patronage of the late Father Matew. Foundation stone
for Parnell. Breakdown. Heart.
White horses with white frontlet plumes came round the Rotunda
corner, galloping. A tinycoffin flashed by. In a hurry to bury. A mourning
coach. Unmarried. Black for the married. Piebald for bachelors. Dun for a nun.
— Sad, Martin Cunningham said. A child.
A dwarf's face mauve and wrinkled like little Rudy's was. Dwarf's body,
weak as putty, in a whitelined deal box. Burial friendly society pays. Penny a
week for a sod of turf. Our. Little. Beggar. Baby. Meant nothing. Mistake of
nature. If it's healthy it's from the mother. If not the man. Better luck next
time.

Figure 3.7. Page 92 from the 1922 *Ulysses*; post-serial additions highlighted
(Modernist Versions Project, University of Victoria, http://web.uvic.ca/~mvp1922/about)

quite different to 'Our little beggar baby'. The innovative punctuation slows the
pace of Bloom's thought to elegiac meditation and helps to communicate the sense
of trauma he has experienced through Rudy's death. The stops force the pathos,
putting weight on every word. Another addition here ('If it's healthy its from the
mother, if not from the man. Better luck next time') reveals a bitterness and wist-
fulness in Bloom's thinking about Rudy, more than eleven years after the death.

Pathos is by no means the only component added to page 92. Joyce also adds a whole paragraph of Bloomian interior monologue which describes a section of the west side of O'Connell Street, at the Parnell Square end:

> Dead side of the street this. Dull business by day, land agents, temperance hotel, Falconer's railway guide, civil service college, Gill's, catholic club, the industrious blind. Why? Some reason. Sun or wind. At night too. Chummies and slaveys. Under the patronage of the late Father Mathew. Foundation stone for Parnell. Breakdown. Heart.

Of course, there is a realism to what Bloom notes: there was a Temperance hotel at 56 O'Connell Street and Gill's book shop, where Haines goes to buy a copy of *The Love Songs of Connacht*, was at 50 O'Connell Street. The shop was allied to the publishing and printing firm of M. H. Gill and Son, a publisher of a Catholic and nationalist mentality, with somewhat conservative values.[177]

O'Connell Street, laid out in the eighteenth century, is Dublin's grandest thoroughfare: its width is designed to be imposing, commanding, emblematic of Dublin's importance within the British empire. In making Bloom note its 'dead side', 'dull' businesses, 'Chummies and slaveys', Joyce is stressing the failure of colonial and commercial culture. More specifically, in noting the statue of 'the late Fr Mathew', the so-called Apostle of Temperance, alongside a mere 'Foundation stone for Parnell', Joyce is drawing attention to the politics of commemoration. The serial version of chapter 6, published in September 1918, only includes one reference to Parnell: the visit of the men to the 'Chief's grave' after Dignam's burial, a visit which suggests both the ongoing importance of Parnell for the group, and Bloom's loneliness and cultural separation (he goes his own way, 'unheeded along his grove').[178] The 1922 text adds two new references to Parnell: the reference to the foundation stone, and Bloom's later musing about how the dead are gradually forgotten: 'Even Parnell. Ivy day dying out' (*U*1922, 106).

The acknowledgement that Parnell's monument is not in place is especially significant. The business of commemorating Parnell was marred by the ongoing bitterness of the deep and acrimonious split in the Irish Parliamentary Party which took place in 1890. Though Parnell died in 1891 (of an apparent 'Breakdown' of the 'Heart' as the revised text acknowledges), plans for the monument were not put in place until 1898, and proved difficult to advance. The ceremony for the laying of the foundation stone in 1899 was heckled by nationalists; most of the Irish Parliamentary Party did not attend, and nor did the Catholic clergy. The statue was not unveiled until 1911, twenty years after Parnell's death. Thus this tiny added detail pushes readers towards a recognition of the politics of cultural memory. The addition of this detail could also be read as an instance of the ways in which the 1922 text requires a more intense kind of engagement from the reader than the serial text.

---

[177] For the history of Gill and Son, see Gillian McIntosh, 'M. H. Gill, Later Gill and Macmillan', in Clare Hutton (ed.) and Patrick Walsh (co-ed.)., *The Oxford History of the Irish Book, 1891–2000* (Oxford: Oxford University Press, 2011), 511–28, and the photos at 229, 230.

[178] *LR*, September 1918, 36. Bloom's moment of solitude is considerably expanded in the 1922 text. See *U*1922, 108f. I discuss this revision in 'The Development of *Ulysses* in Print, 1918–1922', *Dublin James Joyce Journal*, 6:7 (2015), 109–31 (124–6).

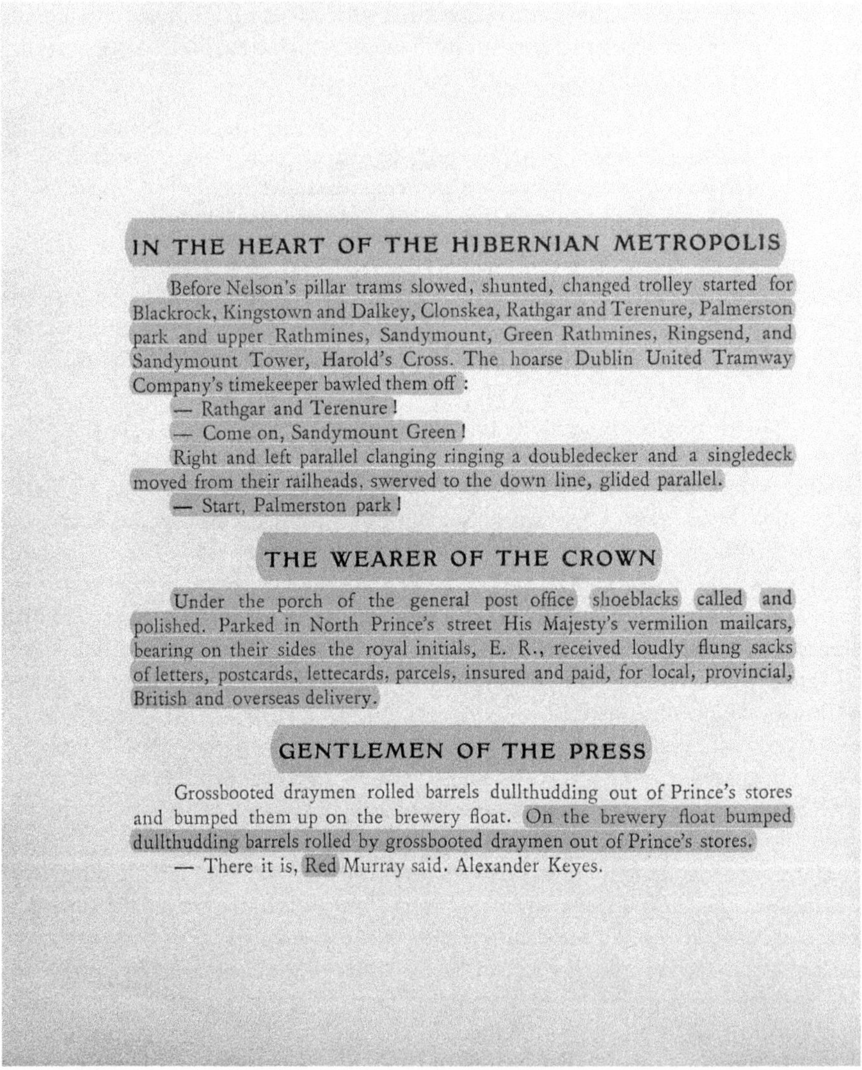

IN THE HEART OF THE HIBERNIAN METROPOLIS

Before Nelson's pillar trams slowed, shunted, changed trolley started for Blackrock, Kingstown and Dalkey, Clonskea, Rathgar and Terenure, Palmerston park and upper Rathmines, Sandymount, Green Rathmines, Ringsend, and Sandymount Tower, Harold's Cross. The hoarse Dublin United Tramway Company's timekeeper bawled them off :
— Rathgar and Terenure !
— Come on, Sandymount Green !
Right and left parallel clanging ringing a doubledecker and a singledeck moved from their railheads, swerved to the down line, glided parallel.
— Start, Palmerston park !

THE WEARER OF THE CROWN

Under the porch of the general post office shoeblacks called and polished. Parked in North Prince's street His Majesty's vermilion mailcars, bearing on their sides the royal initials, E. R., received loudly flung sacks of letters, postcards, lettecards, parcels, insured and paid, for local, provincial, British and overseas delivery.

GENTLEMEN OF THE PRESS

Grossbooted draymen rolled barrels dullthudding out of Prince's stores and bumped them up on the brewery float. On the brewery float bumped dullthudding barrels rolled by grossbooted draymen out of Prince's stores.
— There it is, Red Murray said. Alexander Keyes.

Figure 3.8. Page 112 from the 1922 *Ulysses*; post-serial additions highlighted
(Modernist Versions Project, University of Victoria, http://web.uvic.ca/~mvp1922/about)

Chapter 7 is one of the only places in the text where one can find examples of category 3, pages which exemplify a pattern of extensive post-serial addition. Page 112 (see Figure 3.8) is the opening of chapter 7 and shows that Joyce added completely new paragraphs to the opening of this chapter post-serialization (this 'new' opening being an exception to the general point, made above, that the finished text generally preserves the distinctive openings and closings of the serial version).

'IN THE HEART OF THE HIBERNIAN METROPOLIS' functions as a type of chapter heading by proclaiming the location of the setting, and immediately draws readerly attention to the ways in which typography creates meaning, a particularly apt narrative strategy given the chapter's principal setting in the editorial office and printing works of the *Freeman's Journal* and *Evening Telegraph*. A comparison between this page and the opening page of the serial text, published in the *Little Review* in October 1918, reveals both the visual and hermeneutic impact of Joyce's revision (see Figure 3.9).

The difference between the two textual exemplars is immediately apparent to the eye. In fact, the differences here seem so significant that it is necessary to put forward a more general account of the revisions to this chapter in order to situate and understand the specifics of what has happened to the opening page.

One feature of this page which compels immediate attention is the inadvertent setting of the first line twice, and the glaring typographical corruption of 'dullthudding' ('dullhudding').[179] This is the kind of error one can make in settling to a difficult task. Popovich must have been distracted as he started to typeset a text which represents printing machinery ('The machines clanked in threefour time. Thump, thump, thump'), 'obedient reels feeding in the huge webs of paper', and 'silent typesetters at their cases'.[180] But, as others have noted, Joyce appears to have enjoyed Popovich's error, and seems to have responded to the first erroneous publication. In revising the text he included the sentence as originally written, and then rewrote it with the word order changed, in order to introduce a 'chiastic structure', a chiasmus being a rhetorical criss-cross structure, used for emphasis and effect.[181] The addition 'On the brewery float bumped dullthudding barrels rolled by grossbooted draymen out of Prince's stores' (*U*1922, 112) reverses the elements of the original in order to draw readerly attention to the artistry of the writing, and suggest the ways in which modes of narration affect readerly perception and experience.

Joyce's initial idea for the opening of chapter 7 was to open the scene *in medias res*, more or less, with Bloom inside the newspaper office and in dialogue with 'Red Murray'. In the description of the 'grossbooted draymen' loading beer barrels, the serial text contains just the merest evocation of the scene outside. Indeed, had Popovich followed the typescript here, this rhythmic description of bumping and rolling barrels—evoking men at work and in collaboration, and anticipating the energy and rhythm of the printing room—would have been merely one sentence.[182] What one can see in the new paragraphs which open chapter 7 is a greater commitment to the representation of the street scene which could be experienced in the immediate environs of the newspaper offices, a large building which stretched between Middle Abbey Street, which leads on to O'Connell Street, and Prince's Street, a cul de sac, which also leads on to O'Connell Street. The new paragraphs show Joyce taking the opportunity to insert a kind of geographical and political

---

[179] *LR*, October 1918, 26.   [180] *LR*, October 1918, 27, 28, 29.

[181] Sigler, 'Archival Errors: *Ulysses* in the *Little Review*', 80; see also Daniel Ferrer and Jean-Michel Rabaté, 'Paragraphs in Expansion (James Joyce)', in *Genetic Criticism: Texts and Avant-Textes* (Philadelphia, PA: University of Pennsylvania Press, 2004), 132–51 (139).

[182] For the typescript consigned to Darantiere, a carbon of that consigned to Popovich, see *JJA*, volume 12, 286.

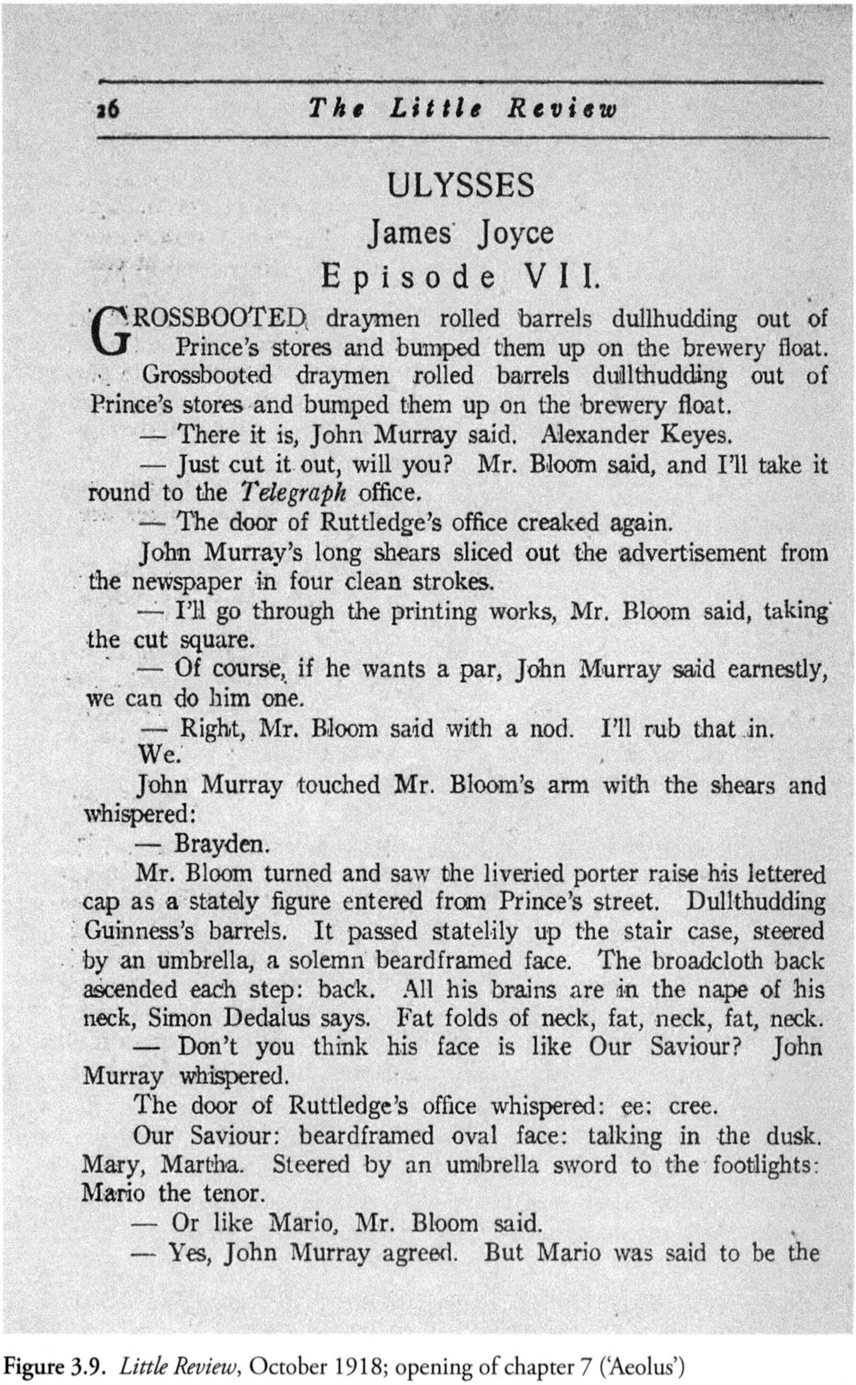

26 *The Little Review*

ULYSSES

James Joyce

Episode VII.

GROSSBOOTED draymen rolled barrels dullhudding out of Prince's stores and bumped them up on the brewery float. Grossbooted draymen rolled barrels dullthudding out of Prince's stores and bumped them up on the brewery float.

— There it is, John Murray said. Alexander Keyes.

— Just cut it out, will you? Mr. Bloom said, and I'll take it round to the *Telegraph* office.

— The door of Ruttledge's office creaked again.

John Murray's long shears sliced out the advertisement from the newspaper in four clean strokes.

— I'll go through the printing works, Mr. Bloom said, taking the cut square.

— Of course, if he wants a par, John Murray said earnestly, we can do him one.

— Right, Mr. Bloom said with a nod. I'll rub that in. We.

John Murray touched Mr. Bloom's arm with the shears and whispered:

— Brayden.

Mr. Bloom turned and saw the liveried porter raise his lettered cap as a stately figure entered from Prince's street. Dullthudding Guinness's barrels. It passed statelily up the stair case, steered by an umbrella, a solemn beardframed face. The broadcloth back ascended each step: back. All his brains are in the nape of his neck, Simon Dedalus says. Fat folds of neck, fat, neck, fat, neck.

— Don't you think his face is like Our Saviour? John Murray whispered.

The door of Ruttledge's office whispered: ee: cree.

Our Saviour: beardframed oval face: talking in the dusk. Mary, Martha. Steered by an umbrella sword to the footlights: Mario the tenor.

— Or like Mario, Mr. Bloom said.

— Yes, John Murray agreed. But Mario was said to be the

Figure 3.9. *Little Review*, October 1918; opening of chapter 7 ('Aeolus')

(*Little Review*, The Modernist Journals Project (searchable database). Brown and Tulsa Universities, ongoing. http://www.modjourn.org)

specificity, in the litany of places for which trams are destined ('Start, Palmerstown park!', *U*1922, 112), and a type of historical and political specificity, in the description of who controls Dublin's postal system ('His Majesty's vermilion mailcars, bearing on their sides the royal initials, E. R.', *U*1922, 112). These additions are highly significant for any kind of historicist or political reading of the text such as that proposed, for example, by Len Platt who sees this chapter as a portrait of the Irish Catholic intelligentsia whose 'empathy is in a shared social status and a shared historical consciousness':

> There is a clannishness about the men in the *Telegraph* office which is not just a matter of acquaintance or friendship. They are a gathering, a gathering of failure and unfulfillment, which is why the energetic Bloom is so famously excluded... Stephen, McHugh, Crawford, O'Molloy and Lenehan are elevated to the status of a quintet of high performance talent. They represent literature, the classics, the press, the law and 'the turf'. But the ironies of these designations are obvious. In reality, these are the underachievers, and wasted potential here is not simply a matter of personal dissipation. The relevant historical context, here, is the collapse of a dynamic middle-class Catholicism.[183]

This kind of engagement with chapter 7 is notably absent from most commentaries—it is a noticeable omission, for example, even from critical works which pursue Joyce's political positions through close reading, such as *Semicolonial Joyce* and *Joyce's Revenge*.[184]

Most commentators focus on the chapter's style and use of rhetoric, usually at the expense of noting the narrative significance of Stephen's editorial welcome in the newspaper office. Crawford tells Stephen: 'I want you to write something for me... Something with a bite in it. You can do it. I see it in your face' (*U*1922, 130). The camaraderie of this culturally charged exchange contrasts quite dramatically with Bloom's treatment in the same environment. Not many of the individuals gathered in this workplace appear to be doing any work, but Bloom's efforts in securing an ad from Keyes are belittled by Crawford who tells Bloom to tell Keyes he 'can kiss my royal Irish arse... Any time he likes, tell him' (*U*1922, 141). As Platt has observed, Stephen thinks briefly about Daniel O'Connell, his oratory, and the legacy of the monster meetings of 1843, which were part of O'Connell's campaign for the repeal of the Union between Britain and Ireland ('Hosts at Mullaghmast and Tara of the Kings. Miles of ears of porches. The tribune's words howled and scattered to the four winds. A people sheltered within his voice. Dead noise', *U*1922, 137–8).[185] This is a key moment within the chapter, pointing, as it does, to the central theme of personal and political failure within the work as a whole. It is all too easy to miss this because the structure of the action—in both the serial and final version—is confusing and difficult to follow. It takes considerable

---

[183] Len Platt, *Joyce and the Anglo-Irish: A Study of Joyce and the Literary Revival* (Amsterdam: Rodopi, 1998), 61.
[184] Derek Attridge and Marjorie Howes (eds.), *Semicolonial Joyce* (Cambridge: Cambridge University Press, 2000); Andrew Gibson, *Joyce's Revenge: History, Politics and Aesthetics in Ulysses* (Oxford: Oxford University Press, 2002).
[185] Platt, *Joyce and the Anglo-Irish*, 61.

determination for the reader to work out where the action is happening, who is speaking to whom, and how what is happening is significant. No one made any comment on this chapter in the 'Reader Critic' column, and Pound, who made many positive comments to Joyce as he read *Ulysses* in typescript, and had so much to say to so many, did not say anything about this chapter, a silence which may suggest confusion, a lack of engagement, or his sense that the chapter was less strong than others.

The interior action begins with Bloom in some sort of cuttings department (where he meets 'John Murray' and finds the original ad placed by Alexander Keyes); thereafter he goes through the 'printing works' ('Through a lane of clanking drums') to discuss the placing of the Keyes ad with Nannetti, foreman of the newspaper, who has his own 'reading closet' (a room within the works).[186] Bloom then goes past the 'caseroom', 'down the house staircase', and into 'the *Evening Telegraph* office' where Ned Lambert, Simon Dedalus, and professor MacHugh are gathered and engaged in desultory chit-chat (an activity justified by Bloom's reflection, 'Rather upsets a man's day a funeral does').[187] This room also contains an 'inner office' which has a phone which Bloom uses to phone Keyes ('*Evening Telegraph* here, Mr. Bloom phoned from the inner office').[188] After this, Bloom leaves for a discussion with Keyes at the auction rooms in Bachelor's walk, and the group of men gathered in the office—now including 'the professor', Lenehan, J. J. O'Molloy, Myles Crawford—watch from a window as Bloom walks along the street followed by a file 'of capering newsboys', 'young guttersnipes' 'Taking off his flat spaugs and the walk'.[189] The narrative focus turns to the conversation between the men who are left behind, a group of four which becomes six once Mr O'Madden Burke arrives with Stephen Dedalus, who is bearing his letter from Garrett Deasy ('I escort a suppliant').[190] Simon Dedalus ('Your governor') and Ned Lambert have already left for a drink at 'the Oval' and Crawford, who is already tipsy ('He's pretty well on'), is keen to join them ('Come on then, Myles Crawford said. Wher's my hat?').[191] But instead of leaving, the group engage in a lengthy conversation which ranges from Lenehan's riddle ('What opera is like a railwayline?'), to Deasy's wife ('The bloodiest old tartar God ever made'), to the legacies of Roman civilization ('a race the acme of whose mentality is the maxim: time is money'), to stories about Ignatius Gallaher's journalism 'in eightytwo, time of the invincibles' ('That's press. That's talent').[192] Crawford is the most powerful figure among those gathered and he is keen to influence and impress Stephen ('Grattan and Flood wrote for this very paper').[193] O'Molloy and MacHugh are also significant conversational presences; MacHugh's long citation of a speech about cultural nationalism by John F. Taylor

---

[186] *LR*, October 1918, 26, 27.   [187] *LR*, October 1918, 30, 31.
[188] *LR*, October 1918, 35.   [189] *LR*, October 1918, 36.
[190] *LR*, October 1918, 37. Platt notes a 'quintet'; the multiple entries and exits are harder to track in the 1922 text.
[191] *LR*, October 1918, 37, 36.   [192] *LR*, October 1918, 37, 38, 40, 41.
[193] *LR*, October 1918, 43.

dominates the latter part of this scene, before the group decides to head for Mooney's pub at Stephen's suggestion ('May I suggest the house do now adjourn?').[194]

As they leave, Stephen begins to tell his story about 'Two old women on the top of Nelson's pillar'.[195] J. J. O'Molloy is trying to borrow money from Crawford, a request which is refused ('Sorry, Jack. With a heart and half if I could'); Crawford is therefore straggling behind the main group ('What's keeping our friend?').[196] He is caught by Bloom for a brief conversation on or near the steps of the offices ('. . . he says he'll give the renewal. But he wants the par. What will I tell him, Mr. Crawford?').[197] As the men proceed across O'Connell Street towards Mooney's, group dialogue—the mode of narration which dominates the chapter—continues and is focused on the conclusion to Stephen's story, responses to it, and the significance of Nelson, who Stephen dubs the 'one handled adulterer', a phrase repeated with adulation by the professor ('I like that. I see the idea. I see what you mean').[198] Bloom sees the group leaving ('All off for a drink') and takes a keen interest in Stephen:

> Wonder is that young Dedalus standing. Has a good pair of boots on him today. Last time I saw him he had his heels on view. Been walking in muck somewhere. Careless chap. What was he doing in Irishtown?[199]

After being snubbed by Crawford, he is left behind, 'weighing the point and about to smile'.[200] If one takes the view that *Ulysses* is about Stephen's search for a symbolic father and Bloom's search for a son, the fact that Bloom notes Stephen so intensely and yet fails to meet him is a significant event in the chapter.

The serial version of this chapter is by no means an easy read, but these events are far easier to follow in that version. The differences between the two versions are, of course, critically instructive; as Baron has argued, chapter 7 'demands that *Ulysses*'s compositional history be taken into account'.[201] Joyce's decision to include the sixty-one headings in the text was a decision to disrupt the naturalistic narrative form of the serial text, thereby obfuscating the significance of the chapter as a portrait of political stasis and cultural failure. The headings, already discussed briefly in Chapter 2, break up the narrative events and comment on what is happening in various ways (through irony or disjunctive counterpoint, for example).[202] They are an adept way of communicating the atmosphere and processes of the newspaper office, and they encourage readers to consider the significance of the ways in which individuals process printed matter almost without thinking, particularly within urban environments.

Joyce himself characterized the revision to this chapter as that of 'recasting' and it is important to note that the primary impulse of his revision to this chapter has been the insertion of the headings.[203] As Groden has observed, Joyce does not

---

[194] *LR*, October 1918, 46.   [195] *LR*, October 1918, 49.
[196] *LR*, October 1918, 49, 48.   [197] *LR*, October 1918, 48, 49.
[198] *LR*, October 1918, 50.   [199] *LR*, October 1918, 49.   [200] *LR*, October 1918, 49.
[201] Baron, 'Beginnings', 64.   [202] See above, p. 73.
[203] '*Eolus* is recast', J to Weaver, 7 October 1921, *L* I, 172.

appear to make many significant revisions to the 'novelistic' aspects of the chapter.[204]
'The reading experience is altered by the headings', as Lawrence has argued, and it
is certainly plausible to suggest that:

> Joyce deliberately altered the chapter to make it predict the antics of the later chapters and
> to give the reader early notice that the form of the novel was becoming obsolete.[205]

It is also crucial to note that Joyce did not begin to insert the headings until *after*
he had seen the first proofs, which were sent to him during August 1921.[206] This
leads to an obvious question: what was it about the sight of the first proofs which
inspired him to 'recast' the chapter in such a significant manner? Joyce may have
wanted to signal his commitment to the stylistic disruptions of the latter part of
the work, but it is also possible that he was dissatisfied with the shape of the chapter in its serial form.

In terms of both narrative technique (naturalism, with multi-speaker male
dialogue) and theme (the cultural, political, and psychological state of post-Parnellite
middle-class Dublin), the serial version of 'Aeolus' is quite close to 'Ivy Day in
the Committee Room'. Joyce's initial narrative interest in the chapter appears to
have resided in the evocation of the internal geography and atmosphere of the
newspaper office, in recording the kinds of conversation and interaction which
took place between groups of men in a workplace of that kind, in recording the
cultural preoccupations of middle-class Catholic nationalism, and in contrasting
the different ways in which Bloom and Stephen Dedalus were received and treated.
But the links and cuts between the mini-scenes in the serial text are rapid and confusing to follow, in sharp contrast to chapter 6 ('Hades') and 'Ivy Day' (for example,
two texts which are obvious points of comparison). In order to understand the
significance of what is happening, it is important for readers to gain a sense of the
complicated geography of the offices, of the difference between the types of negotiation which happen outside Ruttledge's office, the foreman's 'reading closet',
Crawford's 'sanctum', the Oval, and the streets of Dublin. Arguably, the naturalism
of the serial 'Aeolus' does not quite work—either aesthetically or emotionally—
and Joyce chose to revise the weakness out of the chapter by disrupting that
naturalism through the introduction of the headings. The headings may be read as
a kind of disguise—albeit a very effective disguise—which conceal what might
otherwise have remained a weak chapter, an 'After the Race' within *Ulysses*.

In terms of advancing the naturalistic plotlines of the work, one of the functions
of the serial version of this chapter is to reveal Bloom's alienation within Dublin's
cultural world. But Bloom's alienation had already been established within the serial
versions of chapters 4, 5, and 6, was enhanced in the revision of those chapters,
and would be significantly embellished in chapter 12 ('Cyclops'). Thus Joyce could
afford to make that plot element less clear, and to prepare readers for the stylistic

[204] Groden, *Ulysses in Progress*, 102.

[205] Karen Lawrence, *The Odyssey of Style in Ulysses* (Princeton, NJ: Princeton University Press,
1981), 59.

[206] *CSE*III 1914. Groden dates this first placard to 11–13 August (*Ulysses in Progress*, 102).

innovations of the latter part of the work by introducing the headings. Nor is it the case that Bloom's alienation is written out; in fact, some elements of that story are enhanced through the introduction of the headings, 'RETURN OF BLOOM', 'INTERVIEW WITH THE EDITOR', 'K. M. A.', and 'K. M. R. I. A.' ('kiss my royal Irish arse'), which raise (successively, and insistently) and then dash expectations that Bloom might be treated kindly (*U*1922, 140, 141).

Joyce's clarification of the schemata of *Ulysses* was another significant impetus behind the revision of this chapter. He made what is known as the 'Linati schema' available in September 1920, just under two years after the serial version of 'Aeolus' had been published.[207] In it, he lists 'rhetoric' as the art of the chapter; 'red' as its colour; the 'lungs' as its organ; 'the mockery of victory' as its meaning; Aeolus, Sons, Telemachus, Mentor, and Ulysses as its 'people'; 'tropes' and deliberative, forensic, and public oratory as 'technic' (or technique); and various objects as its symbols (machines, wind, hunger, stag beetle, failed destinies, the press, mutability).[208] The Gilbert schema, which Joyce made available to Valery Larbaud in the autumn of 1921, repeated certain elements of the Linati schema but specified solely 'the Editor' as the chapter's symbol, 'enthymemic' as the chapter's 'technic'; and added a range of Homeric correspondences (Crawford—Aeolus; Incest—Journalism; Floating Island—Press).[209] While these schemata have had an enormous shaping impact on the structure of Joycean scholarship, it is also the case that the sincerity and utility of some of their elements is questionable. Nonetheless, it is true that Joyce revised the text of *Ulysses*—and 'Aeolus' in particular—in order to make the work conform with elements denoted in the schemes. Groden makes this argument quite decisively in *Ulysses in Progress*, putting the general argument that Joyce 'filled "Aeolus" with correspondences, adding among other things, all the subheads and many of the wind references and rhetorical devices', and giving particular illustrations:

> Among the new devices are Lenehan's 'Clamn dever' . . . his palindromes 'Madam, I'm Adam. And Able was I ere I saw Elba' and his quips 'Muchibus thankibus', 'I feel a strong weakness' and 'O, for a fresh of breath air!'.[210]

One can see elements of what might be termed 'schematic revision' in the highlighted additions of page 112 (see Figure 3.8, above). The timekeeper of the Dublin United Tramway Company is a public orator, whose oratory we actually hear 'Rathgar and Terenure!', and Joyce has added the detail of 'vermilion mailcars' and changed the name of John Murray, the maker of newspaper cuttings, to 'Red Murray' in line with the idea that red is the colour of this chapter (*U*1922, 112).

---

[207] J to Carlo Linati, 21 September 1920, *L* I, 146.

[208] Reproduced in Richard Ellmann, *Ulysses on the Liffey* (London: Faber, 1974), 183–7. The genesis and transmission of the Linati schema is, in itself, interesting and complicated. The original of this document was in Italian and is in the Buffalo Joyce Collection (V. A. I. a); see Crispi's notes at http://library.buffalo.edu/pl/collections/jamesjoyce/catalog/va1a.htm.

[209] J to Valery Larbaud, [about 15 November 1921], *L* III, 53. Details of Gilbert schema from Ellmann, *Ulysses on the Liffey*, 183–7.

[210] Groden, *Ulysses in Progress*, 64, 105. The cited additions are all post-serial: see *U*1922, 132, 135, 130; cf. *CSE*I 286.10, 284.28, 292.16, 280.14.

The headings emphasize the art of rhetoric in their conspicuous use of tropes ('THE WEARER OF THE CROWN' being a euphemism for 'His Majesty'), and the new sentence 'On the brewery float bumped dullthudding barrels' introduces a chiasmus, as already noted.

Yet Joyce was clearly committed to many of the 'schematic' elements of the chapter in the serial version, and had made a specific set of notes on rhetoric in the early compositional stages.[211] The serial version of the text does not just exemplify the art of oratory by citing the speech of John F. Taylor, it also refers to oratory explicitly ('The finest display of oratory I ever heard', 'a finished orator', and 'That is oratory, the professor said').[212] Similarly, the word 'wind' occurs three times: in Bloom's reflection 'Want to get some wind off my chest first'.; the professor's exclamation ('Enough of the windbag!'); and Dedalus's thoughts about O'Connell and oratory ('Gone with the wind').[213] In revising the text, Joyce enhanced its oratory, but he did not introduce another use of that specific word. On the other hand, he inserted multiple additional uses of the word 'wind' and close variants post-serially: 'They always build one door opposite another for the wind to', 'Windfall when he kicks out', 'What's in the wind, I wonder', 'Reaping the whirl-wind', 'wind of a new opening', 'Windy Arbour', 'scattered to the four winds', 'the sack of windy Troy', 'RAISING THE WIND', 'if I could raise the wind anyhow' (*U*1922, 113, 119, 120, 121, 131, 138, 141). This example reveals that the 'schematic' elements already existed in the serial text. In revision, as Kenner avers, Joyce 'extends the artifice' by embellishing certain 'schematic' elements to which he had already committed.[214]

In a sense this is a pattern which can be identified in page 318, the final textual exemplar to be considered here, and another page, this time from chapter 12 ('Cyclops'), which exemplifies 'extensive revision' (see Figure 3.10). The new paragraph—a parodic interpolation—alters the tempo and tension in one of Bloom's most important and moving moments, the moment when he confronts those who surround him at Barney Kiernan's pub and candidly states his nation ('Ireland, says Bloom, I was born here. Ireland', *U*1922, 317), an utterance which makes the citizen spit, a large spit which looks like a 'Red bank oyster' (*U*1922, 317).[215]

One can see the rising tension in the following excerpt from the serial version, which includes the build-up of the moment just before when Bloom is asked 'what a nation means' (see Figure 3.11). Joyce has inserted a number of embellishing details post-serially: the 'oyster' of spit has become a 'Red bank oyster' (*U*1922, 317); and the citizen, after spitting, introduces 'a handkerchief to swab himself dry' (*U*1922, 317). This creates the opportunity for the parodic narrative voice of this chapter to describe the handkerchief, compare it to an illuminated Irish

---

[211] Joyce's notes on rhetoric (in NLI, 36,639/3, page 27) are described by Wim Van Mierlo, 'The Subject Notebook: A Nexus in the Composition History of *Ulysses*—A Preliminary Analysis', 7 (Spring 2007), www.geneticjoycestudies.org.

[212] *LR*, October 1918, 44, 46.

[213] *LR*, October 1918, 30, 33, 46.   [214] Kenner, *Ulysses*, 63.

[215] The 'Red Bank' was a restaurant at 19 and 20 D'Olier Street, which sold oysters harvested from the red-bank beds in county Clare. See joyceproject.com and Gifford, *Ulysses Annotated*, 181.

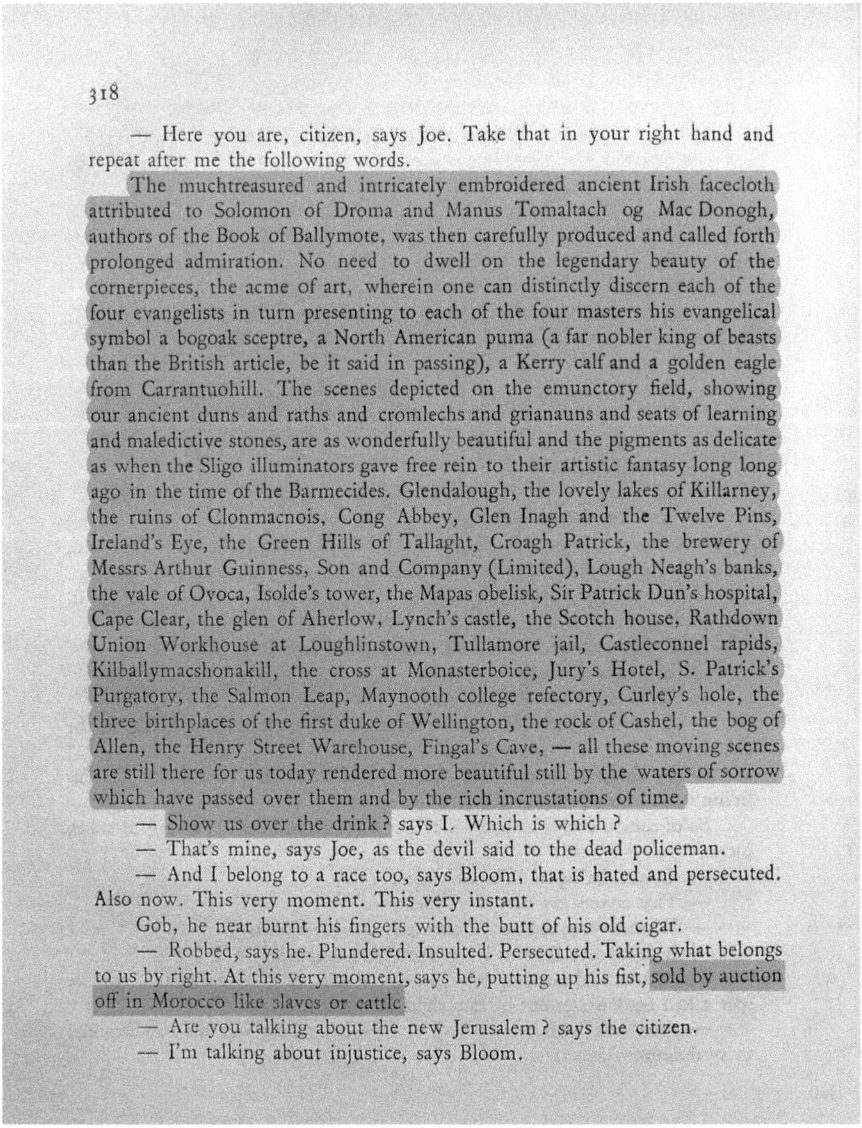

318

— Here you are, citizen, says Joe. Take that in your right hand and repeat after me the following words.

The muchtreasured and intricately embroidered ancient Irish facecloth attributed to Solomon of Droma and Manus Tomaltach og Mac Donogh, authors of the Book of Ballymote, was then carefully produced and called forth prolonged admiration. No need to dwell on the legendary beauty of the cornerpieces, the acme of art, wherein one can distinctly discern each of the four evangelists in turn presenting to each of the four masters his evangelical symbol a bogoak sceptre, a North American puma (a far nobler king of beasts than the British article, be it said in passing), a Kerry calf and a golden eagle from Carrantuohill. The scenes depicted on the emunctory field, showing our ancient duns and raths and cromlechs and grianauns and seats of learning and maledictive stones, are as wonderfully beautiful and the pigments as delicate as when the Sligo illuminators gave free rein to their artistic fantasy long long ago in the time of the Barmecides. Glendalough, the lovely lakes of Killarney, the ruins of Clonmacnois, Cong Abbey, Glen Inagh and the Twelve Pins, Ireland's Eye, the Green Hills of Tallaght, Croagh Patrick, the brewery of Messrs Arthur Guinness, Son and Company (Limited), Lough Neagh's banks, the vale of Ovoca, Isolde's tower, the Mapas obelisk, Sir Patrick Dun's hospital, Cape Clear, the glen of Aherlow, Lynch's castle, the Scotch house, Rathdown Union Workhouse at Loughlinstown, Tullamore jail, Castleconnel rapids, Kilballymacshonakill, the cross at Monasterboice, Jury's Hotel, S. Patrick's Purgatory, the Salmon Leap, Maynooth college refectory, Curley's hole, the three birthplaces of the first duke of Wellington, the rock of Cashel, the bog of Allen, the Henry Street Warehouse, Fingal's Cave, — all these moving scenes are still there for us today rendered more beautiful still by the waters of sorrow which have passed over them and by the rich incrustations of time.

— Show us over the drink? says I. Which is which?

— That's mine, says Joe, as the devil said to the dead policeman.

— And I belong to a race too, says Bloom, that is hated and persecuted. Also now. This very moment. This very instant.

Gob, he near burnt his fingers with the butt of his old cigar.

— Robbed, says he. Plundered. Insulted. Persecuted. Taking what belongs to us by right. At this very moment, says he, putting up his fist, sold by auction off in Morocco like slaves or cattle.

— Are you talking about the new Jerusalem? says the citizen.

— I'm talking about injustice, says Bloom.

Figure 3.10. Page 318 from the 1922 *Ulysses*; post-serial additions highlighted
(Modernist Versions Project, University of Victoria, http://web.uvic.ca/~mvp1922/about)

manuscript (with 'legendary' 'cornerpieces'), and parody the language and conceptual worlds of Irish genealogy (note the mention of the 'Manus Tomaltach og MacDonogh', and the 'Book of Ballymote'); art history ('the pigments as delicate as when the Sligo illuminators gave free rein to their artistic fantasy'); and encyclopaedic travel writing, seen in the addition of the list of famous Irish ecclesiastical sites ('Glendalough … the ruins of Clonmacnois'), intermixed, comically,

—But do you know what a nation means?   says John Wyse.
—Yes, says Bloom.
—What is it? says John Wyse.
—A nation? says Bloom. A nation is the same people living in
the same place.
—By God, then says Ned, laughing, if that's so I'm a nation for
I'm living in the same place for the past five years.
    So of course everyone had a laugh at Bloom and says he,
trying to muck out of it:
—Or also living in different places.
—That covers my case, says Joe.
—What is your nation if I may ask, says the citizen.
—Ireland, says Bloom. I was born here. Ireland.
    The citizen said nothing only cleared the spit out of his gullet
and, gob, he spat an oyster out of him right in the corner.
—After you with the push, Joe, says he.
—Here you are, citizen, says Joe. Take that in your right hand
and repeat after me the following words.
—Which is which? says I.
—That's mine, says Joe, as the devil said to the dead policeman.
—And I belong to a race too, says Bloom, that is hated and perse-
cuted. Also now. This very moment. This very instant.

Figure 3.11. *Little Review*, January 1920; chapter 12 ('Cyclops')

(*Little Review*, The Modernist Journals Project (searchable database). Brown and Tulsa Universities, ongoing. http://www.modjourn.org)

with touristic sites which are not ecclesiastical ('the lovely lakes of Killarney...the Green Hills of Tallaght, the brewery of Messrs Arthur Guinness'). This lengthy addition—which is a journey away from naturalistic representation—distracts readers, at least momentarily, from the tensions of the scene involving Bloom. It is a shift towards a greater commitment to encyclopedism, listing, and narrative disruption.

    The Linati schema—finalized before Joyce had undertaken the major revision of this chapter—specifies 'alternating asymmetry' as its 'technic' and Joyce was certainly committed to intercutting naturalism (narration and dialogue) with parodic inter-polation in the serial version of 'Cyclops'.[216] But the serial version maintained a kind of balance between these different narrative components. In revising the chapter Joyce embellished and extended the parodic interpolations extensively, adding long lists and disquisitions, which tilt readers away from what is happening in terms of plot. He has increased its asymmetries; in fact, he has committed himself to what is described in the later schema (the Gilbert, completed as he was working on the revisions to the chapter) as the 'technic' of 'gigantism'.[217] In that respect, this revision—the addition of the description of the Citizen's handkerchief—can be regarded as 'schematic' (really rather a rough and approximate term, given

---

[216] For the Linati schema, see Ellmann, *Ulysses on the Liffey*, 183–7.
[217] For the Gilbert schema, see Ellmann, *Ulysses on the Liffey*, 183–7.

the two versions of the schema, their multiple components, and the openness of their terms to multiple readings).

How much difference does the extension of the parodies make to a reading of 'Cyclops'? Would readers of the serial and volume versions emerge with a very different sense of what they have read? Does extensive addition always have a significant impact on the meaning of the text, or could it be the case that extensive addition—of the kind one can see in 'Cyclops'—sometimes only has a small her-meneutic impact? While these questions are too large to be considered here, it seems at least plausible that this might be the case: that extensive revisions some-times only make a small difference to the total experience of the work. Similarly, 'minor' revision—involving the addition of a few words here and there—can have a large interpretive impact.

'Cyclops'—which has been singled out for detailed genetic treatment by Groden—points to why it can be challenging to make generalizations about Joyce's revisionary practice.[218] It is one among a number of chapters which contain clutches of pages which are either unrevised post-serialization, or only very minim-ally revised.[219] The opening pages, in which Joyce introduces his distinctive unnamed narrator in dialogue with Joe Hynes ('Lo, Joe, says I. How are you blow-ing? Did you see that bloody chimneysweep near shove my eye out with his brush?'), are unrevised post-serialization. By the moment of serialization Joyce clearly had a very certain sense of how that demotic Dubliner would tell the story, in a manner which is anecdotal, one eyed, and uniquely Dublinese ('says I'). The fact that Joyce did not revise that aspect of 'Cyclops' points to the need to look beyond individual pages, and to study patterns of Ulyssean revision in miniature (within tiny adjustments), in individual paragraphs, and in macro (across whole chapters). It would be impossible to do this for every part of the serial text, but Chapter 4 begins with a general argument about post-serial revisionary practice, and then tests it by selecting a range of chapters for case study.

[218] See Michael Groden, *Ulysses in Progress*, 115–65, and *Ulysses in Focus: Genetic, Textual and Personal Views* (Gainesville, FL: University Press of Florida, 2010), which includes two additional chapters on 'Cyclops', 105–43.

[219] Other chapters with 'unrevised' pages are chapters 9, 10, and 11. See *CSEI* 9.1–130; 10.1043–175; much of chapter 11; and 12.1–67.

4

Paris Departures

Patterns of Post-Serial Ulyssean Revision

INTRODUCTION

Joyce's arrival in Paris early in July 1920, initially planned as a stay of three months ('in order to write the last adventure *Circe* in peace'), brought about new opportunities for his life as a writer, and gave him a new and more confirmed sense that he was a writer of note.[1] Within days he had been lent a furnished flat by an 'admirer', and he had found his way to Shakespeare and Company, where Sylvia Beach was happy to listen to his complaints about material discomforts and put at his disposal the opportunity to browse or borrow from her wide but careful selection of titles in English.[2] Though his plans for where to live had not been settled by December, he had decided to take a lease for six months on a flat with a piano, a telephone, and 'about 100 electric lamps and gas stoves'; in correspondence with Budgen, he was soon gloating about his changed fortunes ('is it not extraordinary the way I enter a city barefoot and end up in a luxurious flat?').[3] The latter months of 1920 also provided new social opportunities, including the opportunity to meet many other writers, including 'Eliot, Wyndham Lewis, Rodker', as he noted in a letter to Stanislaus ('Dinner and lunches are the order of the day').[4] The arrangements for Beach to publish *Ulysses* were in hand early in April 1921, as noted, and his plans for the revision of the text were being realized by June, when the first proofs were produced.[5]

During the period when he was revising and completing *Ulysses* in Paris, Joyce was responding to multiple revisionary impulses and stimuli. In one letter he describes himself as 'working like a lunatic, trying to revise and improve and connect and continue and create all at the one time'.[6] In another, he likens himself to the 'man who used to play several instruments with different parts of his body'.[7] But for all the admitted variety of the text, the process of studying Ulyssean revision—slowly examining significant variations between the serial and volume

---

[1] J to Weaver, 12 July 1920, *L* I, 142.
[2] J to Stanislaus Joyce, 12 July 1920, *L* III, 8. According to Ellmann, Joyce met Beach on 11 July 1920 (*L* III, 3), just two days after arriving in Paris.
[3] J to Budgen, 10 December 1920, *L* I, 151, 152.
[4] J to Stanislaus Joyce, 29 August 1920, *L* III, 17.   [5] *CSE* III 1913. See above, p. 95.
[6] J to Robert McAlmon, 10 October 1921, *L* I, 173.
[7] J to Weaver, 10 December 1921, *SL*, 288.

forms—leads to the view that certain patterns or types of revision recur. These recurring patterns can be summarized, as follows. *First*: if *Ulysses* is considered as a work which evokes different types of specificity, Joyce adds to those specificities in revision; in other words, Joyce thickens the bibliographical, citational, cultural, geographical, historical, linguistic, naturalistic, political, and social specificities of the work as he revises it for publication in volume form. *Second*: Joyce deepens Bloom's imaginative and psychological range by extending his streams of consciousness; he also deepens Stephen's characterization by adding new phrases and streams of consciousness (though to a much lesser extent). *Third*: he makes 'schematic' (but not necessarily overtly Homeric) additions which align the work with the various terms and referents of the Linati and Gilbert schemata; and he systematically inserts connecting phrases, leitmotifs, or 'phrasal ligatures' in order to increase the internal referentiality of the work.[8] *Fourth*: Joyce makes the styles of the work more complicated, diverse, and demanding; what Karen Lawrence characterizes as a 'stylistic odyssey' is enhanced in revision. *Fifth*: Joyce makes the work more suggestive or explicit about the body and sexuality. *Sixth*: he embellishes the micro-narratives which are playing out in the background to the more central elements of the story. *Seventh*: he revises certain elements of speech and narration so that they become more overtly Hibernian or staged.

Writing about Joyce's *Work in Progress* in 1929, Samuel Beckett memorably observed a 'danger in the neatness of identifications' and wished to remind Joyce's readers that 'literary criticism is not book-keeping'.[9] Perhaps this rough classification of seven types of Ulyssean revision is too neat, too much of an oversimplification, or too much like book-keeping. There are, after all, are some obvious fudges here. Specificity, for example, is a very wide-ranging category, and what might be regarded as a 'schematic' revision is open to a wide range of interpretive possibilities, as already noted.[10] There is also the possibility of overlap between categories: revision which might be regarded as 'schematic' (*type 3*, above), such as the added paragraph on the Citizen's handkerchief, might also be regarded as an example of *type 4*: 'complicating the stylistic odyssey'. Nonetheless, it is still useful to explore the view that post-serial Ulyssean revision is essentially patterned. Thus this chapter, which is in three parts, begins, in the first part, by introducing 'Seven Types of Ulyssean Revision' in more detail. The second and third parts test this argument more generally by looking at patterns of minimal revision in chapters 2 ('Nestor') and 11 ('Sirens'); and patterns of macro revision in chapters 5 ('Lotus-Eaters') and 13 ('Nausicaa'). As Joyce himself noted, *Ulysses* proceeds by 'variation'.[11] The aim in selecting these chapters—which represent naturalism ('Nestor' and 'Lotus-Eaters'), the shift away from the initial style ('Sirens' and 'Nausicaa'), a focus on Stephen ('Nestor'), and a focus on Bloom ('Lotus-Eaters', 'Sirens', 'Nausicaa')—is

---

[8] 'Phrasal ligatures' is in Ronan Crowley, 'Fusing the Elements of "Circe": From Compositional to Textual Repetition', *James Joyce Quarterly*, 47:3 (Spring 2010), 341–61 (343).

[9] Samuel Beckett, 'Dante…Bruno…Vico…Joyce', in *Poems, Short Fiction, Criticism*, ed. by Paul Auster (New York: Grove Press, 2006) (Volume IV of the Grove Centenary Edition), 495–510 (495).

[10] See above, p. 181.   [11] J to Weaver, 6 August 1919, *SL*, 242.

to acknowledge such variation, and examine its significance for Ulyssean revision more generally.

SEVEN TYPES OF ULYSSEAN REVISION

Specificities

Specificity of character, place, time, and historical and cultural detail is absolutely central to Joyce's practice in *Ulysses*, and in post-serial revision it is very often possible to identify Joyce adding new details which enhance or deepen the specificities of the work. Some of the political and historicist specificities which are added to chapter 6 ('Hades') have already been suggested.[12] For *type 1*, which is such a broad category, it is worth looking at five additional examples in five different chapters. First, Mulligan in chapter 1 ('Telemachus'). In the serial text, it is made obvious that he is a reader of Yeats. His booming voice recites lines from 'Who goes with Fergus?' as he descends the staircase in the Martello Tower (—And no more turn aside and brood/Upon love's bitter mystery/For Fergus rules the brazen cars').[13] Later in the same chapter he tells Haines that he could supply copy for his collection of folklore, characterizing Haines's finished work as 'Five lines of text and ten pages of notes about the folk and the fishgods of Dundrum'.[14] The reference to Dundrum makes it clear that Mulligan has the Yeats family enterprise of the Dun Emer Press in mind. But the 1922 text makes that bibliographical reference more specific by adding the phrase: '**Printed by the weird sisters in the year of the big wind**'.[15] Elizabeth Corbet Yeats, sister of the poet, printed his *In the Seven Woods*, and closed the work with a triangular colophon commemorating 1903 as 'the year of the big wind'.[16] This bibliographical detail appears to have been drawn from Joyce's actual experience; the subscriber's list for the linen-bound privately printed *In the Seven Woods*, priced 10/6 and sold by advance subscription, records that Oliver St John Gogarty, the model for Mulligan, bought six copies of this edition.[17] Joyce was almost certainly aware of this, and he may have seen the proofs of this historic first edition: Yeats was at work on them early in December 1902, when Joyce, en route to Paris to study medicine, spent a day with Yeats in London.[18] Joyce's second arrival in Paris in 1920—this time to finish *Ulysses*—gave him access to a greater range of books than had been possible in either Zurich or Trieste. It is

---

[12] See above, p. 170.   [13] *LR*, March 1918, 9.   [14] *LR*, March 1918, 12.
[15] *U*1922, 13. Semi-bold font here and subsequently represents text added post-serially.
[16] W. B. Yeats, *In the Seven Woods* (Dublin: Dun Emer, 1903), [64].
[17] Dun Emer Press archive, TCD. For more information on the Dun Emer Press, later known as the Cuala Press, see Gifford Lewis, ' "This Terrible Struggle with Want of Means": Behind the Scenes at the Cuala Press', in Clare Hutton (ed.) and Patrick Walsh (co-ed)., *The Oxford History of the Irish Book, 1891–2000* (Oxford: Oxford University Press, 2011), 529–47.
[18] J to his family, 6 December 1902, *SL*, 9; Yeats to Lady Gregory, 4 December 1902, in John Kelly and Ronald Schuchard (eds.), *The Collected Letters of William Butler Yeats: Volume 3, 1901–1904* (Oxford: Clarendon Press, 1994), 268–9.

possible that this added flourish was inspired by consulting a copy of *In the Seven Woods* at the Bibliothèque Nationale or Shakespeare and Company.

Not all of the instances of Joyce adding specificity to the work are so laboured or elaborate. A second example can be found in a one-word addition to the second sentence of chapter 4 ('Calypso'), which lists Bloom's favoured foods: 'He liked thick giblet soup, nutty gizzards, a stuffed roast heart, liver-slices fried with crust-crumbs, fried cods' roes'.[19] 'Fried cods' roes' becomes 'fried **hen**cods' roes' in the 1922 text (*U*1922, 53): the tiny addition of 'hen' shows Joyce striving for linguistic innovation and precision, and communicates Bloom's exacting culinary preferences. Additions to Bloom's thoughts about Queen Victoria in chapter 8 ('Lestrygonians') provide a third example of enhanced cultural and historical specificity. After meeting Mrs Breen, and hearing about Mrs Purefoy ('She's three days bad now'... 'It's a very stiff birth'), Bloom thinks about her labour ('Phew! Dreadful simply! Child's head too big: forceps. Doubled up inside her trying to butt its way out blindly').[20] He thinks they 'ought to invent something to stop that. Twilight sleep idea: queen Victoria was given that', a reference to the fact that Queen Victoria took a light dose of chloroform during the birth of her eighth child.[21] Joyce embellishes this moment, adding: '**Nine she had. A good layer. Old woman that lived in a shoe she had so many children. Suppose he was consumptive**' (*U*1922, 154), the last phrase being a reference to Albert, and the view that consumptives were thought to be sexually hyperactive. The contemporary diagnosis of Albert's death was typhoid fever, not TB, but the point here is not that kind of specificity, but the record of Bloom's thought process. Joyce has clearly worked at this detail quite carefully, correcting the number of Victoria's children from twelve to nine on proof.[22] Joyce also added further thoughts about Victoria to chapter 6 ('Hades'), in the passage which begins '**Widowhood not the thing since the old queen died**'.[23]

A fourth example of enhanced cultural specificity may be read in an addition to chapter 9 ('Scylla and Charybdis') where a narrative voice reports that 'A. E. has been telling some interviewer'.[24] In revision, this inconclusive sentence—which does not tell us what AE said, but merely reports the fact of his interview—becomes 'A. E. has been telling some **yankee** reviewer'.[25] This sentence echoes an earlier moment in chapter 7 ('Aeolus'), in which J. J. O'Molloy tells Stephen:

> A. E. has been telling some interviewer that you came to him in the small hours of the morning to ask him about planes of consciousness.[26]

The word 'yankee' does not occur in the *Little Review Ulysses*. As though to suggest an awareness that Irish literary and cultural achievements are being recognized in

[19] *LR*, June 1918, 39.   [20] *LR*, January 1919, 34.   [21] *LR*, January 1919, 36.
[22] *CSE* I 338.30.   [23] *U*1922, 98; cf. *CSE* I 208.15.   [24] *LR*, April 1919, 31.
[25] *U*1922, 177; as Gifford notes, Russell (AE) was interviewed by Cornelius Weygandt from the University of Pennsylvania in the summer of 1902, who subsequently compiled *Irish Plays and Playwrights* (1913). Joyce is not named in the book but is identifiable as a 'boy... not yet twenty-one' (*Ulysses Annotated*, 147).
[26] *LR*, October 1918, 44.

the US, and point to the significance of the US serialization and trial, and acknowledge his American friends (Ezra Pound, Sylvia Beach, Robert McAlmon), Joyce adds the word 'yankee' to the 1922 text in three different places: in chapter 7 ('some **yankee** interviewer', *U*1922, 135), in chapter 9 (as noted), and in the phrase of Dedalus's interior monologue, '**Between the Saxon smile and the yankee yawp**' (*U*1922, 180). These additions—and the specific insistence on the word 'yankee'—may have been inspired by Joyce noting that the chapter 12 ('Cyclops') reference to 'one of the smutty yankee pictures' which appeared in the *Police Gazette* had been silently omitted from the December 1919 issue of the *Little Review*. The paragraph details the 'misconduct' of a society belle, the wife of 'Norman W. Tupper' being found in the 'lap' of police officer Taylor 'misconduct-ing herself'.[27] These references were restored in the 1922 text, and made more explicit by the addition of the phrase '**Secrets for enlarging your private parts**' (*U*1922, 310).

Joyce's sense of Americans and of American cultural nationalism became deeper after his first face-to-face meeting with Pound in June 1920, and his subsequent arrival in Paris. He had also begun to see how Irish literary culture (and his own reception) was poised, sometimes quite uncomfortably, between the literary tradi-tions of Britain and the US, between 'the Saxon smile and the yankee yawp', a phrase followed and qualified, tellingly, by another late-stage addition: '**The devil and the deep sea**' (*U*1922, 180).

A fifth and final example of added specificity can be identified in an addition to chapter 10 ('Wandering Rocks'), in the moment when Ned Lambert shows 'the reverend Hugh C. Love' 'the historic council chamber of saint Mary's abbey' (*U*1922, 221). Lambert's speech, which introduces the significance of what had become a gloomy basement, is embellished in the revision for the 1922 text:

—Yes, sir, Ned Lambert said heartily. We are standing in the historic council chamber of saint Mary's abbey where silken Thomas proclaimed himself a rebel in 1534. **This is the most historic spot in all Dublin. O'Madden Burke is going to write something about it one of these days. The old bank of Ireland was over the way till the time of the union and the original jews' temple was here too before they built their synagogue over in Adelaide road.** You were never here before, Jack, were you?   (*U*1922, 221)

As Gifford makes clear, the facts reported here are true: the bank of Ireland was once located close to the ruins of St Mary's Abbey, and there was a synagogue nearby from about 1650; thus Joyce has added a literal and geographic detail to this moment of the text.[28] But can this revision—this designation of Dublin's 'most historic spot'—realistically be compared with 'Printed by the weird sisters

---

[27] See *LR*, December 1919, 59; *U*1922, 310–11; *CSE* II 698.4–11. This omission, almost certainly socially motivated given the suggestive content, complicates the argument about Anderson and Heap as editors, as the omission is not marked or acknowledged. This omission has not been noted in Gaipa et al., *LRU* or Vanderham, *James Joyce and Censorship*, though Vanderham does note that this passage was controversial for US Attorney Samuel Coleman in the early 1930s (176). See http://www.jjon. org/jioyce-s-people/tupper for information about the suggestively named Tupper, and the image from which Joyce was working.

[28] Gifford, *Ulysses Annotated*, 268.

in the year of the big wind', 'hencods' roes', 'Nine she had', and 'some yankee interviewer'? While these additions clearly point in quite different interpretive directions, the answer is, perhaps, a qualified yes. The addition of the 'weird sisters' is an example of Joyce adding bibliographical or citational particularity; 'hencods' roes' adds cultural and culinary specificity; 'Nine she had' acknowledges the historical facts of Victoria's life; and 'yankee', not quite as pejorative in Britain and Ireland as it was in the US, points to the politics of reception, and adds a kind of linguistic and nationalist dimension which complements the cultural essentialism of dubbing someone a 'saxon'.

Streams of Consciousness

Type 2, the deepening of Bloom's consciousness, and, to a lesser extent, Stephen's, cannot be catalogued easily; again it is necessary to make the point in general terms and through the rapid citation of a few examples. As Bloom's extension has already been mentioned in relation to chapter 6 ('Hades'), and will be considered again in relation to chapter 5 ('Lotus-Eaters'), 11 ('Sirens'), and 13 ('Nausicaa'), the alterations to Stephen are worth prioritizing instead, in three examples from three different chapters. The first is to be found at the end of chapter 1 ('Telemachus') in the description of Mulligan swimming. In the serial text, this reads:

> A voice, sweettoned and sustained, called to him from the sea. Turning the curve he waved his hand. It called again. A sleek brown head far out on the water, round.
> Usurper.[29]

After the word 'again', the passage seems to shift from third- to first-person narration: it is probably Stephen who perceives Mulligan's 'sleek brown head' swimming in the distance, and Stephen who identifies Mulligan as a 'usurper' in the final one-word paragraph that concludes the chapter. But Joyce wants the associative structure of Stephen's sensibility to be sharper, and thus introduces a new image in the penultimate sentence, which becomes 'A sleek brown head, **a seal's,** far out on the water, round' (*U*1922, 23). This tiny addition characterizes the way in which Stephen can think like a poet, and clarifies his envy of Mulligan's fluency and fluidity, his shape-changing transformative potentiality.

Another instance of intense linguistic self-consciousness can be observed in one of the revisions to chapter 3 ('Proteus'), in a moment where Stephen recalls dining with Kevin Egan in a Parisian café. The 1922 text records Stephen remembering Egan's clumsy French:

> A jet of coffee steam from the burnished caldron. She serves me at his beck. *Il est irlandais. Hollandais. Non fromage. Deux irlandais, nous, Irlande, vous savez? Ah, oui!* **She thought you wanted a cheese *hollandais.*** Your postprandial, do you know that word? Postprandial. (*U*1922, 43)

This little memory of linguistic confusion may have been inspired by the experience of Joyce trying to make himself understood in one of Paris's many cafés. Joyce

---

[29] *LR*, March 1918, 22.

also enhances the representation of Stephen's poetic sensibility in representing the moment of AE's leave-taking, which significantly interrupts the delivery of Stephen's lecture in chapter 9 ('Scylla and Charybdis'). A paragraph of a composite narrative voice records individuals like R. I. Best, John Eglinton, and T. W. Lyster noting the significance of the Irish Literary Revival by referring to topics such as 'the grand old tongue', 'our younger poets' verses', and the prospects for a 'national epic' (*U*1922, 184–5). The surrounding paragraphs of interior monologue which read: 'See this. Remember' and 'Listen' reveal Stephen urging himself (and readers) to attend to what is being said. But Stephen's train of thought is clearly envious and resentful, and thus the 1922 text introduces an experiment, which distracts him from the scene:

> Stephen looked down on a wide headless caubeen, hung on his ashplanthandle over his knee. My casque and sword. **Touch lightly with two index fingers. Aristotle's experiment. One or two? Necessity is that in virtue of which it is impossible that one can be otherwise. Argal, one hat is one hat.**   (*U*1922, 184)

The addition—with its references to Aristotle—reiterates the significance of Stephen's intellectual ability, but it also communicates his cultural distance from those he is trying to impress, and gestures to the significance of the speeches which he is trying so hard to ignore.

The revisions which Joyce makes to Bloom are more extensive, and, in general, easier to follow (because Bloom is a less intellectual character than Stephen). Before moving on to a discussion of schematic additions (*type 3*), it is worth looking at two examples of Bloom's stream of consciousness being extended: one from chapter 4 ('Calypso'), and one from chapter 8 ('Lestrygonians'). As he walks back along Dorset Street, after his trip to Dlugacz's, Bloom reads a flier he took from a pile of 'cut sheets' on the counter. In the 1922 text, the content of what Bloom reads is made more explicit, because Joyce adds some of the marketing language from the flier, which communicates the significance of the scheme for the development of land in Palestine:

> He walked back along Dorset street, reading gravely. Agendath Netaim: planters' company. **To purchase waste sandy tracts from Turkish government and plant with eucalyptus trees. Excellent for shade, fuel and construction. Orangegroves and immense melonfields north of Jaffa.** You pay eighty marks and they plant a dunam of land for you with olives, oranges, almonds or citrons.   (*U*1922, 58)

This revision is one among a number of post-serial elaborations to chapter 4 which help readers to understand that Bloom is Jewish, as the first hint in the serial text— the moment when Bloom picks up this flier, recognizes that it is about the Zionist project, and recognizes that Dlugacz is also Jewish—would have been all too easy to miss. The serial text simply reads: 'He took a page up from the pile of cut sheets: the model farm at Kinnereth on the lakeshore of Tiberias. I thought he was'.[30] In revision, Joyce adds a reference to Moses Montefiore, a philanthropist who encouraged

---

[30] *LR*, June 1918, 43.

the development of land in Palestine (*U*1922, 57); and he adds the word 'Kosher' in a string of additions which document Bloom's musings about the cat ('**Give her too much meat she won't mouse. Say they won't eat pork. Kosher. Here**', *U*1922, 60). These revisions tighten the representation of Bloom's identity, and make his thought processes slightly easier to follow.

Sometimes the extension of Bloom's inner life involves the introduction of completely new strains of thought. Mr Purefoy, Mina Purefoy's 'Methodist husband', is not spared a consideration in the serial version of chapter 8 ('Lestrygonians'). But a three-word paragraph in the serial text ('Poor Mrs. Purefoy!') expands to become 113 words in the 1922 text:[31]

> Poor Mrs Purefoy! **Methodist husband. Method in his madness.** Saffron bun and milk and soda lunch in the educational dairy. Eating with a stopwatch, thirtytwo chews to the minute. Still his muttonchop whiskers grew. Supposed to be well connected. Theodore's cousin in Dublin Castle. One tony relative in every family. Hardy annuals he presents her with. Saw him out at the Three Jolly Topers marching along bareheaded and his eldest boy carrying one in a marketnet. The squallers Poor thing! Then having to give the breast year after year all hours of the night. Selfish those t.t's are. **Dog in the manger.** Only one lump of sugar in my tea, if you please. (*U*1922, 153)

What exactly is achieved in this addition? What impact does it have locally on chapter 8 ('Lestrygonians'), and on subsequent chapters of the work? Apart from the details of Mr Purefoy's idiosyncrasies (a teetotaller who goes out without a hat, frequents the 'educational dairy', and 'eats with a stopwatch'), the paragraph communicates Bloom's sense of community, and of how Methodism works as a community in Dublin ('One tony relative in every family'). Theodore Purefoy has a cousin 'in Dublin Castle', home to the offices of the chief secretary, and a central institution in Ireland's civic and legal organization (Corny Kelleher is a spy who is 'all the time drawing secret service pay from the castle'; Martin Cunningham works at the castle; and Mortimer Edward Purefoy is in the 'Treasury Remembrancer's Office, Dublin Castle', *U*1922, 155, 236, 400). Bloom's sense of humour is evident in 'Hardy annuals he presents her with', as someone who is 't.t' might well propagate 'hardy annuals' and give them as gifts. But there is a reader trap here: hardy annuals actually refers to the 'squallers' in the huge Purefoy family, named in chapter 14: 'Charley, Mary Alice, Frederick Albert (if he had lived), Mamy, Budgy (Victoria Frances), Tom, Violet Constance Louisa, darling little Bobsy' and the latest 'young hopeful' who 'will be christened Mortimer Edward' (*U*1922, 400). There is an element of disapproval in Bloom's thoughts about this large family: Mr Purefoy is 'selfish', fastidious about how he takes his tea, and inattentive; his 'eldest boy' is left struggling, 'carrying one in a marketnet', a detail which seems to affront Bloom's strong sense of paternal duty. Bloom feels particularly sorry for Mrs Purefoy ('Poor Mrs Purefoy!', 'Poor thing!') and after this extended moment of thought thinks about her on several further occasions (later in chapter 8, and in chapters 10, 11, and 13); the thoughts are usually brief and passing and, with the

---

[31] *LR*, January 1919, 36.

exception of one example, were included in the serial text.[32] Thus this added paragraph of Bloomian interiority, which maps his cognitive environment and anticipates the Purefoy birth scene of chapter 14 ('Oxen of the Sun'), is an example of Joyce embellishing an early element of the work once he had established later elements, a bit of rewriting inspired by looking back on the serial text and making adjustments 'in a kind of retrospective arrangement' (*U*1922, 231).

Schematic and Systematic Additions

As noted earlier, the argument about post-serial 'schematic' and systematic additions (*type 3*)—that Joyce revised the text to align it to the terms of the Linati and Gilbert schema, and in order to increase its inter-referentiality—can open up in a number of directions, and has already been mooted with regard to chapters 7 ('Aeolus') and 12 ('Cyclops'). For the purpose of a slightly fuller illustration, the case will be made with reference to reiterative linguistic usage, landmarks, and statues in chapter 6 ('Hades'); references to food in chapter 8 ('Lestrygonians'); and the systematic introduction of leitmotifs in chapter 10 ('Wandering Rocks').

The Linati schema lists black and white as the colours of chapter 6 ('Hades'), the 'descent to nothing' as its sense, and the 'heart' as its organ.[33] The references to colour are certainly enhanced post-serially; Joyce adds the '**whiteflattened**' nose of the old woman peeping at the passing cortège (*U*1922, 84); the colours of the funereal horses ('**white**' horses for a child, '**Black for the married**', *U*1922, 92), and the detail of '**Blackedged notepaper**' (*U*1922, 100). Joyce also adds several new references to the heart, and phrases associated with the heart, post-serially: Queen Victoria, for example, was '**Vain in her heart of hearts**' (*U*1922, 98); the caretaker tells jokes out of '**pure good-heartedness**' (*U*1922, 103); and Bloom thinks about '**old Ireland's hearts and hands**' '**praying with upcast eyes**' (*U*1922, 98). These additions—references to black, white, and the heart—certainly reflect a commitment to the terms of the schemata. But the commitment in revision is more than simply schematic: it involves a systematic deepening of key words, ideas, and leitmotifs which are not recorded in the jottings of the schemata. Take the words dead and death, for example. There are certainly many instances of these words in the serial text of chapter 6 ('Hades'), but beginning with a phrase of Bloom's reflection ('**Never know who will touch you dead**', *U*1922, 84), Joyce has worked through this chapter adding many more. The additions, often examples of lexical innovation or colloquialism, include the phrases '**Canvassing for death**', '**his deathday**', '**Dead side of the street**', '**Death by misadventure**', '**Dead march from Saul**', '**Dead meat trade**', '**How she met her death**', '**Pomp of death**', '**So much dead weight**', '**More dead for her than for me**', '**dead letter office**', '**Courting death**', '**In the midst of death we are in life**', '**Deathmoths**',

---

[32] For Bloom's thoughts about Mrs Purefoy, see *U*1922, 155, 156, 226, 269, 274, 356. The only one of these references added post-serially is 155 ('Still I got to know that young Dixon who dressed that sting for me in the Mater and now he's in Holles street where Mrs Purefoy'); cf. *CSE* I 342.13.

[33] Details of Linati schema from Ellmann, *Ulysses on the Liffey*, 183–7.

'deadborn child', 'Death's number', 'Shame of death', 'The death struggle', and 'Priests dead against it'.[34]

The repetitive nature of these additions is immediately obvious in a genetically marked-up copy of the text, such as an Adobe-highlighted digital copy of the 1922 text, or a paper copy of Gabler's *Critical and Synoptic Edition*. In fact, the pattern of reiteration is so obvious that it seems as though Joyce has made a list of every phrase and compound word in the English language which uses dead or death, and then found ways to insert them into Bloom's entelechy, his mind, his being-at-work. But if this aspect of the process of compositional revision is schematic, it is also inventive: 'stillborn', the word we might expect, has become 'deadborn' in Bloom's reflection that '**Only a mother and deadborn child ever buried in the one coffin**' (*U*1922, 106). 'Birthday' has an economy not matched in the phrases commonly used to express the anniversary of a death, a point Joyce recognizes in having Bloom invent 'deathday' ('**Smith O'Brien. Someone has laid a bunch of flowers there. Woman. Must be his deathday. For many happy returns**', *U*1922, 90). Similarly, the words of the *Book of Common Prayer* ('In the midst of life we are in death') are subversively rethought by Bloom ('**In the midst of death we are in life**', *U*1922, 104). Lexical inventiveness has ensured that these additions are not in the least bit formulaic, but have instead become part of the chapter's concentrated depiction of funereal atmosphere and ritual. Joyce has deepened death as the leitmotif in the chapter, and thus encouraged readers to look 'beyond and beside linear narrative'.[35] As Katherine O'Callaghan has argued, leitmotif is a key feature of Joycean writing which 'complicates and interrupts the uni-directional flow of the text' and is akin to:

> a sort of linguistic magic-realism whereby coincidences and connections occur not on the level of subject and technique, but on the level of aesthetics and language.[36]

Another leitmotif in the serial text of chapter 6 ('Hades') is the repetitive waymarking of the route followed by the Dignam cortège, beginning in 'Tritonville Road', proceeding along 'Ringsend road', over the 'Dodder bridge', the 'Grand Canal', past the 'Antient Concert Room's, "Elvery"s elephant house', 'Rotunda corner', 'Rutland square', 'Dunphy's corner', Phibsborough Road, Finglas Road, etc.[37] In revising the text Joyce has been even more meticulous in noting the route followed, adding '**Watery lane**', '**Blessington street**', '**Brian Boroimhe house**', '**Jimmy Geary, the sexton's**'.[38] Similarly, while Nelson's pillar is the only political monument noted in the serial text, the 1922 version appears to note all of the commemorations of dead political leaders on O'Connell Street (the '**hugecloaked Liberator's form**', '**Gray's statue**', the '**late Father Mathew**', the '**Foundation stone**

[34] *U*1922, 87, 90, 92, 93, 94, 97, 98, 104, 106, 110. This list is not conclusive.
[35] Katherine O'Callaghan, 'Mapping the "Call from Afar": The Echo of Leitmotifs in James Joyce's Literary Landscape', in Valérie Bénéjam and John Bishop (eds.), *Making Space in the Works of James Joyce* (London: Routledge, 2011), 173–90 (173).
[36] O'Callaghan, 'The Echo of Leitmotifs in James Joyce's Literary Landscape', 173.
[37] *LR*, September 1918, 15, 16, 18, 19, 21, 22, 23, 24, 25. This list is not conclusive.
[38] *U*1922, 85, 93, 96. This list is not conclusive.

for Parnell') and 'Sir Philip Crampton's Memorial Fountain', which was on the junction between College Street and D'Olier Street.[39] These encyclopaedic mnemonics of political, geographical, and historicist specificity leaven the representation of Bloom's interior world and force reading to a slower pace, a pace which is constantly being pulled back to linger on detail. In some respects it is possible to argue that the cultural memory of the 1922 text is more exhaustive, more plural than that of the serial text.

Joyce specified the 'esophagus' as the organ of chapter 8 ('Lestrygonians'), 'peristaltic prose' as its 'technic', and 'dejection' as its sense or meaning.[40] It is immediately obvious that multiple references to food, eating, digestion, and diet have been added at proof stage. For example, Bloom spies 'Dedalus' daughter there still outside Dillon's auctionrooms' and notices that her dress 'is in flitters':

> Underfed she looks too. **Potatoes and marge, marge and potatoes.** Its after they feel it. **Proof of the pudding.** Undermines the constitution.   (*U*1922, 145)

The simple repetition and inversion ('Potatoes and marge, marge and potatoes') mimetically evokes the daily attempt to serve the same things in different ways, and confirms the monotony of the Dedalus family diet. Bloom often thinks in terms of idiom, and '**proof of the pudding**' is apt; its addition seems to suggest that Joyce has thought about phrases used in relation to food, and compiled a list, or perhaps even reached for a dictionary of phrase and fable, such as Brewer's, which was first published in 1870 and was in a 'new edition' by 1900. Other added idiomatic food phrases include: '**Eat you out of house and home**', '**Appetite like an albatross**', '**Our staple food**', '**Pillar of salt**', '**My heart's broke eating dripping**', '**For what we have received may the Lord make us**', '**muttonchop whiskers**', '**Goosestep**', '**A punch in his dinner**', '**Drop him like a hot potato**', '**Michelmas goose**', '**Penny roll and a walk with the band**', '**No grace for the carver**', '**Built on bread and onions**', '**Eaten a bad egg**', '**Poached eyes on ghost**', '**No meat and milk together**', '**God made food, the devil the cooks**', '**Devilled crab**', '**Too much fat on the parsnips**', '**Jugged hare**', '**Curly cabbage *à la duchesse de parme***', '**Too many drugs spoil the broth**', '**Do ptake some ptarmigan**', '**You can make bacon of that**', '**if you're worth your salt**', etc.[41]

Joyce also makes notable extensions to Bloom's interior monologues, by including new thoughts about the culture of eating. The changes made to Bloom's perception of the scene at the Burton are illustrative. The serial text read:

> His heart astir he pushed in the door of the Burton restaurant. Stink gripped his trembling breath: pungent meatjuice, slush of greens.
>   Men, men, men.

---

[39] *LR*, September 1918, 22; *U*1922, 90, 91, 92, 89.
[40] Details of Linati schema from Ellmann, *Ulysses on the Liffey*, 183–7.
[41] *U*1922, 145, 147, 148, 153, 154, 155, 156, 157, 163, 164, 165, 166, 167, 169, 170. This list is not conclusive. Several of these phrases were written in on typescript, rather than proof, and were thus planned rather than spontaneous; the planning suggests Joyce being systematic, and perhaps working from a list.

Perched on high stools by the bar, hats shove back, at the table calling for more bread no charge, swilling wolfing gobfuls of sloppy food, their eyes bulging, wiping wetted moustaches. A man with an infant's napkin tucked round him spooned gurgling soup down his gullet. A man spitting back on his plate: gristle gums: no teeth to chew it. Chump chop he has. Sad booser's eyes.[42]

This is certainly an effective representation of the scene, and of the sights and smells in the atmosphere that repel Bloom. The meatjuice is 'pungent'; the men are to be seen 'wolfing gobfuls' and one man with 'no teeth to chew' is 'spitting' a 'chump chop' 'back on this plate'.[43] 'Sad booser's eyes' is a strong example of Joycean lyric intensity and achieves a particular impact by being a short sentence placed at the end of the paragraph. In a sea of lengthy written detail, readers tend to pay particular attention to the beginning and end of paragraphs.

Joyce makes the decision to make some significant changes here, intensifying the atmosphere, and actually specifying the animalistic nature of the scene by including the phrase, 'See the animals feed':

> His heart astir he pushed in the door of the Burton restaurant. Stink gripped his trembling breath: pungent meatjuice, slop of greens. **See the animals feed.**
>
> Men, men, men.
>
> Perched on high stools by the bar, hats shoved back, at the tables calling for more bread no charge, swilling, wolfing gobfuls of sloppy food, their eyes bulging, wiping wetted moustaches. **A pallid suetfaced young man polished his tumbler knife fork and spoon with his napkin. New set of microbes.** A man with an infant's **sauces-tained** napkin tucked round him **shovelled** gurgling soup down his gullet. A man spitting back on his plate : **halfmasticated** gristle : no teeth to **chewchewchew** it. Chump chop **from the grill. Bolting to get it over.** Sad booser's eyes. **Bitten off more than he can chew. Am I like that? See ourselves as others see us. Hungry man is an angry man. Working tooth and jaw. Don't! O! A bone! That last pagan king of Ireland Cormac in the schoolpoem choked himself at Sletty southward of the Boyne. Wonder what he was eating. Something galoptious. Saint Patrick converted him to Christianity. Couldn't swallow it all however.**   (*U*1922, 161)

'Chewing', evoked in the ingenious '**chewchewchew**', '**halfmasticated**', the deliberately flat cliché of '**Bitten off more than he can chew**' (*U*1922, 161), and in Theodore Purefoy's '**Thirtytwo chews to the minute**' (*U*1922, 153), has become a leitmotif in the chapter. The most lyrical and intense reference to chewing, Bloom's erotic memoir—'Softly she gave me in my mouth the seedcake warm and chewed'—is in the serial version but two other chewing references are added post-serially ('**Slight spasm, full, chewing the cud**' and '**Never know whose thoughts you are chewing**', *U*1922, 161, 162).[44] The embellishment of the chewing reference in this Burton passage moves well beyond the toothless man, towards Bloom's half-remembered account of a 'schoolpoem' about Cormac, the 'last pagan king'. The fluidity of Bloom's mental processing and free association means that Joyce has been able to introduce a completely new idea: the story of Ireland's conversion to Christianity, and the continuing vestiges of paganism which could not be completely

---

[42] *LR*, January 1919, 42.   [43] *LR*, January 1919, 42.   [44] *LR*, January 1919, 47.

'swallowed' by the new order. In a sense Joyce is responding to two types of revisionary impulse simultaneously: *type 1*, deepening cultural specificity, and *type 3*, schematic rewriting. It could also be argued that this is an example of *type 2* (deepening streams of consciousness) and *type 4*, complicating the stylistic odyssey. The move of 'sad booser's eyes' into the midst of the paragraph seems a particular loss.

After the systematic addition of death references to chapter 6 ('Hades'), wind references to chapter 7 ('Aeolus') and food references to chapter 8 ('Lestrygonians'), Joyce's commitment to the terms of the schemata seems to wax and wane, and is not so easy to identify in patterns of revision. For example, chapter 9 ('Scylla and Charybdis') does not become more overtly literary or 'dialectic' in revision, though Joyce does add quite a number of new references to Shakespeare. Nor would it be absolutely accurate to say that chapter 11 ('Sirens') becomes more musical (because the musical theme is very carefully established in the serial version). But there are some interestingly systematic patterns of revision revealed by the discovery that Joyce added the phrase 'agenbite of inwit' to chapter 10 ('Wandering Rocks'). Stephen meets his sister Dilly and remorsefully thinks about the poverty in the family household. The 1922 text reads as follows:

> She is drowning. **Agenbite.** Save her. **Agenbite.** All against us. She will drown me with her, eyes and hair. Lank coils of seaweed hair around me, my heart, my soul. Salt green death.
> We.
> **Agenbite of inwit. Inwit's agenbite.**
> Misery! Misery!　(*U*1922, 233)

Apparently derived from *Ayenbite of Inwyt* (1340), 'a medieval manual of virtues and vices intended to remind the layman of the hierarchy of sins', this phrase occurs five times in the 1922 text: twice in chapter 1 ('Telemachus'), twice in chapter 9 ('Scylla and Charybdis'), and on this occasion in chapter 10.[45] This phrase is a key leitmotif for Stephen, and leitmotifs, as O'Callaghan argues, 'have a resonance beyond their function on the naturalistic level: collectively they sound a tone which gathers momentum throughout the works'.[46]

'Agenbite of inwit' only occurs once in the serial text: in chapter 9 ('Scylla and Charybdis'), where the phrase is introduced by Stephen in his speech about Anne Hathaway's sudden turn to 'gospellers' in 'old age'.[47] The implication of Stephen's theory is that Hathaway trapped Shakespeare in marriage by becoming pregnant ('He was chosen, it seems to me. If others have their will Ann hath a way. By cock, she was to blame').[48] Then, in 'exhausted whoredom', she repented and turned to religion: 'Venus has twisted her lips in prayer. Agenbite of inwit: remorse of conscience'.[49] The phrase has a kind of linguistic supercharge, a poetic puissance

---

[45] Gifford, *Ulysses Annotated*, 22; *U*1922, 16, 17, 181, 198, 233.

[46] O'Callaghan, 'The Echo of Leitmotifs in James Joyce's Literary Landscape', 173.

[47] *LR*, May 1919, 25.

[48] *LR*, April 1919, 37. See Timothy Martin, *Joyce and Wagner* (Cambridge: Cambridge University Press, 1991), 156 and *passim* for an important discussion of leitmotif and 'agenbite of inwit'.

[49] *LR*, May 1919, 25.

which is not fully unleashed in this context because it is buried within a range of other complex intertextual elaborations. Thus Joyce chose to reuse it, placing it more prominently in chapter 1 ('Telemachus'), where it occurs as part of Stephen's interior monologue. It was written in to the text post-serially, on the second set of proofs, along with two other 'sayings' Stephen contemplates for Haines's collection:

Speaking to me. **They wash and tub and scrub. Agenbite of inwit. Conscience. Yet here's a spot.** (*U*1922, 16)

The 1922 text also includes 'agenbite of inwit' in the description of Mulligan dressing, though this reading, identified by Gabler as a 'misplaced insertion', is in doubt: 'His hands plunged and rummaged in his trunk while he called for a clean handkerchief. **Agenbite of inwit.** God, we'll simply have to dress the character'.[50]

Stephen's 'sayings' are inherently quotable, as Haines and Joyce realize, and three others are added, post-serially, to chapter 1 ('Telemachus'): '**Horn of a bull, hoof of a horse, smile of a Saxon**' (*U*1922, 23). This string, which ties up with the 'saxon smile and Yankee yawp' (*U*1922, 180), reveals a pattern of Joyce adding leitmotific phrases which increase the connections and references between chapters, thus deepening the structure and meaning of the work overall. Joyce also added the phrase 'agenbite of inwit' to Stephen's reflection on the 'whoredom' of Georgina Johnson's bed:

Go to! You spent most of it in Georgina Johnson's bed, clergyman's daughter. **Agenbite of inwit.** (*U*1922, 181)

But 'agenbite of inwit' is perhaps most effectively positioned in its last appearance in the book (in chapter 10, as cited), in its association with Stephen's thoughts about his family, where the reiteration of 'agenbite' communicates the idea of conscience biting again, an idea reiterated lyrically by the repetition of 'Misery! Misery!' which closes the scene. It is a curious fact that Joyce inserted this instance of the leitmotif last, on the sixth set of chapter 10 proofs, which were completed between 7 and 12 October 1921.[51] Nor is this the only example of an important late-stage addition. 'One thinks of Homer' (*U*1922, 208), voiced by Mulligan in chapter 9 ('Scylla and Charybdis') and added on the first proofs, is perhaps the most knowing 'schematic' addition to the text, a subtle hint that readers should look for Telemachus in Stephen and Odysseus in Bloom, Hades in Glasnevin, and Ithaca in Eccles Street.

Complicating the Stylistic Odyssey

The argument in support of Ulyssean revision *type 4*, complicating the stylistic odyssey, has already been generally suggested in several ways: with regard to the changing form of chapter 7 ('Aeolus'); the increased length and density of the interpolations in chapter 12 ('Cyclops'); and the lengthening of Bloom's interior monologues (such as that which considers Doady Purefoy). Bloom's monologues

---

[50] *U*1922, 17; *CSE* III 1756 (Historical Collation).   [51] *CSE* III 1914.

can be considered from the perspective of stylistic complication. This one is from the serial version of chapter 6 ('Hades'), and follows the burial of Dignam:

> Mr. Bloom walked unheeded along his grove. Who passed away. Who departed this life. As if they did it of their own accord. Got the shove, all of them. Rusty wreaths hung on knobs, garlands of bronzefoil. Better value that for the money. Still, the flowes are more poetical. The other gets rather tiresome, never withering. Expresses nothing.[52]

Opening with a sentence of third-person narration, but then shifting in the second sentence to the representation of Bloom's interiority, this paragraph of fifty-eight words and ten sentences invites readers to consider Bloom's train of thought as he walks among a set of gravestones. He thinks about: the banal euphemisms used to describe death ('Who departed this life'); the fact that people delude themselves into thinking that they control the hour of their passing ('Got the shove all of them'); and the merits of perpetual 'bronzefoil' wreaths against flowers which are 'more poetical'. Popovich's typo—flowes instead of flowers—might cause momentary confusion but all in all this short moment of meditation is not difficult to follow once readers have worked out how to negotiate the rapid and unannounced shift from third- to first-person narration, and have become accustomed to Bloom's mindstyle.

The 1922 version of this paragraph is considerably more challenging. Consisting of 258 words and forty sentences—each sentence being a unit of sense which an attentive reading needs to assimilate—the extended version asks readers to process a much wider range of information, and to concentrate for longer (before the cognitive break which comes at the end of a paragraph):

> Mr Bloom walked unheeded along his grove **by saddened angels, crosses, broken pillars family vaults, stone hopes praying with upcast eyes, old Ireland's hearts and hands. More sensible to spend the money on some charity for the living. Pray for the repose of the soul of. Does anybody really? Plant him and have done with him. Like down a coalshoot. Then lump them together to save time. All souls' day. Twentyseventh I'll be at his grave. Ten shillings for the gardener. He keeps it free of weeds. Old man himself. Bent down double with his shears clipping. Near death's door.** Who passed away. Who departed this life. As if they did it of their own accord. Got the shove, all of them. **Who kicked the bucket. More interesting if they told you what they were. So and so, wheelwright. I travelled for cork lino. I paid five shillings in the pound. Or a woman's with her saucepan. I cooked good Irish stew. Eulogy in a country churchyard it ought to be that poem of whose is it Wordsworth or Thomas Campbell. Entered into rest the protestants put it. Old Dr Murren's. The great physician called him home. Well it's God's acre for them. Nice country residence. Newly plastered and painted. Ideal spot to have a quiet smoke and read the Church Times. Marriage ads they never try to beautify.** Rusty wreaths hung on knobs, garlands of bronzefoil. Better value that for the money. Still, the flowers are more poetical. The other gets rather tiresome, never withering. Expresses nothing. **Immortelles.**   (*U*1922, 108–9)

[52] *LR*, September 1918, 36.

Of the ten sentences included in the *Little Review*, only the first is changed. Joyce extends the opening moment of third-person narration, and invites readers to visualize the scene in detail: the lonely Bloom, among the bric-à-brac of gravestones and 'family vaults'. 'Saddened angels' and 'stone hopes praying with upcast eyes' have a vividness which suggest that the person perceiving the scene is no longer an impersonal narrator but Bloom, whose sensibility colours the scene. The other original sentences are split into two groups and then surrounded with new writing. Subsequent additions include a passage in which Bloom thinks about what people really do after a death ('Pray for the repose of the soul of. Does anybody really?'); a passage when he thinks about going to visit his father's grave ('Twentyseventh I'll be at his grave'); a passage when he thinks about what it would be like if the gravestones announced the dead person's occupation; a deliberately muddled allusion to Thomas Gray's 'Elegy in a Country Churchyard'; some further proverbs about dying ('Entered into rest the protestants put it'); thoughts about the different rituals and mentalities of protestant burial ('it's God's acre for them'); and the concluding one-word sentence 'Immortelles', which refers to both a long-lasting flower arrangement placed on a grave and various species of flower. 'Immortelles' and the allusive reference to 'Wordsworth or Thomas Campbell' pose a new level of hermeneutic challenge: readers have to know or find out certain facts in order to make sense of these moments in Bloom's interiority. It is easy to miss the first reference to Bloom's father's death ('Poor papa!... perhaps it was best for him', *U*1922, 73), and to fail to see the significance of subsequent references ('That afternoon of the inquest', *U*1922, 93); any reader who has missed out on the fact of Bloom's father's death will be confused by 'Ten shillings for the gardener' and left to consider what they have missed.

But if this passage, and the additions to chapters 7 ('Aeolus') and 12 ('Cyclops'), may be read as evidence of the styles of *Ulysses* becoming more challenging in revision, it is also important to bear in mind that *Ulysses* had moments of considerable stylistic difficulty before it was revised post-serially. Consider, for example, the moment when the serial version of chapter 7 ('Aeolus') suddenly segues into an Edwardian prose style (at the word 'Messenger'):

Pause. J. J. O'Molloy took out his cigarettcase.

False lull. Something quite ordinary.

Messenger took out his matchbox thoughtfully and lit his cigar.

I have often thought since on looking back over that strange time that it was that small act, trivial in itself, the striking of a match, that determined the whole aftercourse of both our lives.

J. J. O'Molloy resumed, moulding his words[.][53]

What exactly are the two 'Messenger' paragraphs, with their 'peculiar shifts in time and tone', doing here?[54] How do they relate to Stephen's interior monologue which

[53] *LR*, September 1918, 43.
[54] Thomas Jackson Rice, '*Ulysses*, Chaos and Complexity', *James Joyce Quarterly*, 31:2 (Winter 1994), 41–54 (41).

records a 'false lull' in the discussion? Stephen has been asked by Crawford 'to write something for me' and it is possible to view these paragraphs as Stephen practising for that occasion, as an 'exercise in false narration, a critique through parody of pretentious narrative technique'.[55] But it is also important to note that this moment of stylistic disruption and complication existed in the serial text: it serves as a reminder that Joyce was committed to stylistic difficulty before he revised the serial text, and before he inserted the headings to this particular chapter. What he does in revision is to simply increase the level of stylistic difficulty and complication.

Suggestiveness, Sexuality, and Candour

The argument for *type 5*, Joyce revising the text so that it becomes more suggestive, candid, or explicit about the body and sexuality, has already been suggested in relation to chapter 4 ('Calypso'), the moment where Bloom sits 'calm above his own rising smell'.[56] There is significant evidence of this kind of revision in chapter 5 ('Lotus-Eaters'), 11 ('Sirens'), and 13 ('Nausicaa'), which will be considered forthwith. Thus just three examples, exemplifying the point in other chapters, serve to make the general argument here. Molly's reading in chapter 4 ('Calypso') is a good place to begin. Though she asks Bloom to explain the meaning of a word in her book ('metempsychosis'), the book itself, '*Ruby*: a tale of circus life', is named but not described in the *Little Review*.[57] In the 1922 text, Molly's novel becomes the more suggestive *Ruby: the Pride of the Ring*, and Bloom's interior monologue records his impressions of the illustrations:

> He turned over the smudged pages. *Ruby: the Pride of the Ring*. Hello. Illustration. Fierce Italian with carriagewhip. Must be Ruby pride of the on the floor naked. Sheet kindly lent. The monster Maffei desisted and flung his victim from him with an oath.
> (U1922, 62)

Joyce introduces a master-slave narrative here (Maffei vs Ruby) and a suggestion of sadomasochism and bondage in the reference to the 'carriagewhip' and Ruby's nakedness. He was drawing on a real bibliographical source, Amy Reade's *Ruby: A Novel: Founded on the Life of a Circus Girl* (1889), and is inspired in particular by one of the illustrations, labelled 'The monster desisted and threw his victim from him with an oath'. This depicts the circus master—Signor Enrico in the novel—with a whip or baton in hand, standing over a woman on the floor who would be naked but for the thin covering of a sheet.[58] Though the idea that this work contains the word 'metempsychosis' is an invention, Joyce was obviously aware of this source when he wrote the serial text; he exploited the sexual subtexts of the original to a much greater extent in revision, but also continued to work with artistic licence, changing the title so it would be more suggestive. This addition anticipates many of the details in chapter 15 ('Circe'), including Signor Maffei's introduction

---

[55] Bernard Benstock, *Narrative Contexts in Dubliners* (London: Macmillan, 1994), 9.
[56] *U*1922, 66; see above, p. 159.   [57] *LR*, June 1918, 47.
[58] Mary Power, 'The Discovery of *Ruby*', *James Joyce Quarterly*, 18:2 (Winter 1981), 115–21. This article includes illustrations from Reade's novel.

of Ruby, pride of the ring (*U*1922, 431) and Bloom's transformation into Ruby Cohen (who is lectured and spanked by Bello; *U*1922, 505). Thus this set of additions also exemplifies the systematic way in which the relationships between the chapters are thickened in revision.

Another instance of Bloom's thought pattern becoming more sexually explicit can be identified in chapter 8 ('Lestrygonians') in the moment where he suddenly contemplates the idea that Boylan could transmit a venereal disease to Molly: 'If he....? O! Eh? No.....No. I don't believe it. He wouldn't surely?' (*U*1922, 147). The significance of what Bloom is thinking is difficult to pick up, particularly in the serial version: the clue is in the previous paragraph in the reference to 'That quack doctor for the clap used to be stuck up in all the greenhouses'.[59] Joyce has added another reference to venereal disease (**'Some chap with a dose burning him'**) in the 1922 text (*U*1922, 146). This makes Bloom's train of thought slightly clearer because 'dose' and 'burning' are strong and unignorable words; it is also significant that the new phrase is introduced at the end of the paragraph, a key position for an interpretive cue.

Sometimes Joyce changes the text post-serially in ways which are sexually suggestive, rather than explicit. This can be seen in relation to Bloom, who obviously spends a good deal of time thinking about Milly, and worrying about her developing sexuality. In chapter 6 ('Hades'), he contemplates making 'a walking tour' and visiting her 'as a surprise', a scheme he suddenly rethinks:

> She mightn't like me to come that way without letting her know. Must be careful about women. **Catch them once with their pants down. Never forgive you after.** Fifteen.
>
> (*U*1922, 97)

In another addition to Bloom's thinking about Milly, at the moment in chapter 4 ('Calypso') when he remembers her finding a mirror in professor Goodwin's hat, Joyce is more explicit: he adds the sentence **'Sex breaking out even then'** (*U*1922, 61). The word 'pants' and the idea of 'pants down' is more subtle but may be read as part of the same tendency—of the work becoming more candid in revision.

Embellishing Micro-Narratives

A sense of the ways in which Joyce embellishes the micro-narratives of the work (*type 6*) can be seen by briefly surveying some of the tiny post-serial additions which Joyce made to chapter 4 ('Calypso'). In the serial text, Bloom simply pours out 'Milk for the pussens'. In the 1922 version, readers are told that the milk is **'warmbubbled'** and comes **'from the jug Hanlon's milkman had just filled for him'** (*U*1922, 54), a detail which communicates a sense of Bloom's community, and establishes a correspondence with the delivery of the milk at the Martello tower. In the serial text Bloom simply goes to the hall and takes his hat from the peg; the 1922 text insists on noting **'his initialled heavy overcoat and his lost**

---

[59] *LR*, January 1919, 30.

property office secondhand waterproof' (*U*1922, 55); again, this detail gives a sense of Bloom's community, and establishes a correspondence with Dedalus, who is dressed in Mulligan's 'secondhand breeks' (*U*1922, 6). In the serial text Bloom acknowledges Larry O'Rourke, the publican, and remembers one of his jokes ('Do you know what: the Russians, they are an only an eight o'clock breakfast for the Japanese').[60] The 1922 text adds Bloom's thoughts about the 'competition' from other Dublin pubs, '**Adam Findlaters or Dan Tallons**', and muses '**Good puzzle would be cross Dublin without passing a pub**' (*U*1922, 56). While queuing to be served at the counter of Dlugacz's, Bloom stands 'near the next door girl'.[61] In the 1922 text Joyce embellishes this detail by naming the neighbour: '**Woods his name is. Wonder what he does. Wife is oldish**' (*U*1922, 57). Bloom also spies 'whatdoyoucallhim' in the 1922 text: '**There's whatdoyoucallhim out of. How do you? Doesn't see. Chap you know just to salute a bit of a bore**' (*U*1922, 58). The 1922 text also adds '**Kearney**', the guarantor for Bloom's membership at the Capel street library (*U*1922, 62), and '**O'Brien**', the chap in the '**paybox**' at Tara street baths who '**got James Stephens away**' (*U*1922, 66). Individuals such as Hanlon, Woods, Kearney, and 'whatdoyoucallhim' do not feature in latter chapters of the work and can barely be described as characters. Nor would it be accurate to classify the vignettes which they suggest as stories. But it is significant that Joyce has added these figures; these additions may be read as part of a general revisionary impulse of embellishing micro-narrative, and of Joyce becoming committed to the representation of a more thorough and encyclopaedic sense of the Blooms' community. The addition of 'Hanlon's milkman' and of the 'secondhand waterproof' are also examples of *type 3*, 'schematic' and systematic revision, being instances of Joyce increasing the internal referentiality of the work.

Within the suite of Bloom-focused naturalistic chapters—chapters 4 to 8 ('Calypso' to 'Lestrygonians') in the serial version—Joyce establishes multiple micro-narratives, including major psychological events which structure Bloom's emotional life, such as the death of his father, the death of Rudy, and the fact of Molly's impending affair with Boylan. It is worth considering how these particular micro-narratives are embellished in chapter 6 ('Hades') and chapter 8 ('Lestrygonians'), beginning with Bloom's father. While readers of the serial version ought to pick up on the fact of Bloom's father's death ('Poor papa! Poor man! I'm glad I didn't go into the room to look at his face'), the circumstances of his death are not so clear.[62] In revising chapter 6 ('Hades'), Joyce adds the phrase which expresses the coroner's verdict: '**Death by misadventure**' (*U*1922, 93), and adds a string of Bloomian reflection on suicide ('**They have no mercy on that here or infanticide. Refuse christian burial**', *U*1922, 93), Martin's Cunningham's acknowledgement that the purpose of Bloom's trip to Clare is the anniversary ('**You heard him say he was going to Clare. Anniversary**', *U*1922, 98), Bloom's

---

⁶⁰ *LR*, June 1918, 42.   ⁶¹ *LR*, June 1918, 42.
⁶² *LR*, July 1918, 42. The most explicit hint of Bloom's father's death in the serial version is in *LR*, September 1918, 23, the passage about 'That afternoon of the inquest' [...] 'Verdict: overdose'.

reflection that his father went away for the suicide ('**Also poor papa went away**', *U*1922, 106), as well as the thoughts about visiting the grave (*U*1922, 105, noted above). Bloom's thoughts about his father are also developed post-serially in chapter 8 ('Lestrygonians'), in a moment when he is thinking about Milly taking up in the photography business: '**Now photography. Poor papa's daguerreotype atelier he told me of. Hereditary taste**' (*U*1922, 148).

The fact of Rudy's death is carefully established in the serial text, in the moment which follows Bloom reading his letter from Milly: Mrs Thornton 'knew from the first poor little Rudy wouldn't live. Well, God is good, sir. She knew at once. He would be eleven now if he had lived'.[63] In revision, Joyce builds on these details. In chapter 6, ('Hades'), after hearing Simon Dedalus talk about Stephen ('Noisy selfwilled man. Full of his son'), Bloom imagines what it would have meant to see Rudy beside Molly, and adds '**in an Eton suit**' (*U*1922, 86). '**Our. Little. Beggar. Baby**' (*U*1922, 92), discussed in Chapter 3, is also an addition which reflects on Rudy, whose death has had a profound impact on the Blooms' sexual intimacy, a fact which is added in the following passage in chapter 8 ('Lestrygonians'):

> I was happier then. Or was that I? Or am I now I? Twentyeight I was. She twentythree. **When we left Lombard street west something changed. Could never like it again after Rudy.** Can't bring back time. (*U*1922, 160)

Apart from increasing the sense of pathos, the added details deepen the plot: they help readers to understand that sexual frustration is a factor in Molly's plan to have an affair with Boylan.

Most of the hints which suggest Molly's plans for a liaison are included in the serial version of chapter 4 ('Calypso'), including, for example, the receipt of the letter from Boylan (which causes Bloom's 'quickened heart' to slow 'at once'); the arrangements to meet ('He's bringing the programme'); and the representation of Bloom's sense of how inevitable the trajectory of events is: 'A soft qualm, regret, flowed down his backbone, increasing. Will happen, yes. Prevent. Useless, can't move'.[64] But Joyce opts to add a few extra hints, including Bloom's acknowledgement that he feels 'desolation' because he '**Got up wrong side of the bed**' (*U*1922, 59), that Boylan is a '**Friend of the family**' (*U*1922, 64), and, most significantly, that he may be seen as the '**Worst man in Dublin**' (*U*1922, 89). Boylan's presence is communicated through a series of leitmotifs, including those that describe his physical appearance, 'Straw hat in sunlight. Tan shoes. Turnedup trousers' (*U*1922, 174), and his association with the song 'Seaside Girls', which is first mentioned in Milly's letter to Bloom (*U*1922, 64). Every echo of this song—and there are many—is a reminder of Boylan's presence in the lives of both Milly and Molly. One is added to chapter 6 ('Hades') in a passage where Bloom is thinking about graves:

> But they must breed a devil of a lot of maggots. Soil must be simply swirling with them. Your head it simply swirls. **Those pretty little seaside gurls.** (*U*1922, 105)

[63] *LR*, June 1918, 49.   [64] *LR*, June 1918, 45, 46, 50.

In terms of psychology, the plot involving Boylan is carefully established in the serial version of chapter 8 ('Lestrygonians'), with Bloom thinking about the possibility of Molly contracting a venereal disease ('If he.......?'); remembering the moment when he, Molly, and Boylan were together walking 'down by the Tolka'. ('He other side of her. Elbow, arm. He. *Glowworm's lamp is gleaming, love.* Touch. Fingers. Asking. Answer. Yes.'); being haunted by the thought of the coming affair ('Stop. Stop. If it was it was. Must.'); Nosey Flynn asking Bloom about Molly's 'big tour' ('Who's getting it up?'), and asking Bloom 'Isn't Blazes Boylan mixed up in it?' while scratching his groin; and Bloom urging himself to not think about what is happening ('Today. Today. Not think.').[65] Martin Cunningham sees and salutes Boylan as the cortège travels to Dignam's funeral.[66] Bloom also sees him both before and after his lunch at Davy Byrne's (*U*1922, 158, 174); the significance of the second of these three sightings is enhanced in a post-serial revision:

> And there he is too. Now that's really a coincidence: secondtime. **Coming events cast their shadows before.** (*U*1922, 158)

This hardly makes the significance of what is happening clear; but it is certainly the case that Joyce adds hints to the text post-serially which make this aspect of the plot more obvious, particularly for a re-reader.

Joyce did not make extensive post-serial additions to chapter 10 ('Wandering Rocks'), a 'micro' revised chapter, as noted, which increased from approximately 11,441 words to 12,670 words, an increase of 10.7 per cent or thereabouts.[67] The pattern of rewriting in this chapter is quite distinctive, in that much of the text prepared for serial publication is undisturbed. But Joyce does add blocks of new writing, which often amplify the work's micro-narratives. For example, Tom Kernan does not simply walk 'down the slope of Watling street'; he notes 'Some Tipperary bosthoon endangering the lives of the citizens', as follows:

> Mr Kernan turned and walked down the slope of Watling street **by the corner of Guinness's visitors' waitingroom. Outside the Dublin Distillers Company's stores an outside car without fare or jarvey stood, the reins knotted to the wheel. Damn dangerous thing.** Some Tipperary bosthoon endangering the lives of the citizens. **Runaway horse.** (*U*1922, 231)

The excerpt in which Bloom selects *Sweets of Sin* for Molly is also revised. Joyce adds a reference to Denis J. Maginni: a description of him crossing O'Connell bridge (**'On O'Connell bridge many persons observed the grave deportment and gay apparel of Mr Denis J Maginni, professor of dancing & c.'**, *U*1922, 226).[68] He also adds a description of an **'elderly female'** leaving the courts of chancery (*U*1922, 227). These additions pitch the naturalistic and stylistically sophisticated manner of representing Bloom's experiences within the bookshop against an encyclopaedic and documentary impulse, which is concerned with mapping a broader sense of

---

[65] *LR*, January 1919, 30, 40, 41, 44, 45; *LR*, February–March 1919, 59.
[66] *LR*, September 1918, 19.   [67] See above, p. 139.
[68] The two other references to Maginni were also added post-serially (*U*1922, 211, 243).

what other events are happening in the city of Dublin at the same time. The shift of register is very striking:

> Mr Bloom read again: *The beautiful woman.*
>
> Warmth showered gently over him, cowing his flesh. Flesh yielded amid rumpled clothes. Whites of eyes swooning up. His nostrils arched themselves for prey. Melting breast ointments (for him! For Raoul!). Armpits' oniony sweat. Fishgluey slime (her heaving embonpoint!). Feel! Press! Crished! Sulphur dung of lions!
>
> Young! Young!
>
> **An elderly female, no more young, left the building of the courts of chancery, king's bench, exchequer and common pleas having heard in the lord chancellor's court the case in lunacy of Potterton, in the admiralty division the summons, exparte motion, of the owners of the Lady Cairns versus the owners of the barque Mona, in the court of appeal reservation of judgment in the case of Harvey versus the Ocean Accident and Guarantee Corporation.**
>
> Phlegmy coughs shook the air of the bookshop, bulging out the dingy curtains.
>
> (*U*1922, 227)

In respect of this particular instance of post-serial embellishment of micro-narrative, what exactly is gained? Why has Joyce chosen to lift details of actual cases reported in the *Freeman's Journal* of 16 June 1904?[69] Has the desire for an encyclopaedic representation overwhelmed Joyce's (better) naturalism? Or does the reminder that the city has a set of courts, with a train of pleas, cases, summons, and motions, add something which is aesthetically worthwhile? Would this be a better addition if Joyce had gone against his own rules for deviation from standard forms and insisted on 'Courts', 'Chancery', 'King's Bench', 'Lord Chancellor', 'In Lunacy', 'Admirality', 'Appeal', and *ex parte*, etc.? Might it be the case that the introduction of a legalistic strain here reflects on Joyce's own deeper experience of litigious process, including the trial of the *Little Review* editors, which was set in train in September 1920? The dates for this supposition would work, in that the serial version of chapter 10 was en route to publication in February 1919, and this addition was not added until the first proofs of the chapter, at some point between 3 and 27 August 1921.[70] Whatever one decides, the embellishing of micro-narrative, as exemplified, is a significant factor here.

Hibernicism and the Revision of Speech

Type 7, the revision of certain elements of speech and narration so that they become more overtly Hibernian or staged, is a revisionary impulse associated with certain speakers, such as Buck Mulligan and Simon Dedalus. As the argument has already been implied with regard to Mulligan, and the insertion of the phrase 'Is there gaelic on you?', a discussion of Simon Dedalus should come first.[71] Stephen's father, with his sudden and unpredictable shifts in mood, is an important secondary character for the development of plot, and for thematic realization. It is through

---

[69] See Gifford, *Ulysses Annotated*, 272.
[70] J to Weaver, 25 February 1919, *L* II, 436; *CSE* III, Table 1, 1914.   [71] See above, p. 167.

him, within chapter 6, that we begin to understand more of Bloom and Stephen. The first revision to his speech is in the moment when Bloom sees Stephen and points him out to his father: 'There's a friend of yours gone by' (*U*1922, 85). This immediately elicits the response:

> Was that Mulligan cad with him? His *fidus Achates!* (*U*1922, 85)

As used here the Latin tag, added post-serially, means loyal friend; it suggests learnedness and sarcasm, and adds a frisson of dramatic tension to what ought to be a sombre journey, a journey shared by four men (Bloom, Dedalus, Cunningham, and Power) en route to a colleague's funeral in an uncomfortably 'cramped' (*U*1922, 97) and crumb-strewn carriage. Later in the same exchange, Joyce revises Dedalus's speech about Mulligan so that it becomes:

> —He's in with a lowdown crowd, Mr Dedalus snarled. That Mulligan is a contaminated **bloody doubledyed** ruffian **by all accounts**. His name stinks all over Dublin. But with the help of God and His blessed mother **I'll make it my business** to write a letter one of those days to his mother or his aunt or whatever she is that will open her eye as wide as a gate. I'll tickle his catastrophe, believe you me. (*U*1922, 85–6)

The addition of '**bloody doubledyed**' and '**by all accounts**' gives the sentence deeper rhetorical energy and force. Joyce also changed 'I am going to write' to '**I'll make it my business to write**', a substitution which makes the intention seem sharper and more real. These revisions are not Hibernicisms per se, but they have the impact of making Dedalus a more obvious stage Irishman, because they enhance the dramatic or 'staged' elements of his behaviour, a pattern which can be identified in several other examples. 'Can't complain', the original response to Ned Lambert's greeting ('How are you, Simon.... Haven't seen you for a month of Sundays?'), becomes the rather more buoyant '**Never better**'.[72] This is an odd thing to say at a funeral, but Dedalus is a store of 'most amusing expressions', as Bloom muses (*U*1922, 100). Later in the exchange with Lambert, a fellow Corkonian, the two men talk of their friend, Dick Tivy, becoming bald. Dedalus's response to this in the serial version ('For God's sake—! Mr Dedalus said. Dick Tivy bald?') becomes '**By the holy Paul! Mr Dedalus said in subdued wonder. Dick Tivy bald?**'.[73] Similarly, Dedalus's response to the mention of 'Reuben J' shifts from 'That hobbledehoy is it?' in the serial to 'That **confirmed bloody** hobbledehoy is it?' in the 1922 text.[74]

As noted earlier, Joyce's plan for the revision of *Ulysses*, as outlined in November 1920, envisaged putting in 'insertions', which he described as 'chiefly verbal or phrases'. This is an apt description of several of the additions made to Dedalus, in the latter part of chapter 6 ('Hades'), in chapter 7 ('Aeolus'), and in chapter 10 ('Wandering Rocks'). Examples include:

> —O, that be damned for a story, Mr Dedalus said. **Pullman car and saloon diningroom.**
>
> (*U*1922, 95)

---

[72] *LR*, September 1918, 27; *U*1922, 98.   [73] *LR*, September 1918, 27; *U*1922, 99.
[74] *LR*, September 1918, 21; *U*1922, 91.

—First round Dunphy's, Mr Dedalus said, nodding. **Gordon Bennett Cup.**

(*U*1922, 95)

—**Though lost to sight, Mr Dedalus said, to memory dear.** (*U*1922, 96)

—Bathe his lips, Mr Dedalus said. **Blessed and eternal God! Yes? Is he taking anything for it?** (*U*1922, 121)

—Stand up straight for the love of the lord Jesus, Mr Dedalus said. Are you trying to imitate your uncle John, the cornetplayer, head upon your shoulder? **Melancholy God!**

(*U*1922, 228)

—Wait awhile, Mr Dedalus said threateningly. You're like the rest of them, are you? An insolent pack of little bitches since your poor mother died. But wait awhile. You'll all get a short shrift and a long day from me. **Low blackguardism! I'm going to get rid of you. Wouldn't care if I was stretched out stiff. He's dead. The man upstairs is dead.** (*U*1922, 228)

Simon Dedalus is certainly funny, and full of sayings in the serial text, but as this list establishes, Joyce intensifies those traits in revision.

Some of Joyce's revisions to Buck Mulligan in chapter 9 ('Scylla and Charybdis') relate quite specifically to knowledge of literary culture, and particularly to the culture of the Irish Literary Revival, which Mulligan mocks almost every time he speaks. His 'wailing rune', a parody of J. M. Synge, who is mentioned several times in the discussion at the National Library, is enhanced in revision:

—***Pogue mahone! Acushla machree!*** It's destroyed we are from this day! It's destroyed we are surely! (*U*1922, 197)

Joyce may not have invested a great deal of time in the serious academic study of the Irish language, but he was a brilliant linguist, and he knew enough Irish to use it for tokenistic effect. 'Póg mo thóin' and 'A chuisle mo chroí', Irish phrases meaning 'Kiss my arse' and 'O pulse of my heart', are inserted here to intensify the impact of Mulligan's performance. Syngean locutions are also intensified in the speech which describes Mulligan and Haines waiting for Dedalus at the pub:

—It's what I'm telling you, mister honey, it's queer and sick we were, Haines and myself, the time himself brought it in. **'Twas murmur we did for a gallus potion would rouse a friar, I'm thinking, and he limp with leching.** And we one hour and two hours and three hours in Connery's sitting civil waiting for pints apiece. (*U*1922, 191)

Joyce also enhances the Hibernian element of Mulligan's speech by inserting references to Yeats, including 'Printed by the weird sisters in the big wind' (*U*1922, 13), as noted, and the following:

—O, the chinless Chinaman! **Chin Chon Eg Lin Ton.** We went over to their playbox, Haines and I, the plumbers' hall. **Our players are creating a new art for Europe like the Greeks or M. Maeterlinck.** Abbey theatre! I smell the public sweat of monks.[75]

(*U*1922, 207)

---

[75] *U*1922, 207. The reading is 'pubic', not public, in Gabler.

'Chin Chon Eg Lin Ton', one of the many word plays on John Eglinton's name, could be seen as an example of revision *type 4*, complicating the stylistic odyssey. 'Our players are creating...' is a mocking echo of the type of public statement Yeats was accustomed to make with regard to the Irish National Theatre Society.

A strain of Hibernian intensification can also be identified in the revisions to chapter 12 ('Cyclops'), where there are multiple instances of Joyce inserting new phrases of Irish, and Dublinese idioms and proverbs. Both the narrator and the Citizen use phrases of actual and translated Irish for dramatic and tokenistic effect. This feature of the text is well established in the serial version, in words and phrases like: 'Barney mavourneen's', 'Doing the rapparee', 'Arrah', 'begob', '*a chara*', 'honourable person', '*Bi i dho husht*', '*Sinn Fein!* says the citizen. *Sinn fein amhain!*', '*Slan leat*', '*The Sluagh na h-Eireann*', '*Na bacleis*', 'God save you', '*Raimeis*'.[76] In revision Joyce strengthens the impact of these spoken phrases and narrative descriptions by including new tags, such as 'cruiskeen lawn', an anglicized form of 'crúiscín lán', meaning full jug (and implying a full jug of whiskey), in the following:

—There he is, says I, in his gloryhole, with his **cruiskeen lawn and his** load of papers, working for the cause.   (*U*1922, 283)

A few lines later, Joyce adds 'Rory of the hill', a pseudonym adopted for the signing of letters in the 1880s by tenants engaged in the Land War.[77] Thus a reference to 'rapparee' (an anglicized version of 'rapairí', the plural of robber) becomes: 'Doing the rapparee **and Rory of the hill**' (*U*1922, 283). In both the serial and volume versions of this chapter, Joyce makes frequent use of a fairly extreme example of stage Irish: the words 'gob' and 'begob', 'gob' being both the Irish for mouth and a shortened version of 'begob' which is a corruption of 'by God' (the etymology has been identified by Dolan, and is perhaps not entirely firm).[78] In the serial version, in the moment where Alf Bergan is told that Dignam has 'paid the debt of nature', Joyce uses the word 'Begod': 'Begod he was what you might call flabbergasted'.[79] It may only be the difference of one letter, but it makes a difference to see (and hear) this as: '**Begob** he was what you might call flabbergasted' (*U*1922, 288). The tiny adjustment—from 'begod' to 'begob'—makes the falsity in the narration sound truer, and more assured.

Other post-serial intensifications of this chapter include the addition of the Irish word for friend in the sentence: '—I will, says he, **a chara,** to show there's no ill feeling', the use of '**howandever**', a very Dublin phrase, and the introduction of multiple proverbs, idioms, and phrases, such as '**that'd put the fear of God in you**', '**The tear is bloody near your eye**', '**phenomenon with a back on her like a ballal-ley**', '**Ireland sober is Ireland free**', '**Do you see any green in the white of my eye?**', '**All wind and piss like a tanyard cat**', '**May your shadow ever grow less**', '**Goodbye Ireland I'm going to Gort**', '**Not as much as would blind your eye**', '**Cute as a**

[76] *LR*, November 1919, 39, 41, 43, 44, 50; *LR*, December 1919, 51, 52, 55, 60. This is a rough list from the first two of the four instalments in which chapter 12 was published.

[77] Gifford, *Ulysses Annotated*, 320.

[78] T. P. Dolan, *A Dictionary of Hiberno-English* (Dublin: Gill and Macmillan, 1998), 127, 24.

[79] *LR*, November 1919, 46.

shithouse rat', 'the curse of Cromwell on him', and **'to tear him limb from limb'**.[80] Read alongside the added references to food and death, this list, which is by no means complete, shows that the adding of idiomatic phrases and proverbs— whether they deepen the stream of consciousness, fit with the schemata, enhance the leitmotific structure of the work, or intensify its dramatic and Hibernian elements—is a highly significant aspect of Ulyssean revision.

Thus far, the argument that there are seven types of Ulyssean revision has been tested in relation to nine of the thirteen chapters which were serialized in the *Little Review* (1, 3, 4, 6, 7, 8, 9, 10, and 12). The emphasis on Bloom-focused naturalism has been unavoidable, because naturalism dominates the serialized portion of the work, and the Bloom chapters are the most heavily revised. But by looking at a Dedalus chapter, a Bloom chapter, and two non-naturalistic chapters, the case studies (on chapters 2, 5, 11, and 13) will attempt to rebalance that emphasis and consider, in particular, whether the seven types of Ulyssean revision hold true for non-naturalistic chapters. At the same time, the chapter case studies offered in the next two sections will attempt to confront the bigger question underpinning the study of Ulyssean revision. What is the cumulative effect of Joyce's revision? Is one type of revision more significant and transformative than another? How does the revision of *Ulysses* change the shape and reading of the work as a whole?

MINIMAL REVISION: THE CASE OF 'NESTOR' AND 'SIRENS'

With fewer than 200 words added, chapter 2 ('Nestor') is the most minimally revised chapter of all: in both serial and final form, it is also the shortest chapter in the work and essentially contains four scenes. It opens with Stephen teaching his class; after the class leaves for hockey, Stephen helps Cyril Sargent who is struggling with his sums; thereafter he goes to the study of the headmaster, Garret Deasy, to be paid; finally, after an intense set of exchanges about money, Irish history, and politics, Stephen leaves the school and wanders 'down the gravel path under the trees, hearing the cries of voices and crack of sticks from the playfield' (*U*1922, 35). All four of these scenes are included in both serial and final text, and in the transition between the two versions none appears to have been significantly altered.

In terms of advancing the narratives and arguments of the work, this chapter gives readers a deeper sense of Stephen Dedalus, his psychology, and the denominational contours which shape his sense of history. It also introduces the politics of the period, through the character of Deasy whose belief in the value of preserving political union between Britain and Ireland is made clear through details such as the display of a portrait of 'Albert Edward, prince of Wales' (*U*1922, 31) and his characterization of Dedalus as a 'Fenian' ('You Fenians forget some things', *U*1922, 31). Given that the pattern of revision is so minimal, and that Joyce rarely introduces completely new paragraphs, it is particularly significant that Joyce adds

---

[80] *U*1922, 299, 298, 287, 290, 293, 298, 308, 314, 317, 321, 323, 326, 327, 330.

a whole paragraph which expresses Stephen's response to Deasy's orange version of nineteenth-century Irish history. This addition is placed within a moment when Deasy is speaking and needs to be read in context:

> —You think me an old fogey and an old tory, his thoughtful voice said. I saw three generations since O'Connell's time. I remember the famine in '46. Do you know that the orange lodges agitated for repeal of the union twenty years before O'Connell did or before the prelates of your communion denounced him as a demagogue? You fenians forget some things.
>
> **Glorious, pious and immortal memory. The lodge of Diamond in Armagh the splendid behung with corpses of papishes. Hoarse, masked and armed, the planters covenant. The black north and true blue bible. Croppies lie down.**
>
> Stephen sketched a brief gesture.   (*U*1922, 31)

Every greyscale phrase here is replete with cultural and historical meaning, beginning with Stephen's half-memory of the Orangeman's toast to William ('To the glorious, pious and immortal memory of the Great and Good King William III, who saved us from popery, slavery, arbitrary power, brass money and wooden shoes').[81] He also thinks of the Planters' Covenant, an Elizabethan initiative which consolidated control of land in Protestant hands; the clashes between Catholics and Protestants in Armagh, which culminated in the Battle of the Diamond in 1795; and the fate of the 'croppies'—the name given to the Irish rebels in 1798.

In expressing Stephen's perception of Deasy, the added paragraph deepens and clarifies Deasy's characterization. It reads as Stephen's mental retort to being designated a 'fenian' and is a nudge to readers to attend to the specificities of Irish history, and to understand the complicated power dynamics which are at work. Stephen may not be able to say much in response to Deasy—he can only sketch a 'brief gesture'—but the response which Joyce has added is mentally strong, and insists, as Andrew Gibson has noted, on recognizing and remembering the barbarity of the English invasion of Ireland in the 1590s ('masked and armed'), as well as the violence of the nascent Orange order in the 1790s ('behung with corpses of papishes').[82] This revision to the text—which expresses Stephen's disesteem and sense of the injustice so adeptly—tips power in his direction. At the very moment when Stephen is accused of forgetting, the addition, added to the second set of chapter proofs of the 1922 text in late June 1921, directs readers to see what he is remembering.[83]

From the perspective of style, the way in which this passage works is particularly interesting. From the outset, the chapter has a high level of repetition, with many words and phrases being repeated in close proximity ('blank', 'sir', 'fabled', 'pier', 'riddle', 'Kingstown', '*Weep no more*', 'history', 'nightmare', 'money', 'fight', etc.). Such repetitions—strung insistently through the text, like a set of worry-beads—are a means by which readers come to understand the significance of what is

---

[81] Gifford, *Ulysses Annotated*, 36.

[82] Andrew Gibson, *Joyce's Revenge: History, Politics and Aesthetics in Ulysses* (Oxford: Oxford University Press, 2002), 36.

[83] *CSE* I 62.36f; *CSE* III 1914.

happening. The classroom scene draws attention to patterns of repetition through the recitation of *Lycidas*, and Stephen saying his riddle twice ('lines were repeated', *U*1922, 27). In such a context, moments of lexical variation stand out, and the passage of 'glorious, pious and immortal memory'—in a chapter in which memory and forgetting are leitmotifs—is exactly such a moment. In response to the designation as 'Fenian'—which is only used once in *Ulysses*—the added paragraph introduces another three words which are only used once: behung, papishes, and covenant. Stephen professes that he is trying to wake himself from the nightmare of history, but his consciousness refuses to forget the spectre of behung papishes, and the cynical terms of the Planter's Covenant, which saw the planters of the 1590s covenanting loyalty to the English Crown in return for the grant of forfeited Catholic land.

Joyce makes other small but significant revisions which tilt the power dynamic of the chapter towards Stephen, by altering the characterization of Deasy. He adds the phrase 'backstairs influence' to the moment when Deasy asks Stephen to help with regard to the placing of his letter about foot and mouth disease ('I want that to be printed and read', *U*1922, 33). Deasy confesses that he needs Stephen's advocacy because he is 'surrounded by difficulties, by... intrigues by... **backstairs influence by...**' (*U*1922, 33). Another instance of Joyce adding what corpus linguists would call a *hapax legomenon*—a word which is only used once within a single text—'backstairs influence' is a crucial facet of Dublin's public and cultural sphere, which Deasy cannot access (but Stephen can, a point reiterated later in chapter 7, where Stephen is invited to write something for the newspaper, and Deasy is derided by Crawford as 'that old pelters', *U*1922, 127).[84] Deasy knows that Stephen thinks him 'an old fogey and an old Tory' (*U*1922, 31) but attempts to claim an alliance with him by announcing 'I have rebel blood in me too' (though it is only on the 'spindle side', i.e. less important because through 'the female line of descent').[85] In the 1922 text, Deasy recalls that 'I am descended from sir John Blackwood who voted for the union'. He continues:

—*Per vias rectas*, Mr Deasy said firmly, was his motto. He voted for it and put on his topboots to ride to Dublin from the Ards of Down to do so. (*U*1922, 31)

The sharp-eyed reader will note the irony of this claim. If Deasy wants to impress Stephen with his 'rebel blood', why is he pointing to an ancestor who voted in favour of the 1800 Act of Union between Great Britain and Ireland? This is exactly as one would have expected; the ancestor was not a rebel, and Deasy has simply inherited the political views of his forebears.

The Tories were known officially as the Conservative and Unionist party: in pointing to an ancestor who was clearly not a rebel, Deasy has shown himself to be exactly the labels he has denied, both an old fogey (who cannot get his stories straight) and an old Tory. The subtexts deployed here are very neat, though it needs

[84] The study of *hapax legomenon* or 'unique' words has been helped enormously by digital tools and is discussed briefly in Hammond, *Literature in the Digital Age*, 90.
[85] OED online; 'spindle side', usually hyphenated, is rarely used, and is only used once in *Ulysses*.

to be borne in mind that Deasy's putative ancestor, Sir John Blackwood (1722–99), was a real historical figure, MP from 1761 to 1797, who did in fact oppose the union of British and Irish parliaments, though he died before he could get to Dublin to cast his vote.[86] In the serial version, Joyce preserves some of that historical fact: 'I am descended from Sir John Blackwood who voted *against* the union'; 'He voted *against* it'.[87] The post-serial revision, which simply involves changing 'against' to 'for' (twice), is an instance of Joyce loosening the text from the grip of fact, loosening the propagandistic force of Deasy's argument, making Deasy seem confused, and thus tipping the power dynamic in the relationship between Deasy and Stephen towards Stephen.

A specifically linguistic and Hibernian register enters the chapter in the phrase 'one pair brogues', a typescript addition to the list of things Stephen owes his friends:

> Mulligan, nine pounds, three pairs of socks, **one pair brogues**, ties. Curran, ten guineas. McCann, one guinea. Fred Ryan, two shillings. Temple, two lunches. Russell, one guinea, Cousins, ten shillings, Bob Reynolds, half a guinea, Koehler, three guineas, Mrs MacKernan, five weeks' board. The lump I have is useless.   (*U*1922, 31)

'Brogue' is one of the few loan words from Irish into English: in modern Irish 'bróg' simply means shoe. In English, by the early twentieth century, brogue had thrown off its sense of a 'rude kind of shoe generally made of untanned hide, worn by the inhabitants of the wilder parts of Ireland and the Scottish highlands', and had come to mean a strong leather shoe, with ornamental leather work, the kind of shoe which the younger Joyce might only borrow or be given.[88] Clearly this addition develops the second-hand economy of clothing already established in chapter 1 of the serial text, where Mulligan remarks to Stephen: 'Ah, poor dogsbody! he said in a kind voice. I must give you a shirt and a few noserags. How are the secondhand breeks?'.[89] It could also be a knowing biographical joke: on the first occasion that Joyce met T. S. Eliot, in Paris in August 1920, Eliot was charged with handing him a brown-paper parcel from Pound. To Joyce's embarrassment, this contained 'a fairly presentable pair of old brown shoes'.[90]

It is interesting that Joyce inserts the word brogue rather than shoe in this context because, as a noun, brogue had an entirely other and more historically established meaning, specifying the 'peculiarities that generally mark the English speech of Ireland': in 1878 William Black noted that 'the very stones of Westminster Hall are saturated with Irish brogue'.[91] OED's etymologists have struggled to understand the association of shoes with Irish speech, but Dolan cites historical evidence for the view that speakers with a brogue could be so unintelligible that 'the effect was as if they had a shoe on their tongue'.[92] 'Is there gaelic on you?' in the revision of Mulligan (*U*1922, 14), alongside the introduction of 'brogue' here, and such

[86] thepeerage.com; see also Gifford, *Ulysses Annotated*, 36.
[87] *LR*, April 1918, 40. Italics mine.
[88] OED online, 2016. Some elements of this entry were written in 1888 and have not yet been fully updated.
[89] *LR*, March 1918, 6.   [90] Ellmann, *James Joyce*, 493.   [91] OED online, 2016.
[92] T. P. Dolan, *A Dictionary of Hiberno-English* (Dublin: Gill and Macmillan, 1998), 42.

charged words as 'papishes' and 'croppies', points again to Ulyssean revision *type 7*: Joyce revising *Ulysses* with a renewed attentiveness to the peculiarities, historicities, and cultural ironies of Hiberno-English. Boots and brogues are a leitmotif in the chapter: once the classroom has emptied for hockey, the narrator listens to the 'clamour of their boots and tongues' (*U*1922, 27); the 'topboots' of 'Sir John Blackwood' are mentioned three times (*U*1922, 31, 32). The brogue references are submerged, however: in Stephen's half-remembered toast to William ('who saved us from popery, slavery, arbitrary power, brass money and *wooden shoes*'), and in the song, 'The Rocky Road to Dublin', which Stephen thinks of in relation to Sir John ('*Lal the lal the ra/The Rocky Road to Dublin*', *U*1922, 31). A later moment of the same song contains the lines: 'With a pair of bran new brogues, I rattled o'er the bogs—/Sure I frightened all the dogs on the rocky road to Dublin'.[93]

As Luca Crispi and others have made clear, Joyce composed and revised from notebook sources, where he had jotted down rough citations harvested from his broad reading.[94] It may be that the idea for the insertion of 'brogues' emerged from re-reading (or recalling) the lyrics of 'The Rocky Road to Dublin' and it is certainly the case that another addition to this chapter—the addition of a reference to saint Columbanus in a passage of Dedalus monologue—is an instance of what might be described as 'submerged citation', inspired by Joyce's reading. The addition is the phrase **'His mother's prostrate body the fiery Columbanus in holy zeal bestrode'** (*U*1922, 28), a phrase of rhetoric (particularly evident in 'prostrate', 'fiery', 'zeal', and 'bestrode'), with a non-natural word order which evokes translated liturgical texts, such as prayers and saints' lives. As Ronan Crowley and Geert Lernout have established—by studying one of Joyce's working notebooks in the National Library of Ireland, and then working backward from there to find the source using internet searches—Joyce's source for this moment is Joseph McCabe's *The Religion of Women* (1905).[95] Interestingly, the source which Joyce read ('St Columban, accordingly, stepped over the prostrate form of his mother as she clung to the door-posts to keep him from the dreaded monastery') does not contain the word 'bestrode', another instance of a unique word added to chapter 2 post-serially.

Stephen likens himself to Columbanus in chapter 3 ('You were going to do wonders, what? Missionary to Europe after fiery Columbanus', *U*1922, 42), a reference which was included in the serial version of the text.[96] The addition represents a retroactive inter-referential thickening of texture: the reference in chapter 3 ('Proteus') is not so hard to interpret given the earlier mention in chapter 2 ('Nestor'). The submerged citation has helped Joyce to create the effect of Stephen remembering the way in which he learned, or perhaps was forced to learn, the life of Columbanus; the moment even appears to recall overtly rhetorical phrases— such as 'in holy zeal bestrode'. Thanks to the detective work of Crowley and

---

[93] Wikipedia, version of the song reported by Manus O'Connor in 1901.

[94] Crispi, 'The Notescape of *Ulysses*', *passim*.

[95] Ronan Crowley and Geert Lernout, 'Joseph McCabe in *Ulysses*', Genetic Joyce Studies, 12 (Spring 2012), 8; www.geneticjoycestudies.org.

[96] *LR*, May 1918, 36.

Lernout, it now appears that that rhetorical flourish is Joyce's imaginative creation and not a derivation from any particular bibliographical source.[97]

In thinking about Sargent, Stephen thinks about Sargent's mother:

> But for her the race of the world would have trampled him underfoot, a squashed boneless snail. She had loved his weak watery blood drained from her own. Was that then real? The only true thing in life? **His mother's prostrate body the fiery Columbanus in holy zeal bestrode.** She was no more: the trembling skeleton of a twig burnt in the fire, an odour of rosewood and wetted ashes.   (*U*1922, 28)

Particular pathos arises here from the idea of the mother who 'had saved him from being trampled underfoot' being 'prostrate'. Stephen is haunted by the hubris of his association with Columbanus, by the denial of his mother's wishes, and by the memory of his failure to kneel at her deathbed when she lay 'groaning vomiting' (*U*1922, 6). The serial text establishes all of these leitmotifs (Stephen's association with Columbanus, the deathbed scene, the role of mothers generally, the association of Stephen's mother with rosewood and wetted ashes): what this addition has succeeded in doing is to take what is already an intense associative lyrical structure and intensify it yet more.

For serial readers chapter 2, labelled 'Episode II' and presented without any introductory or editorial comment, contained particular challenges. Alongside some very obvious typos ('breat' instead of breath, 'sopybook' instead of copybook, 'tehir' instead of their), readers had to contend with missing punctuation marks, and confusing omissions in phrases introduced by Popovich (owing to 'eyeskip', the text reads 'Mr. Deasy stared sternly for moments over the mantel-box' rather than 'Mr Deasy laughed with rich delight, putting back his savingsbox' and 'to the Mr. Field, M. P.' rather than 'I wrote last night to Mr Field, M. P.').[98] In addition to these corruptions, readers had to work out how to negotiate ruptures in novelistic continuity. It is not, for example, immediately obvious where the action is set and how it relates to the first chapter. The opening dialogue specifies Stephen's involvement, but readers might otherwise feel that they have been left to flounder in a sea of detail. Multiple facts from chapter 1 need to be recalled: that Dedalus has been in Paris, that his mother is dead, that he works in a school and is due to be paid, that Haines intends to make 'chapbook' of his sayings, that he is friends with Mulligan. The dropped-in italicized quotations are disjunctive and hard to follow (particularly '*The harlot's cry from street to street/Shall weave old England's windingsheet*').[99] Where does this come from? Who, within the narrative, voices it and how is it relevant? Why is Deasy obsessed with Jews and 'Old England'? What is the significance of the cultural and generational tensions which seem so central to Stephen's relationship with Deasy? When one begins to think about the text

[97] An observation which brings to mind the thought that *Ulysses* has researcher traps, just as it has reader traps. The economies of submerged Ulyssean citation and creativity are closely connected—phrases which look citational are sometimes original, and phrases which look original are sometimes citational.

[98] *LR*, April 1918, 39, 44.

[99] *LR*, April 1918, 42. The lines are from Blake's 'Auguries of Innocence'.

from this perspective, that of the serial reader—who read *Ulysses* from month to month, without annotations and guidebooks to ease the way—it is easy to empathize with 'S. S. B.', from Chicago, who wrote in to complain in June 1918, after reading the first two or three chapters:

> Really now: Joyce! what does he think he is doing? What do you think he is doing? I swear I've read his 'Ulysses' and haven't found out yet what it's about, who is who and where. Each month he's worse than last. I consider myself fairly intelligent. I have read more than most. There are some few things I expect of a writer. One of them is coherence. Joyce will have to change his style if he wants to get on. Very few have the time or patience to struggle with this impressionistic stuff—to get nothing out of it even then.[100]

Presumably S. S. B. had given up by August 1919, when the *Little Review* published the first instalment of chapter 11 ('Sirens'). By that juncture comment on *Ulysses* by 'ordinary' readers had all but disappeared from the journal's discussion column, and had been replaced by comments from *littérateurs* and writers who were more obviously 'in the know', such as William Carlos Williams, Marsden Hartley, and John Rodker. In September 1919, for example, Williams was gushingly appreciative of both Joyce and Dorothy Richardson:

> Their form lives!…It lives in its today. They plunge naked into the flaming cauldron of today.…What can one care if Joyce is lewd and in the street, if Richardson is charming and in a girl's bedroom?[101]

Similarly, Israel Solon, a regular *Little Review* contributor, thought Joyce 'the most sensitive stylist writing in English. There is enough skill and matter in a single Episode of "Ulysses" to equip a regiment of novelists'.[102] But such views were by no means universal. Responding to the receipt of the chapter typescript, the normally reticent Harriet Shaw Weaver told Joyce that she thought that 'Sirens' had been 'affected to some extent by your worries; I mean that this episode seems to me not quite to reach your usual pitch of intensity'.[103] Pound was also uncertain about this chapter, candidly telling Joyce that it was 'too long', that he had had enough of Bloom ('Bloom has been disproportionately on'…'Where in hell is Stephen Tellemachus? all the bloody mackintosh while'), and his *'obsessions* arseor-ial'. He had particular reservations about the opening section and the leitmotific non sequiturs of what is conventionally thought of as the chapter's 'overture' which needed, in Pound's view, 'a few signposts' which would 'clarify' and 'even improve the 1st. page'. He thought such stylistic innovation and excess would 'bitch' the American market 'which had begun to take "Portrait" seriously' and instructed Joyce to relay 'relentings' (or revisions) to the chapter direct to the offices of the *Little Review*.[104]

Joyce paid little heed to Pound's response, dismissing it as being 'based on grounds which are not legitimate'.[105] On the other hand, Weaver's reservations tipped him into a state of 'blank apathy' because he had finally established that she was the

[100] *LR*, June 1918, 54.   [101] *LR*, September 1919, 38.   [102] *LR*, January 1920, 30.
[103] Weaver to J, 6 July 1919, Firth (ed.), 'Harriet Weaver's Letters to James Joyce', 182.
[104] Pound to J, 10 June 1919, *EP-JJ*, 158, 159.   [105] J to Weaver, 20 July 1919, *L* I, 129.

source of several large financial donations, including the very considerable sum of £5,000, given in May 1919.[106] To discover her subsequent disapproval of 'Sirens' was thus particularly difficult, a point made evident in a letter to her from Joyce, which was only partially published in the first volume of Joyce's correspondence:

> *I have felt during these last days of waiting an added sense of perplexity due to the fact that at the moment when I have the very great pleasure of knowing that it was you who have aided and are aiding me so munificently* you write me that the last episode sent seems to you to show a weakening or diffusion of some sort. Since the receipt of your letter I have read this chapter again several times. It took me five months to write it and always when I have finished an episode my mind lapses into a state of blank apathy out of which it seems that neither I nor the wretched book will ever more emerge.... I must ask you to add to the great favours which you have given me also that of long suffering. If the Sirens have been found so unsatisfactory I have little hope that the Cyclops or later the Circe episode will be approved of... I confess that it is an extremely tiresome book but it is the only book which I am able to write at present.... *During these last two years when I have received your gifts I have always had the foreboding (now proved false) that each episode of the book as it advanced would alienate gradually the sympathy of the person who was helping me.*[107]

From a psychological perspective, this letter treads several fine lines, managing, as it does, to express 'perplexity', gratitude for 'aiding me so munificently', disappointment ('blank apathy'), and frustration ('wretched book'). Such a wide range of emotions could hardly be sincere or lasting, and it is testament to a deep and cussed resilience on Joyce's part that he put all reservations to one side, continued with his writing, and made no immediate changes to the serial text of 'Sirens', even if it had (in fact) temporarily alienated Weaver's sympathies.

In terms of content and form, the *Little Review* version of 'Sirens', split into the issues of August 1919 and September 1919, is strikingly similar to that of the 1922 text. An earlier draft shows that Joyce was not sure how to include Bloom in the Ormond, but this problem was settled by the moment of serialization.[108] Serial readers had been prepared for narrative disjunction by the final pages of chapter 9 ('Scylla and Charybdis') and the multiple and apparently disconnected sections of chapter 10 ('Wandering Rocks'), but they had not had the warning—and hermeneutic jolt—served by the headings of chapter 7 ('Aeolus'), not added, as noted, until 1921. In some respects, therefore, the idea that the work might depart from a narrative norm had yet to be fully established, making the challenge thrown

---

[106] Weaver to J, 6 July 1919 in Firth (ed.), 'Harriet Weaver's Letters to James Joyce', 182.

[107] J to Weaver, 20 July 1919, *L* I, 128, 129; additional text in italic is in BL Add Ms 57345, and is published in *SL*, 240. Weaver (1876–1961) was alive when the first volume of Joyce's correspondence was prepared for publication (in 1957) and did not wish to have her identity as Joyce's patron made public.

[108] See Daniel Ferrer, 'What Song the Sirens Sang...Is No Longer Beyond All Conjecture: A Preliminary Description of the New "Proteus" and "Sirens"', *James Joyce Quarterly*, 39:1 (Fall 2001), 53–68. Ferrer is discussing NLI MS 7B. Noting the absence of Bloom from the preliminary draft, he suggests that Joyce might have 'had in mind something like the present structure of "Nausicaa": a simple cinematographic shot-reverse-shot, with the second part of the episode given over entirely to Bloom' (60).

up by the non sequiturs of the opening section all the more considerable (and the consternation of Weaver and Pound more understandable). What exactly could serial readers make of sentences such as 'Imperthnthn thnthnthn', 'Trilling, trilling: Idolores', 'Jingle jingle jaunted jingling', 'Will lift your tschink with tschunk', and 'Rrrpr. Kraa. Krandl'?[109]

The Linati schema characterizes the ear as the organ of this chapter and 'fuga per canonem' as its 'technic'.[110] For immediate purposes, it is perhaps more useful to understand that the interior action takes place within three different rooms of the Ormond Hotel (the bar, where drinks are served by Miss Lydia Douce and Miss Mina Kennedy; the 'saloon', where the singsong involving Simon Dedalus, Ben Dollard, and Fr Cowley occurs; and the 'diningroom', where Bloom dines with Richie Goulding, and writes his letter to Martha).[111] The hotel, located on the North side of the Liffey, was at 8 and 9 Upper Ormond Quay; and the exterior action of the chapter maps Bloom and Boylan en route to the hotel, and then Boylan's journey by hackney car to 7 Eccles Street for his assignation with Molly. The asterisks between the multiple sections in chapter 10 ('Wandering Rocks') usefully signal a change in narrative focus, and serve the function of readerly orientation. The interpolations—such as the 'skiff' which runs down the Liffey 'under the loopline bridge' at the moment when Katey and Boody Dedalus discuss 'peasoup' and 'Our father, who art not in heaven'—are not difficult to follow either, because they are short and occur frequently, and thus gradually (and incrementally) direct readers to see that the narration is describing multiple moments of action occurring more or less simultaneously.[112]

Joyce's interest in simultaneity and coincidence continues in chapter 11—in the narration of events within the three rooms at the Ormond, and the interpolations which track what is happening on the quays and en route to Eccles Street—but the narration does not explicitly foreground the many changes in focus and scene. Nor can a reader be oriented by the implicit instruction carried in the asterisks of chapter 10. Pound complained that the chapter is 'so all bloodily fricasseed!'—an observation which certainly seems justified on a first reading.[113] Because the chapter makes extensive use of lexical innovation, inference, indirect and unfinished narrative action, and leitmotif, the coherence of event only becomes clear on sustained re-reading. The chapter's multifocal nature is absolutely deliberate, of course, because Joyce is interested in creating a stylistically innovative total picture, a picture which depicts the two barmaids (Dublin's version of Homer's 'Sirens'), the camaraderie and musical culture of the Ormond, Boylan's position in that world, Bloom's distance from it, and the pain which Bloom experiences in knowing that the affair

[109] *LR*, August 1919, 41, 42.
[110] Details of Linati schema from Ellmann, *Ulysses on the Liffey*, 183–7. Much has been written about the significance of Joyce describing this chapter as a 'fuga per canonem'. The NLI's 'coverless copybook' (NLI MS 7B) casts considerable light on this issue: see Susan Brown, 'The Mystery of the Fuga Per Canonem Solved', *Genetic Joyce Studies*, 7 (Spring 2007), www.geneticjoycestudies.org.
[111] For a very useful account of the chapter's micro-topography and a conjectural floorplan of the hotel as Joyce imagines it, see Harald Beck, 'Joyce's Ormond Hotel', www.jjonline.org.
[112] *LR*, June 1919, 41.
[113] Pound to J, 10 June 1919, *EP-JJ*, 159.

between Molly and 'the worst man in Dublin' (*U*1922, 89) is about to happen ('I feel so sad today. La ree. So lonely', *U*1922, 268).

The serialized text runs to approximately 11,540 words, as noted in Chapter 3, and only increased by about 793 words in 1922, a percentage increase of 6.8 per cent, or thereabouts.[114] The pattern of revision is of small adjustments—added words and phrases inserted throughout the whole, but nothing major or extensive, such as a new paragraph, or extensive rewriting within a paragraph. One of the notable patterns in rewriting is that of *type 4*, enhancing stylistic complication. This can be observed, for example, in the revision of paragraph openings, where the simple form of Bloom or Bloom's is altered: '*Bloom* went by Moulang's pipes' becomes '**Bloowho** went by Moulang's pipes'; '*Bloom's* dark eye read Aaron Figatner's name' becomes '**Bloowhose** dark eye read Aaron Figatner's name'; and 'Winsomely she smiled on *Bloom*' becomes 'Winsomely she on **Bloohimwhom** smiled'.[115] Bloom's name, as it appeared in the serial instance of each example, directs readers to understand the narrative action. In revision, Joyce has chosen to disrupt that specificity by creating neologisms which fuse a foreshortened version of Bloom's name with a relative pronoun ('Bloowho', 'Bloowhose', 'Bloohimwhom'). Perhaps momentarily confusing, these new words—examples of lexical creativity—are part of the text's strategy of 'defamiliarisation', a strategy which 'forces on the reader a fresh conceptualisation of the ordinary', as Katie Wales has argued.[116] There are numerous examples of Joyce playing with names, and two other instances of names becoming more complicated in revision are worth citing here: '*Leopold Bloom* with letter for Mady, naughty Henry' becomes '**Up the quay went Lionelleopold,** naughty Henry with letter for Mady' and 'Sparkling bronze azure eyed *Blazes*' skyblue bow and eyes' becomes 'Sparkling bronze azure eyed **Blazure's** skyblue bow and eyes'.[117] Joyce's interest in noting and playing with names runs throughout the work, and is particularly evident in chapter 9 ('Scylla and Charybdis'), with 'littlejohn Eglinton', 'Mageeglinjohn', 'John Eclecticon', and 'Mr Secondbest Best' (*U*1922, 186, 200, 205, 195). This trend is superabundant in chapter 11, which exploits the lexical potentiality of Boylan ('Boylan with impatience'), Blazes ('Come on to blazes, said Blazes Boylan, going'), Lydia Douce ('Lidlydiawell', *U*1922, 266), and Mina Kennedy ('minagold', *U*1922, 277), and unites the listeners in the saloon by reducing them to one-syllable versions of their names ('Lid, De, Cow, Ker, Doll' instead of Lidwell, Dedalus, Cowley, Kernan, Dollard, *U*1922, 278).[118]

Some of the new stylistic flourishes added to the text are intensely lyrical, and reflect Bloom's isolation. For example, as he listens to Simon Dedalus perform 'M'appari' from von Flotow's aptly named 'Martha', Bloom's strain of thought

[114] See above, p. 139.

[115] *LR*, August 1919, 43; cf. *U*1922, 247; *LR*, August 1919, 44; *U*1922, 249; *LR*, August 1919, 49; cf. *U*1922, 253, italics mine.

[116] Katie Wales, *The Language of James Joyce* (London: Macmillan, 1992), 113.

[117] *LR*, August 1919, 43, 44, 49; *LR*, September 1919, 53; cf. *U*1922, 247, 249, 253 276.

[118] Boylan's surname is repeated twenty-six times within the chapter, and his association with impatience is reiterated four times (*U*1922, 252, 256, 259, 265).

becomes charged with eroticism: 'warm jamjam lickitup secretness' and 'The joy the feel the warm the' (*U1922*, 263). A sentence added to this paragraph—**'Tipping her tepping her tapping her topping her'**—appears to mix thoughts of Bloom, Molly, and Boylan, and shows how dramatically meaning alters by the change of just one vowel. Tipping in music is 'the action of striking the tongue against the palate so as to produce a staccato effect in playing certain wind-instruments' (similar to tonguing); tepping is Joyce's invention; tapping and topping carry sexual subtexts.[119] The only vowel sound omitted from the sentence is the 'u' which produces 'tup', slang for copulation, associated with sheep (as in *Othello*, 'An old blacke Ram is tupping your white Ewe'), a word which was included within this passage in the serial text (and in the opening section: 'Full tup. Full throb').[120] The addition of the new phrase, a kind of reference to the 'A. E. I. O. U.' pattern of chapter 9 (*U1922*, 182), is an elaboration from 'tup', and enhances the stylistic impact of the paragraph, by drawing further attention to its artistry:

> Bloom. Flood of warm jimjam lickitup secretness flowed to flow in music out, in desire, dark to lick flow, invading. **Tipping her tepping her tapping her topping her.** Tup. Pores to dilate dilating. Tup. The joy the feel the warm the. Tup. To pour o'er sluices pouring gushes. Flood, gush, flow, joygush, tupthrop. Now! Language of love. (*U1922*, 263)

The chapter may be seen as a portrait of different types of sound and music, and 'tup' is the sound Bloom hears in his mind as he contemplates Boylan's arrival at Eccles Street.

A similar kind of revisionary impulse—involving the enhancement of stylistic effect—can be observed in Bloom's thoughts about Molly's hair. 'Hair uncombed' in the serial becomes '**Her wavyavyeavyheavyeavyevyevy** hair un comb:'d'.[121] Hair is one of the chapter's preoccupations: the colour of the barmaid's hair (bronze and gold) is reiterated on multiple occasions; Miss Kennedy is seen 'twining a loose hair behind an ear' (*U1922*, 247), and Bloom sees a poster of a 'swaying mermaid' with her hair 'streaming' (*U1922*, 253). Feminine pubic hair ('Maidenhair', *U1922*, 275) is also a preoccupation and one of the post-serial addition likens pubic hair to shreds of tobacco, in a revision which could be seen as exemplifying *type 3*, additions which align the work with the terms of the schema. 'He fingered shreds **of hair, her maidenhair, her mermaid's** into the bowl' (*U1922*, 251) describes Dedalus filling his pipe as he engages in flirtatious conversation with Miss Douce, and enhances the 'Sirens' theme of the chapter. Mermaid's was the name of a popular brand of tobacco—a point implied later in 'mermaid coolest whiff of all' (*U1922*, 277)—thus there is a submerged reference to a brand in this addition.[122] The introduction of 'maidenhair' is also an example of revision *type 5*—increasing sexual suggestiveness—an impulse which can be identified in several examples, including one of Miss Douce's responses to Dedalus which shifts from 'Yes, I don't think' to '**You must have been a doaty**', and a moment which involves Lenehan and Boylan at the

[119] OED.   [120] OED; *LR*, August 1919, 41.   [121] *LR*, August 1919, 61; *U1922*, 266.
[122] Gifford, *Ulysses Annotated*, 296. GoogleImages has illustrations of the brand dating from the period.

bar.[123] Lenehan watches Douce reaching 'high to take a flagon, stretching her satin arm, her bust. —O! O! jerked Lenehan, gasping at each stretch. O!'.[124] In revision, the first of these phrases becomes: 'Miss Douce reached high to take a flagon, stretching her satin arm, her bust, **that all but burst, so high**' (*U*1922, 254).

An element of Hibernian intensification (*type 7*) can be identified in one of the revisions of Dedalus's speech. The example involves the introduction of some translated Irish, 'machree' being 'mo chroí' (my heart), and a colloquial phrase. 'He is, said Mr. Dedalus, clapping Ben's fat back shoulderblade. He has a lot of a adipose dispose tissue concealed about his person' becomes:

> —**Ben machree**, said Mr Dedalus, clapping Ben's fat back shoulderblade. **Fit as a fiddle only** he has a lot of adipose tissue concealed about his person.[125]

Bloom obviously has a strong sense of how Simon Dedalus speaks. From his vantage point in the dining room, he cannot see that it is Dedalus singing 'M'appari', but identifies him from the tone of his voice, in a passage of interior monologue which introduces 'brogue' in the sense of speech, and a number of other post-serial embellishments:

> Glorious tone he has still. **Cork air softer also their brogue.** Silly man! Could have made oceans of money. **Singing wrong words.** Wore out his wife: now sings. But hard to tell. Only the two themselves. If he doesn't break down. **Keep a trot for the avenue. His hands and feet sing too.** Drink. Nerves overstrung. Must be abstemious to sing. **Jenny Lind soup: stock, sage, raw eggs, half pint of cream. For creamy dreamy.** (*U*1922, 263)

The potentiality of brogue had obvious appeal for Joyce; the word occurs nine times throughout *Ulysses* as a whole, perhaps most memorably (and ironically) in the phrase 'Ignorant as a kish of brogues' (*U*1922, 167) in Bloom's reflection on Micky Hanlon, a fishmonger from Dublin's Moore Street.[126] 'Keep a trot for the avenue', i.e. keep the horse going for the sake of show, is another example of a colloquial phrase added post-serially, and the recipe for Jenny Lind soup, named in honour of Lind (1820–87), a popular soprano from Sweden, was included in Beeton's *Book of Household Management* (1861), as Gifford notes.[127] The additions to this paragraph can be seen as exemplifying *type 2*, deepening the stream of consciousness, and *type 1*, deepening the specificities of the work.

It would certainly be possible to go on cataloguing interesting post-serial revisions to 'Sirens', and to show how selected examples reveal particular trends in Ulyssean revision. But there are deeper questions about patterns of minimal revision. Do such revisions make a *significant* difference to the reading of the two chapters selected for case study? In the case of chapter 2 ('Nestor'), the changes in

---

[123] *LR*, August 1919, 46; *U*1922, 250.   [124] *LR*, August 1919, 50.
[125] *LR*, September 1919, 52; *U*1922, 275. Joyce did not write the word 'dispose'; this is another instance of corruption in the serial text.
[126] For brogue in *Ulysses* see *U*1922, 31, 167, 191, 263, 284, 397, 426, 470, 500, 702. Kish is an anglicized form of cis, Irish for basket.
[127] Gifford, *Ulysses Annotated*, 303.

Deasy's characterization are small but highly significant: Dedalus's response to his Unionism is sharper and more assured in 1922, and Deasy's grip on the significance of his 'rebel blood' is weakened, knowingly, in order to make the 'old fogey' look confused about the specificities of his own cultural identity. These revisions reflect the considerably stronger position of Irish nationalism which prevailed in the closing months of 1921, when Joyce was finishing the book, than was the case in April 1918, when this chapter was serialized. The general election of December 1918 returned seventy-three seats for Sinn Féin, six for the Irish Parliamentary Party, and just twenty-six for the Unionists. The War of Independence, which ensued in 1919, ended with a truce between the IRA and the British army in July 1921. Unionism continued to be a considerable force within the island of Ireland, but it had not succeeded in stopping the first meeting of Dáil Eireann in April 1919. Negotiations which led to the creation of Northern Ireland and the Irish Free State in January 1922 began in October 1921.[128] Joyce may have been in Paris, but followed these momentous developments with interest. His revision of Deasy—completed by September 1921—is a microcosm which reflects changing political structures and changing sensibilities.[129] In the case of chapter 11 ('Sirens'), the post-serial revisions are moving, lyrical, and interesting in various ways, but their interest is more local and only impacts a close reading of the chapter *in situ*, rather than the shape of the work as a whole.

MACRO REVISION: THE CASE OF 'LOTUS-EATERS' AND 'NAUSICAA'

In serial form, chapter 5 ('Lotus-Eaters'), published in July 1918, was the second shortest chapter of all (after chapter 2, 'Nestor'), at approximately 4,541 words, as noted.[130] Its extensive post-serial revision—which saw the text expand by approximately 1,865 words—may be seen as part of a drive to even out the lengths of the early Bloom chapters a little by giving readers a deeper portrait of the community in which Bloom lives, a deeper sense of his imaginative world, and a deeper sense of his characteristic thought processes. With the exception of post-serial revision *type 7*—Hibernian intensification—all of the types of Ulyssean revision can be identified in the rewriting of this chapter. The omission of Hibernian intensification is not a particularly surprising find as the chapter does not contain a great deal of speech: there are only three dialogues, those being the ones that involve Bloom talking to M'Coy (*U*1922, 70–3), the chemist (*U*1922, 81), and Bantam Lyons (*U*1922, 82). In linguistic terms, Bloom's speech patterns and thought processes are not particularly marked examples of Hiberno-English, and thus this type of revision does not pertain to Bloom. Joyce could have chosen to revise M'Coy but he must have been happy with the version of M'Coy he had achieved, and the

---

[128] Dates and figures from the chronology in R. F. Foster, *Modern Ireland, 1600–1972* (London: Penguin, 1988), 613, 614.
[129] *CSE* III 1914.   [130] See above, p. 139.

brilliant way in which M'Coy delays Bloom by telling the inconsequential story of how he heard about Dignam:

> —I was with Bob Doran, he's on one of his periodical bends, and what do you call him Bantam Lyons. Just down there in Conway's we were....
>
> —And he said: *Sad thing about our poor friend Paddy! What Paddy?* I said. *Poor little Paddy Dignam*, he said....
>
> —*Why?* I said. *What's wrong with him?* I said....
>
> —*What's wrong with him?* he said. *He's dead*, he said. And, faith he filled up. *Is it Paddy Dignam?* I said. I couldn't believe it when I heard it. I was with him no later than Friday last or Thursday was it in the Arch. *Yes*, he said. *He's gone. He died on Monday, poor fellow.*[131]

By turning the 'I said' tag into the more common Dublin inversion of 'says I', Joyce could have opted to revise these speeches. But 'says I', which can sound staged, is reserved for the narrator of chapter 12 ('Cyclops', in phrases like 'Hoho begob, says I to myself, says I', *U*1922, 306) where it is a defining narrative affectation. Joyce has not opted to use the form here because it would over-elaborate the text: his inner ear has calculated that this portrait is good enough.

Instead, his revisionary impulse has set to work on enhancing the sexualized nature of Bloom's thought processes, a conspicuous feature in the rewriting of this chapter. As M'Coy speaks, Bloom stares at a well-off man and woman about to mount an 'outsider' (a two-wheeled carriage for a single horse, in which the passengers faced to the side, outward over the wheels); the couple are on the opposite side of Westland Row, outside the Grosvenor Hotel (*U*1922, 70). Bloom is keen to catch a glimpse of her 'silk flash rich stockings' as she climbs up ('Watch! Watch!') but does not succeed in this because a tram passes and obscures his view ('Always happening like that. The very moment', *U*1922, 71). In revision, his thoughts about this woman, with her 'stylish kind of coat' and 'careless stand', are embellished. She reminds him of '**that haughty creature at the polo match**'; if only he could '**possess her once**' that would '**take the starch out of her**' (*U*1922, 71). As Bloom contemplates the woman's boots, he notices that she appreciates his gaze:

> High brown boots with laces dangling. Wellturned foot. What is he fostering over that change for? **Sees me looking. Eye out for other fellow always. Good fallback. Two strings to her bow.** (*U*1922, 71)

Bloom is ultimately frustrated that he runs into M'Coy; the letter from Martha is half open in his pocket, and he wants to 'get rid of him quickly' (*U*1922, 70). His reservations about M'Coy, expressed in the serial text ('Wonder is he pimping after me?'), become more explicit in the 1922 text ('**Think he's that way inclined a bit. Against my grain somehow**').[132]

Bloom had wanted to walk behind the 'nextdoor' servant girl on his return from Dlugacz's ('behind her moving hams. **Pleasant to see first thing in the morning**' *U*1922, 57). Though he had not succeeded in actually trailing her, this moment is

---

[131] *LR*, July 1918, 39, 40. Italics in the original.   [132] *LR*, July 1918, 41; cf. *U*1922, 73.

imagined again in an addition to chapter 5: '**How did she walk with her sausages? Like that something**' (*U*1922, 69). Similarly, after the disappointment of not seeing the woman mounting the outsider, Bloom thinks back on another moment of frustrated voyeurism, also introduced post-serially:

> Always happening like that. The very moment. **Girl in Eustace street hallway Monday was it settling her garter. Her friend covering the display of.** *Esprit de corps.* **Well, what are you gaping at?** (*U*1922, 71)

One of the points of comedy in this chapter is Bloom's response to the rituals of Catholicism. The scene in All Hallows Church (*U*1922, 77–80) is revised quite extensively. In the serial text, Bloom thinks twice about how he and Martha could meet 'one Sunday after mass'.[133] In the 1922 text this becomes 'one Sunday after **the rosary**'. The rosary was more likely to be said later in the day and thus affords a better opportunity for a clandestine meeting, in a fantasy which is developed:

> Meet one Sunday after **the rosary.** Do not deny my request. **Turn up with a veil and black bag. Dusk and the light behind her.** She might be here with a ribbon round her neck and do the other thing all the same on the sly. (*U*1922, 78)

Bloom seems to be thinking that he could write to Martha, proposing a plan that they meet and asking her to wear a veil and carry a black bag, so that he can recognize her, but it is easy to misread this; the confusion, which hints at Bloom's interest in cross-dressing—*he* might be the one wearing the 'black veil'—is a deliberate anticipation of chapter 15 ('Circe').

In the scene within the church, the serial text describes the priest ministering communion: 'Women knelt in the benches with crimson halters round their necks, heads bowed. A batch knelt at the altar rails. The priest went along by them, murmuring, holding the thing in his hands'.[134] The 1922 text embellishes this moment by including Bloom's thoughts about the fact that not many people are in the church:

> Something going on: some sodality. **Pity so empty. Nice discreet place to be next some girl. Who is my neighbour? Jammed by the hour to slow music. That woman at midnight mass. Seventh heaven.** (*U*1922, 77)

Joyce is keen to promote the view that Catholicism gives individuals the opportunity to engage in fantasy and illicit behaviour, and is particularly drawn to thinking about penance, punishment, and what happens in a confession box. Revisions to the following moment of Bloom's interior monologue, which occurs as mass is ending, are emblematic in this regard. He is thinking about the Catholic church:

> Wonderful organisation certainly, goes like clockwork. **Confession. Everyone wants to. Then I will tell you all. Penance. Punish me, please. Great weapon in their hands. More than doctor or solicitor. Woman dying to. And I schschschschsch. And did you chachachachacha? And why did you? Look down at her ring to find an excuse.**

---

[133] *LR*, July 1918, 43, 45.   [134] *LR*, July 1918, 44–5.

Whispering gallery walls have ears. Husband learn to his surprise. God's little joke. Then out she comes. Repentance skindeep. Lovely shame. Pray at an altar. Hail Mary and Holy Mary. Flowers, incense, candles melting. Hide her blushes. Salvation army blatant imitation. Reformed prostitute will address the meeting. How I found the Lord. Squareheaded chaps those must be in Rome: they work the whole show.

(*U*1922, 79–80)

The serial version introduces just one of the important ideas: the power of the Catholic church as an institution. The 1922 text is richer and funnier, and makes the strain of Bloom's thinking much more detailed, overt, and sexualized.[135] What do people say in confession boxes? Do they talk about sexual indiscretions in an explicit way? Do priests use the cover of the confession box to ask prurient questions? Bloom knows little about Catholicism, but is a careful observer of what he sees, and has a keen sense of denominational difference. Joyce exploits these traits in multiple ways, and for comic effect. He picks out details which are suggestive, such as the sinner's desire for punishment ('Punish me, please'), the uplifting and narcotic effect of 'flowers, incense, candles melting', and the comfort derived from being in a state of 'lovely shame'. Bloom's stray thought of a 'reformed prostitute' addressing a Salvation army meeting is also titivating and suggestive.

In addition to making the text more sexually suggestive and overt, and including a deeper portrait of Bloom's impressions of Catholicism, the 1922 version of chapter 5 includes details which document social deprivation, especially as it relates to children. As suggested in Chapter 3, this is particularly noticeable in the opening paragraph, which includes a description of two children from Brady's cottages, a street he passes, in a highly effective mix of first- and third-person narration:[136]

He turned from the morning noises of the quayside and walked through Lime street. By Brady's cottages a boy for the skins lolled, his bucket of offal linked, smoking a chewed fagbutt. A smaller girl with scars of eczema on her forehead eyed him, listlessly holding her battered caskhoop. Tell him if he smokes he won't grow. O let him! His life isn't such a bed of roses! Waiting outside pubs to bring da home. Come home to ma, da. Slack hour : won't be many there.   (*U*1922, 68)

Much of *Ulysses* is concerned with interiority, the world of the mind, and emotions. Additions of this kind ensure that Joyce's naturalism records the public as well as the private sphere. There is another example of a child being written in later in chapter 5, near the 'ruins and tenements' in Cumberland street, where Bloom goes to read his letter from Martha:

No-one. Meade's timberyard. Piled balks. Ruins and tenements. With careful tread he passed over a hopscotch court with its forgotten pickeystone. Not a sinner. Near the timberyard a squatted child at marbles, alone, shooting the taw with a cunnythumb.   (*U*1922, 74)

---

[135] This passage is also discussed by Groden. See *Ulysses in Progress*, 28–9.
[136] See above, p. 135.

A similar kind of pattern—the post-serial addition of details which suggest Dublin's squalor—can be perceived in chapter 6 ('Hades'). Joyce adds the details of '**open drains and mounds of rippedup roadway before the tenement houses**' (*U*1922, 85) and he describes how the Royal Canal has '**beds of weeds**', '**slime, mudchoked bottles**', and '**carrion dogs**' (*U*1922, 96). He also introduces two extra tramps to the 1922 version of chapter 6: one who sits on '**the curbstone before Jimmy Geary's**' and empties '**the dirt and stones out of his huge dustbrown yawning boot**' (*U*1922, 96), and another, a talented eccentric, who plays the street organ as the Dignam cortège passes:

> As they turned into Berkeley street a streetorgan near the Basin sent over and after them a rollicking rattling song of the halls. Has anybody here seen Kelly? Kay ee double ell wy. Dead March from *Saul*. He's as bad as old Antonio. He left me on my ownio. Pirouette! (*U*1922, 94)

It is clear from the pattern of these additions—which glimpse tramps, slums, tenements, and deprived children who are hanging around aimlessly—that Joyce has rewritten the text with a view to giving a more encyclopaedic and naturalistic portrayal of the city, one which insists on representing the social realities faced by Dublin's underclass.

Revision *type 3*, the addition of material suggested by the terms of the schemata, can also be noted in the rewriting of chapter 5 ('Lotus-Eaters'). The point of Homeric origin is the moment in book 9 of *The Odyssey* when Odysseus visits the land of the Lotus-eaters, where those of his crew who ate the lotus 'lost all desire to send a message back.../their only wish to linger there with the Lotus-eaters,/...all memory of the journey home/dissolved forever'.[137] The Gilbert schema characterizes the 'cab-horses, communicants and soldiers' as Lotus-eaters, and the Linati schema lists the chapter's symbols as 'host, penis in bath, foam, flower, drugs, castration and oats'.[138] If the chapter is read with these terms in mind and as one of 'forgetfulness and drugged lethargy', as Groden avers, then it is certainly possibly to see those elements being enhanced in rewriting: this revisionary impulse is evident, for example, in the paragraph describing the children of Brady's cottages: the boy is '**lolling**' while the girl eyes him '**listlessly**' (*U*1922, 68).[139] The word 'lethargy'—a leitmotif in the chapter—is inserted at the moment of the text in which Bloom contemplates the chemist at Sweny's, in a passage of stream of consciousness writing which more than doubled in length post-serialization.[140] The insertion of '**Drugs age you after mental excitement. Lethargy then. Why?**' (*U*1922, 81) is an example of the revised text specifically using a word ('drugs') included in the Linati schema. '**Lethargy**' is also inserted into the paragraph in which Bloom thinks about 'Ceylon brands'; in fact the whole idea of substances, and the act of

---

[137] Homer, *The Odyssey*, translated by Robert Fagles (London: Penguin, 1996), 214.
[138] Details of Linati and Gilbert schema from Ellmann, *Ulysses on the Liffey*, 183–7.
[139] Groden, *Ulysses in Progress*, 28.
[140] *LR*, July 1918, 47; *U*1922, 81; cf. *CSE*I 168.18–32.

communion, having a lethargizing or stupefying effect is enhanced in post-serial revision, in words and phrases like '**Cigar has a cooling effect. Narcotic**', '**Good idea the Latin. Stupefies them first**', and '**Chloroform. Overdose of laudanum**'.[141] These additions may be read as instances of Joyce systematically revising the text in a way which reflects the terms and preoccupations of the schema. 'Flower', Bloom's epistolary name, is included in the serial text, and so is the 'yellow flower with flattened petals' which Martha sends.[142] But numerous additional references to flowers and botany are inserted post-serially, including: '**His life isn't such a bed of roses**', '**flowery meads**', '**Flowers of idleness**', '**Hothouse in Botanic gardens**', '**Waterlilies**', '**Walk on roseleaves**', and '**No roses without thorns**'.[143]

It is also notable that flower references are increased in the lengthy paragraph in which Bloom thinks about Martha's letter:

> He tore the flower gravely from its pinhold **smelt its almost no smell** and placed it in his heart pocket. **Language of flowers. They like it because no-one can hear. Or a poison bouquet to strike him down.** Then, walking slowly forward, he read the letter again, murmuring here and there a word. **Angry tulips with you darling manflower punish your cactus if you don't please poor forgetmenot how I long violets to dear roses when we soon anemone meet all naughty nightstalk wife Martha's perfume.** Having read it all he took it from the newspaper and put it back in his sidepocket.
>
> (*U*1922, 75)

The insertions—which all relate to the idea of flowers—complicate the narrative form: Joyce has taken what was a description of action, written in the third person, and intercut first-person narration, which is much more stylized, imaginative, and harder to follow. The 'angry tulips' sentence represents Bloom trying to imagine Martha's thought processes as he rereads the letter: the sentence represents the reading by actually reiterating several words contained in the letter, which is, of course, included earlier in the text: '*angry*' as in 'I am awfully angry with you'; *darling* and *naughty* as in 'Goodbye now, naughty darling'; *punish* as in 'I do wish I could punish you for that'; *please* as in 'Please tell me what is the real meaning of that word'; *poor* as in 'poor little naughty boy' and 'poor me'; *long* and *meet* as in 'O how I long to meet you'; *wife* and *perfume* as in 'tell me what kind of perfume does your wife use' (*U*1922, 74, 75). The additions here exemplify four different types of revisionary impulse simultaneously: *type 2*, deepening the stream of consciousness; *type 3*, schematic addition; *type 4*, stylistic complication; and *type 5*, making the work more sexually suggestive or explicit (in the addition of words such as 'punish', 'naughty', and 'nightstalk').

Another type of revision not yet noted in respect of the rewriting of chapter 5 is that of *type 6*, embellishing micro-narratives, an impulse that can be identified in several examples, including the scene involving M'Coy. The mention of the drowning case is not included in the serial text:

---

[141] *U*1922, 75, 77, 81.   [142] *LR*, July 1918, 38, 42.   [143] *U*1922, 68, 69, 75.

—Tell you what, M'Coy said. You might put down my name at the funeral, will you? I'd like to go but I mightn't be able, you see. **There's a drowning case at Sandycove may turn up and then the coroner and myself would have to go down if the body is found.** You just shove in my name if I'm not there, will you? (*U*1922, 72)[144]

Given so much rewriting, and extensive evidence of the work conforming, roughly, to the rough theory of seven types of post-serial Ulyssean revision, the more interesting argument to pursue here is either that of a counter-argument—pointing to a body of revisions which does not conform—or a bigger picture, which stands back from the detail and looks at the more global impact of the revisions to this chapter. The addition of detail which insists on the squalor of Dublin in 1904—the pathos and stylistic achievement of a child playing with a '**battered caskhoop**' and uttering a sentence like '**Come home to ma, da**' (*U*1922, 68)—is perhaps the most singular element of post-serial revision which can be identified in this chapter, and only conforms to the seven-types argument through the accommodation of *type 1*, enhancing the specificities of the work (in this case enhancing naturalistic specificities).

The evidence of rewriting contradicts the stance Joyce took in the *Dubliners* dispute of 1906, when he resolutely told Grant Richards that 'I cannot alter what I have written'.[145] Even allowing for the fact that Joyce made that statement in the context of a dispute which turned on Richards wishing to change the text by deleting the word 'bloody', the strength of feeling and emphasis in Joyce's response is notable, and seems to suggest the arrival at an aesthetic *credo*:

> I have written it for the most part in a style of scrupulous meanness and with the conviction that he is a very bold man who dares to alter in the presentment, still more to deform, whatever he has seen and heard. I cannot do any more than this. I cannot alter what I have written.[146]

A little more than a decade later, the continuing tribulation of his work being rewritten for him hardened Joyce's determination to have things just so, a point which comes across in a letter to Forrest Reid, written after chapter 4 ('Calypso') had been 'mutilated' in print: 'I shall see that the few passages excised are restored if it costs me another ten years'.[147] But Joyce did not simply wish to restore the 'mutilated' parts of *Ulysses*, he wanted to rewrite, and the evidence of the two versions of chapter 5 points to significant aesthetic reshaping. The serial version is an achieved and careful portrait, which is split between third-person narration, moments of dialogue, and Bloom's interior monologue. In revision, the passages of interior monologue are expanded, often extensively, and the rhythm of the text

---

[144] Other micro-narratives which are embellished include the mention of Molly's father (Tweedy) who is identified as a mason: '**A mason, yes**'; the story of M'Coy and the valise ('**Bob Cowley lent his for the Wicklow regatta**', etc.); and the mention of Bloom's schooling ('**that old dame's school**') (*U*1922, 70, 73, 74).

[145] J to Grant Richards, 5 May 1906, *L* II, 134.

[146] J to Grant Richards, 5 May 1906, *L* II, 134.

[147] J to Forrest Reid, 1 August 1918, *L* I, 117.

alters as the monologues become more complicated and time consuming to decode, a point that can be seen if one compares the before and after states of the paragraph documenting Bloom's response to Martha's letter:

He tore the flower gravely from its pinhold and placed it in his heart pocket. Then, walking slowly forward, he read the letter again, murmuring here and there a word. Having read it all he took it from the newspaper and put it back in his sidepocket.[148]	He tore the flower gravely from its pinhold smelt its almost no smell and placed it in his heart pocket. **Language of flowers. They like it because no-one can hear. Or a poison bouquet to strike him down.** Then, walking slowly forward, he read the letter again, murmuring here and there a word. **Angry tulips with you darling manflower punish your cactus if you don't please poor forgetmenot how I long violets to dear roses when we soon anemone meet all naughty nightstalk wife Martha's perfume.** Having read it all he took it from the newspaper and put it back in his sidepocket. (*U*1922, 75)

The serial version has an immediacy, which partly comes from the fact that it is shorter and easier to follow. It also has a sensuousness and delicacy, in details like the 'heart pocket' and the word 'murmuring'. The 1922 text has a more complicated rhythm and pace, and requires a more intense intellectual and emotional commitment on the part of the reader. It is more involved in recording Bloom's psychological response to the letter from Martha, and there are non sequiturs which are difficult to decode. What is it that 'no-one can hear' and what is the significance of a 'poison bouquet'? The exact meaning and significance of the 'angry tulips' sentence is elusive.

It is possible to argue, in this instance, that the serial text is less modernist than the 1922 text. It is also possible to argue that the 1922 text is working to distance the reader, an effect which can be noted in multiple other examples, and which has been described, in narratology, as 'distanciation'.[149] It would also obviously be possible to pursue an evaluative argument here. Can it be said that Joyce has always improved chapter 5 in every aspect of its revision? Or do some of the additions look like hastily written padding? Perhaps it is easiest to fudge this, by simply suggesting that the texts are incommensurate, each with their own points of value and interest. Sometimes Joyce improves the text; sometimes he seems to weaken it. Every example is different. Perhaps the truth is 'midway', like Stephen's literary argument about *Hamlet* (*U*1922, 204).

As he prepared the text for serialization, Joyce had not fully understood the extent to which stream of consciousness could be used as a method of characterization.

---

[148] *LR*, July 1918, 43.
[149] Monika Fludernik, 'Narrative and Its Development in *Ulysses*', *Journal of Narrative Technique*, 16 (1986), 15–40 (24).

Nor had he fully appreciated the extent to which he wanted to move his writing beyond naturalism and towards radical stylistic experiment. But by the time he came to prepare for publication in volume form—a point when his career as a writer was more assured because of the financial support of individuals like Weaver and Beach—the writing could be more stylistically experimental and more risky. He knew Beach would publish *Ulysses*, come what may. Thus Bloom's streams of consciousness became more overtly sexualized, more detailed, more difficult to follow, and more stylized.

Following *Dubliners* (1914) and *A Portrait of the Artist as a Young Man* (1916), the representation of Bloom and his community was a new creative departure for Joyce, a journey away from the Dublin he knew at absolute first hand, a journey away from fiction based on his own immediate cultural and biographical experiences. In the effort to establish that world, and to do so with conviction, Joyce had omitted to include much detail of Dublin's social deprivation. Revision gave him the opportunity to redress that omission—to alter what he had written—and to create a naturalistic style which is layered, contrapuntal, multivalent, a style which developed quite significantly from what Joyce himself described as the 'initial style', and a style with density and richness which could only be achieved through the incremental process of writing for serialization, reconsidering, and then rewriting for publication in volume form.

Chapter 13 ('Nausicaa') was published in three instalments in the *Little Review*: April 1920, May–June 1920, and July–August 1920. Within the serialization, it was the third lengthiest chapter of the work, at approximately 14,211 words (after chapter 12, 'Cyclops', 16,642 words and chapter 14, 'Oxen of the Sun', 19,320 words). Joyce added approximately 2,476 words post-serially, a percentage increase of 17.4 per cent.[150] In terms of structure, this chapter is in two distinct parts, split roughly 60/40, the first part (*U*1922, 331–51) being a stylized third-person narration which describes the evening scene on Sandymount strand and the thoughts and aspirations of Gerty McDowell. Much has been written about the style and significance of this section, including an argument by Andrew Gibson which suggests that Gerty is 'representative of Irish girlhood on the threshold of modern consciousness', and an argument by Katherine Mullin who suggests that the chapter 'argues for the belatedness and obsolescence of social purity's imagined "young person"'.[151] Joyce's own comments on the style of this first part are also useful. In correspondence with Budgen, sorely missed after Joyce's return to Trieste from Zurich in October 1919, Joyce characterized chapter 13 as being written in a 'specially new fizzing style':

Nausikaa is written in a namby-pamby jammy marmalady drawersy (alto là) style with effects of incense, Mariolatry, masturbation, stewed cockles, painter's palette, chitchat, circumlocutions, etc etc.[152]

---

[150] See above, p. 139.

[151] Andrew Gibson, *Joyce's Revenge: History, Politics and Aesthetics in Ulysses* (Oxford: Oxford University Press, 2002), 142; Katherine Mullin, *James Joyce, Sexuality and Social Purity* (Cambridge: Cambridge University Press, 2003), 144.

[152] J to Budgen, [December 1919]; J to Budgen, 3 January 1920, *SL*, 245, 246.

'Drawersy' only characterizes the first part, however. Virtually all of the second part (*U*1922, 351–65) consists of Bloom's interior monologue, recording his state of mind after orgasm, and his thoughts on the day as the evening draws in. In respect of style, this part recalls earlier chapters of the work, notably chapters 4, 5, 8, a few sections of chapter 10, and chapter 11. As in those earlier chapters, there are a few sentences of third-person narration, which open paragraphs and orient readers by setting the scene. Examples include: 'Mr Bloom watched as she limped away', 'Mr. Bloom with careful hand recomposed his wet shirt', 'A long lost candle wandered up the sky from Mirus bazaar in search of funds for Mercer's hospital and broke, drooping, and shed a cluster of violet but one white stars', and 'The clock on the mantelpiece in the priest's house cooed where Canon O'Hanlon and the reverend John Hughes S. J. were taking tea and sodabread and butter' (*U*1922, 351, 353, 361, 364).

Joyce made post-serial revisions to all of the different narrative elements of the chapter, including significant additions to the section which characterizes Gerty, significant additions to Bloom's interior monologue, and a few minimal adjustments to moments of third-person narration. In summary, the additions to the Gerty section include: adjustments to the style which enhance its clichéd nature; the addition of details which deepen her characterization through greater specificity (particularly through reference to the language of advertising); and the addition of detail which makes it clearer that she is aware of Bloom, and of the significance of what is happening. *Ulysses* as a whole gives a much deeper account of Bloom and his imaginative range, and thus his revisions cover a wider canvas. Joyce enhances the Bloom section by making the text more explicit (including more overt acknowledgement of Bloom's masturbation, and more detailed consideration of women's periods). Other additions to the Bloom section could be characterized as more detail about the shaping biographical facts of his life, more sadness, more lyricism, and more random ruminations on this and that (which are so typical of Bloom).

The narrative focus in the Gerty section of this chapter flips between describing what is happening on the beach with Gerty, her friends, and Bloom, and what is happening in the 'men's temperance retreat' which is taking place nearby at the Star of the Sea Church (this is the 'Mariolatry' and 'effects of incense' promised to Budgen). Joyce is keen to communicate a sense of the retreat which does not, on this occasion, involve a mass, but is instead a three-part event with a 'rosary, sermon and benediction of the Most Blessed Sacrament' (*U*1922, 338). The benediction involves placing the consecrated communion host in a monstrance, blessing it, and then allowing for its display and contemplation, accompanied by readings, prayers, the singing of traditional Latin hymns, and moments of silent prayer. Joyce is keen for readers to gain a specific sense of the retreat, and the particular significance of its emphasis on temperance for Gerty:

> How sad to poor Gerty's ears! Had her father only avoided the clutches of the demon drink, **by taking the pledge or those powders the drink habit cured in Pearson's Weekly**, she might now be rolling in her carriage, second to none.   (*U*1922, 338)

This is an example of Joyce deepening Gerty's characterization and communicating a deeper sense of the 'dull **aching void** in her heart' (*U*1922, 334), by introducing the language of advertising, which he has located in a specific bibliographical source. As Gifford notes, *Pearson's Weekly* was a London penny magazine which advertised patent medicines including promised cures for alcoholism.[153] Gerty's consciousness and fashion sensibility is shaped by what she has read in magazines, an impression which Joyce enhances in revision:

> Gerty was dressed simply but with **the** instinctive taste **of a votary of Dame Fashion** for she felt that there was just a might that he might be out. A neat blouse of electric blue, selftinted by dolly dyes **(because it was expected in the Lady's Pictorial that electric blue would be worn)**, with a smart vee opening **down to the division** and kerchief pocket[.] (*U*1922, 335)

Once again, this addition has a specific bibliographical referent, the *Lady's Pictorial*, identified in Gifford as the 'leading ladies' paper': Joyce possibly made this addition after looking at copies in Paris. Another journal which Gerty reads is *The Princess's Novelettes*, which contained serialized stories or novels and advertising which has:

> advised her to try eyebrowleine which gave that haunting expression to the eyes, so becoming in leaders of fashion, and she had never regretted it. **Then there was blushing scientifically cured and how to be tall increase your height and you have a beautiful face but your nose?** That would suit Mrs Dignam because she had a button one. But Gerty's crowning glory was her wealth of **wonderful** hair. (*U*1922, 334)

'Blushing scientifically cured' is almost certainly an instance of submerged citation from a magazine of the period, and may be read as another case of the specific language of advertising being increased post-serially.

The circumstances and aspirations of Gerty's life are made clearer in the 1922 text. She may have been suffering from some sort feminine health issue. She is taking 'iron jelloids' which:

> had done her a world of good **much better than the Widow Welch's female pills** and she was much better of those discharges she used to get **and that tired feeling.** (*U*1922, 333)

She has a dream that she might become '**Mrs Reggy Wylie T. C. D.**' ('**It would be like heaven**') and:

> they would go on the continent for their honeymoon (three wonderful weeks!) and then, when they settled down in a nice snug and cosy little homely house, every morning they would both have brekky, **simple but perfectly served**, for their own two selves and before he went out to business he would give **his dear little wifey** a good hearty hug and gaze for a moment deep down into her eyes. (*U*1922, 337)

As these fantasies and aspirations intensify and become more elaborate, Gerty becomes more aware of Bloom who leans 'back against the rock behind' with a

---

[153] Gifford, *Ulysses Annotated*, 388.

gaze of 'whitehot passion' 'fastened upon her' which 'set her pulses tingling' (*U*1922, 350, 349). In the 1922 text, her fantasies about Bloom are enhanced:

> Here was that of which she had so often dreamed. **It was he who mattered and there was joy on her face because she wanted him because she felt instinctively that he was like no-one else.** The **very** heart of the girlwoman went out to him, **her dreamhusband because she knew on the instant it was him.** (*U*1922, 342)

She looks at him carefully, and the narrative reports her keen sense of his physical appearance, which is more detailed in the 1922 text:

> She could see at once by his dark eyes **and his pale intellectual face** that he was a for-eigner **the image of the photo she had of Martin Harvey, the matinée idol, only for the moustache which she preferred because she wasn't stagestruck like Winny Rippingham that wanted they two to always dress the same on account of a play** but she could not see whether he had an aquiline nose **or a slightly retroussé** from where he was sitting. (*U*1922, 342)

Gerty may not understand that Bloom is masturbating, but she certainly appreci-ates the connection between them, and the narrator nudges readers to understand the significance of the moment, which is described in the text as a '*Tableau*', a word which acquires an exclamation mark in revision, which emphasizes its significance ('*Tableau!*', *U*1922, 352).[154] An abbreviation of *tableau vivant*, this popular form of theatrical performance was strongly associated with Irish cultural nationalism and erotic entertainment (though not at the same time), and involved posed silent costumed actors, acting in a mannered gestural style, relying on the audience to pick up key interpretive clues.

Mullin's reading of the chapter in relation to the cultural history of the muto-scope is rich and suggestive, but it is also possible to read the text as a series of linked tableaux, with the moment of Bloom's climax being the most important of all.[155] Heap's defence of the action ('Art and the Law', discussed in Chapter 2) omits to acknowledge the fact of Bloom's masturbation, simply describing his stream of consciousness as a record of 'unfocused sex thoughts'.[156] In revision, and almost certainly in response to such vagueness, Gerty's narrator is more specific:

> At last they were left alone without the others to pry and pass remarks and she knew he could be trusted to the death, steadfast, **a sterling man,** a man of inflexible honour to his fingertips. **His hands and face were working and a tremour went over her.** She leaned back far to look up where the fireworks were and she caught her knee in her hands[.] (*U*1922, 349)

This implies that Gerty's 'tremour' comes about as a result of her awareness of Bloom's working 'hands and face' (*U*1922, 349). Coupled with added references to

---

[154] *LR*, July–August 1920, 45.

[155] See Mullin, 'Making a Spectacle of Herself: Gerty MacDowell through the Mutoscope', in *James Joyce, Sexuality and Social Purity*, 140–70. As Mullin explains, a mutoscope was a 'contemporary motion picture device containing a sequential series of photographs mounted on a cylinder. When the viewer looked through a peephole, inserted a coin and turned a handcrank, these cards could be rotated to produce the effect of movement' (145).

[156] Jane Heap, 'Art and the Law', *LR*, September–December 1920, 6. See above, p. 119.

'**wondrous revealment**', and 'the cry of young girl's love, a little strangled cry, wrung from her, that cry that has rung through the ages' (*U*1922, 350), this addition makes the significance of the *tableau vivant* harder to evade. Gerty leans back to reveal her 'graceful beautifully shaped legs' and 'she saw that he saw'; she 'was trembling in very limb' and he '**had a full view** high up above her knee where no-one ever **not even on the swing or wading** and she wasn't ashamed' (*U*1922, 350). These post-serial embellishments increase the way in which this chapter teases the reader, and force attention to detail: Gerty flashes her legs at Bloom deliberately and enjoys the fact that she is giving him 'a full view'. Her awareness is suggested in the following:

> Bertha Supple told her once in **dead** secret and made her swear she'd never about the gentleman lodger that was staying with them out of the **Congested Districts Board** that had pictures cut out of papers of those skirtdancers **and highkickers** and she said he used to do something not very nice that you could imagine sometimes in the bed.
> (*U*1922, 349)

Though it is not clear what the 'gentleman lodger' does in the bed, it is tantalizing that Gerty associates that memory with the spectacle of Bloom, though 'this was **altogether** different from a thing like that' and 'besides there was absolution so long as the didn't do the other thing before being married' (*U*1922, 349). In the end, the text adeptly refuses to be drawn on the question of how knowing Gerty really is. But it is evidently the case that Joyce has increased the number of suggestions and hints, so that *readers* can appreciate the significance of what happens, even if Gerty sees things differently in this 'chapter of glances'.[157]

A drive to greater explicitness can also be discerned in the Bloom section of the chapter. As noted in Chapter 3, a letter from Pound to Quinn indicates that Pound had made deletions to the typescript en route to the *Little Review*, including deleting the word 'wet', which should have appeared before 'shirt' in the phrase 'Mr Bloom with careful hand recomposed his shirt'.[158] In what can be seen as an explicit reaction to the trial of the *Little Review* editors, Pound's intervention, and Heap's vague suggestion that the *Little Review* was 'being prosecuted for printing the thoughts in a young girl's mind', Joyce adds phrases and words which restore Bloom's wet shirt, and clarify the fact of his orgasm.[159] There are several examples, but perhaps the most obvious is the addition of the word 'foreskin' in the following: 'This wet is very unpleasant. **Stuck. Well the foreskin is not back. Better detach.** Ow!' (*U*1922, 356). The specificity of 'foreskin', which is only used once in the 1922 text, ensures that readers cannot be confused about the significance of what has happened. Joyce also adds other stray thoughts to Bloom's musings as he thinks back over his day: 'Anyhow I got the best of that. **Damned glad I didn't do it in the bath this morning over her silly I will punish you letter**', an addition which reflects on the letter from Martha, and which is matched by a similar

---

[157] Fritz Senn, 'Nausicaa', in *James Joyce's 'Ulysses': Critical Essays*, ed. Clive Hart and David Hayman (Berkeley, CA: University of California Press, 1974), 310.
[158] *LR*, July–August 1920, 46; see above, p. 162.
[159] *LR*, September–December 1920, 6.

addition to chapter 5: '**Also I think I. Yes. Do it in the bath. Curious longing I. Water to water. Combine business with pleasure**' (*U*1922, 81). This is more evidence of Joyce revising the text systematically, creating ligatures between the chapters, and links which might be seen by readers whom he envisions reading the work 'five, ten or twenty times'.[160]

The typescript of chapter 5 ('Lotus-Eaters') had included an explicit reference to Martha's period ('Has her monthlies probably') which had been deleted before serial publication.[161] In revising chapter 13, Joyce is keen to include clearer acknowledgement of monthly bleeding and the impact it has on behaviour. Gerty justifies her display on Sandymount strand by thinking that 'it was on account of that other thing coming on the way it did' (*U*1922, 349), an idea which is echoed by Bloom: 'Devils they are when that's coming on them' who muses that 'Molly often told me feel things a ton weight' (*U*1922, 352). These ideas are clear enough in context, but lest there is any doubt, Joyce elaborates: '**Turns milk, makes fiddlestrings snap**' (*U*1922, 352), and he adds significantly to the first moment of Bloom's stream of consciousness:

> **How many women in Dublin have it today? Martha, she. Something in the air.** That's the moon. But then why don't all women menstruate at the same time with same moon, I mean? Depends on the time they were born, I suppose. **Or all start scratch then get out of step. Sometimes Molly and Milly together.**   (*U*1922, 351)

All of these revisions are examples of revision *type 5*, of the work becoming more suggestive, candid, or explicit about the body and sexuality. Another distinctive revisionary pattern is the embellishing of Bloom's musings on the specificities of Catholicism (thus *type 1*, deepening the specificities of the work). Bloom is fascinated by the idea of celibacy, and the fact that priests have a different (and non-sexual) type of 'mansmell' which women find attractive:

> Women buzz round it like flies round treacle. **Railed off the altar get on to it at any cost. The tree of forbidden priest.** O father, will you? Let me be the first to.
> (*U*1922, 358)

He also spends time thinking about what happens in convents, and muses that '**Virgins go mad in the end I suppose**' (*U*1922, 351). The chapter draws an analogy between the Exposition of the Blessed Sacrament—a rite which has something in common with tableau, being gestural and silent in places—and the exposition of Bloom and Gerty. But Bloom, of course, does not fully appreciate the significance of what was happening in the Star of the Sea, and makes the predictable mistake of thinking that what he had overheard was a mass:

> Mass seems to be over. **Could hear them all at it. Pray for us. And pray for us. And pray for us. Good idea the repetition. Same thing with ads. Buy from us. And buy from us.** Yes, there's the light in the priest's house.   (*U*1922, 360)

---

[160] Joyce in conversation, cited in Ronan Crowley, 'Fusing the Elements of "Circe": From Compositional to Textual Repetition', *James Joyce Quarterly*, 47:3 (Spring 2010), 341–61 (341).
[161] See above, p. 162.

The deepening of Bloom's response to Catholicism is a revisionary pattern which works across the Bloom chapters, and may be seen as an aspect of deepening Bloom's characterization, adding to the humour of the work as a whole, and encouraging readers to recognize the extent of Bloom's alienation within the cultural world of Dublin in 1904.

All of Bloom's streams of consciousness are extended significantly in the revision of this chapter. Compared with the chapter 5 'Language of flowers' example discussed above, the extensions tend not to introduce stylistic complication, but are more predictable, more of the same, often introducing small additional snippets of biographical, plot, or timing detail, which clarify the micro-narratives in the work. It is worth looking at the moment when Bloom closes his eyes for a short nap, at the very end of the chapter:

Short snooze now if I had. And she can do the other. Did too. And Belfast. I won't go. Let him. Just close my eyes a moment. Won't sleep though. Bat again. No harm in him. Just a few.[162]	Short snooze now if I had. **Must be near nine. Liverpool boat long gone. Not even the smoke.** And she can do the other. Did too. And Belfast. I won't go. **Race there, race back to Ennis.** Let him. Just close my eyes a moment. Won't sleep though. **Half dream. It never comes the same.** Bat again. No harm in him. Just a few. (*U*1922, 364)

The serial version comprises eleven short sentences which communicate that Bloom is thinking about Molly ('she'), about what might be going on at home, about her affair with Boylan, her plans to go to Belfast with him, his attitude to that planned trip ('Let him'), his need for a light sleep, and the bat who is circling in the sky ('No harm in him'). The inference of 'Just a few' is that Bloom is planning just a few minutes of sleep, but he begins to drowse before the plan is fully formed, literally drifting off in the middle of a sentence. This is the last we witness of Bloom's active conscious mind in this chapter: the next paragraph reports his dream, and thereafter a stylized third-person narrator records the chiming of the cuckoo clock in the priest's house 'where Canon O'Hanlon and Father Conroy and the reverend John Hughes S. J. were taking tea and sodabread and fried mutton chops' (*U*1922, 365).

The 1922 text intercuts what existed by adding an additional six sentences. Of these, four help to specify elements of the plot, including the time ('Must be near nine') and Bloom's way of working out the time given that his watch has stopped (he looks on the horizon for the smoke from the Liverpool steamer; it left Dublin's North Wall every day at 8 p.m.).[163] 'Race there, race back to Ennis' reintroduces Molly's plans to sing at what Bloom had earlier described as 'a swagger affair in the Ulster hall, Belfast on the twentyfifth' (*U*1922, 72), and Bloom's planned trip to Ennis for his father's anniversary ('Twentyseventh I'll be at his grave', *U*1922, 109).[164] The date of the trip to Clare was added post-serially, thus 'Race there, race back to

---

[162] *LR*, July–August 1920, 57.   [163] Gifford, *Ulysses Annotated*, 404.
[164] *CSE* I 230.22. For the serial instance of Molly's 'swagger affair', see *LR*, July 1918, 40.

Ennis' is an instance of Joyce tightening the plot post-serially. Bloom realizes the travel arrangements will be too tight. Thus, in a moment which reveals his pragmatism, emotional strength, and expedience, he has decided not to go to Belfast. 'Half dream' orients a reading of the next paragraph, by preparing readers for what is coming. 'It never comes the same' reveals that Bloom has a desire for a particular dream to recur. The impact of these additions is hard to evaluate. For a re-reader, the 1922 text is, in this instance, easier, throwing out more links and points of orientation. But the serial version is, perhaps, slightly more assured. The very short sentences capture and communicate a sense of fading consciousness, of Bloom's desperation to blot things out and dream for a moment.

What would be different about readings of the work if Joyce had made no revisions to the two 'macro revised' chapters which have been selected for case study, chapter 5 ('Lotus-Eaters') and chapter 13 ('Nausicaa')? Certainly *Ulysses* would be less rich, less funny, and Bloom would not be such a deep or compelling character. It would also be less explicit, and here an understanding of the genesis and reception of the text as a serial is formative, because Joyce obviously rewrote the text with a detailed understanding of how it had been greeted by its very first readers. With respect to the portion of chapter 13 which was deemed controversial—the third instalment which appeared in July–August 1920—Heap's reading was something of an evasion and misnomer. Joyce had little sense of Heap in the months leading up to the trial, and he did not recognize that 'Art and the Law' was trying to both defend the work and evade prosecution, a thin and fraught line which made it necessary for her to fail to acknowledge the fact of Bloom's masturbation.[165]

Writing in private, John Quinn proved to be a more important source of readerly engagement. As noted in Chapter 2, the letters which Quinn sent to Joyce via Pound in October 1920—twenty-three typed pages in all, dated 16 and 21 October respectively—included a list of the 'things in different pages…that are objected to' in the 'Nausicaa' instalment.[166] This list, compiled after Quinn's 'tactful talk' with Sumner of 15 October 1920, shows that both men had attended to the instalment very carefully, identifying every suggestive and salacious detail they could find.[167] It also shows that the lawyer for the defence (Quinn) had been heavily influenced by the lawyer for the prosecution (Sumner). Had Joyce been perspicuous and proactive at this point—around 10 November 1920 when he received Quinn's letters and list—he might have sought a better and more sympathetic lawyer who could defend his text as it appeared in the *Little Review*.[168] But he was too far away, too involved in the ongoing material struggle to actually write the work, and was thus inclined to just let things take their course. After the trial, and once he was assured of support from Beach, Joyce's attitude changed. He responded to the obscenity judgment and evidence of reading which Quinn had put in his hand by upping the *ante* and making *Ulysses* more suggestive, more candid, and more explicit.

[165] J to Weaver, 25 February 1920, *SL*, 249.
[166] Quinn to Pound, 16 October 1920, Carbondale. See above, p. 120–121, and Appendix 2.
[167] Quinn to Pound, 16 October 1920, Carbondale.
[168] J to Weaver, 10 November 1920, *L* I, 149 acknowledges receipt of Quinn's letters.

Conclusion

Writing in 2010, Michael Groden, one of the world's leading textual Joyceans, offered a candid and reflective account of the role he had played in the construction and reception of Gabler's three-volume *Ulysses: A Critical and Synoptic Edition* (1984). Among the many thought-provoking comments in that essay—offered as a turn to 'life-writing'—a few stand out. One is that Gabler's edition has never 'completely recovered from Kidd's attack on it', and that the arguments in the 174 pages of Kidd's 'An Inquiry into *Ulysses: The Corrected Text*' were 'scattered' and did not try to 'confront what Gabler did on his own terms'.[1] Another is that Gabler's response to Kidd, the remarkable 'What *Ulysses* Requires' (something of a page-turning thriller as articles on editorial theory go), has barely been noticed by Joyce scholars.[2] As Groden observes, Kidd's attack:

> deflected attention away from the three-volume Critical and Synoptic Edition, with its synoptic presentation and apparatus that scholars assumed would be the focus of attention, and toward the one-volume reading text, which is isolated from the editorial principles and procedures that produced it.[3]

The problem is that what was intended as a window into the textual pluralities of *Ulysses* (the three-volume synoptic edition) segued all too quickly into being marketed as a one-volume 'corrected text'. Nonetheless, Groden hailed the edition for being 'an impressive, even brilliant, amalgamation of Anglo-American and German editorial theory and practice applied to an extremely complex text'.[4] At the same time, he concedes:

> I am much more aware now that its theory and execution are alien and counterintuitive to many readers: that it is flawed both in theory and execution, although no more flawed than any human endeavour, and certainly it is not the only way in which *Ulysses* might and should be edited.[5]

While this is not the context to reopen the whys and wherefores of the Joyce wars, it is worth making a few additions to Groden's welcome and balanced comments,

---

[1] Michael Groden, '*The James Joyce Archive* and Hans Walter Gabler's Edition of *Ulysses*: A Personal History', in *Ulysses in Progress: Genetic, Textual and Personal Views* (Gainesville, FL: University of Florida Press, 2010), 81–104.

[2] Hans Walter Gabler, 'What *Ulysses* Requires', *Proceedings of the Bibliographical Society of America*, 87:2 (1993), 187–248.

[3] Groden, '*The James Joyce Archive* and Hans Walter Gabler's Edition of *Ulysses*', 97.

[4] Groden, '*The James Joyce Archive* and Hans Walter Gabler's Edition of *Ulysses*', 104.

[5] Groden, '*The James Joyce Archive* and Hans Walter Gabler's Edition of *Ulysses*', 104.

in order to conclude and point to the significance of my own study. First, it is a very great shame that Gabler's edition is out of print, and is thus inaccessible to many, though Ronan Crowley and Joshua Schäuble have recently begun to make their digital version of the Gabler edition available online (at ulysses.online), a welcome and transformative scholarly initiative. Second, one of the things the debate about editions still requires is a clear and comprehensive bibliographical account of the status and historicity of the Rosenbach manuscript, and particularly a discussion of the differences between that 'fair copy' and the volume edition of 1922. In our age of automatic collation, this enquiry should be easy to compile. Third, and most importantly, the most significant contribution of the Gabler edition is that of its orientation 'towards the written and the changing text', and the access it provides 'to distinct versions of that text'.[6] As long ago as 1985, Jerome McGann hailed the edition as 'postmodern' and claimed that 'it should remove forever that illusion of fixity and permanence we normally take from literary works because they so often come to us wearing their masks of permanence'.[7] In short, the most important element of the three-volume edition of Gabler is that it enables readers to identify the textual indeterminacy of *Ulysses*, and to study indeterminacy for critical purposes.

Gabler's rationale, sigla, and apparatus will never be easy for readers to decode, which is one among several reasons for the emphasis in this monograph on the study of the variations which exist between the two editions of *Ulysses* with which Joyce was most involved: the serial text of the *Little Review* and the volume text of February 1922. These variant editions may not be the ones which Joyce intended, but they are nonetheless the ones he managed to achieve. Their multiple points of corruption and divergence are points of critical interest. As Sebastian Knowles has argued, unedited texts are worthy of critical study because *Ulysses* itself demonstrates that 'errors are inevitable' and 'are not only forgivable but necessary'.[8] The notice of Dignam's funeral includes a 'line of bitched type' ('*eatondph 1/8 ador dorador douradora*'), gives Simon Dedalus a B.A., includes the name of one person who did not attend (C. P. M'Coy), and dubs the 'the chap in the macintosh' as M'Intosh (*U*1922, 106, 602).[9] Another value of studying *Ulysses* through its first editions is that of studying the work in its original historic context, and of bringing textual and historicist issues into contact with one another. This is much easier to do now that digital facsimiles of the two texts have become available, now that we live in an age of digitality—of the digital genetic, an era which is enabling a new kind of hermeneutic enquiry, of a kind that is more fine-grained, more attentive to style, and more historicist.

---

[6] Hans Walter Gabler, 'What *Ulysses* Requires', *Proceedings of the Bibliographical Society of America*, 87:2 (1993), 187–248 (190, 191).

[7] Cited by Groden, '*The James Joyce Archive* and Hans Walter Gabler's Edition of *Ulysses*', 103.

[8] Cited by Groden, '*The James Joyce Archive* and Hans Walter Gabler's Edition of *Ulysses*', 103.

[9] This passage is of particular genetic interest. See *CSE* III 1412.25f. The 1922 text fails to get Bloom's name wrong, and omits to include Stephen Dedalus in the list of attendees, two passively authorized errors which complicate Joyce's point about 'the usual crop of nonsensical howlers of misprints' (*U*1922, 602).

Literary scholarship before theory positioned bibliography, textual criticism, literary criticism, and literary history as firmly separate activities. But the distinctions between those different types of enquiry no longer seem so pertinent. In this regard the interventions of D. F. McKenzie, who reconceived of bibliography as a 'sociology of texts', have been especially important. As he argued, 'in the pursuit of historical meanings, we move from the most minute feature of the material form of the book to questions of authorial, literary and social context'.[10] Certainly this has been an underpinning methodological consideration throughout this study, which has moved from questions of book history (or periodical history) (in Chapter 1) to compositional and legal history (in Chapter 2) and textual criticism (in Chapters 3 and 4). In excavating the compositional, publication, and reception circumstances of the first iterations of *Ulysses* in print, this study has located the origins of the text within a different cultural geography and temporality than that of Paris in February 1922. Between November 1917, when Sykes set to work on typing the first chapter, and June 1920, when the typed copy of chapter 14 ('Oxen of the Sun') was read by Pound in Italy's Sirmione, the serial *Ulysses* was being written and prepared for publication in Locarno, and then Zurich and then Trieste. The serial *Ulysses* is *Ulysses* before Paris, and a *Ulysses* which was published during the First World War (in the case of chapters 1 to 7), and in its confused political aftermath (in the case of chapter 8 to the first portion of chapter 14). Because of the *Little Review*, the serial *Ulysses* is also a *Ulysses* in New York, and must therefore be located within the context of an evolving American Modernism—alongside writings by figures such as William Carlos Williams, Wallace Stevens, Amy Lowell, Djuna Barnes, Sherwood Anderson, Marianne Moore, as well as the more obvious 'men of 1914': T. S. Eliot and Pound. All of these writers appeared in the *Little Review* and alongside *Ulysses*. In fact, Leopold Bloom and his cat made their first entry on to the world's literary stage in the 'American Number' of the *Little Review*—an issue edited by Jane Heap—and 'offered as a resumé of a representative group...all at present living and working in America'.[11] This rich and original serial context is certainly worthy of further study, and is something of a cultural irony given the Hibernian specificities of some aspects of *Ulysses*, the fact that Joyce never visited the US, his initial reception as European modernist, and, more recently, his reception as the most notable novelist among the many produced by Ireland in the twentieth century.

McKenzie's *Bibliography and Sociology of Texts* pointed to the fact that 'readers inevitably make their own meanings' and that 'each reading is peculiar to its occasion'.[12] In a similar vein, and at much the same time, Jerome McGann advocated that critics draw a distinction between the 'double helix of perceptual codes' which exist in every literary work: 'the linguistic codes, on one hand, and the bibliographical codes on the other'.[13] In seeking to uncover the bibliographical and linguistic codes of the serial *Ulysses*, this study has also located the work's very

[10] D. F. McKenzie, *Bibliography and the Sociology of Texts* (1986; Cambridge: Cambridge University Press, 1999), 13, 23.
[11] *LR*, June 1918, 62.   [12] McKenzie, *Bibliography and the Sociology of Texts*, 19.
[13] Jerome McGann, *The Textual Condition* (Princeton, NJ: Princeton University Press, 1991), 77.

first readers: its typists and production intermediaries—Pound, Weaver, Anderson, Heap, and Popovich. The work has also sought to understand the reading experiences of those who first encountered *Ulysses* as a serial, a group which included luminaries such as John Butler Yeats, T. S. Eliot, and Virginia Woolf. In fact, Woolf's experience as a reader of *Ulysses* began at Hogarth House as early as April 1918. Katherine Mansfield, who visited at the time, and heard Woolf's initial response, presciently suggested that that moment is one that 'should figure I suppose in this history of literature'.[14] Indeed Woolf's reading of the text—in typescript, as a serial, and in volume form—constitutes what McKenzie characterized as an 'informative history', and is a history of genetic significance which is worth recounting here, as part of a more general conclusion.[15]

Woolf was offered the opportunity to publish *Ulysses* by Harriet Shaw Weaver, who called at the newly established Hogarth Press on 14 April 1918, at the suggestion of T. S. Eliot. Woolf confided to her diary that she did her very best to make Miss Weaver 'reveal herself' but Weaver:

> remained inalterably modest judicious & decorous. Her neat mauve suit fitted both soul & body; her grey gloves laid straight by her plate symbolised domestic rectitude; her table manners were those of a well bred hen. We could get no talk to go. Possibly the poor woman was impeded by her sense that what she had in the brownpaper parcel was quite out of keeping with her own contents. But then how did she ever come in contact with Joyce & the rest? Why does their filth seek exit from her mouth? Heaven knows.[16]

One might think from this emphasis on 'filth' that Woolf was looking at the completed *Ulysses*; in fact, all that she (and Weaver) had to hand was the first four chapters of the text in typescript, in the version consigned for serialization.[17] The projected plans to publish in book form were certainly premature, though of course they are a testimony of Weaver's determination to support Joyce.

Woolf did not share Weaver's enthusiasm. She told a correspondent that she would hesitate to put the typescript into the hands of even 'a married woman. The directness of the language, and the choice of the incidents, if there *is* any such choice...—have raised a blush even upon such a cheek as mine'. Is this, she wondered, 'an Irish quality?'[18] Thinking that Joyce should be nowhere near the next visitors due at Hogarth House, a deputation from the Mothers' Co-operative Guild, she firmly placed the typescript, in its brown-paper wrapper, in 'the drawer of her inlaid cabinet'.[19] But she could not resist getting it out for other visitors.

[14] Leonard Woolf (ed.), *A Writer's Diary: Being Extracts from the Diary of Virginia Woolf* (London: The Hogarth Press, 1969), 363 (entry for 15 January 1941).

[15] McKenzie, *Bibliography and the Sociology of Texts*, 19.

[16] Anne Olivier Bell (ed.), *The Diary of Virginia Woolf: Volume I: 1915–1919* (London: The Hogarth Press, 1977), 140 (entry for 18 April 1918).

[17] Evidence in Weaver to J, 19 June 1918, in John Firth, 'Harriet Weaver's Letters to James Joyce, 1915–1920', *Studies in Bibliography*, 20 (1967), 151–88 (180).

[18] VW to Nicholas Bagenal, 15 April 1918, in Nigel Nicolson (ed.), *The Question of Things Happening: The Letters of Virginia Woolf: Volume II: 1912–1922* (London: The Hogarth Press, 1976), 231.

[19] Leonard Woolf (ed.), *A Writer's Diary* (entry for 15 January 1941), 363.

These included Desmond McCarthy who, late at night, took to reading Joyce's typescript aloud, and imitating the 'modern imitation of a cat's miau', a game which Woolf found herself capable of enjoying.[20]

Prompted by Weaver to respond, Woolf turned down *Ulysses* in May 1918, citing the length, a projected 300 pages, as a matter of 'insuperable difficulty' for a press with such limited printing equipment.[21] This response was not entirely candid. Though she found *Ulysses* 'interesting as an experiment', Woolf told Roger Fry that she was worried that Joyce 'hadn't got anything very interesting to say...after all the p-ing of a dog isn't very different from the p-ing of a man. Three hundred pages of it might be boring'.[22] Meanwhile, Leonard Woolf had consulted with two printers—who might potentially have printed the text on behalf of the Hogarth Press—and was told that the publication of the novel would lead to prosecution.[23]

Woolf's next encounter with *Ulysses* came about in the spring of 1919, when she set herself the task of reading modern fiction in order to write what would be the leading article in the *Times Literary Supplement* of 10 April 1919, her essay on 'Modern Novels', which, as Andrew McNeillie has noted, is an essay in which the creator of *Jacob's Room* and its successors is 'clearly present as in no other piece of criticism to have come from her pen by this date'.[24] In preparation for writing this essay, Woolf read the first seven chapters of *Ulysses* as a serial, those that appeared between March 1918 and October 1918.[25] She was no ordinary reader of course, and was reading with critical purpose. In her notes, she identified the serial *Ulysses* as an attempt to represent 'psychology' and to 'get thinking into literature', possibly, she added, 'like a cinema that shows you very slowly'.[26] Woolf also notes the strangeness of the 'convention that makes us believe that people talked or felt or lived as Jane Austen and Thackeray and Dickens make them'; 'the only thing' she concedes is 'that we're used to it'.[27] These realizations quickly found critical formulation in her *TLS* essay, in which she attacked the methods of Edwardian novelists such as H. G. Wells, John Galsworthy, and Arnold Bennett for failing to represent 'likeness to life', and singled out Joyce for bravely 'discarding most of the conventions which are commonly observed' and revealing the 'flickerings of that

[20] Bell (ed.), *The Diary of Virginia Woolf (Volume I)*, 145 (entry for 28 April 1918).

[21] Woolf to Weaver, 17 May 1918 in Nicolson (ed.), *Letters of Virginia Woolf (II)*, 242. Weaver had probably calculated 300 pages on the basis that *Ulysses* would be the length of *A Portrait of the Artist as a Young Man*, a detail which suggests how little she (or indeed anyone) knew of Joyce's plans at this stage in the genesis of the text.

[22] VW to Roger Fry, [24 April 1918], Nicolson (ed.), *Letters of Virginia Woolf (II)*, 234.

[23] VW to Harriet Shaw Weaver, 17 May 1918, Nicolson (ed.), *Letters of Virginia Woolf (II)*, 242, 243n.

[24] 'Modern Novels', *The Times Literary Supplement*, 10 April 1919, 1–2, reprinted in Andrew McNeillie (ed.), *The Essays of Virginia Woolf: Volume III, 1919–1924* (London: The Hogarth Press, 1988), 33–4 (33).

[25] The evidence of Woolf's reading is recorded in her reading notebook on 'Modern Novels' (Berg Collection, New York Public Library). See also Brenda R. Silver, *Virginia Woolf's Reading Notebooks* (Princeton, NJ: Princeton University Press, 1983), 155–7.

[26] VW's reading notes on *Ulysses* quoted by Harvena Richter, *The 'Ulysses' Connection: Clarissa Dalloway's Bloomsday*, Studies in the Novel, 21:3 (Fall 1989), 305–19 (305).

[27] Silver, *Virginia Woolf's Reading Notebooks*, 157.

242 *Serial Encounters*

innermost flame which flashes its myriad messages through the brain'.[28] The same passage invokes writers to 'record the atoms as they fall upon the mind in the order in which they fall, let us trace the pattern, however disconnected and incoherent in appearance, which each sight or incident scores upon the consciousness'.[29] As noted in Chapter 1, some of these comments were picked out by Anderson and Heap, and republished in the *Little Review* in the 'Reader Critic' column of September–December 1920, the last number in which an instalment of *Ulysses* would appear.[30]

This history of textual reading and recirculation is an instance of what McGann would describe as 'radial reading', a reading which 'involves decoding one or more of the contexts that interpenetrate the scripted and physical text'.[31] With regard to the serial *Ulysses*, radial reading leads in multiple directions: towards the historicity of a range of specific cultural moments; towards the reading of adjacent literary and non-literary texts; towards biography, annotation, and the post-serial genesis of the text. For the moment, though, let's stick with Woolf, who found her serial encounter with *Ulysses* to be one of disappointment. In 'Modern Novels', she compared Joyce to Conrad and Hardy, noting, in Joyce, 'the comparative poverty of the writer's mind', and finding 'flashes of deep significance succeeded by incoherent inanities'.[32] The essay in which these comments appeared was published anonymously (like much criticism in the *TLS* during this era); thus neither Joyce nor the editors of the *Little Review* could trace the comments back to Woolf. But, as Dirk Van Hulle notes, Joyce did notice the phrase 'terrible poverty of mind' in the *Little Review* and included it in one of the notebooks he prepared in the early stages of writing *Finnegans Wake*, in preparation for the phrase 'your horrible awful poverty of mind' in the final text.[33]

However disheartened Woolf may have been from reading the early chapters of the serial *Ulysses*, the experience did not dissuade her from tackling the finished work. By April 1922 she had come to the view that it was 'necessary' to read *Ulysses* and she parted with £4 for a copy of the 'blue paper book', which had been praised a great deal by Eliot, a regular visitor at Hogarth House at this time.[34] She read the text in fits and starts over that summer, 'with spasms of wonder, of discovery and...long lapses of intense boredom'.[35] She had finished it by early October, and concluded that the book as a whole was a 'misfire':

> Genius it has, I think; but of the inferior water. The book is diffuse. It is brackish. It is pretentious. It is underbred, not only in the obvious sense, but in the literary sense. A first rate writer, I mean, respects writing too much to be tricky; startling; doing stunts. I'm reminded all the time of some callow board school boy, full of wits and powers, but so self-conscious and egotistical that he loses his head, becomes extravagant,

28 'Modern Novels', *TLS*, 10 April 1919, 1–2.
29 'Modern Novels', *TLS*, 10 April 1919, 1–2.   30 *LR*, September–December 1920, 93–4.
31 McGann, *The Textual Condition*, 119.   32 'Modern Novels', *TLS*, 10 April 1919, 1–2.
33 Dirk Van Hulle, *James Joyce's 'Work in Progress': Pre-Book Publications of Finnegans Wake* (London: Routledge, 2016), 5.
34 VW to David Garnett, 9 April 1922, Nicolson (ed.), *Letters of Virginia Woolf (II)*, 519; Woolf (ed.), *A Writer's Diary*, 363 (entry for 15 January 1941).
35 Woolf (ed.), *A Writer's Diary*, 363 (entry for 15 January 1941).

mannered, uproarious, ill at ease, makes kindly people feel sorry for him and instead ones merely annoyed; and one hopes he'll grow out of it.[36]

At exactly this time she was reviewing the proofs of *Jacob's Room*, which would be published by the Hogarth Press in October 1922. She found the text of *Jacob* 'thin and pointless...the words scarcely dint the paper' and was planning *Mrs Dalloway*, a work with many obvious correlations to *Ulysses* (all set in one day, involving the meeting of unconnected characters in a city, and containing streams of consciousness).[37]

The structure of *Mrs Dalloway*, which was published by the Hogarth Press in May 1925, was planned in notes written just after Woolf had completed reading *Ulysses*, and brings to mind its structure. By Woolf's account, *Dalloway* was a book of 'six or seven chapters, each complete separately. Yet there must be some sort of fusion! And all must converge upon the party at the end'.[38] This is one of Woolf's moments of negative capability: the experience of encountering the finished *Ulysses*, published when Joyce was forty (a detail which Eliot probably relayed from Paris), enabled her to forge ahead with the evolution of a more confident version of her own style in the summer of 1922, at the very moment when she was reading *Ulysses*:

> There's no doubt in my mind that I have found out how to begin (at 40) to say something in my own voice; and that interests me so that I feel I can go ahead without praise.[39]

These rich and dateable histories of reading position the first printed iterations of *Ulysses* within the nexus of a more general genesis of modernist literature, a genesis which could certainly be explored at greater length. But let's switch from radial reading to another of McGann's precepts: the reading of bibliographical and linguistic codes. One of the remarkable things about the first volume edition of *Ulysses* is the way its bibliographical codes appear to have established the terms for the reception of the work more generally. Joyce's prefatory note, which 'asks the reader's indulgence for typographical errors unavoidable in the exceptional circumstances' (*U*1922, [viii]), sent critics, editors, and readers in pursuit of a corrected version of the text. Beach had promised a version of *Ulysses* 'complete as written' but the evident typographical corruptions of the 'blue paper book' immediately suggested that this objective had not been realized.[40] Similarly, the acknowledgement that the work had been 'suppressed four times during serial publication' and produced in 'exceptional circumstances', alongside its evident biographical components, unleashed intense biographical interest in Joyce's formation, which continues to this day.[41] 'One thinks of Homer' (*U*1922, 208), an inspired last-minute post-serial addition, coupled with the eventual release of the schemata, persuaded readers that they should attempt to decode the work's Homeric substructures.

---

[36] Woolf (ed.), *A Writer's Diary*, 49 (entry for 6 September 1922).

[37] Woolf (ed.), *A Writer's Diary*, 49 (entry for 6 September 1922).

[38] Stella McNichol (ed.), *Mrs Dalloway's Party: A Short Story Sequence* (London: The Hogarth Press, 1973), 15.

[39] Woolf (ed.), *A Writer's Diary*, 47 (entry for 16 August 1922).

[40] Prospectus advertising the first edition, reproduced in Katherine McSharry (ed.), *A Joycean Scrapbook from the National Library of Ireland* (Dublin: Wordwell, 2004), 102.

[41] Shakespeare and Company prospectus, McSharry (ed.), *A Joycean Scrapbook*, 102.

Ulysses enthusiasts are drawn from a wide range of what Stanley Fish would describe as 'interpretive communities'.[42] A diversity in critical approach is necessary and welcome. Yet most readers of *Ulysses* come to recognize two facts about the history of the book: that it has a tangled and troubled textual history (usually associated with the Gabler edition), and that the work could only be freely published following legal action—namely the 'Monumental Decision of the United States District Court rendered December 6 1933 by Hon. John M. Woolsey lifting the ban on *Ulysses*'—a decision which was printed in full in the Random House edition of 1934.[43] As Mullin has observed, the continued republication of the Woolsey decision framed 'the novel as a crucial social document in the war between philistine prudery and artistic freedom'.[44] This study—which is both a history of the early composition and publication of the book, and a textual response to it—has located interest in the instructive corruptions and divergences of a much earlier text, that of the serial *Ulysses*, and an earlier trial, that of the *Little Review* editors in New York in February 1921. A particular justification for this emphasis is that these experiences—of serialization and legal action against the *Little Review*—played a formative shaping role in the completion of *Ulysses* in 1922.

From the perspective of the sociology of texts, *Ulysses* presents a unique case of book history for three reasons. First, the work was published twice: once as a serial, and once in volume form. Within literary history, particularly the history of nineteenth-century British fiction, this is not so unusual. But it does mean that the work went through two separable processes of publication and reception, each with a particular (and in this instance) quite different temporality and cultural geography. Second, the serial text was subject to successful legal action, and was deemed obscene. Although there were a number of obscenity cases in the era—the era of the social purity movement—it was unusual for a literary work which had yet to be finished to be deemed obscene (and this decision had far-reaching implications for the subsequent publishing history of *Ulysses* in the English-speaking world, and for Joyce's copyright in *Ulysses*, a topic explored at length by Spoo).[45] Third, the work was rewritten extensively in preparation for publication in volume form. The theory of seven types of Ulyssean revision, offered as an initial way of reading textual variation, shows that Joyce was responding to multiple revisionary imperatives: to the opportunities provided by Beach's generous offer to fund multiple proofs; to an evolved sense of what the style and structure of the work could and should be; to a greater range of bibliographical resources which residence in Paris made available. But Joyce was also using the opportunity to rewrite in response to the first reception of the text in the *Little Review*. The evidence of the work becoming more suggestive and explicit about the body and sexuality is extensive, and can be positioned as an instance of socially motivated rewriting, a rewriting inspired by

[42] Stanley Fish, *Is There a Text in This Class? The Authority of Interpretive Communities* (Cambridge, MA: Harvard University Press, 1980).

[43] James Joyce, *Ulysses* (New York: Random House, 1934), [ix].

[44] Katherine Mullin, *James Joyce, Sexuality and Social Purity* (Cambridge: Cambridge University Press, 2003), 2.

[45] Robert Spoo, *Without Copyright: Piracy, Publishing and the Public Domain* (Oxford: Oxford University Press, 2013).

the circumstances of the work's interim reception. In this respect, in combination of all three factors, the material history of *Ulysses* is unique, and offers an extension to McKenzie's 'sociology of texts', a process which acknowledges the social elements of production, but has not, hitherto, encompassed socially motivated revision.

With radial reading, bibliographical codes, the sociology of texts, and the sociology of editing and revision all in view, let's focus on two final textual details, which point to the importance of the 1922 text and its precursor for interpretation. The first detail relates to the date of the famine; the second to Mulligan's reading of Yeats. In the serial version of chapter 2 ('Nestor'), published in April 1918, Deasy tells Stephen: 'I remember the famine in '46'.[46] Readers might wonder about the prominence and reliability of this date. There were several famines in Ireland in the 1830s, but the Great Famine began in 1845, and had its worst year in 1847. Joyce seems to be making a point in having Deasy remember an odd year. As noted in Chapter 4, the conversation between Deasy and Dedalus was revised significantly for the 1922 text, and includes a whole paragraph of Dedalus remembering various atrocities in Irish history.[47] The 1922 text omits the date of the famine ('I remember the famine', *U*1922, 31). This is almost certainly because the date ('in '46') was added to the typescript by hand: a letter from Joyce to Sykes of December 1917 reveals him relaying this instruction.[48] The insertion was evidently copied onto the typescript relayed to the *Little Review*, but appears to have been omitted in the copy relayed to Darantiere in 1921. But why did Joyce omit this detail in the proofs which he saw and approved? Unless further evidence comes to light, it is impossible to answer this question: what we have in this instance is a transmissional variant which may or may not be authorially intended. Gabler restores 'in '46' on the basis of the letter to Sykes of 1917 but it is not possible to say that that is a correct reading, a fact which again shows how the variant texts of *Ulysses* are editorially problematic but critically instructive.[49]

Mulligan's rewriting of Yeats is a textual crux of a different kind. In the second instalment of chapter 9 ('Scylla and Charybdis'), published in May 1919, Mulligan trills what is clearly his set-piece, a re-working of the first eight lines of 'Baile and Aillinn', which was written in an awkward iambic tetrameter. His version of this poem catches the atmosphere, rhythm, and over-elaborate syntax of Yeats's original with cruel effectiveness:

> —I hardly hear the purlieu cry
> Or a Tommy talk as you pass one by
> Before my thoughts begin to run
> On F. M'Curdy Atkinson,
> The same that had the wooden leg
> And that filibustering filibeg
> That never dared to slake his drought,
> —Magee that had the chinless mouth...[50]

---

[46] *LR*, April 1918, 40.   [47] See above, p. 210.
[48] J to Sykes, [? 16 December 1917], *L* II, 413.   [49] *CSE* I 60.32; *CSE* III 1730.
[50] *LR*, May 1919, 32.

The ellipses which conclude this citation indicate Mulligan's energy and voice trailing away: he is dancing as he recites these words, and descending the staircase at the National Library. In revision, Joyce saw the opportunity to respond explicitly to Sumner and the New York Society for the Suppression of Vice who found the fact of Bloom's activity on Sandymount Strand so problematic and difficult to discuss. Perhaps remembering that Corrigan had referred to the third instalment of 'Nausicaa' as 'the episode where the man went off in his pants', Joyce added two further lines to the parody of Yeats, which move away from the subtle fireworks of 'Nausicaa' and insist on explicitly naming and acknowledging a sexual act.[51] The revised lines, which indicate Joyce's determination to be hung for a sheep as a lamb, and his willingness to accept the charge as offered, can be almost the last word:

> I hardly hear the purlieu cry
> Or a Tommy talk as I pass one by
> Before my thoughts begin to run
> On F. M 'Curdy Atkinson,
> The same that had the wooden leg
> And that filibustering filibeg
> That never dared to slake his drouth,
> Magee that had the chinless mouth.
> **Being afraid to marry on earth**
> **They masturbated for all they were worth.**   (*U*1922, 207)

The chapter in which these lines are uttered, in which Yeats is treated so mercilessly, contains many other hermeneutic snares. It features, after all, a debate about Shakespeare in Ireland's *national* library, thus commenting on the anglicized nature of Irish educational experience and culture, and suggesting what it was like for an author of Joyce's disposition to be exposed to the Irish literary revival and its institutions. George Russell, a key figure in that movement, and in the chapter, is portrayed as an 'oracle', whose utterances include the statement that 'The supreme question about a work of art is out of how deep a life does it spring' (*U*1922, 177). This is the issue Dedalus explores in relation to Shakespeare, ironically, and in reductive and biographical terms. The author of *Ulysses* could see things with greater insight and subtlety; he rewrote his text in partial response to the conditions of its stalled serial publication, in response to its first editors, printers, and readers, and its reception in the New York legal system in 1920 and 1921.

---

[51] Quinn to Pound, 21 October 1920, Carbondale.

APPENDIX 1

The Genesis of *Ulysses* in Typescript
(to Chapter 14)

Although scholars know little about the production of *Ulysses* in typescript, and a complete run of the typescripts does not survive, chapter typescripts were clearly a crucial component in the authorship of the text, and its transmission to serial publication. They represented a state of interim finality for the evolving text, and are worthy of genetic study in their own right. It is not generally possible to date the typescripts and their moments of transition to exact days, but it is possible, using the evidence of correspondence between Joyce, Weaver, and Pound, to establish the month in which the individual chapter typescripts were received by either Weaver or Pound (and thus to know *when* Joyce considered each chapter complete enough for serial publication). For ease of reference, and to facilitate further scholarship, this table, which should be read in conjunction with the detailed evidence presented in Chapter 2 (especially pp. 86 to 90), summarizes the dateable evidence of typescript receipt by either Weaver or Pound to the nearest month.

During the process of serialization Joyce seems to have asked his typists to produce three copies of each typescript (a top copy and two carbons); he then kept a copy for his own use after submitting one (or two) for serial publication. The typescripts which survive in Buffalo generally include post-serial additions and other markings indicating that they were sub-mitted to Darantiere, printer of the Shakespeare and Company volume edition of February 1922. The typescripts submitted to the *Little Review* do not appear to have survived, but for one fragment: the portion of chapter 14 ('Oxen of the Sun') which was not published in the *Little Review* (owing to the halt in serialization because of the trial and obscenity judgment of February 1921). More detailed information on the genetic dossier of *Ulysses* can be found in the appendices to Luca Crispi, *Becoming the Blooms: Joyce's Creative Process and the Construction of Characters in Ulysses* (Oxford: Oxford University Press, 2015), 281–320.

Chapter #	Homeric title	Month of confirmed typescript receipt by Weaver and/or Pound	Known surviving exemplars	Publication in the *Little Review*
1	Telemachus	December 1917	none	March 1918
2	Nestor	January 1918	Buffalo: 1 page	April 1918
3	Proteus	February 1918	Buffalo: 1 page	May 1918
4	Calypso	late March/early April 1918	Buffalo: 3 partial copies	June 1918
5	Lotus-Eaters	April 1918	none	July 1918
6	Hades	July 1918	Buffalo: 1 partial copy	September 1918
7	Aeolus	August 1918	Buffalo: 1 complete copy	October 1918

(*continued*)

Continued

Chapter #	Homeric title	Month of confirmed typescript receipt by Weaver and/or Pound	Known surviving exemplars	Publication in the *Little Review*
8	Lestrygonians	October 1918	Buffalo: 1 complete copy	January 1919 February–March 1919
9	Scylla and Charybdis	January/February 1919	Buffalo: 1 complete copy	April 1919 May 1919
10	Wandering Rocks	February 1919	Buffalo: 2 partial copies	June 1919 July 1919
11	Sirens	June 1919	Buffalo: 1 complete copy	August 1919 September 1919
12	Cyclops	October 1919	Buffalo: 2 partial copies	November 1919 December 1919 January 1920 March 1920
13	Nausicaa	February 1920	Buffalo: 1 complete and 1 partial copy	April 1920 May–June 1920 July–August 1920
14	Oxen of the Sun	June 1920	Buffalo: 1 complete and 2 partial copies; UWM: 1 partial copy	September– December 1920 *LR* publishes first portion only

APPENDIX 2

Excerpts from a Letter by John Quinn
to Ezra Pound

From John Quinn's letter to Ezra Pound, 16 October 1920 (by kind permission of the Special Collections Research Center, Southern Illinois University, Carbondale). This a copy of what appears in the letter, including Quinn's transcriptional errors.

Quinn describes this as a 'list of the things in different pages that are objected to'. It refers to the third instalment of chapter 13 ('Nausicaa'), as it appeared in the *Little Review* in July–August 1920.

EXTRACTS FROM 'ULYSSES' Episode XIII (Continued)

L. R. p. 43
She said he used to do something not very nice that you could imagine sometimes in the bed.

L. R. p. 45
Not little devil all the same. Near her monthlies, I expect, makes them feel ticklish...Where did I put the letter?...But then why don't all women menstruate at the same time with same moon. Depends on the time they were born, I suppose...Yours for the asking...Felt for the curves inside her <u>deshabille</u>. Excites them also when they're...vindictive too for what they can't get. Devils they are when that's coming on them.

L. R. p. 46
Scratch the sole of my foot. O that way! O, that's exquisite! Feel it myself too. Wonder if it's bad to go on with them then. Safe in one way. Something about withering plants I read in a garden. Besides they say if the flower withers she wears she's a flirt...Gently does it. Dislike rough and tumble...Pretty girls and ugly man marrying...Ten bob I got for Molly's combings when we were on the rocks in Holles Street. Why not? Suppose he gave her money, why not? All a prejudice. She's worth ten, fifteen, more a pound...All that for nothing. Was that just when he, she?
O, he did. Into her. She did. Done...
Mr Bloom with careful hand recomposed his shirt. O lord, that little limping devil. Begins to feel cold and clammy. After effect not pleasant. They don't care. Good job I let off there behind coming out of Dignam's. Cider that was.

L. R. p. 47
That's what they enjoy. Taking a man from another woman. French letter still in my pocketbooks...Fifteen she told me. But her breasts were developed. Fell asleep then.
My fireworks. Up like a rocket, down like a stick...

L. R. p. 48
Did she know what I? Course. Like a cat sitting beyond a dog's jump...a picture of Venus with all his belongings on show. His wife had her work cut out for her...man at the corner of Cuffe Street was goodlooking, thought she might like, twigged at once he

had a false arm... Still she was game. Lord, I am wet. Devil you are. Swell of her calf. Transparent stockings, stretched to breaking point... White. Wow! Beef to the heel. She smelt an onion. Darling I saw your. I saw all.

Lord!

... For this relief much thanks.

L. R. p. 50

This wet is very unpleasant...

Because that was about the time he... Cat's away the mice will play... when you hold out the form. Come. Come. Tip. Woman and man that is. Fork and steel... let you see more and defy you if you are a man to see and legs, look, look and. Tip. Have to let fly. But lots of them can't kick the beam, I think. Keep that thing up for hours. Kind of a general all around over me and half down my back.

... Took its time in coming like herself, slow but sure.

L. R. p. 51

And they're always spinning out of them, fine as anything. Rainbow colors with out knowing it, Clings to everything she takes off. Vamp of her stockings, Warm shoes. Stays. Drawers: little kick taking them off... Also the cat likes to sniff in her shift on the bed... There or the armpits or under the neck... Some women, for instance, warn you off when they have their period. Come near. Then get a hogo you could hang your hat on. Like what? Potted herrings gone stale. Boof! Please keep off the grass.

Perhaps they get a man smell off us. Mansmell, I mean. Must be connected with that because priests are supposed to be different. Women buzz around it like flies around treacle. O father, will you. Let me be the first to. That diffuses itself all through the body, permeates. Source of life. And it's extremely curious that smell. Celery sauce. Let me.

L. R. p. 53

He gets the plums and I the leavings...

Tired I feel now. Drained all the manhood out of me, little wretch. She kissed me. My mouth. Never again. Only once it comes. Or hers... Like kids your second visit to a house. The new I want... His gun rusty from the dew.

L. R. p. 55

And then their stomachs clean... Her first stays I remember... Little paps to begin with. Left one is more sensitive, I think. Mine too. Nearer the heart... Frightened she was when her nature came on her first.

L. R. p. 57

O, exhausted that female has me. Not so young now. Will she come here tomorrow? Will I? But it was lovely... Made me feel so young.

short snooze now if I had. And she can do the other.

Bibliography

PRINCIPAL VERSIONS AND EDITIONS OF *ULYSSES*

Little Review (in twenty-three instalments from March 1918 to December 1920). A complete run of the *Little Review* (12 vols) is available in printed facsimile (New York: Kraus Reprint, 1967); the first nine vols (1914–22) are available in digital facsimile: Modernist Journals Project, http://modjourn.org.

The Little Review Ulysses, edited by Mark Gaipa, Sean Latham, and Robert Scholes (New Haven, CT: Yale University Press, 2015).

Ulysses (Paris: Shakespeare and Company, 1922). Available as digital facsimile at http://web. uvic.ca/~mvp1922/portfolio/ulysses-shakespeare-co-1922-1st-edn.

Ulysses: A Critical and Synoptic Edition, edited by Hans Walter Gabler, 3 vols (1984; London and New York: Garland, revised edn, 1986).

ARCHIVAL AND UNPUBLISHED SOURCES

Beinecke Rare Book and Manuscript Library, Yale University:
Ezra Pound Papers, YCAL MSS 43.
British Library, Manuscripts Collections:
Correspondence, literary and business papers of Harriet Shaw Weaver.
Cornell University Library, Rare and Manuscript Collections:
The Cornell Joyce Collection.
Lilly Library, Bloomington, Indiana:
Ezra Pound MSS, 1919–24.
Morris Library, Southern Illinois University, Carbondale:
Croessman Collection of James Joyce.
New York Public Library, Manuscripts and Archives Division:
John Quinn Memorial Collection.
University at Buffalo Libraries:
The James Joyce Collection.
University of Wisconsin-Milwaukee Libraries, Archives Department:
Little Review Records, 1914–64.

DIGITAL AND PRINTED SOURCES

Anderson, Margaret. *My Thirty Years' War* (1930; New York: Horizon Press, 1969).
Anderson, Margaret. 'Conversation', *Prose*, 2 (1971), 5–21.
Anderson, Sherwood. 'Real—Unreal', *The New Republic*, 11 June 1930.
Archive Consultants. 'History of Monuments: O'Connell Street Area' (Report Commissioned by Dublin City Council, November 2003), https://www.dublincity.ie.
Arnold, Bruce. *The Scandal of Ulysses: The Life and Afterlife of a Twentieth Century Masterpiece* (1991; Dublin, The Liffey Press, rev edn, 2004).
Attridge, Derek. 'Reading Joyce', in Derek Attridge (ed.), *The Cambridge Companion to James Joyce* (1990; Cambridge: Cambridge University Press, 2nd edn, 2006), 1–27.

Attridge, Derek. 'Joyce's Pen', in Richard Brown (ed.), *Joyce, Penelope and the Body* (Amsterdam: Rodopi, 2006), 47–62.

Attridge, Derek and Marjorie Howes (eds.). *Semicolonial Joyce* (Cambridge: Cambridge University Press, 2000).

Backus, Margot Gayle. *Scandal Work: James Joyce, the New Journalism and the Home Rule Newspaper Wars* (Notre Dame, IN: University of Notre Dame, 2013).

Baggett, Holly A. 'The Trials of Margaret Anderson and Jane Heap', in Susan Albertine (ed.), *A Living of Words: American Women in Print Culture* (Knoxville, TN: University of Tennessee Press, 1995), 169–88.

Baggett, Holly A. (ed.). *Dear Tiny Heart: The Letters of Jane Heap and Florence Reynolds* (New York: New York University Press, 2000).

Banta, Melissa and Oscar A. Silverman. *James Joyce's Letters to Sylvia Beach* (Oxford: Plantin, 1987).

Barnet, Andrea. *All-Night Party: The Women of Bohemian Greenwich Village and Harlem, 1913–1930* (Chapel Hill, NC: Algonquin Books, 2004).

Baron, Scarlett. 'Beginnings', in Sean Latham (ed.), *The Cambridge Companion to Ulysses* (Cambridge: Cambridge University Press, 2014), 51–68.

Barsanti, Michael (comp.). *Ulysses in Hand: The Rosenbach Manuscript* (Philadelphia, PA: Rosenbach Museum, 2000).

Beach, Sylvia. *Shakespeare and Company* (1959; Lincoln, NE: University of Nebraska Press, 1991).

Beck, Harald. 'Joyce's Ormond Hotel', www.jjonline.org.

Beckett, Samuel. 'Dante…Bruno…Vico…Joyce', in Samuel Beckett, *Poems, Short Fiction, Criticism*, ed. by Paul Auster (New York: Grove Press, 2006) (Volume IV of the Grove Centenary Edition), 495–510.

Bell, Anne Olivier (ed.). *The Diary of Virginia Woolf: Volume I: 1915–1919* (London: The Hogarth Press, 1977).

Benstock, Bernard. *Narrative Contexts in Dubliners* (London: Macmillan, 1994).

Berkman, Alexander and Emma Goldman. *Trial and Speeches of Alexander Berkman and Emma Goldman in the United States District Court, in the City of New York July 1917* (New York: Mother Earth Publishing Association, 1917).

Birmingham, Kevin. *The Most Dangerous Book: The Battle for James Joyce's Ulysses* (New York: The Penguin Press, 2014).

Bishop, Edward L. 'The "Garbled History" of the First-Edition *Ulysses*', *Joyce Studies Annual*, 9 (1998), 3–36.

Blamires, Harry. *The New Bloomsday Book: A Guide Through Ulysses* (1966; London: Routledge, 2nd edn, 1988).

Blondel, Natalie (ed.). *The Journals of Mary Butts* (New Haven, CT and London: Yale University Press, 2002).

Bonapfel, Elizabeth and Tim Conley (eds.). *Doubtful Points: Joyce and Punctuation* (Amsterdam: Rodopi, 2014).

Bowker, Gordon. *James Joyce: A Biography* (London: Weidenfeld and Nicolson, 2011).

Brooker, Peter and Andrew Thacker (eds.). *The Oxford Critical and Cultural History of Modernist Magazines: Volume 1: Britain and Ireland, 1880–1955* (Oxford: Oxford University Press, 2009).

Brooker, Peter and Andrew Thacker (eds.). *The Oxford Critical and Cultural History of Modernist Magazines: Volume II, North America, 1894–1960* (Oxford: Oxford University Press, 2012).

Brown, Susan. 'The Mystery of the Fuga Per Canonem Solved', *Genetic Joyce Studies*, 7 (Spring 2007), www.geneticjoycestudies.org.

Bryant, John. 'Witness and Access: The Uses of the Fluid Text', *Textual Cultures*, 2:1 (2007), 16–42.

Bryer, Jackson Robert. '"A Trial-Track for Racers": Margaret Anderson and the *Little Review*' (PhD Dissertation, University of Wisconsin, 1965).

Budgen, Frank. *James Joyce and the Making of Ulysses* (1934; Bloomington, IN: Indiana University Press, 1960).

Bulson, Eric. '*Ulysses* by Numbers', *Representations*, 127 (Summer 2014), 1–32.

Bulson, Eric. *Little Magazine, World Form* (New York: Columbia University Press, 2016).

Cao, Nan and Weiwei Cui. *Introduction to Text Visualisation* (Paris: Atlantis Press, 2016).

Carr, Helen. '*Poetry: A Magazine of Verse* (1912–1936), Biggest of Little Magazines', in Peter Brooker and Andrew Thacker (eds.), *The Oxford Critical and Cultural History of Modernist Magazines: Volume II, North America, 1894–1960* (Oxford: Oxford University Press, 2012), 40–60.

Chauncey, George. 'Long-Haired Men and Short-Haired Women: Building a Gay World in the Heart of Bohemia', in Rick Bear and Leslie Cohen Berlowitz (eds.), *Greenwich Village: Culture and Counterculture* (New Brunswick, NJ: Rutgers University Press, 1993), 151–64.

Churchill, Suzanne W. and Adam McKible (eds.). *Little Magazines and Modernism: New Approaches* (Aldershot: Ashgate, 2007).

Cloud, Gerald W. *John Rodker's Ovid Press: A Bibliographical History* (New Castle, DE: Oak Knoll Press, 2010).

Collier, Patrick. 'What Is Modern Periodical Studies?', *The Journal of Modern Periodical Studies*, 6:2 (2016), 92–111.

Crispi, Luca. 'A First Foray into the National Library of Ireland's Joyce Manuscripts: Bloomsday 2011', *Genetic Joyce Studies*, 11 (Spring 2011), www.geneticjoycestudies.org.

Crispi, Luca. *Becoming the Blooms: Joyce's Creative Process and the Construction of Characters in Ulysses* (Oxford: Oxford University Press, 2015).

Crispi, Luca. 'The Notescape of *Ulysses*', in Ronan Crowley and Dirk Van Hulle (eds.), *New Quotatoes: Joycean Exogenesis in the Digital Age* (Leiden: Brill, 2016), 75–87.

Crispi, Luca and Ronan Crowley. 'Proof ^ Finder: Page Proofs', *Genetic Joyce Studies*, 8 (Spring 2008), www.geneticjoycestudies.org.

Crispi, Luca and Ronan Crowley. 'Proof ^ Finder: Placards', *Genetic Joyce Studies*, 8 (Spring 2008), www.geneticjoycestudies.org.

Crispi, Luca and Ronan Crowley. 'Proof ^ Finder: Proofs by Episode', *Genetic Joyce Studies*, 8 (Spring 2008), www.geneticjoycestudies.org.

Crowley, Ronan. '"The Hand that Wrote *Ulysses*" and the *Avant-Texte* of "Wandering Rocks"', *Genetic Joyce Studies*, 7 (Spring 2007), www.geneticjoycestudies.org.

Crowley, Ronan. 'Fusing the Elements of "Circe": From Compositional to Textual Repetition', *James Joyce Quarterly*, 47:3 (Spring 2010), 341–61.

Crowley, Ronan. '"It Is Hard to Believe in Typescript": The Typewriter and Transmissional Departure in Joyce's *Ulysses*', unpublished typescript.

Crowley, Ronan and Geert Lernout. 'Joseph McCabe in *Ulysses*', *Genetic Joyce Studies*, 12 (Spring 2012), www.geneticjoycestudies.org.

Cuddon, J. A. *A Dictionary of Literary Terms and Literary Theory* (Oxford: Blackwell, 2013).

de Grazia, Edward. *Girls Lean Back Everywhere: The Law of Obscenity and the Assault on Genius* (New York: Random House, 1992).

Dent, R. W. *Colloquial Language in Ulysses* (London and Toronto: Associated University Presses, 1994).

Deppman, Jed, Daniel Ferrer and Michael Groden (eds.). *Genetic Criticism: Texts and Avant-Textes* (Philadelphia, PA: University of Pennsylvania Press, 2004).

Dolan, T. P. *A Dictionary of Hiberno-English* (Dublin: Gill and Macmillan, 1998).

Driver, Clive (ed.). *James Joyce, Ulysses: A Facsimile of the Manuscript*, 3 vols (Philadelphia, PA: Rosenbach Foundation, 1975).

Drouin, Jeffrey. 'Close- and Distant-Reading Modernism: Network Analysis, Text Mining, and Teaching *The Little Review*', *The Journal of Modern Periodical Studies*, 5:1 (2014), 110–35.

Eberly, Rosa A. *Citizen Critics: Literary Public Spheres* (Chicago, IL: University of Illinois Press, 2000).

Egoist, The, January 1914–December 1919. A complete run (3 vols) is available in printed facsimile (New York: Kraus Reprint Corporation, 1967), or see Modernist Journals Project, http://modjourn.org.

Eliot, Valerie (ed.). *The Letters of T. S. Eliot*, vol 1: 1898–1922 (London: Harcourt Brace, 1988).

Ellmann, Richard. *Ulysses on the Liffey* (London: Faber, 1974).

Ellmann, Richard. *James Joyce* (1959; Oxford: Oxford University Press, rev edn, 1982).

Eve, Martin Paul. 'Close Reading with Computers: Genre Signals, Parts of Speech and David Mitchell's *Cloud Atlas*', *SubStance*, 46:3 (2017), 76–104.

Feather, John. *A History of British Publishing* (London: Routledge, 1988).

Feldman, Paula R. 'Margaret Anderson', in Karen Lane Rood (ed.), *American Writers in Paris, 1920–1939*, Dictionary of Literary Biography, vol. 4 (Detroit, MI: Gale Research, 1980), 3–10.

Ferrer, Daniel. 'What Song the Sirens Sang...Is No Longer beyond All Conjecture: A Preliminary Description of the New "Proteus" and "Sirens"', *James Joyce Quarterly*, 39:1 (2001), 53–68.

Ferrer, Daniel. 'The Joyce of Manuscripts', in Richard Brown (ed.), *A Companion to James Joyce* (Oxford: Blackwell, 2008), 286–99.

Ferrer, Daniel and Jean-Michel Rabaté. 'Paragraphs in Expansion', in Jed Deppman, Daniel Ferrer, and Michael Groden (eds.), *Genetic Criticism: Texts and Avant-Textes* (Philadelphia, PA: University of Pennsylvania Press, 2004), 132–51.

Firth, John (ed.). 'Harriet Weaver's Letters to James Joyce, 1915–1920', *Studies in Bibliography*, 20 (1967), 151–88.

Firth, John. 'James Pinker to James Joyce, 1915–1920', *Studies in Bibliography*, 21 (1968), 205–25.

Fish, Stanley. *Is There a Text in This Class? The Authority of Interpretive Communities* (Cambridge, MA: Harvard University Press, 1980).

Fludernik, Monika. 'Narrative and Its Development in *Ulysses*', *Journal of Narrative Technique*, 16 (1986), 15–40.

Fordham, Finn. 'Biography', in John McCourt (ed.), *James Joyce in Context* (Cambridge: Cambridge University Press, 2009), 17–26.

Foster, R. F. *Modern Ireland, 1600–1972* (London: Penguin, 1988).

Gabler, Hans Walter. 'What *Ulysses* Requires', *Proceedings of the Bibliographical Society of America*, 87:2 (1993), 187–248.

Gabler, Hans Walter. 'The Genesis of *A Portrait of the Artist as a Young Man*', in Philip Brady and James F. Carens (eds.), *Critical Essays on James Joyce's A Portrait of the Artist as a Young Man* (New York: G. K. Hall, 1995), 83–112.

Gammel, Irene. *Baroness Elsa von Freytag-Loringhoven: Gender, Dada, and Everyday Modernity: A Cultural Biography* (Cambridge, MA: MIT Press, 2002).

Gammel, Irene and Suzanne Zelazo (eds.). *Body Sweats: The Uncensored Writings of Elsa von Freytag-Loringhoven* (Cambridge, MA: MIT Press, 2011).

Gaskell, Philip. *A New Introduction to Bibliography* (Oxford: Clarendon Press, 1972).

Genette, Gérard. *Paratexts: Thresholds of Interpretation*, translated by Jane E. Lewin (Cambridge: Cambridge University Press, 1997).

Gibson, Andrew. *Joyce's Revenge: History, Politics and Aesthetics in Ulysses* (Oxford: Oxford University Press, 2002).

Gifford, Don with Robert J. Seidman. *Ulysses Annotated: Notes for James Joyce's Ulysses* (1974; London: University of California Press, 2nd rev edn, 1989).

Gilbert, Martin. *The First World War: A Complete History* (London: Phoenix, 2008).

Gillers, Stephen. 'A Tendency to Deprave and Corrupt: The Transformation of American Obscenity Law from *Hicklin* to *Ulysses II*', *Washington University Law Review*, 85:2 (2007), 215–96.

Glaister, Geoffrey Ashall. *Encyclopedia of the Book*, 2nd edn with a new introduction by Donald Farren (New Castle, DE: Oak Knoll Press; London: The British Library, 1996).

Golding, Alan. '*The Dial, The Little Review*, and the Dialogics of Modernism', *American Periodicals: A Journal of History, Criticism, and Bibliography*, 15.1 (2005), 42–55.

Golding, Alan. 'The Little Review', in Peter Brooker and Andrew Thacker (eds.), *The Oxford Critical and Cultural History of Modernist Magazines: Volume II, North America, 1894–1960* (Oxford: Oxford University Press, 2012), 61–84.

Gorman, Herbert. *James Joyce: A Definitive Biography* (London: John Lane, The Bodley Head, 1941).

Green, Michelle Erica. 'Making No Compromises with Critical Taste: The War for the *Little Review*', http://www.littlereview.com/mca/mcapaper.htm.

Greg, W. W. 'The Rationale of Copy-Text', *Studies in Bibliography*, 3 (1950).

Groden, Michael. *Ulysses in Progress* (Princeton, NJ: Princeton University Press, 1977).

Groden, Michael (ed.). *James Joyce Archive*, 63 vols (New York: Garland, 1977–9).

Groden, Michael. 'A Textual and Publishing History', in Zack Bowen and James F. Carens (eds.), *A Companion to James Joyce* (London: Greenwood Press, 1984), 71–129.

Groden, Michael. 'Before and After: The Manuscripts in Textual and Genetic Criticism of *Ulysses*', in Michael Patrick Gillespie and A. Nicholas Fargnoli (eds.), *Ulysses in Critical Perspective* (Gainesville, FL: University Press of Florida, 2006), 152–70.

Groden, Michael. 'Joyce at Work on "Cyclops": Towards a Biography of *Ulysses*', *James Joyce Quarterly*, 44:2 (Winter 2007), 217–47.

Groden, Michael. *Ulysses in Focus: Genetic, Textual and Personal Views* (Gainesville, FL: University Press of Florida, 2010).

Gunn, Ian and Clive Hart with Harald Beck. *James Joyce's Dublin: A Topographical Guide to the Dublin of Ulysses* (London: Thames and Hudson, 2004).

Hamilton, Ian. *The Little Magazines: A Study of Six Editors* (London: Weidenfeld and Nicolson, 1976).

Hammond, Adam. *Literature in the Digital Age* (Cambridge: Cambridge University Press, 2016).

Hancher, Michael. 'Re:Search and Close Reading', in Matthew K. Gold and Lauren F. Klein (eds.), *Debates in the Digital Humanities* (Minneapolis, MN: University of Minnesota Press, 2016), 118–38.

Hassett, Joseph M. *The Ulysses Trials: Beauty and Truth Meet the Law* (Dublin: The Lilliput Press, 2016).

Hayman, David and Sam Slote (eds.). *Genetic Studies in Joyce* (Amsterdam: Rodopi, 1995).

Herring, Philip F. (ed.). *Joyce's Ulysses Notesheets in the British Museum* (Charlottesville, VA: Bibliographical Society, 1972).

Herring, Philip F. (ed.). *Joyce's Notes and Early Drafts for Ulysses: Selections from the Buffalo Collection* (Charlottesville, VA: Bibliographical Society, 1977).

Herring, Philip F. *Djuna: The Life and Work of Djuna Barnes* (London: Viking, 1995).

Herring, Philip F. (ed.). *Djuna Barnes: Collected Stories* (Los Angeles, CA: Sun and Moon Press, 1996).

Himber, Alan (ed.). *The Letters of John Quinn to William Butler Yeats* (Ann Arbor, MI: UMI Research Press, 1983).

Homer. *The Odyssey*, translated by Robert Fagles (London: Penguin, 1996).

Hutton, Clare. 'Joyce and the Institutions of Revivalism', *Irish University Review*, 33 (2003), 117–32.

Hutton, Clare. 'Chapters of Moral History: Failing to Publish *Dubliners*', *Papers of the Bibliographical Society of America*, 97:4 (December 2003), 495–519.

Hutton, Clare (ed.). *The Irish Book in the Twentieth Century* (Dublin: Irish Academic Press, 2004).

Hutton, Clare. 'The Development of *Ulysses* in Print, 1918–1922', *Dublin James Joyce Journal*, 6:7 (2015), 109–31.

Hutton, Clare (ed.) and Patrick Walsh (co-ed.). *The Oxford History of the Irish Book, 1891–2000* (Oxford: Oxford University Press, 2011).

Joost, Nicholas. *Schofield Thayer and The Dial: An Illustrated History* (Carbondale, IL: Southern Illinois University Press, 1964).

Joost, Nicholas. *Years of Transition: The Dial, 1912–1920* (Barre, MA: Barre Publishers, 1967).

Joyce, James. *Dubliners*, edited by Hans Walter Gabler and Walter Hettche (New York: Vintage, 1993; London: Garland, 1993).

Joyce, James. *Ulysses* (New York: Random House, 1934).

Joyce, James. *Letters of James Joyce*, vol. 1 edited by Stuart Gilbert (New York: Viking, 1957); vols 2 and 3 edited by Richard Ellmann (New York: Viking, 1966).

Joyce, James. *Selected Letters of James Joyce*, edited by Richard Ellmann (London: Faber, 1975).

Joyce, James. *Ulysses* (The Corrected Text), edited by Hans Walter Gabler with a New Preface by Richard Ellmann (London: Penguin in association with the Bodley Head, 1986).

Joyce, James. *Poems and Shorter Writings*, edited by Richard Ellmann, A. Walton Litz, and John Whittier-Ferguson (London: Faber, 1991).

Joyce, James. *Finnegans Wake*, with an introduction by Seamus Deane (London: Penguin Books, 1992).

Joyce, James. *Ulysses*, edited by Declan Kiberd (London: Penguin, 1992).

Joyce, James. *Ulysses* (The 1922 Text), edited by Jeri Johnson (Oxford: World's Classics, 1993).

Joyce, James. *Occasional, Critical, and Political Writing*, edited by Kevin Barry (Oxford: Oxford University Press, 2000).

Joyce, Stanislaus. *My Brother's Keeper* (New York: The Viking Press, 1958).

Kidd, John. 'An Inquiry into *Ulysses: The Corrected Text*', *Proceedings of the Bibliographical Society of America*, 82 (1988), 411–584.

Killeen, Terence. *Ulysses Unbound* (Dublin: Wordwell, 2004).

Killeen, Terence. 'Myths and Monuments: The Case of Alfred H. Hunter', *Dublin James Joyce Journal*, 1 (2008), 47–53.

Killeen, Terence. 'Marion Hunter Revisited: Further Light on a Dublin Enigma', *Dublin James Joyce Journal*, 3 (2010), 144–51.

Kenner, Hugh. *Ulysses* (1980; Baltimore, MD: Johns Hopkins University Press, rev edn, 1987).

Lappin, Linda. 'Jane Heap and Her Circle', *Prairie Schooner*, 78:4 (2004), 5–25.

Latham, Sean. 'Unpacking My Digital Library: Programs, Modernisms, Magazines', in Dean Irvine, Vanessa Lent, and Bart Vautour (eds.), *Making Canada New: Editing Modernism and New Media* (Toronto: University of Toronto Press, 2017), 31–60.

Latham, Sean and Robert Scholes. 'The Rise of Periodical Studies', *PMLA*, 121:2 (2006), 517–31.

Lawrence, Karen. *The Odyssey of Style in Ulysses* (Princeton, NJ: Princeton University Press, 1981).

Lewis, Gifford. '"This Terrible Struggle with Want of Means": Behind the Scenes at the Cuala Press', in Clare Hutton (ed.) and Patrick Walsh (co-ed.), *The Oxford History of the Irish Book, 1891–2000* (Oxford: Oxford University Press, 2011), 529–47.

Lidderdale, Jane and Mary Nicholson. *Dear Miss Weaver: Harriet Shaw Weaver, 1876–1961* (New York: The Viking Press, 1970).

Litz, A. Walton. *The Art of James Joyce* (London: Oxford University Press, 1961).

Maddox, Brenda. *Nora: A Biography of Nora Joyce* (London: Hamish Hamilton, 1988).

Mao, Douglas and Rebecca L. Walkowitz. 'The New Modernist Studies', *PMLA*, 123:3 (May 2008), 737–48.

Marek, Jayne E. *Women Editing Modernism: Little Magazines and Literary History* (Lexington, KY: University Press of Kentucky, 1995).

Marshik, Celia. *British Modernism and Censorship* (Cambridge: Cambridge University Press, 2006).

Martin, Timothy. *Joyce and Wagner* (Cambridge: Cambridge University Press, 1991).

Materer, Timothy (ed.). *The Selected Letters of Ezra Pound to John Quinn* (Durham, NC and London: Duke University Press, 1991).

McCourt, John. *The Years of Bloom: James Joyce in Trieste, 1904–1920* (Dublin: The Lilliput Press, 2000).

McCourt, John (ed.). *James Joyce in Context* (Cambridge: Cambridge University Press, 2009).

McGann, Jerome. *The Textual Condition* (Princeton, NJ: Princeton University Press, 1991).

McKenzie, D. F. *Bibliography and the Sociology of Texts* (1986; Cambridge: Cambridge University Press, 1999).

McKenzie, D. F. *Making Meaning: 'Printers of the Mind' and Other Essays*, edited by Peter D. McDonald and Michael F. Suarez (Boston, MA: University of Massachusetts Press, 2002).

McNeillie, Andrew (ed.). *The Essays of Virginia Woolf: Volume III, 1919–1924* (London: The Hogarth Press, 1988).

McNichol, Stella (ed.). *Mrs Dalloway's Party: A Short Story Sequence* (London: The Hogarth Press, 1973).

McSharry, Katherine (ed.). *A Joycean Scrapbook from the National Library of Ireland* (Dublin: Wordwell, 2004).

Moody, A. David. *Ezra Pound: A Portrait of the Man and His Work: Volume 1, The Young Genius, 1885–1920* (Oxford: Oxford University Press, 2007).

Moretti, Franco. 'The Slaughterhouse of Literature', *Modern Language Quarterly*, 61:1 (2000), 207–28.

Moretti, Franco. *Graphs, Maps, Trees: Abstract Models for a Literary History* (London: Verso, 2005).

Morris, Catherine. *Alice Milligan and the Irish Cultural Revival* (Dublin: Four Courts Press, 2013).

Morrisson, Mark S. *The Public Face of Modernism: Little Magazines, Audiences, and Reception, 1905–1920* (Madison, WI: University of Wisconsin Press, 2001).

Morton, Marian J. *Emma Goldman and the American Left: Nowhere at Home* (New York: Twayne Publishers, 1992).

Mullin, Katherine. *James Joyce, Sexuality and Social Purity* (Cambridge: Cambridge University Press, 2003).

Mullin, Katherine. 'Joyce through the Little Magazines', in Richard Brown (ed.), *A Companion to James Joyce* (Oxford: Blackwell, 2008), 374–89.

Nicholson, C. Bríd. *Emma Goldman: Still Dangerous* (London: Black Rose Books, 2010).

Nicholson, Robert. *The Ulysses Guide: Tours Through Joyce's Dublin* (1988; Dublin: New Island, 2002).

Nicolson, Nigel (ed.). *The Question of Things Happening: The Letters of Virginia Woolf: Volume II: 1912–1922* (London: The Hogarth Press, 1976).

Norris, Margot. *Virgin and Veteran Readings of Ulysses* (New York: Palgrave Macmillan, 2011).

Norris, Margot. 'Character, Plot and Myth', in Sean Latham (ed.), *The Cambridge Companion to Ulysses* (Cambridge: Cambridge University Press, 2014), 69–80.

O'Callaghan, Katherine. 'Mapping the "Call from Afar": The Echo of Leitmotifs in James Joyce's Literary Landscape', in Valérie Bénéjam and John Bishop (eds.), *Making Space in the Works of James Joyce* (London: Routledge, 2011), 173–90.

Owen, Rodney Wilson. *James Joyce and the Beginnings of Ulysses* (Ann Arbor, MI: UMI Research Press, 1983).

Pease, Allison. *Modernism, Mass Culture, and the Aesthetics of Obscenity* (Cambridge: Cambridge University Press, 2000).

Pethica, James. 'Yeats's Perfect Man', *The Dublin Review*, 35 (Spring 2009), https://thedublinreview.com/article/yeatss-perfect-man.

Platt, Len. *Joyce and the Anglo-Irish: A Study of Joyce and the Literary Revival* (Amsterdam: Rodopi, 1998).

Plock, Vike Martina. *Joyce, Medicine and Modernity* (Gainesville, FL: University Press of Florida, 2010).

Pound, Ezra. 'Small Magazines', *English Journal*, 19:9 (November 1930), 689–704.

Power, Mary. 'The Discovery of *Ruby*', *James Joyce Quarterly*, 18:2 (Winter 1981), 115–21.

Quillian, William H. 'Shakespeare in Trieste: Joyce's 1912 "Hamlet" Lectures', *James Joyce Quarterly*, 12:1–2 (Fall 1974–Winter 1975), 7–63.

Rainey, Lawrence. 'Consuming Investments: Joyce's *Ulysses*', *James Joyce Quarterly*, 33:4 (Summer 1996), 531–67.

Read, Forrest (ed.). *Pound/Joyce: The Letters of Ezra Pound to James Joyce with Pound's Essays on Joyce* (New York: New Directions, 1965).

Reid, B. L. *The Man from New York: John Quinn and His Friends* (New York: Oxford University Press, 1968).

Reiman, Donald. *Romantic Texts and Contexts* (Columbia, MO: University of Missouri Press, 1987).

Rice, Thomas Jackson. '*Ulysses*, Chaos and Complexity', *James Joyce Quarterly*, 31:2 (Winter 1994), 41–54.

Richter, Harvena. *The 'Ulysses' Connection: Clarissa Dalloway's Bloomsday*, Studies in the *Novel*, 21:3 (Fall 1989), 305–19.

Rose, Danis (ed.). *The Dublin Ulysses Papers*, 6 vols (Dublin: House of Breathings, 2012).

Ross, Shawna and James O'Sullivan. *Reading Modernism with Machines: Digital Humanities and Modernist Literature* (London: Palgrave Macmillan, 2016).

Scholes, Robert E. (ed.). 'Grant Richards to James Joyce', *Studies in Bibliography*, 16 (1963), 139–60.

Scholes, Robert E. and Richard M. Kain (eds.). *The Workshop of Daedalus: James Joyce and the Raw Materials for A Portrait of the Artist as a Young Man* (Evanston, IL: Northwestern University Press, 1965).

Scholes, Robert E. and Clifford Wulfman. *Modernism in the Magazines: An Introduction* (Princeton, NJ: Yale University Press, 2010).

Schreibman, Susan and Amit Kumar and Jarom McDonald. 'The Versioning Machine', *Literary and Linguistic Computing*, 18:1 (2003), 101–7.

Schwartzman, Myron (ed.). ' "Quinnigan's Quake": John Quinn's Letters to James Joyce, 1916–1920', *Bulletin of Research in the Humanities*, 81:2 (Summer 1978), 216–60.

Schwartzman, Myron. ' "Quinnigan's Quake!": John Quinn's Letters to James Joyce, 1921–1924', *Bulletin of Research in the Humanities*, 83:1 (Spring 1980), 27–66.

Scott, Bonnie Kime. 'The Young Girl, Jane Heap, and Trials of Gender', in Vincent Cheng, Kimberly J. Devlin, and Margot Norris (eds.), *Joycean Cultures/Culturing Joyces* (Newark, DE: University of Delaware Press, 1998), 78–95.

Scott, Thomas L. and Melvin J Friedman (eds.). *Pound/The Little Review: The Letters of Ezra Pound to Margaret Anderson: The Little Review Correspondence* (New York: A New Directions Book, 1988).

Senn, Fritz. 'Nausicaa', in Clive Hart and David Hayman (eds.), *James Joyce's 'Ulysses': Critical Essays* (Berkeley, CA: University of California Press, 1974).

Senn, Fritz. 'Genetic Fascination', *Genetic Joyce Studies*, Special Issue (2002), www.genetic-joycestudies.org.

Shillingsburg, Peter. *From Gutenberg to Google* (Cambridge: Cambridge University Press, 2006).

Sigler, Amanda. 'Archival Errors: *Ulysses* in the *Little Review*', in Matthew Creasy (ed.), *Errears and Erroriboose: Joyce and Error* (European Joyce Studies, 20) (Amsterdam: Rodopi, 2011), 73–87.

Sigler, Amanda. 'In Between the Sheets: Sexy Punctuation in American Magazines', in Tim Conley and Elizabeth Bonapfel (eds.), *Doubtful Points: Joyce and Punctuation* (European Joyce Studies 23) (Amsterdam: Rodopi, 2014), 43–66.

Silver, Brenda R. *Virginia Woolf's Reading Notebooks* (Princeton, NJ: Princeton University Press, 1983).

Slote, Sam. *Ulysses in the Plural: The Variable Editions of Joyce's Novel* (Dublin: National Library of Ireland, 2004).

Sova, Dawn B. *Literature Suppressed on Sexual Grounds* (New York: Facts on File, 2006).

Spoo, Robert. *Without Copyrights: Piracy, Publishing and the Public Domain* (New York: Oxford University Press, 2013).

State of New York. *Consolidated Laws of the State of New York* (New York: Lyon State Printers, 1909).

Sullivan, Hannah. *The Work of Revision* (Cambridge, MA: Harvard University Press, 2013).

Sumner, John S. 'The Truth about "Literary Lynching" ', *The Dial*, July 1921.

Van Hulle, Dirk. *James Joyce's 'Work in Progress': Pre-Book Publications of Finnegans Wake* (London: Routledge, 2016).

Van Mierlo, Wim. 'Reading Joyce In and Out of the Archive', *Joyce Studies Annual*, 13 (Summer 2002), 32–63.

Van Mierlo, Wim. 'The Subject Notebook: A Nexus in the Composition History of *Ulysses*—A Preliminary Analysis', 7 (Spring 2007), www.geneticjoycestudies.org.

Vanderham, Paul. *James Joyce and Censorship: The Trials of Ulysses* (London: Macmillan, 1998).

Vaughn, Stephen. *Encyclopedia of American Journalism* (New York: Routledge, 2008).

Wales, Katie. *The Language of James Joyce* (London: Macmillan, 1992).

Walsh, Keri (ed.). *The Letters of Sylvia Beach* (New York: Columbia University Press, 2010).

Weir, David. 'What Did He Know, and When Did He Know It: *The Little Review*, Joyce, and *Ulysses*', *James Joyce Quarterly*, 37 (Spring/Summer 2000), 389–412.

Williams, William Carlos. *Autobiography* (1948; New York: McGibbon and Key, 1968).

Woolf, Leonard (ed.). *A Writer's Diary: Being Extracts from the Diary of Virginia Woolf* (London: The Hogarth Press, 1969).

Wright, David G. *Dubliners and Ulysses: Bonds of Character* (Novi Ligure, Italy: Edizioni Joker, 2013).

Yanella, Philip R. 'James Joyce to the *Little Review*', *Journal of Modern Literature*, 1:3 (1971), 393–8.

Yeats, W. B. *In the Seven Woods* (Dublin: Dun Emer, 1903).

Yeats, W. B. 'A General Introduction for My Work', *Essays and Introductions* (London: Macmillan, 1961).

Yeats, W. B. *The Collected Letters of William Butler Yeats: Volume 3, 1901–1904*, edited by John Kelly and Ronald Schuchard (Oxford: Clarendon Press, 1994).

Index